5 STEPS TO A 5™

AP Comparative Government & Politics

5 STEPS TO A 5™

AP Comparative Government & Politics

3RD EDITION

Suzanne Bailey, NBCT

New York   Chicago   San Francisco   Athens   London   Madrid
Mexico City   Milan   New Delhi   Singapore   Sydney   Toronto

1 2 3 4 5 6 7 8 9   LHS   27 26 25 24 23 22

ISBN   978-1-264-48674-8
MHID   1-264-48674-X

e-ISBN   978-1-264-48803-2
e-MHID   1-264-48803-3

McGraw Hill products are available at special quantity discounts to use as premiums and sales or for use in corporate training programs. To contact a representative, please visit the Contact Us pages at www.mhprofessional.com.

McGraw Hill is committed to making our products accessible to all learners. To learn more about the available support and accommodations we offer, please contact us at accessibility@mheducation.com. We also participate in the Access Text Network (www.accesstext.org), and ATN members may submit requests through ATN.

CONTENTS

STEP 5 Build Your Test-Taking Confidence

PREFACE

Congratulations on deciding to take the AP Comparative Government and Politics exam!

This is a challenging and engaging AP course that will introduce you to the dynamics of government and politics around the world. By focusing on six case studies, you will have the opportunity to apply the comparative method to gain insight into how political systems operate and transition. The six countries covered in this course are the United Kingdom, Iran, Russia, China, Mexico, and Nigeria. Studying them will help you learn to evaluate political events as a global citizen, and at the same time, you will better understand political activity in the United States.

We prepared this volume to provide you with a resource beyond your textbook and classroom material to help you master the material and confidently take the AP Comparative Government and Politics exam.

Good luck!

ACKNOWLEDGMENTS

I would like to dedicate this book to my students, past, present, and future: Thank you for taking on the challenge of an elective AP course and traveling this journey with me. Special thanks to my friends in the AP Comparative Reading world with whom I have so many cherished memories. Finally, thank you to my amazing husband and children for all your love and support.

SUZANNE BAILEY

ABOUT THE AUTHOR

Suzanne Bailey teaches AP Comparative and U.S. Government and Politics, along with AP Micro and Macroeconomics at Virgil I. Grissom High School in Huntsville, Alabama. She has served as the College Board Advisor for AP Comparative Government and Politics, as well as a member of its Test Development Committee. In addition, she has participated in the AP Exam Reading for this course since 2004, serving as Table Leader and Question Leader. A College Board consultant for both Comparative and U.S. Government and Politics, she has led sessions at APAC and NCSS as well as conducting one-day and weeklong training sessions. She earned her National Board Certification in 2004 and renewed in 2014.

INTRODUCTION: THE FIVE-STEP PREPARATION PROGRAM

This book is organized as a five-step program to prepare you for success on the exam. These steps are designed to provide you with the skills and strategies vital to the exam and the practice that can lead you to that perfect 5. Each of the five steps will provide you with the opportunity to get closer to that prize trophy 5. Here are the five steps.

Step 1: Set Up Your Study Program

In this step you'll get an overview of the AP Comparative Government and Politics exam to gain an understanding of the format of the exam, the topics covered, and the approximate percentage of the exam that will test knowledge of each topic. You will also find advice to help you set up your preparation program. Three specific options are discussed:

- Full school year: September through May
- One semester: January through May
- Six weeks: Basic training for the exam

Step 2: Determine Your Test Readiness

In this step you'll take a diagnostic exam in AP Comparative Government and Politics. This test should give you an idea of how prepared you are to take the real exam before beginning to study for it. The diagnostic test closely matches the real test, so time yourself and discover what taking the test will be like.

- Go through the diagnostic exam question by question to find out how prepared you are for the exam.
- Review the correct answers and explanations.

Step 3: Develop Strategies for Success

In this step you will learn strategies that will help you do your best on the exam. These strategies cover both the multiple-choice and free-response sections of the exam. Some of these tips are based upon an understanding of how the questions are designed, and others have been gleaned from years of experience helping students prepare for the exam and reading (grading) the AP Comparative Government and Politics exam.

- Learn how to answer multiple-choice questions, including whether or not to guess.
- Learn how to plan and write answers to the free-response questions.

Step 4: Review the Knowledge You Need to Score High

In this step you will learn or review the material you need to know for the test. This review takes up the bulk of this book. It contains:

- A comprehensive review of the concepts you'll need to know for the AP Comparative Government and Politics exam

- Key terms, which are listed at the beginning of each chapter and then defined in the chapter text (look for the boldfaced terms)
- Reviews of the government and politics of the six countries included in the test: the United Kingdom, Iran, Russia, China, Mexico, and Nigeria

Step 5: Build Your Test-Taking Confidence

In this step you will complete your preparation by testing yourself on practice exams. This book provides you with two complete exams, answers, explanations, and rubrics. Be aware that these practice exams are *not* reproduced questions from actual AP U.S. Government and Politics exams, but they mirror both the material tested by AP and the way in which it is tested.

Introduction to the Graphics Used in This Book

To emphasize particular skills and strategies, we use several icons throughout this book. An icon in the margin will alert you that you should pay particular attention to the accompanying text. We use three icons:

 This icon points out a very important concept that you should not pass over.

 This icon calls your attention to a strategy that you may want to try.

 This icon indicates a tip that you may find useful.

5 STEPS TO A 5™

AP Comparative Government & Politics

STEP 1

Set Up Your Study Program

CHAPTER 1

What You Need to Know About the AP Comparative Government and Politics Exam

IN THIS CHAPTER

Summary: Learn what topics are tested, how the test is scored, and basic test-taking information.

Key Ideas

✪ A score of 3 or above on the AP exam may allow you to get college credit for your AP course; each college sets its own AP credit policy.
✪ Multiple-choice questions account for one-half of your total score.
✪ Free-response questions account for one-half of your total score.
✪ Your composite score on the two test sections is converted to a score on the 1-to-5 scale.

Frequently Asked Questions About the AP Comparative Government and Politics Exam

The AP Comparative Government and Politics exam and the U.S. Government and Politics exams were both introduced in 1989. Far more students take the U.S. Government exam (319,000) than do the Comparative exam (22,000). So, if you are reading this book, realize that you are one of the lucky few to be able to study six contemporary political systems to increase your understanding of how governments work.

Why Take the Comparative Government and Politics Exam?

The main reason to take the exam is to earn college credit. Many schools require that you earn a 4 or a 5 on the exam to receive credit for an introductory Comparative Government and Politics course, but some schools will accept a 3. Earning college credit will allow you more flexibility in scheduling courses, either because you will have fulfilled a requirement or can advance more quickly into a higher-level course. Even if you do not earn a passing score, the fact that you enrolled in an AP course signals to admission committees that you are willing to challenge yourself and take advantage of opportunities, which are the traits of a successful college student.

What Is the Format of the AP Comparative Government and Politics Exam?

The following table summarizes the format of the AP Comparative Government and Politics exam.

SECTION	NUMBER OF QUESTIONS	TIME LIMIT
I. Multiple Choice	55	60 minutes
II. Free Response	4	90 minutes

What Is the Distribution of Grades on the AP Comparative Government and Politics Exam?

The score distribution of the 2021 AP Comparative Government and Politics exam from the Chief Reader's Report is listed in the table below. This exam was given in both paper and digital form.

SCORE	PERCENT OF TEST TAKERS
5	16.6%
4	24.5%
3	30.7%
2	14.9%
1	13.3%

Who Writes the AP Comparative Government and Politics Exam?

Development of each AP exam is a multiyear effort that involves many education and testing professionals and students. At the heart of the effort is the AP Comparative Government and Politics Test Development Committee, a group of college and high school government teachers who are typically asked to serve for three years. The committee creates a large pool of multiple-choice questions. With the help of testing experts at Educational Testing Service (ETS), these questions are then pretested with college students enrolled in introductory Comparative Government and Politics classes for accuracy, appropriateness, clarity, and assurance that there is only one possible answer. The results of this pretesting allow these questions to be categorized as easy, average, or difficult. After more months of development and refinement, Section I of the exam is ready to be administered.

The free-response essay questions that make up Section II go through a similar process of creation, modification, pretesting, and final refinement so that the questions cover the necessary areas of material and are at an appropriate level of difficulty and clarity. The committee also makes a great effort to construct a free-response exam that will allow for clear and equitable grading by the AP readers.

At the conclusion of each AP reading and scoring of the exams, the exam itself and the results are thoroughly evaluated by the committee and by ETS. In this way, the College Board can use the results to make suggestions for course development in high schools and to plan for future exams.

What Is Going to Appear on the Exam?

The College Board, after consulting with teachers of comparative government and politics, develops a curriculum that covers material that college professors expect to cover in their first-year classes. Based on this outline of topics, the multiple-choice exams are written such that those topics are covered in proportion to their importance to the expected government and politics understanding of the student. For example, if 15 percent of the curriculum in an AP Comparative Government and Politics class is about political and economic change, then you can expect 15 percent of the multiple-choice exam to address political and economic change. Below is a general outline for the AP Comparative Government and Politics exam. Remember this is just a guide and each year the exam differs slightly in the percentages.

I. Political Systems	23%
II. Political Institutions	30%
III. Participation	13%
IV. Parties and Elections	14%
V. Political and Economic Change	20%

How Is My Multiple-Choice Exam Scored?

The multiple-choice section of each Comparative Government and Politics exam is 55 questions and is worth one-half of your final score. Your answer sheet is scored by a computer that adds up your correct responses. No points are deducted for incorrect answers. Your score is based solely on the number of questions answered correctly, which are then multiplied to reach a weighted average based on 60 points. No points are awarded (or deducted) for unanswered questions or for questions answered incorrectly.

How Are My Free-Response Essays Scored?

The new version of the AP Comparative Government and Politics exam has standardized rubrics, meaning the number of rubric points per free-response question is fixed. There are four free-response questions on the exam. Question 1 is based on conceptual analysis, Question 2 requires quantitative analysis, and Question 3 assesses the skill of comparative analysis. Question 4 is an argument essay requiring you to develop a thesis and provide supporting evidence and reasoning. The chart below shows the percentage of your total score each question accounts for.

QUESTION #	TYPE OF QUESTION	POINTS	% OF TEST SCORE
1	conceptual analysis	4	11.0%
2	quantitative analysis	5	12.5%
3	comparative analysis	5	12.5%
4	argument essay	5	14.0%

A sample calculation chart can be found with each of the sample exams in this book.

Who Scores the Essays on My Exam?

Every June a group of government teachers gathers for a week to score the exams. Each of these "faculty consultants" spends a day or so getting trained on one question. Because each reader becomes an expert on that question, and because each exam book is anonymous, this process provides a very consistent and unbiased scoring of that question. During a typical day of grading, a random sample of each reader's scores is selected and cross-checked by other experienced "table leaders" to ensure that consistency is maintained throughout the day and the week. Each reader's scores on a given question are also analyzed statistically to make sure that no reader is giving scores that are significantly higher or lower than the mean scores given by other readers of that question. All measures are taken to maintain consistency and fairness for your benefit.

Will My Exam Remain Anonymous?

Absolutely. Even if your high school teacher happens to randomly read your booklet, there is virtually no way he or she will know it is you. To the reader, each student is a number, and to the computer, each student is a bar code.

How Is My Final Grade Determined, and What Does It Mean?

The maximum possible composite score for the AP Comparative Government and Politics exam is 120. The composite score is determined by adding the score from the multiple-choice section to the score from the essay section and rounding that sum to the nearest whole number.

Over the years there has been an observable trend indicating the number of points required to achieve a specific grade. Although the 2020 exam is a new format, data released from previous AP Comparative Government and Politics exams, which show the approximate ranges for the five scores, are summarized in the following table:

COMPOSITE SCORE RANGE	AP GRADE	INTERPRETATION
Mid 70s–120	5	Extremely well qualified for college credit
Mid 60s–mid 70s	4	Well qualified
Low 50s–low 60s	3	Qualified
Mid 30s–low 50s	2	Possibly qualified
0–mid 30s	1	Not qualified

The ranges change from year to year—use this only as an approximate guideline.

How Do I Register, and How Much Does It Cost?

If you are enrolled in AP Comparative Government and Politics in your high school, your teacher is going to provide you all of these details, but a quick summary will not hurt. After all, you do not have to enroll in the AP course to register for and complete the AP exam. When in doubt, the best source of information is the College Board's website: http://apstudent .collegeboard.org.

Currently the fee for taking the AP Comparative Government and Politics exam is $94. Students who demonstrate a financial need may receive a partial refund to help offset the cost of testing. There are also several optional fees that must be paid if you want your scores rushed to you or if you wish to receive multiple grade reports.

The coordinator of the AP program at your school will inform you where and when you will take the exam. If you live in a small community, your exam may not be administered at your school, so be sure to get this information.

What About the Permission Box on the Back?

The College Board uses some exams to help train high school teachers so that they can help the next generation of AP Comparative Government and Politics students avoid common mistakes. If you check this box, you simply give permission to use your exam in this way. Even if you give permission, your anonymity is still maintained.

What Should I Bring to the Exam?

On exam day, you should bring the following items:

- Several pencils and an eraser that does not leave smudges
- Black or blue colored pens for the free-response section
- A watch so that you can monitor your time. You never know if the exam room will have a clock on the wall. Make sure that you turn off the beep that goes off on the hour.
- Your school code
- Your photo identification and social security number
- Tissues
- Your quiet confidence that you are prepared and ready

What Should I NOT Bring to the Exam?

Leave the following items at home:

- A cell phone, beeper, PDA, walkie-talkie, or calculator.
- Books, a dictionary, study notes, flash cards, highlighting pens, correction fluid, a ruler, or any other office supplies.
- Portable music of any kind. No CD players, MP3 players, or iPods are allowed.
- Panic or fear. It is natural to be nervous, but you can comfort yourself that you have used this book and you do not need to fear the exam. Let this test be an opportunity to show what you have learned this year!

CHAPTER 2

How to Plan Your Time

IN THIS CHAPTER

Summary: The right preparation plan for you depends on your study habits, your own strengths and weaknesses, and the amount of time you have to prepare for the test. This chapter recommends some study plans to get you started.

Key Ideas

✪ Preparing for the exam is important. It helps to have a plan—and stick with it!

✪ You should create a study plan that best suits your situation and prioritize your review based on your strengths and weaknesses.

✪ The first step in creating your study plan is to take the diagnostic test in the next chapter. This will tell you what the test is actually like and identify what your priorities for practice should be.

Three Approaches to Preparing for the AP Comparative Government and Politics Exam

It's up to you to decide how you want to use this book to study for the AP Comparative Government and Politics exam. This book is designed for flexibility; you can work through it in order or skip around however you want. In fact, no two students who purchase this book will probably use it in exactly the same way. Chapters 6 through 10 focus on the concepts that you need to master for the exam, and Chapters 11 through 16 are the case studies that provide you with country-specific examples of these political concepts.

The first step in developing your plan is to take the diagnostic test in the next chapter. This is a practice exam that closely mirrors the actual exam. By taking the diagnostic test, you'll find out exactly what the exam is like and what you are reasonably good at and what things you need to practice. Identify your weaknesses and focus on these first.

The Full School-Year Plan

Choose this plan if you like taking your time going through the material. Following this plan will allow you to practice your skills and develop your confidence gradually. This book is filled with practice exercises. Beginning to work through them at the beginning of the school year will allow you to get to all the practice exercises in the book and maximize your preparation for the exam.

You should go through the chapters in the book as you go through the units of your course. Take the diagnostic exam during Christmas break, even though you will not have covered all of the material you'll be tested on. This will show you exactly what the exam is like so you will know what you're up against. Then take the first practice exam during spring break, and the final practice exam a few days before the actual exam. You will be able to see your progress!

The One-Semester Plan

Starting in the middle of the school year should give you ample time to review and prepare for the test. Of course, if you also need to prepare for other AP exams, or if you are super-busy with extracurricular activities, your time will be more limited.

Regardless of how much time you are able to devote to prepping for the AP Comparative Government and Politics exam, you should start by taking the diagnostic test in the next chapter. This will give you an accurate idea of what the test is like. You'll get a sense of how hard the test will be for you, how much time you need to devote to practice, and which types of questions or tasks you most need to work on. Skip around in this book, focusing on the chapters that deal with the types of questions/tasks you find most difficult. At the end of this book are two practice tests that closely match the actual exam. Take the first practice exam during spring break and the final practice exam a few days before you take the actual test.

The Six-Week Plan

OK, maybe you procrastinated a bit too long. But this might not be a problem if you are doing well in your AP Comparative Government and Politics class and just need to familiarize yourself with the types of questions and tasks on the exam. In fact, preparation for the test is included in most AP Comparative Government and Politics classes. So you may be more ready for the exam than you realize.

Start by taking the diagnostic test in the next chapter to find out what the actual test will be like and to identify the types of questions or tasks you most need to practice. Skip around in the book, prioritizing the chapters the diagnostic test identified as most in need of your careful review. Whatever you do, save time to take both practice exams at the end of this book. Even if you do well on the diagnostic test and don't need further practice with the tasks involved, taking the practice tests will give you experience in pacing yourself within the time limits of the exam.

When to Take the Practice Exams

You should take the diagnostic test in Chapter 3 when you begin your test preparation, unless you opted for the full school year of review for the test. It will show you what the exam is like and, based on your performance, you can identify your strong points as well as any weaknesses you'll need to focus on. Take the first practice test at the end of this book midway through your test preparation to measure your progress and see if your priorities should change. Take the final practice exam a few days before the actual test.

The practice tests are perhaps the most important part of this book. Taking them will do all of the following:

- Give you practice with all the different types of questions and tasks on the AP Comparative Government and Politics exam
- Allow you to measure your progress and identify areas you need to focus on in your test preparation
- Allow you to practice pacing yourself within the time limits imposed on the test

Below are some things to remember as you plan your test-prep effort, regardless of when you start and how long you plan to practice:

- Establish a calendar of review and start as early as you can.
- Use your mobile phone to time yourself every time you take a timed test or practice exercise.
- Be sure you know your Comparative Government and Politics concepts along with specific examples from each of the six required countries.
- Take advantage of the practice tests in this book. They are your friends.
- Don't stay up the night before the test trying to do some last-minute cramming; this may be counterproductive.

Good luck!

STEP **2**

Determine Your Test Readiness

CHAPTER **3** Diagnostic Test

CHAPTER 3

Diagnostic Test

IN THIS CHAPTER

Summary: In the following pages, you will find a diagnostic exam that is modeled on the actual AP exam. It is intended to give you an idea of your level of preparation in AP Comparative Government and Politics. After you have completed both the multiple-choice and the free-response questions, check your answers to the multiple-choice questions against the given answers and read over the sample rubrics for the free-response questions.

Key Ideas

✪ Practice the kind of multiple-choice and free-response questions you will be asked on the real exam.

✪ Answer questions that approximate the coverage of topics on the actual exam.

✪ Check your work against the given answers and the free-response rubrics.

✪ Determine your strengths and weaknesses.

✪ Mark the concepts that you must give special attention.

How to Take the Exam

When you take the diagnostic exam, try to reproduce the actual testing environment as closely as possible. Find a quiet place where you will not be interrupted. Do not listen to music or watch a movie while taking the exam! Set the timer on your cell phone and stop working when the 90 minutes are up. If you don't finish, note how far you get so you can learn to pace yourself, but then take the extra time to complete all the questions so you can find your areas of weakness. One more thing: Tear out the answer sheet provided and fill in the correct ovals with a #2 pencil. The AP Environmental Science exam is a paper-and-pencil test.

After Taking the Diagnostic Exam

Following the exam, you'll find not only the answers to the test questions, but also explanations for each answer. Don't just read the explanations for the questions you missed; you also need to understand the explanations for the questions you got right but weren't sure of. In fact, it's a good idea to read through the explanations for all the questions. Finally, complete the chapter-by-chapter analysis of your test results by filling in the boxes for the questions you missed. Then you have it—the chapters you most need to review.

AP Comparative Government and Politics
Diagnostic Test

Section I: Multiple-Choice Questions

ANSWER SHEET

1 (A) (B) (C) (D)	16 (A) (B) (C) (D)	31 (A) (B) (C) (D)	46 (A) (B) (C) (D)
2 (A) (B) (C) (D)	17 (A) (B) (C) (D)	32 (A) (B) (C) (D)	47 (A) (B) (C) (D)
3 (A) (B) (C) (D)	18 (A) (B) (C) (D)	33 (A) (B) (C) (D)	48 (A) (B) (C) (D)
4 (A) (B) (C) (D)	19 (A) (B) (C) (D)	34 (A) (B) (C) (D)	49 (A) (B) (C) (D)
5 (A) (B) (C) (D)	20 (A) (B) (C) (D)	35 (A) (B) (C) (D)	50 (A) (B) (C) (D)
6 (A) (B) (C) (D)	21 (A) (B) (C) (D)	36 (A) (B) (C) (D)	51 (A) (B) (C) (D)
7 (A) (B) (C) (D)	22 (A) (B) (C) (D)	37 (A) (B) (C) (D)	52 (A) (B) (C) (D)
8 (A) (B) (C) (D)	23 (A) (B) (C) (D)	38 (A) (B) (C) (D)	53 (A) (B) (C) (D)
9 (A) (B) (C) (D)	24 (A) (B) (C) (D)	39 (A) (B) (C) (D)	54 (A) (B) (C) (D)
10 (A) (B) (C) (D)	25 (A) (B) (C) (D)	40 (A) (B) (C) (D)	55 (A) (B) (C) (D)
11 (A) (B) (C) (D)	26 (A) (B) (C) (D)	41 (A) (B) (C) (D)	
12 (A) (B) (C) (D)	27 (A) (B) (C) (D)	42 (A) (B) (C) (D)	
13 (A) (B) (C) (D)	28 (A) (B) (C) (D)	43 (A) (B) (C) (D)	
14 (A) (B) (C) (D)	29 (A) (B) (C) (D)	44 (A) (B) (C) (D)	
15 (A) (B) (C) (D)	30 (A) (B) (C) (D)	45 (A) (B) (C) (D)	

AP Comparative Government and Politics
Diagnostic Test

Section I: Multiple-Choice Questions

Time—60 minutes

55 Questions

Directions: Each of the questions or incomplete statements below is followed by four answer choices. Select the one that best answers each question and then fill in the corresponding oval on the answer sheet.

Questions 1 and 2 refer to the following passage.

Source: Reuters Business News, "Mexico President Says No More Pemex Oil Joint Ventures for Now," February 21, 2019

MEXICO CITY (Reuters)—President Andres Manuel Lopez Obrador said on Thursday Mexico will not offer more oil joint ventures between private companies and state energy company Pemex indefinitely, raising doubts about auctions set for October. In reply to a question about the contracts, known in the industry as "farm-outs," Lopez Obrador said the country would not offer more until existing projects began producing oil. Credit ratings agency Fitch downgraded Pemex in January, citing precarious finances and a collapse in oil output. Lopez Obrador is betting on raising oil production through service contracts mainly with Mexican companies to squeeze more oil from existing shallow water and onshore fields. He has long been a critic of his predecessor's liberalization of the energy industry, which allowed private and foreign companies to bid for oil exploration and production both alone and in association with Pemex. Lopez Obrador, who is from oil-producing state Tabasco, has previously said he will give companies three years to start producing before he decides whether to allow more auctions. He has not been clear whether this also applies to Pemex joint ventures.

1. Which of the following statements is supported by the main idea of the passage?
   (A) President Lopez Obrador is suspicious of efforts to privatize Pemex and allow more foreign direct investment in the industry.
   (B) President Lopez Obrador is quickly moving to re-nationalize the oil industry in Mexico.
   (C) The Mexican oil company, Pemex, is in strong financial shape with plenty of investment capital to spend.
   (D) President Lopez Obrador is not familiar with oil production and is delegating decisions about the future of Mexico Mexican oil production to his subordinates.

2. Which of the following statements is an implication of the argument presented in the passage?
   (A) The neoliberal economic policies of former President Pena Nieto may be reversed by President Lopez Obrador.
   (B) President Lopez Obrador is critical of the traditional role that Pemex has played in the Mexican economy and seeks to privatize the company.
   (C) The Mexican government will not allow any private or foreign direct investment in Pemex.
   (D) The Mexican government is a rentier state and receives the majority of its government revenue from the sale of oil.

GO ON TO THE NEXT PAGE

Questions 3 and 4 refer to the following passage.

Source: Freedom in the World Report 2019. Democracy in Retreat. www.freedomhouse.org

In 2018, Freedom in the World recorded the 13th consecutive year of decline in global freedom. The reversal has spanned a variety of countries in every region, from long-standing democracies like the United States to consolidated authoritarian regimes like China and Russia. The overall losses are still shallow compared with the gains of the late 20th century, but the pattern is consistent and ominous. Democracy is in retreat.

In states that were already authoritarian, earning Not Free designations from Freedom House, governments have increasingly shed the thin façade of democratic practice that they established in previous decades, when international incentives and pressure for reform were stronger. More authoritarian powers are now banning opposition groups or jailing their leaders, dispensing with term limits, and tightening the screws on any independent media that remain. Meanwhile, many countries that democratized after the end of the Cold War have regressed in the face of rampant corruption, antiliberal populist movements, and breakdowns in the rule of law. Most troublingly, even long-standing democracies have been shaken by populist political forces that reject basic principles like the separation of powers and target minorities for discriminatory treatment.

3. Which of the following statements is supported by the main idea of the passage?
   (A) The world now has more authoritarian governments than democratic governments.
   (B) Once a country has democratized, there is very little likelihood that it will regress to authoritarianism.
   (C) Authoritarian governments feel less pressure to appear like they are protecting the civil liberties and political rights of their citizens.
   (D) Populist movements always push for more protection of civil liberties of all citizens.

4. Which of the following statements is an implication of the argument presented in the passage?
   (A) External pressure from institutions like the United Nations and the International Monetary Fund to respect democratic norms has had no effect on global governance.
   (B) Internal pressure from social movements has the power to force governments to make reforms, so authoritarian governments often restrict civil society.
   (C) Dispensing with term limits gives voters more control over elections and the selection of their leaders.
   (D) Controlling the media allows governments to protect their citizens from fake news.

Questions 5, 6, and 7 refer to the following table.

Presidential Election Results

Candidate A	38%
Candidate B	32%
Candidate C	25%
Candidate D	5%

5. According to the rules of presidential elections in Nigeria, what happens next?
   (A) Candidate A has a plurality of the votes, so Candidate A becomes the president.
   (B) Because no candidate has a majority, a run-off between Candidate A and Candidate B will be scheduled.
   (C) Candidate A will become the president and Candidate B will become the vice president.
   (D) Because no candidate has a majority, the House of Representatives will appoint a president.

6. According to the rules of presidential elections in Mexico, what happens next?
   - (A) Candidate A has a plurality of the votes, so Candidate A becomes the president.
   - (B) Because no candidate has a majority, a run-off between Candidate A and Candidate B will be scheduled.
   - (C) Candidate A will become the president and Candidate B will become the vice president.
   - (D) Because no candidate has a majority, the House of Representatives will appoint a president.

7. What is the most significant challenge facing Candidate A if it is possible to win the presidency with a simple plurality of the vote?
   - (A) Candidate A will only control 38% of the lower house in the legislature, making it difficult to pass legislation.
   - (B) Candidate A will only be able to appoint 38% of the members of the cabinet so that it will be difficult to pass legislation.
   - (C) With only 38% of the vote, Candidate A does not have a mandate from the voters, making it more difficult to pass legislation.
   - (D) With only 38% of the vote, Candidate A lacks legitimacy and will soon lose a vote of confidence in the legislature.

Questions 8, 9, and 10 refer to the following table.

Fragile State Index (FSI) 2019

COUNTRY	FSI (highest possible score is 120)	CATEGORY
CHINA	71.1	Elevated Warning
IRAN	83	High Warning
MEXICO	69.7	Warning
NIGERIA	98.5	Alert
RUSSIA	74.7	Elevated Warning
UNITED KINGDOM	36.7	Very Stable

Source: The Fund for Peace

8. According to the data in the table, which country is the most fragile?
   - (A) China
   - (B) Iran
   - (C) Mexico
   - (D) Nigeria

9. Which of the following statements is the best description of a fragile state?
   - (A) A fragile state is one with a weak economy and a high percentage of its people living in poverty.
   - (B) A fragile state is one with an authoritarian government and few protections for civil liberties.
   - (C) A fragile state is one with a number of coinciding cleavages that cause political conflict.
   - (D) A fragile state is one with political, economic, and social weaknesses caused by poverty, social unrest, and a corrupt government.

10. Which of the following is the best reason why the United Kingdom is considered very stable?
    (A) The UK has a long history of democratic consolidation combined with a strong economy and a welfare state.
    (B) The UK has a large military force with nuclear weapons and is a member of NATO.
    (C) The UK is leaving the European Union, which will reduce domestic unrest.
    (D) The UK has a constitutional monarchy with a very popular Queen to rally national support.

Questions 11, 12, and 13 refer to the following table.

European Union (EU) Referendum in the UK

July 2016   Voter Turnout 72%

	LEAVE	REMAIN
UK	51.9%	48.1%
ENGLAND	53.4%	46.6%
N. IRELAND	44.2%	55.8%
SCOTLAND	38%	62%
WALES	52.5%	47.5%

Source: BBC

11. According to the data in the chart, which of the following best summarizes the results of the EU referendum?
    (A) An overwhelming majority of British voters chose to leave the EU.
    (B) Only English voters wanted to leave the EU.
    (C) Only Scottish voters wanted to remain in the EU.
    (D) A bare majority of voters wanted the UK to leave the EU.

12. What is a major limitation of the data as presented in this chart?
    (A) It is not clear how many actual voters chose to leave the EU.
    (B) It is not clear whether a voter turnout rate of 72% is a typical turnout rate in the UK for a referendum.
    (C) There is no reference to the overseas vote on the referendum.
    (D) It is not clear what question was specifically listed on the ballot.

13. What were the implications of the results of this EU referendum on British politics?
    (A) The clear voter mandate made it impossible for the government to ignore the results.
    (B) The lack of a clear consensus made it difficult for the government to negotiate a withdrawal from the EU.
    (C) The vote marked a clear victory for Conservative Prime Minister David Cameron.
    (D) The devolved parliaments in Scotland, Wales, and Northern Ireland were quick to ratify the results of the referendum.

14. Which of the following pairs of countries have sharia as part of their formal legal structures?
    (A) Mexico, Nigeria
    (B) Russia, China
    (C) Great Britain, Mexico
    (D) Iran, Nigeria

GO ON TO THE NEXT PAGE

15. A one-party system is one in which:
    (A) election law prohibits the formation of any party except the ruling party
    (B) multiple parties compete in elections, but the same party is continuously assured of a large majority
    (C) two major parties continuously win because of the use of single-member districts
    (D) all parties have the power to nominate one candidate without a primary

16. Why is Iran characterized as a rentier state?
    (A) Because Iran is a member of OPEC and its government follows the agreement of the cartel
    (B) Because the Iranian government earns a sizable percentage of its revenue from the sale of oil to foreign companies
    (C) Because Iran is considered by the World Bank to be a developing nation with a low GDP
    (D) Because Iran has a high percentage of people living in poverty

17. According to the Chinese constitution, the government institution that formally has the most power is:
    (A) National People's Supreme Court
    (B) National Party Congress
    (C) National People's Congress
    (D) the Politburo Standing Committee

18. Which of the following is a correct statement about how Mexican presidents are selected?
    (A) They are elected to a four-year term and cannot be reelected.
    (B) They are appointed by the prime minister.
    (C) They are directly elected to a single six-year term.
    (D) They must receive a majority of votes in each of the Mexican states or face a runoff.

19. Which of the following is only a characteristic of an authoritarian regime?
    (A) A dominant party system
    (B) Independent media
    (C) Separation of powers
    (D) Patronage appointments

20. Which of the following is a normative statement?
    (A) Industrial economies face labor shortages and use migrant workers to help.
    (B) Many developing countries have a young median age and require more schools.
    (C) Postindustrial economies should be preparing to deal with an aging population.
    (D) Many authoritarian regimes have engaged in economic liberalization.

21. What kind of interest group system is characterized by a government selecting a few peak associations to negotiate over public policy?
    (A) Authoritarianism
    (B) Corporatism
    (C) Imperialism
    (D) Pluralism

22. Which of the following groups of countries has a directly elected president?
    (A) Mexico, Iran, Russia
    (B) Great Britain, China, Nigeria
    (C) China, Iran, Russia
    (D) Mexico, Great Britain, Nigeria

23. Sovereignty is:
    (A) only present in a constitutional monarchy
    (B) centralized in the national government in a unitary state
    (C) completely lost by any country that joins the European Union
    (D) only legitimate if granted through competitive elections

24. If a state were to adopt a proportional representation (PR) system with a low threshold, what kind of party system should it expect to foster?
    (A) One-party system
    (B) Two-party system
    (C) Multiparty system
    (D) Dominant party system

25. Which of the following is an appointed position in the Iranian political system?
    (A) President of Iran
    (B) Supreme Leader of Iran
    (C) Member of the Majlis
    (D) Member of the Assembly of Experts

GO ON TO THE NEXT PAGE

26. The purpose of a structural adjustment program (SAP) is to:
    (A) address serious economic problems by liberalizing trade practices
    (B) devolve more power to subnational governments
    (C) increase the power of the judiciary
    (D) cause a regime change from an authoritarian to a democratic government

27. Which of the following is a correct statement about British political parties?
    (A) The Conservatives have their strongest level of support in northern urban areas.
    (B) Sinn Fein is a Northern Irish party with strong Catholic support.
    (C) Labour won the 2017 general election and holds a majority of seats in the House of Commons.
    (D) The Liberal Democrats were part of a coalition government with the Scottish National Party.

28. What kind of statement is the following quote, "Vladimir Putin has an 81 percent approval rating"?
    (A) Normative
    (B) Empirical
    (C) Causal
    (D) A correlation

29. An example of transparency is:
    (A) when a government requires that all citizens carry identification with them in public places
    (B) when a government mandates that all families send their children to school
    (C) when a congressional committee holds a closed hearing on national security
    (D) when a bureaucratic agency publishes its budget

30. A consequence of a market economy is:
    (A) an efficient allocation of resources
    (B) equality of income
    (C) a system of government price controls
    (D) a ban on private property

31. Which of the following pairs of countries are federal?
    (A) Iran and China
    (B) Great Britain and Russia
    (C) Mexico and Nigeria
    (D) Russia and Iran

32. In a parliamentary system, the prime minister is selected:
    (A) directly by the voters
    (B) by all the leaders of the regional governments
    (C) by a unanimous vote in the legislature
    (D) by being the leader of the majority party in the legislature

33. An advantage of a federal system of government over a unitary system of government is that in a federal system:
    (A) the national government makes uniform policies for all local governments
    (B) voters have access to many more policy-makers than in a unitary system
    (C) all sovereignty is centralized in the national government
    (D) local governments lack the authority to develop local policies

34. Unicameral legislatures are:
    (A) more likely to gridlock than bicameral legislatures
    (B) likely to have more women legislators than bicameral legislatures
    (C) more likely to be dominated by two political parties than bicameral legislatures
    (D) more likely to pass a law than a symmetrical bicameral legislature

35. What type of election system is used in elections for the House of Commons?
    (A) First past the post
    (B) Proportional representation with a 5 percent threshold
    (C) Proportional representation with a 7 percent threshold
    (D) A mixed election system

GO ON TO THE NEXT PAGE

36. Which of the following political ideologies is committed to individual freedom and a market economy?
    (A) Communism
    (B) Socialism
    (C) Liberalism
    (D) Conservatism

37. Which of the following is a political party on the ideological right?
    (A) CCP
    (B) PDP
    (C) PRI
    (D) UKIP

38. Which of the following countries was corporatist but is now pluralist?
    (A) China
    (B) Great Britain
    (C) Iran
    (D) Russia

39. Which of the following is indicative of a robust civil society?
    (A) The existence of many nonpolitical community organizations
    (B) A state-controlled media
    (C) A government agency that censors political bloggers
    (D) A corporatist interest group system

40. Which of the following is an ethnic cleavage in Mexico?
    (A) Hausa vs. Yoruba
    (B) Uyghur vs. Han
    (C) Persian vs. Azeri
    (D) Mestizo vs. Amerindian

41. Which of the following do Great Britain and China have in common?
    (A) Both countries are constitutional monarchies.
    (B) Both countries have weak upper houses in the legislature.
    (C) Both countries have independent judiciaries.
    (D) Both countries belong to the WTO.

42. Which of the following is the best indicator to use to measure income inequality?
    (A) GDP per capita
    (B) Literacy rates
    (C) Population growth rates
    (D) GINI index

43. Which of the following countries has experienced both a regime change and a change in government since 1999?
    (A) China
    (B) Iran
    (C) Mexico
    (D) Russia

44. Which of the following is a reason why Iran reserves seats for minority religious groups in the Majlis?
    (A) It was a requirement to join OPEC.
    (B) Religious minority groups own substantial oil reservoirs.
    (C) It contributes to the legitimacy of the representative body.
    (D) Minority religious voters are concentrated in Tehran.

45. Why is the Nigerian cabinet an example of the federal character principle?
    (A) All members of the cabinet must represent a different ethnic group.
    (B) All members of the cabinet must be selected from the Senate.
    (C) There must be a member of the cabinet from each of the 36 states.
    (D) There must be a member of the cabinet from each of the major cities.

46. What is an advantage of being a rentier state?
    (A) Reliance on one resource increases exposure to fluctuating commodity prices.
    (B) Governments feel less need to diversify the economy.
    (C) Certain sectors of the economy develop more quickly than others.
    (D) Increased government revenue can be used for internal improvements.

GO ON TO THE NEXT PAGE

47. The Chinese government made many policy changes to become an export-driven economy. Which of the following changes had the greatest impact on increasing global trade?
    (A) The creation of Township and Village Enterprises in rural areas to encourage entrepreneurship
    (B) The creation of special economic zones with foreign direct investment
    (C) The establishment of a household responsibility system
    (D) The nationalization of many private businesses in large cities

48. How can an independent court strengthen democracy?
    (A) It can rule in accordance with the stated wishes of the executive.
    (B) It can refuse to hear controversial discrimination cases.
    (C) It can enforce rule of law according to constitutional principles.
    (D) It can assess the will of the people by studying public opinion polls.

49. Why did the British Parliament devolve power to Scotland, Wales, and Northern Ireland in the 1990s?
    (A) British MPs decided that it was time for the regions to handle their own affairs.
    (B) The Labour Party responded to regional demands for more local authority.
    (C) The Conservative Party pushed for more local autonomy to increase support for its party.
    (D) Regional parties boycotted Westminster until they could govern themselves.

50. Which of the following is NOT a power of the Iranian supreme leader?
    (A) Appoint the cabinet
    (B) Appoint six clerics of the Guardian Council
    (C) Appoint the chief judge
    (D) Appoint the commander of the armed forces

51. Which of the following was a dominant party and is now part of a multiparty system?
    (A) PRI
    (B) SNP
    (C) United Russia
    (E) APC

52. What was the major cause for the 2011–2012 protests in Russia?
    (A) Falling oil prices that led to a recession and high unemployment
    (B) The excessive cost of preparing for the Sochi Olympics
    (C) Putin's successful invasion of Crimea
    (D) Rigged State Duma elections in favor of United Russia

53. The president of which of the following countries faces a no-reelection principle?
    (A) China
    (B) Iran
    (C) Mexico
    (D) Nigeria

54. Why did the British government create the Supreme Court of the United Kingdom?
    (A) To prevent losing sovereignty to the European Court of Justice
    (B) To increase transparency by removing the Law Lords from the House of Lords
    (C) To create an independent court of justice that follows rule of law
    (D) To devolve power to an English institution instead of a Scottish one

55. Globalization is:
    (A) a system of regional governments centered around one national government
    (B) a system of international sporting leagues, like the Olympics
    (C) an international system of banking and currency exchange
    (D) an interconnected system of worldwide trade, communications, and culture

STOP: END OF SECTION I.

Section II: Free Response

Time—1 Hour and 30 Minutes

Directions: The Free-Response Section includes four questions. You need to answer all parts of all four questions. Write your answers on a separate sheet of paper, making sure to number your answers as the questions are numbered below. Before answering an essay question, take a few minutes to plan and outline your answer. Include specific examples in your answers to the essay questions where appropriate.

1. (A) Define resource curse.
   (B) Describe a problem caused by the resource curse.
   (C) Explain how governments typically deal with the problem of a resource curse.
   (D) Explain why countries with a resource curse tend to be economically underdeveloped.

2. Use the following table to complete your answer.

INDICATORS	COUNTRY ALPHA	COUNTRY BETA
GDP per Capita	$5,000	$35,000
Adult Literacy Rate	65%	99%
GINI Index	.46	.41
Population	75 million	100 million

   (A) Using the data in the table, identify which country is more economically developed.
   (B) Using the data in the table, describe how you determined your answer in (A).
   (C) Define public policy.
   (D) Explain why political scientists study economic development.
   (E) Explain what public policy Country Alpha should use to increase its literacy rate.

3. Compare how federal states handle violent uprisings in two different AP Comparative Government and Politics countries.
   (A) Define federalism.
   (B) Describe the goals of a violent group in a subnational government in two different federal AP Comparative Government and Politics countries.
   (C) Explain how the federal government in each of the two countries in (B) responded in a similar fashion to the conflict.

4. Develop an argument as to whether an independent press or an independent judiciary is more important in constraining executive power in a democratic state.
   Use one or more of the following course concepts in your response:

   • Transparency
   • Rule of Law
   • Sovereignty

In your response, you should do the following:

- Respond to the prompt with a defensible claim or thesis that establishes a line of reasoning using one or more of the provided course concepts.
- Support your claim with at least TWO pieces of specific and relevant evidence from one or more course countries. This evidence should be relevant to one or more of the provided course countries.
- Use reasoning to explain why your evidence supports your claim or thesis, using one or more of the provided course concepts.
- Respond to an opposing or alternate perspective, using refutation, concession, or rebuttal.

STOP: END OF SECTION II.

› Answers and Explanations

Section I: Multiple Choice

1. **A.** President Lopez Obrador campaigned against the privatization of Pemex. This article confirms that he is reluctant to continue the policies of former President Pena Nieto.

2. **A.** President Lopez Obrador may reverse the neoliberal economic policies, particularly those concerned with foreign direct investment.

3. **C.** The Freedom in the World report argues that authoritarian regimes are less constrained in restricting civil liberties than they used to be. The report acknowledges that authoritarian governments have not replaced democracies, but that a trend away from democratization is evident, noting that some populist movements have illiberal goals.

4. **B.** Increasingly, authoritarian regimes are restricting civil society by reducing press freedom or by banning civil society groups. These coercive measures would not be necessary if the internal forces were not effective.

5. **B.** Nigerian presidential elections require candidates to win a majority. In this case, the top 2 candidates would compete in a runoff election.

6. **A.** Mexican presidential elections award the office to the winner with the most votes. Candidate A has the plurality and thus would win.

7. **C.** With only 38% of the vote, Candidate A lacks a mandate from the voters. A lack of a mandate reduces the power of the president and makes it more difficult to enact legislation. But the president is still legitimate and will serve a fixed presidential term and not face a vote of confidence.

8. **D.** Nigeria has the highest score of 98.5/120.

9. **D.** A fragile state faces multiple challenges; in fact options A, B, and C are all components of a fragile state. The best description is the one that combines all the factors.

10. **A.** The UK is "very stable" because it has a long history of democratic consolidation with a responsive legislature that provides services to its population. Although the other factors are significant, they only support democratic consolidation.

11. **D.** 51.9% voting to leave is a bare majority of voters.

12. **A.** It is not clear how many actual voters chose to leave the EU. Eighty percent of the population of the UK lives in England, so actual population numbers would be a good addition to the graph to show the magnitude of support for Leave or Remain.

13. **B.** The lack of a clear consensus made it difficult for the government to get Brexit done. PM David Cameron and PM Theresa May both resigned before PM Boris Johnson was able to get the votes to pass the legislation.

14. **D.** Iran's legal code is based on sharia or Islamic law. Nigeria has a common-law tradition from its British colonial past, but to appease religious cleavages, the government has allowed northern states to adopt sharia in addition. No other states use sharia law.

15. **A.** A one-party system is the only party allowed by law. China has a one-party system.

16. **B.** The definition of a rentier state is one in which the government earns most of its revenue from the export and sale of a natural resource.

17. **C.** All formal power in the Chinese constitution resides in the NPC or National People's Congress.

18. **C.** Mexican presidents serve one 6-year term called a sexano after being directly elected in a plurality vote.

19. **A.** Authoritarian governments restrict voters' ability to participate in a fair, competitive election. A dominant party can only exist if elections are rigged in some manner. Democratic regimes, however, do have patronage appointment, usually to high-level bureaucratic agencies, along with separation of powers and an independent media.

20. **C.** Normative statements are statements of opinion or prescriptions of what the government should do. All the other statements are empirical or factual statements.

21. **B.** Corporatism is an interest group system characterized by a government selecting a few peak associations to negotiate public policy.

22. **A.** Mexico, Iran, and Russia, along with Nigeria, have directly elected presidents. Great Britain doesn't have a president, and China's president is appointed.

23. **B.** Sovereignty or the ultimate authority over a territory is centralized in the national government in a unitary state. Sovereignty is shared in a federal state.

24. **C.** A state that adopts a PR system of voting with a low threshold is seeking to establish a multi-party system where numerous parties can secure at least a small percentage of the popular vote.

25. **B.** The supreme leader is an appointed position. He is appointed by the Assembly of Experts. All the other offices listed are elected directly by the people of Iran.

26. **A.** The purpose of an SAP is to economically liberalize an economy by lowering trade barriers and reducing state intervention in a domestic economy.

27. **B.** Sinn Fein is a Northern Irish Catholic party. The Conservative Party is strongest in the south of England and won the most seats in the 2017 election but has had to form a coalition with the Democratic Unionists. Plaid Cymru is a Welsh party.

28. **B.** This is an empirical or factual statement based on a public opinion poll. Public opinion polls results are empirical, not normative. There is no cause given, and so there is no causal connection. There is no assertion about a relationship over time or with another variable, so it is not a correlation.

29. **D.** Transparency is when the government allows citizens to view the policymaking process, so publishing a budget is an example of transparency. Simply stating a law is not enough, to be transparent a government needs to hold open hearings about the bill and allow dissenting voices to be heard.

30. **A.** A consequence of a market economy, in theory, is an efficient allocation of resources. Adam Smith's "invisible hand" marshals the forces of supply and demand to determine price and quantity so that there is an adequate supply of goods. Price controls and lack of private property would prohibit market clearing action.

31. **C.** Mexico and Nigeria are federal, as is Russia. China, Great Britain, and Iran are unitary.

32. **D.** In a parliamentary system, the prime minister is selected as the head of the majority party in the legislature.

33. **B.** An advantage of a federal system is that shared sovereignty allows local officials the ability to make local policies, thereby increasing the number of policymakers that a voter has access to as opposed to a unitary system where power is centralized.

34. **D.** Unicameral legislatures are more likely to pass a law than a symmetrical bicameral legislature where a bill must pass each house by a majority, which is an intra-branch check. Unicameral legislatures only need a majority vote to pass a bill. The number of parties or women is more dependent on election laws as opposed to the type of legislature. Federal systems use a bicameral system to allow the subnational units' representation in the upper house and the people in the lower house.

35. **A.** The House of Commons uses a first-past-the-post or single-member district voting system.

36. **C.** Because of its roots in the Enlightenment, liberalism is the political ideology that emphasizes individual freedom and a market economy. Countries that intend to become more democratic or capitalistic pursue policies of political and economic liberalization.

37. **D.** UKIP is a far-right British party dedicated to Brexit. The CCP is the Chinese Communist Party, which is on the ideological left, as is A Just Russia. The PDP of Nigeria and PRI of Mexico are moderate parties.

38. **B.** Great Britain had a corporatist system until it was dissolved by Margaret Thatcher. It now practices pluralism.

39. **A.** Civil society is defined as the space where voluntary organizations can form free from government control. Restrictions of civil liberties do not help civil society develop.

40. **D.** The main ethnic cleavage in Mexico is between Mestizos and Amerindian.

41. **D.** Both countries belong to the WTO. Great Britain is a constitutional monarchy with a weak upper house and an independent judiciary. China staffs its bureaucracy using nomenklatura.

42. **D.** The GINI index specifically measures income inequality. The others do not.

43. **C.** Mexico moved to a full democracy in 2000 and has had several changes in presidents. Russia underwent a regime change in 1993, China in 1949, Iran in 1979, and Great Britain in 1689.

44. **C.** There are specific seats for religious minorities in the Majlis to demonstrate the legitimacy of the body in representing these groups in society. These seats are only reserved for other "People of the Book" and do not include the Baha'i.

45. **C.** The Nigerian federal character principle is to ensure that all government appointments reflect the diversity of the country. So each of the 36 states must be represented in the cabinet.

46. **D.** The main advantage of being a rentier state is increased revenue to the government that could be used to improve infrastructure. Unfortunately, the funds are usually diverted to corrupt purposes and not used to reinvest in the economy.

47. **B.** The greatest impact on China's becoming an export-driven global economy was the creation of special economic zones where foreign direct investment boosted exports. TVEs and the household responsibility system increased domestic output.

48. **C.** An independent court strengthens democracy by following rule of law and interpreting the law according to constitutional principles. An independent court will have impartial judges to make decisions.

49. **B.** The British Parliament devolved power to Scotland, Wales, and Northern Ireland after Prime Minister Tony Blair offered each region its own referendum on establishing a regional parliament. Blair was fulfilling a Labour Party manifesto election promise to gain support for the 1997 general election.

50. **A.** The president of Iran appoints the cabinet, and the Majlis approves his appointments. The supreme leader appoints the six clerics to the Guardian Council, the chief judge, the commander of the armed forces, and the head of radio and TV networks.

51. **A.** The PRI was the dominant party in Mexico until 2000 and is now part of a multiparty system dominated by the PRI, PRD, and PAN parties. United Russia is a dominant party. The SNP (Scottish National Party), Liberal Democrats (in either Great Britain or Russia), and the Nigerian APC are not dominant parties.

52. **D.** The 2011–2012 protests in Russia were triggered by the 2011 parliamentary elections that resulted in a win for United Russia despite public outrage over the Putin-Medvedev switch.

53. **C.** The president of Mexico can serve only one 6-year term. Until recently, all political offices in Mexico faced a no reelection principle. Although members of the legislature may now serve more than one consecutive term, the president cannot. The presidents of China, Iran, Nigeria, and Russia may serve two consecutive terms.

54. **B.** The British government created the Supreme Court of the United Kingdom to physically separate the Law Lords from the House of Lords by moving them into a separate building across the street from the Palace of Westminster. Although the Law Lords by tradition ruled as an independent court and the new Supreme Court did not have any new powers, this modernization of the institution was part of a series of reforms by the Blair government.

55. **D.** Globalization is an interconnected system of worldwide trade, communications, and culture. It is more than simply an economic or political phenomenon.

Section II: Free Response

Note: *The examples here are not the only correct answer to the free-response questions. There almost always exists more than one correct answer for each part of the free-response questions. Gaining full credit for a response requires answering all parts of the question.*

1. (4 points possible)

   (A) The resource curse occurs in countries that rely on the export of a natural resource for export and fail to use the revenue to diversify the economy and instead enrich political leaders. (1 point)

   (B) The revenue earned from the sale of the resource often leads to government corruption. Political leaders get personally wealthy instead of investing the money into infrastructure or education to help the economy grow. (1 point)

   (C) The government dealing with a resource curse is often the problem. Anti-corruption policies will be enacted to placate voters but often are not effective because the financial incentive is strong. (1 point)

   (D) Countries with a resource curse tend to be economically underdeveloped because the revenue earned by the sale of the resource is not used to invest in new industries or training. Nigeria is an example of a country with a resource curse. The government leaders enrich themselves and fail to develop policies to diversify the economy. (1 point)

2. (5 points possible)

   (A) Country Beta is more economically developed. (1 point)

   (B) Beta is more developed because it has a higher GDP per capita and literacy rate, both signs of economic development. (1 point)

   (C) Public policy is an action taken by a government (new law, executive order) to address a problem. (1 point)

   (D) Political scientists study economic development because the strength of an economy is a source of legitimacy for a government. If the economy is growing because of government policies, political leaders will be rewarded with popular support. (1 point)

   (E) Country Alpha has a low literacy rate. It should increase funding for public schools and teachers to address the issue. (1 point)

3. (5 points possible)

   (A) Federalism is the formal sharing of sovereignty by a national and subnational government. (1 point)

   (B) In Mexico, the Zapatistas fought for more autonomy in the state of Chiapas as well as more protection for indigenous rights. (1 point)
   In Nigeria, groups like MEND fought for a larger share of oil revenue to be spent in the Niger Delta, an area with widespread poverty and environmental degradation. (1 point)

   (C) In both countries, the government responded with force. In Mexico, troops were sent to Chiapas to put down the rebellion. (1 point). In Nigeria, troops were sent to the Niger Delta to stop the violence. (1 point). In both cases, the violence was stopped temporarily but the issue has not been completely resolved.

4. (5 points possible)
   An independent judiciary is more important in constraining executive power in a democracy than a free press because only the judiciary has the power to ensure executive compliance with rule of law. Rule of law is upheld when no one is above the law, including the executive. A free press is needed to be a watchdog over executive activity, but only the judiciary has the power to rule against an executive decision. (1 point)

Nigeria has a free press that serves an important role in holding the executive accountable to expose corruption. It is only the Supreme Court, however, who has the power to rule against the president, as it did when Obasanjo wanted to try for a third term. (1 point)

The UK has a robust free press environment that relishes its watchdog role. But here as well, it is the independent Supreme Court who has the ability to rule that the British government could not carry out Brexit without a vote from Parliament, thus ensuring parliamentary sovereignty over the government of the day. (1 point)

Separation of powers between the executive and judicial branches serves as a critical element of rule of law. In a democracy, executive authority must be constrained, and a truly independent judiciary is well positioned to accomplish that by checking executive action by either overturning it or requiring an adjustment in executive policymaking. (1 point)

Critics may charge that only a truly independent press will ensure that a government is transparent in its actions to the voters. By playing the watchdog role, a vigilant free press will hold the executive account- able. The problem remains, though, that simply highlighting the problem is not enough to stop it. A truly independent judiciary will retain the power of the law to constrain the executive. (1 point)

Scoring Conversion

You can get a rough approximation of your score on the AP Comparative Government and Politics exam. Use the answer explanations to award yourself points on the free-response questions. Then compute your raw score using the worksheet below. Finally, refer to the table to translate your raw score to an AP score of 1 to 5.

Section I: Multiple Choice

Number of questions correctly answered _____ × 1.0909 = (a) _____

Section II: Free Response

Points Earned Question 1 (4 possible) _____ × 3.3 = _____
Points Earned Question 2 (5 possible) _____ × 3 = _____
Points Earned Question 3 (5 possible) _____ × 3 = _____
Points Earned Question 4 (5 possible) _____ × 3.36 = _____

TOTAL points earned on Section II   (b) _____

RAW SCORE: Add lines (a) and (b) = _____

Conversion Table

RAW SCORE	APPROXIMATE AP SCORE
Mid 70s–120	5
Mid 60s–mid 70s	4
Mid 50s–mid 60s	3
Mid 30s–mid 50s	2
0–mid 30s	1

Assessing Your Performance and Then Prioritizing

One strategy you can use to maximize your score is to focus on the content you most need to review. It is now time to assess how you did on the diagnostic exam and devise a study plan that prioritizes the content with which you had the most trouble.

Look at each question you missed on the multiple-choice section of the exam and shade in the box below corresponding to that question. This should help you determine what chapters you need to prioritize in reviewing for the exam. Do you need more practice with concepts or with country-specific information? What countries or concepts do you need to focus your review on?

Chapter 6: Political Systems, Regimes, and Governments

5	6	20	23	28	29	31	33	43

Chapter 7: Political Institutions

14	17	18	22	25	32	32	34

Chapter 8: Political Culture and Participation

36	40

Chapter 9: Party and Election Systems and Citizens Organization

15	19	21	24	37	38	39	51

Chapter 10: Political and Economic Change and Development

7	8	16	26	30	41	42	46	49	55

Chapter 11: United Kingdom

1	2	9	27	35	37	38	41	49	54

Chapter 12: Iran

14	16	22	25	44	50

Chapter 13: Russia

22	52

Chapter 14: China

3	4	10	17	41	47

Chapter 15: Mexico

18	22	31	40	43	51	53	41	49	54

Chapter 16: Nigeria

14	22	31	45

STEP **3**

Develop Strategies for Success

CHAPTER 4

Strategies to Approach the Multiple-Choice Questions

IN THIS CHAPTER

Summary: Use these question-answering strategies to raise your score on the multiple-choice questions.

Key Ideas

✪ Familiarize yourself with the patterns of multiple-choice questions on the AP exam.

✪ Review general guidelines for answering multiple-choice questions.

✪ Learn the skill of eliminating incorrect answer choices.

✪ Practice your strategies on the multiple-choice section of a practice exam.

The Multiple-Choice Section of the Exam (Section I)

The Basics

For this first section of the Comparative Government and Politics exam, you are allotted 60 minutes to answer 55 objective questions. Some questions will be on general political concepts, while others will require you to have country-specific information from the six required case studies of China, United Kingdom, Iran, Mexico, Nigeria, and Russia. It is not expected that everyone will know the answer to every question; however, you should try to answer as many questions as you can. The AP Comparative Government and Politics questions always have four answer choices. Points are given for every correct answer. No points are given or deducted for blank answers or incorrect answers.

Types of Multiple-Choice Questions

The multiple-choice questions on the AP Comparative Government and Politics exam do not all follow the same format. The AP test makers employ several basic patterns. Some questions may involve general identification, while others may depend on analysis. Here are the types of multiple-choice questions you will encounter:

NO-STIMULUS QUESTIONS (40–44)

1. **Knowledge-Based:** these questions will test your ability to identify or define political principles, institutions, processes, policies, or behaviors.
2. **Concept Application:** these questions require you to apply political concepts to the six core course countries.
3. **Comparison Questions:** these questions ask you to explain the similarities and differences regarding political concepts and the six core course countries.

STIMULUS-BASED QUESTIONS (11–15)

1. **Quantitative Analysis:** these questions require you to analyze data presented in a table, chart, or graph. There will be three sets of these questions with 2–3 questions each.
2. **Qualitative Analysis:** these questions require to analyze text-based material. There will be two sets of these questions with 2–3 questions each.

Be sure to practice with each of these question types. None of these formats should be a surprise to you on test day.

Strategies for Answering the Multiple-Choice Questions

How to Begin

Take a quick look at the entire multiple-choice section. This will put your mind at ease because you will be more aware of what is expected. Do not spend too much time on this. Remember, this is a timed exam.

Pace Yourself

Finding the best pace for yourself is a key to getting a high score. Here are the important points to keep in mind:

- Always maintain an awareness of the time. Wear a watch. Some students like to put their watch directly in front of themselves on the desk.
- Watch the time and pace yourself. Work at a pace that is comfortable but will get you through the most questions. This should not be your first encounter with the multiple-choice section of the test. You've probably been practicing timed exams in class; in addition, this book provides you with three such experiences. Use the practice exams to practice your pacing.
- Don't spend too much time on one question. You want to make sure you answer all the questions you know before you run out of time.
- Don't rush. There are no bonus points for finishing early.

Read the Question Carefully

Reading the questions and answer choices carefully is a requirement for achieving a high score. Here are some things you can do to get a better score:

- Read the *entire* question. Don't try to guess what the question is asking.
- Read *all* the answer choices. Don't jump at the first answer choice. Consider all the choices in a given question; this will keep you from jumping to false conclusions. You may find that your first choice is not the best or most appropriate choice.
- Pay special attention to key terms.
- Watch for analytical terms such as "the best" or "the most likely to" as these require you to differentiate between several potentially correct answers.
- Don't get thrown off by the length or appearance of a question. There is no correlation between the length or the appearance of a question and the difficulty of the question.

Use the Process of Elimination

The process of elimination is your primary tool when you don't immediately know the answer. Here are the steps:

1. Don't panic if you do not know the answer to a question. You do not need to get all the questions right to get a 5. Just use the process of elimination and do your best.
2. Read the four choices again and eliminate answer choices that are:
   - Obviously wrong
   - Too narrow or too broad to answer the question
   - Illogical
   - Synonymous (identical, but phrased differently)

Remember that all parts of an answer must be correct for the answer to be correct.

3. If you've narrowed it down to two answers that are close, you may be able to do one of the following:
   - Find one that is general enough to cover all aspects of the question.
   - Find the one that is limited enough to be the detail the question is looking for.
4. If you can't narrow it down to only one choice, make an educated guess. You have a wealth of skills and knowledge. A question or choice may trigger your memory. Have confidence to use the educated guess as a valid technique.

Guessing

On the multiple-choice section of the AP Comparative Government and Politics exam, no points are deducted for incorrect answers. Therefore, it is to your advantage to guess on every question when you are not sure of the correct answer. Don't leave any questions blank on your answer sheet; if time is running out, fill in an answer choice for each question.

General Tips

- **Work in order.** This is a good approach because it's easy and clear and you will not lose your place on the scan sheet. There may be a logic to working sequentially that will help you answer previous questions. But this is your call; if you are more comfortable moving around the exam, do so.
- **Write in the exam booklet.** Mark it up! Make it yours. Interact with the test. You can cross out incorrect answers when using the process of elimination. You can also mark questions you want to come back to if you have time at the end. But don't make any marks on the answer sheet other than to fill in the correct oval.

- **Be careful on the answer sheet.** The multiple-choice section of the exam is taken on a scan sheet that is run through a computer to be scored. But if you haven't completely erased an answer choice you've changed, or if you've made any errant marks in an oval, the computer might not recognize which answer you intended. Even if it seems clear to a human eye what you intended, remember that no human eyes will look at this, only the computer.

CHAPTER 5

Strategies to Approach the Free-Response Questions

IN THIS CHAPTER

Summary: Use these question-answering strategies to raise your score on the free-response essays.

Key Ideas

✪ Review the themes that may be covered on the free-response essays.
✪ Learn how the essays are scored.
✪ Review key vocabulary found in essay prompts.
✪ Acquire strategies for responding to the essay prompts.
✪ Become familiar with rubrics.

Introduction to the Free-Response Section of the Exam (Section II)

The AP Comparative Government and Politics exam consists of four free-response questions. Each of the four questions is designed to measure a specific skill along with content knowledge.

Question 1: Concept Application (4 rubric points, 11% of total exam score)

- You will be asked to define a concept. Concepts can be about political systems, principles, institutions, processes, policies, or behaviors.
  - o Be sure to be precise in your definition.
- You will also be asked to describe and explain these concepts.

- o You do not have to give a country-specific example, but feel free to add one to enhance your description and explanation.
- It is recommended that you take 10 minutes to answer this question.

Question 2: Quantitative Analysis (5 rubric points, 12.5% of the total exam score)

- You will be asked to analyze the data presented in the table, chart, or graph.
  - o Be sure to read the data carefully and include the numbers in your answer.
  - o Remember that trends occur over time and are not a single data point.
- You will also be asked to define or describe a concept about political systems, principles, institutions, processes, policies, or behaviors.
- You will then explain how the data relates to this concept.
- It is recommended that you take 20 minutes to answer this question.

Question 3: Comparison (5 rubric points, 12.5% of the total exam score)

- You will be asked to compare two course countries based on their political systems, principles, institutions, processes, policies, or behaviors.
  - o These comparisons will either be about similarities or differences between the two course countries.
- You will then be asked to explain the implications of this comparison.
- It is recommended that you take 20 minutes to answer this question.

Question 4: Argument Essay (5 rubric points, 14% of the total exam score)

- You will be asked to develop an argument using evidence from one or more course countries to substantiate your claim.
  - o It is imperative that you state a claim or thesis.
  - o You must develop a strong and consistent argument to support your thesis.
  - o You must include one of the provided course concepts in your argument.
  - o You must have two pieces of evidence.
    - ▪ You can use two separate pieces of evidence from one country or you can use one piece of evidence from one country and a second piece of evidence from another country.
  - o You must provide reasoning to explain how your evidence backs up your claim.
  - o You must respond to an opposing/alternate perspective using refutation, concession, or rebuttal.
  - o It is recommended that you take 40 minutes to answer this question.

Frequently Asked Questions

What Is a Free-Response Essay?

The free-response questions are specific; therefore, your responses must be focused. You must pay close attention to what is being asked. To gain the highest possible score, your essay must answer the specific questions that are asked. However, responses do not necessarily require a thesis statement.

Remember that there is a general order to the tasks within the question. Organize your essay to answer the question or address the tasks in the order asked.

What Is the Purpose of the Free-Response Essay?

The free-response essay assesses your ability to think critically and analyze the topics studied in Comparative Government and Politics. The essays allow students to demonstrate an understanding of the linkages among the various elements of government.

What Are the Pitfalls of the Free-Response Essay?

The free-response question can be a double-edged sword. Students can experience test anxiety (what's "free" in the free response?) or suffer from overconfidence because of the open nature of this essay. The greatest pitfall is *the failure to plan.* Remember to pace yourself; you want to earn as many rubric points as possible. *Plan your strategy for answering each question and stick to it.* Don't ramble in vague and unsupported generalities. Rambling may cause you to contradict yourself or make mistakes. Even though your time is limited, creating a general outline may help you in this section.

How Should I Prepare for the Free-Response Essay?

You need to begin preparing for the free-response essay as soon as the course begins. Focus on your writing skills, and practice as if you were writing for the AP exam every time you are assigned an essay in your comparative government and politics class. Determine your strengths and weaknesses, and work to correct areas of weakness. Your teacher will probably give you plenty of opportunities to complete these types of essays. Some other things you can do are:

- Broaden your knowledge base by reading your textbook and supplemental texts. They will give you basic information to draw from when writing the free-response essay. Do not skim the text—READ—paying attention to details and focusing on people, events, examples, and linkages between different concepts and the six case study countries. Watch the news and pay attention to events in China, Great Britain, Iran, Mexico, Nigeria, and Russia.
- Pay attention in class to lectures and discussions. Take notes and study them.
- Take advantage of practice writing whenever possible. Watch and correct grammar, spelling, and punctuation in classroom essays. Check out previous years' free-response questions, rubrics, and sample scored student essays on https://apstudent.collegeboard.org. (You will have to register to access the specific course sites, but it is worth your time.)

Types of Free-Response Essay Prompts

Free-response questions are generally straightforward and ask you to perform certain tasks. Understanding exactly what the prompt (question) is asking you to do will help you perform the task correctly. The types of prompts you can expect to encounter on the AP Comparative Government and Politics exam are described as follows.

Define

When you see the "define" prompt, briefly tell what something is or means. Make sure that the definition is specific enough to define only the term given.

TASK	PROBLEMATIC RESPONSE	CORRECT RESPONSE
Define unitary government.	Unitary governments have national and subnational levels of government.	Unitary governments centralize all sovereignty in the national government.
	Problem: Federal systems also have national and subnational levels of government.	Key to unitary versus federal systems of government is which level of government has sovereignty.

Identify

The "identify" prompt requires you to briefly list terms or actions. Be careful not to offer more than the number of terms that are being identified. The AP Comparative Government and Politics exam has a decision rule: **If a student provides more than the number of examples that are asked for in a question, and any of the responses are wrong, then a wrong answer cancels out the correct answer, and the student does not earn a point.** Don't risk it! Only provide exactly what the prompt requires.

TASK	PROBLEMATIC RESPONSE	CORRECT ANSWER
Identify one country in the AP Comparative Government and Politics course that has a directly elected president.	United Kingdom, China, and Iran	Iran has a directly elected president.
	Problem: Only Iran has a directly elected president. The United Kingdom and China are incorrect answers. The wrong answer cancels out the correct answer and the student does not earn a point.	The questions asked for one country—select only one country.

Describe

When you see the "describe" prompt, use words to create a mental picture by using details or examples. Be sure not to simply identify the term; you have to write a more complete description.

TASK	PROBLEMATIC RESPONSE	CORRECT ANSWER
Describe how the cabinet is selected in Great Britain.	The prime minister picks it.	The prime minister selects the cabinet from among the senior members of her party in the House of Commons. These ministers retain their MP seat and are also members of the cabinet.
	Problem: What does the prime minister do to select a cabinet?	Be as complete as possible in your description.

Compare

If you are asked to "compare," point out similarities and/or differences between the two terms. Be sure to include specific references to both terms. Your answer should be as complete as possible.

TASK	PROBLEMATIC RESPONSE	CORRECT ANSWER
Compare the role of the judiciary in a democracy and an authoritarian regime.	An independent judiciary is essential to a democracy but not to an authoritarian regime.	An independent judiciary is essential to a democracy because it protects civil liberties, whereas in an authoritarian regime, the judiciary is often a tool of the government and does not enforce rule of law.

| | Problem: Why is it essential to a democracy, and why isn't it essential to an authoritarian regime? | In order to compare, you must completely explain your point for both terms in the question. |

Explain

To respond to a prompt asking you to "explain," you should give evidence to show why or how something happens. Be sure to include an example that you can use as evidence. An example by itself is not an explanation, but it can clarify your explanation to help you earn the point.

TASK	PROBLEMATIC RESPONSE	CORRECT ANSWER
Explain why a government would offer a referendum.	Governments offer referendums to find out how people feel about an issue.	Governments offer referendums to allow the people a direct vote on a public policy issue. For example, the British government allowed the people in Scotland to vote for or against Scottish independence.
	Problem: This explanation is not complete enough. It could be explaining a public opinion poll.	The example can help you fully explain your answer.

Identify a Trend

To identify a trend you need to show what happened to the variable over time. Be sure not to simply identify a single data point. Describe the trend so that the reader could draw it from your description.

TASK	PROBLEMATIC RESPONSE	CORRECT ANSWER
Identify a trend on the graph of President Putin's public approval ratings from 2000 to 2017.	In 2011, Putin's approval rating dropped.	From 2000 to 2017, President Putin's public approval ratings have consistently stayed higher than 70%.
	Problem: A trend is more than a single data point.	A trend is over time, so include the dates. Also include data drawn directly from the graph.

Develop an Argument

The challenge of developing an argument is the most important task in Free-Response #4 because all the other points are earned from supporting the claim or thesis that you develop. Clearly make your claim and state your reason for your position. It is often helpful to include the word "because" in your answer. Readers want to know why you selected the choice that you did.

TASK	PROBLEMATIC RESPONSE	CORRECT ANSWER
Develop an argument as to whether the use of coercion by an authoritarian state is effective or not effective at maintaining stability.	Coercion is effective at maintaining stability in an authoritarian state.	Coercion is effective at maintaining stability in an authoritarian state because the use of force allows the government to maintain its sovereignty.
	Problem: What is coercion? Why is coercion effective?	**Be sure to clearly state what coercion is and why you believe it to be effective.**

Strategy for Developing the Free-Response Essay

You've learned what the essay is and the tasks that you might be asked to perform in the essay. It's time to write the essay. Here is a step-by-step guide that provides a comprehensive strategy for developing the free-response essay.

A Step-by-Step Guide to Writing the Free-Response Essay

1. **Read the question carefully**, in its entirety, and determine what you are being asked to write about. Analyze the question and identify the topics, issues, and key terms that define your task (define, discuss, explain). Underline key terms to focus your attention.
2. **Brainstorm ideas.**
3. **Organize ideas and outline your essay** before you begin to write. Use the blank space in your test booklet to plan. (Brainstorming and outlining should take about five to eight minutes per question.)
4. **Write the essay.** Be sure to include the exact words of the prompt in your answer to help ensure that you are answering the specific question that is being asked. Pay attention to the prompt task verb to make sure that you are providing enough information. Try to provide examples.
5. **Reread the question and your essay** to determine if you answer the question or questions. NOTE: Many of the free-response questions will have several parts; make sure you answer them all.
6. **Proofread** for grammar, spelling, and punctuation errors. Even though these errors will not count against you, they can make your essay harder to read and can make your answer less understandable. You want to be sure that the reader can read your essay. Consider printing your answer if your handwriting is difficult to read.

Example

Question: Describe a function of political parties in a democracy.

Your thoughts:

- "Describe" means to create a mental picture.
- A function of political parties is to provide cues for voters about the party's candidates and their position on public policies.
- "In a democracy" means that elections are fair and competitive.

Your response:

> *A function of political parties in a democracy is to help make sure that elections are competitive so that voters have real choices about who they want to represent them. So political parties provide cues for voters about the party's candidates and their position on public policies, thereby ensuring that people can make an informed vote between the choices.*

Some Final Helpful Tips

When writing your free-response essays, consider these dos and don'ts.

DON'T

- **Don't** use words that you are uncomfortable using or not familiar with. Readers are not impressed if you use "big words" but don't understand what they mean or use them incorrectly.
- **Don't** try to "fake out" the reader. They are government professors and teachers. Trying to do this will *always* hurt you more than help you.
- **Don't** preach, moralize, editorialize, or use "cute" comments. Remember, you want the reader to think positively about your essay.
- **Don't** "data dump" or create "laundry lists." Do not provide information (names or policies) without explanation or relevant link to the question.

DO

- **Do** write neatly and legibly. Write or print in blue or black ink (not pencil; it's harder to read) as clearly as you can.
- **Do** use correct grammar, spelling, and punctuation. They make your essay much easier to read and understand.
- **Do** answer all questions and all parts of each question. You may answer the questions in any order. Answer the questions you feel you know best first. That way, if you run out of time and don't finish, no harm is done. Even though the essays are graded on different scales, they are weighted and together count for half your total score (60 out of 120 points).
- **Do** support your essay with specific evidence and examples. If the question asks for examples, supply not only the example but also a discussion of how that example illustrates the concept. Provide however many examples the question asks for; hypothetical examples may sometimes be used if they are backed up with facts.
- **Do** pay attention to dates. When time frames are used, keep your evidence and examples within that time frame. For example, if the question says "since 2000 in Russia," that would not include the presidency of Boris Yeltsin.
- **Do** stop when you finish your essay. If you ramble on after you have answered the question completely, you might contradict yourself, causing the reader to question your answer. When you finish, *proofread!*

Note: Just remember that your free-responses are one-half of your overall score. Be sure to frequently practice answering sample prompts. In each chapter of Step 4 you will find a set of four sample test-like free-response questions you can use to hone your skills. If you want more examples than are provided in this book, review past exams on www.apstudent.collegeboard.com.

STEP 4

Review the Knowledge You Need to Score High

CHAPTER 6

Political Systems, Regimes, and Governments

IN THIS CHAPTER

Summary: Political science is the study of the struggle for power and the choices that governments make. The main focus of study are political systems and the institutions, laws, ideas, and procedures that are used to govern society. There are different specialties within the field. Americanists study the United States; comparativists focus on the domestic politics of countries other than the United States, whereas someone interested in international relations would study how states interact with each other. As an AP Comparative Government and Politics student, you will be using the internal political struggles of the six selected countries as case studies to help you develop a deeper understanding of political concepts.

To do this successfully, you will need to master two things:

The comparative method: You must learn how to compare the similarities and differences between states in order to gain deeper understanding of political forces.

Content vocabulary: It is important when you want to compare something that you carefully define what it is that you would like to compare. This will require precise attention to detail. The concepts that you must master in the AP Comparative Government and Politics course are arranged about four basic themes:

- ✪ Power and Authority
- ✪ Legitimacy and Stability
- ✪ Democratization
- ✪ Internal/External Forces

Key Terms

authoritarian	governments	reform
authority	illiberal	regime
causation	legitimacy	representation
consolidated democracy	nation	revolution
correlation	normative	rule of law
coup	political culture	sovereignty
democratic consolidation	political socialization	state
democratization	political stability	transitional
devolution	qualitative	transparency
empirical	quantitative	unitary
federalism	random sample	

The Comparative Method

The study of comparative politics relies heavily on understanding the similarities and differences between the political systems, institutions, and behaviors of two or more countries. In order to do this, it is important to be systematic in determining not only what to compare, but also how to make these comparisons. Deciding what to compare is critical. Comparativists use both inductive and deductive reasoning techniques to develop hypotheses and gather evidence with the goal of identifying patterns of behavior. Sources of political inquiry include those that are **qualitative** and descriptive (political speech, interview, cartoon) or **quantitative** and measurable (voter turnout rates, literacy rates). Throughout your study of AP Comparative Government and Politics you should seek out comparative data from such sites as *Gapminder, Freedom House,* and *the World Bank.*

One of the most common methods of political analysis used to obtain information is by employing surveys. A properly conducted survey using a **random sample** can provide important insights about political behavior. Oftentimes there will be an apparent association, or **correlation**, between two variables, but it is difficult to prove **causation** where one variable directly led to a change in the other variable. Causation is always a challenge because there are often several variables that could have an indirect effect on either or both of the variables being studied. Causation is particularly difficult to prove in comparative politics because of the small number of states available for study and the lack of comparable data. Combined with the difficulty of conducting surveys in repressive authoritarian environments or surmounting language barriers, comparativists also must be wary of selection bias. Yet despite the challenges, comparative inquiry is a fascinating way to approach the study of politics, not only because of the **empirical** or factual conclusions that can be drawn from the evidence, but also the **normative** or value-related assertions that may be made about political behavior. On the AP exam, you may be asked to identify statements as being empirical or normative or to provide your own examples of these concepts.

For example:

Which of the following statements makes an empirical conclusion? Which is a normative statement?

A. Sixty-three percent of Nigerians have a favorable view of China.

B. The Chinese government should continue to fund development programs in Nigeria.

Statement A is empirical because it is a factual, descriptive statement drawn from a Pew Global poll, whereas Statement B is normative because it is a prescriptive assertion about what the Chinese government should do.

Which of the following is a statement showing a correlation? Which one is a causal statement?

C. A majority of people in both Nigeria and China have a favorable view of China.

D. An increase in foreign direct investment boosts economic growth in a country.

Statement C shows a correlation in that there is an apparent relationship between the two populations about a favorable view of China. Statement D is a causal statement in that it asserts that one action, an increase in foreign direct investment, has a direct effect on economic growth.

Sovereignty, Authority, and Power

Harold Laswell defines politics as "who gets what, when, and how." Subsequently, one can think about politics as the power to get what you want, when you want, and how you want. Many actors within a society exert power, so in studying political institutions, the focus is on **authority** or the right to use power. The basic political institution that you will study in AP Comparative Government and Politics is the state, which has been the basis for political comparison since the Treaty of Westphalia in 1648. A **state** is a unified political entity that has a monopoly on the use of force within its borders. In other words, states have **sovereignty**, or ultimate authority over their territory. **Governments** are the individuals who exercise authority for the state. These leaders run the political institutions that make public policy. Consequently a change in government is when there is a change in political leaders, such as when Boris Johnson replaced Theresa May as the British prime minister.

The six states in the AP Comparative Government and Politics course are as follows:

AS IDENTIFIED ON THE AP EXAM	OFFICIAL STATE NAME
China	The People's Republic of China
United Kingdom	The United Kingdom of Great Britain and Northern Ireland
Iran	The Islamic Republic of Iran
Mexico	United Mexican States
Nigeria	Federal Republic of Nigeria
Russia	Russian Federation

The Difference Between Nation and State

It is important to note that there is a difference between a state and a nation. A **nation** is a self-identified group that shares a common culture, ethnicity, language, or religion and aspires for political control. Many of the AP Comparative six countries are multination states that struggle to accommodate the demands of the various groups within their territory. A state's ability to use its power to control conflict is often a key to its legitimacy.

Goals of a Government

The study of government and politics, therefore, is about how the political actors in a state acquire authority to make decisions that the citizens of a state will find legitimate. **Legitimacy** is when the people accept the government's authority to make policy. According to sociologist Max Weber, there are three sources of legitimacy:

- *Traditional legitimacy:* Traditions are long-standing procedures with historical or religious precedence that give credibility to government decision making because they have been in place for an extended period. The British monarchy would be an example of a political institution strengthened by traditional legitimacy. Putin's close connection to the leaders of the Russian Orthodox church would be an example of using religious authority to strengthen political position.
- *Charismatic legitimacy:* Charismatic legitimacy is found in the personal appeal of an individual with a compelling vision that attracts multiple followers. In particular, revolutionary leaders such as Mao Zedong in China or the Ayatollah Khomeini in Iran gained power through their charisma.
- *Rational-legal legitimacy:* Rational-legal legitimacy is found in adherence to a set of laws or procedures, the most fundamental of which is a country's constitution.

An important way for a state to maintain its legitimacy is to provide **political stability**. Political stability ensures that the government is in control. By maintaining sovereignty over both internal actors, such as separatist groups, or external actors, such as multi-national corporations (MNCs), a government can effectively use its authority to make policy.

Compare Types of Political Systems

Although all states have sovereignty, they vary in where they get their source of authority. A **regime** is the prevailing pattern of politics in a state over time. Typically, a regime is classified as democratic or authoritarian, although the term *hybrid* or *transitional* is used to describe a state that displays elements of both. Therefore, a regime change occurs when a political system moves from a democratic system to authoritarianism or vice versa. Assessing the degree to which a state is democratic is a common challenge on the AP Comparative Government and Politics exam. Therefore it is imperative that you are able to describe the characteristics of a democratic regime and to compare them with the characteristics of an authoritarian regime. In the following chart, note well how the various sources of power are differentiated in the three regime types.

	LIBERAL CONSOLIDATED DEMOCRACY	TRANSITIONAL OR HYBRID DEMOCRACY	AUTHORITARIAN
Source of Power	People	Mixed	Hereditary, military, religion
Elections	Fair, frequent, competitive Leaders can be voted out of office	Illiberal—elections take place, but they are neither free nor fair and may not be competitive	Rubber stamp—if held Not competitive
Media/Press Freedom	Independent—opposing views are expressed—multiple outlets	Limited—may allow some opposition outlets but state control of main sources of information	Restricted—either state owned or controlled—opposition is not tolerated Propaganda arm of government

Rule of Law	Upheld—constitutional government that follows formal procedures	Limited—may have a constitution but rules may be manipulated	Restricted—may have a constitution but rules are arbitrarily applied to consolidate power
Civil Society	Civil liberties are protected—freedom of speech, assembly, religion Free to form voluntary organizations outside state control Right to protest	Limited—may form nonpolitical voluntary organizations but political groups are restricted	Civil liberties are restricted—limits on speech, assembly, and religion State-approved organizations State-sponsored protest
Judiciary	Independent—courts act as effective check on executive/legislative actions	Limited—not an effective check on executive/legislative action	Not independent—controlled by authority—serve as repressive arm
Executive-Legislative Relationships	Provide true checks and balances to limit power	Limited checks and balances to control executive power	Executive authority prevails with few checks on power
Transparency	Transparent—government allows citizens to access information about its decision-making process—open hearings, published budgets	Limited—some access to policymaking process	Opaque—government restricts access to its policymaking process—closed proceedings, censorship, secrecy

Once you have mastered the differences between regime types, it is also important that you understand how regimes transition from being considered authoritarian to democratic. If a system becomes democratic, you will be asked to evaluate whether the state has undergone **democratic consolidation**, a process that occurs over a period of time as a state deepens its commitment to free and fair elections and protecting civil liberties.

Typically, the study of political change focuses on **democratization** or political liberalization. This is the process of a state becoming more responsive to the consent of the governed. The questions to ask are: To what degree does the government of a state respond to public pressure? Are elections free, fair, and competitive? Is there an independent judiciary and a press? Is the government limited by effective checks and balances? Does civil society flourish? If the answer is no, how did the state repress the demand for change? If the answer is yes, then how and why did it happen?

Often, democratization is the result of one of three types of political change:

- **Revolution:** The most dramatic form of change in which a large popular movement often violently causes a regime change.
- **Coup:** A small group of elites, often military officers, seize control of the government but make no fundamental change to the regime.
- **Reform:** The most common type of change where adjustments are made to institutions or rules using constitutional procedures.

Reforms often involve two types of state responses:

- **Recognition:** A group's status is acknowledged by the government regarding land, language, or religious rights.
- **Representation:** A group is given the opportunity to participate more fully in the political system through extending suffrage opportunities, power-sharing agreements, or devolution.

TYPE OF POLITICAL CHANGE	CHINA	UNITED KINGDOM	IRAN	MEXICO	NIGERIA	RUSSIA
Revolution	1949 Communists led by Mao		1979 Led by Ayatollah Khomeini	1910 Led by Madero, Villa		1917 Communists led by Lenin
Coup			1953 PM Mosaddegh overthrown	1913, 1920 By generals	Series of military coups from 1966–1993	1991 attempt to overthrow Gorbachev 1993 Yeltsin shuts down Parliament
Reform	1983 Constitution	*Evolution not revolution*	1979 Islamic Republic Constitution	1917 Constitution	1999 Constitution	1993 Constitution
	Grant ethnic minorities language rights Require elections at village level Protect private property in Constitution	Devolution Human Rights Act Referendums		Creation of an independent election commission Mixed election system	Federal character Informal power-sharing agreement between North and South Accommodating sharia in the North	
Regime Status	Authoritarian	Consolidated Democracy	Authoritarian	Democratic	Democratic	Authoritarian

Compare Levels of Government

Political systems not only vary by regime type, but also by how power is either centralized or decentralized geographically. Most states have both national and subnational levels of government. Deciding which vertical power level should exercise sovereignty is a critical choice in state formation.

- **Unitary government:** A system of government in which all sovereignty is centralized in the national government. Most countries in the world are unitary governments because of the efficiency of uniform policy development. It is important to note that there are often numerous subnational governments in a unitary system. Oftentimes, the national government will transfer power to a lower level of government to address regional concerns in a process called **devolution.**
- **Federalism:** A system of government in which sovereignty is formally shared between the national and subnational governments. Federalism's main advantage is that it allows for decentralized decision making, where local governments have flexibility in developing policy to meet local concerns. On the other hand, the increased level of complexity can lead to an uneven access to government services.

	CHINA	UNITED KINGDOM	IRAN	MEXICO	NIGERIA	RUSSIA
Level of Government	Unitary	Unitary devolved	Unitary	Federal	Federal	Federal

› Review Questions

Multiple Choice

1. Which of the following is a correct description of the relationship between correlation and causation?
   - (A) Correlation refers to two events occurring together, while causation refers to one event causing another.
   - (B) Correlation is used in quantitative research, while causation is used in descriptive case study research.
   - (C) Correlation refers to one event preceding another, while causation refers to events occurring at the same time.
   - (D) Correlation refers to the likelihood of an event occurring, while causation refers to the potential significance of the event.

2. An empirical statement is:
   - (A) a statement of what should be done
   - (B) a statement of fact
   - (C) a counterfactual statement
   - (D) a predictive statement about the future

3. Transparency refers to:
   - (A) the ability of foreign corporations to compete with domestic firms
   - (B) the ability of individuals to cross political borders
   - (C) the ability of citizens to observe government decision making
   - (D) the ability of candidates to switch political parties

4. A hybrid political system is one that combines elements of:
   - (A) presidential and parliamentary systems
   - (B) colonial and post-independence political systems
   - (C) winner-take-all and proportional representation election systems
   - (D) democratic and authoritarian systems

5. Which of the following is an example of rational-legal legitimacy?
   - (A) Members of Mexico's PAN party use images of Our Lady of Guadalupe to attract followers.
   - (B) The Iranian constitution specifically details which aspects of the Iranian government are democratic.
   - (C) Many Russians like President Putin's strong tsar-like image.
   - (D) President Xi of China is encouraging the Chinese people to embrace Confucian values.

6. An advantage of a unitary system of government over a federal system of government is that in a unitary system:
   - (A) the national government makes uniform policies for all local governments
   - (B) local governments have sovereignty to develop policies to address local concerns
   - (C) there are no regional governments to disrupt policymaking → *Devolution of powers*
   - (D) voters have access to many more policy-makers than in a federal system

7. Which of the following is an example of a coup?
   - (A) Environmentalists protest the building of a government pipeline.
   - (B) Citizens reject a referendum on independence.
   - (C) Military generals remove the president from office.
   - (D) The legislature votes to impeach the president.

6/7

Free Response

1. (A) Define democratic consolidation. *[handwritten: The process of becoming a democratic country through increasing dem norms over time.]*
   (B) Describe the difference between a democratic and an authoritarian state. *[handwritten: Dem → free/fair, rights/libs, reps. Auth → oppressive, restrictive, control]*
   (C) Explain why it takes time for democratic consolidation to be established. *[handwritten: Takes a while to implement policies and for people to use them]*
   (D) Explain how external forces can help maintain democratic consolidation. *[handwritten: ~ legitimacy and transparency]*
   [handwritten: ~ Supernational Organizations - country, military force, etc. People in power are not very willing to give it up]

2. Use the following table to complete your answer.

Freedom in the World 2019 Report:

COMPONENTS OF A POLITICAL SYSTEM	FREEDOM HOUSE SURVEY RESULTS
ELECTIONS	Over the last 4 years, electoral processes have declined more than any other measure of freedom.
TERM LIMITS	Leaders in 34 countries have tried to revise term limits in the last 13 years and were successful 31 times.
FREEDOM OF EXPRESSION	Freedom of expression, already in decline has taken a steeper downturn in the past 6 years.

   (A) Using the data in the table, identify a trend about global democratization.
   (B) Describe a limitation of the data presented in the table.
   (C) Describe the difference between correlation and causation.
   (D) Explain why a political scientist would study global trends about elections, term limits, and freedom of expression.
   (E) Explain why it is easier to report correlations than it is to make causal conclusions.

3. Compare the process of regime change with that of a change in government in two different AP Comparative Government and Politics course countries. In your response, you should do the following:
   (A) Describe the difference between a regime change and a change in government.
   (B) Describe a regime change and a change in government in two different AP Comparative Government and Politics course countries.
   (C) Explain how the regime change in (B) for each country affected political stability more than the change in government in (B).

4. Develop an argument as to whether a federal or unitary system is more efficient at policymaking.

   Use one or more of the following course concepts in your response.
   • Devolution
   • Political participation
   • Political efficacy

   In your response, you should do the following:
   • Respond to the prompt with a defensible claim or thesis that establishes a line of reasoning using one or more of the provided course concepts.
   • Support your claim with at least TWO pieces of specific and relevant evidence from one or more course countries. This evidence should be relevant to one or more of the provided course countries.
   • Use reasoning to explain why your evidence supports your claim or thesis, using one or more of the provided course concepts.
   • Respond to an opposing or alternate perspective, using refutation, concession, or rebuttal.

❯ Answers and Explanations

Multiple Choice

1. **A.** Correlation means there is an apparent association between variables, but causation means one variable caused an effect on another variable.

2. **B.** An empirical statement is a statement of fact drawn from evidence.

3. **C.** Transparency is a critical component of democratic states because citizens are allowed to have access to the process of government decision making.

4. **D.** A hybrid system is a combination of two regime types, democratic and authoritarian systems.

5. **B.** Rational-legal legitimacy is based on established laws like a constitution. The other examples are based on traditional or charismatic legitimacy.

6. **A.** The major advantage of a unitary system is that all sovereignty is centralized in the national government. This allows a uniformity of policy across the state. It is important to remember that a unitary system does not mean that there is only one government because all unitary states have subnational governments. These regional or local governments often have elected officials as well with administrative authority. Policymaking authority, however, is retained by the national government unless devolved to the subnational government. This means that, unlike in a federal system, local governments have less ability to develop policies to address local concerns and therefore voters have less access to policymakers.

7. **C.** A coup is when an elite group, often military, seizes control of the government through nonconstitutional means. Impeaching and removing a president would not constitute a coup.

Free Response

1. (4 points possible)

   (A) Democratic consolidation is the process of strengthening the democratic norms in a society over time. (1 point)

   (B) The difference between a democratic state and an authoritarian state is about the source of power and how that power is used. A democratic state derives its power from the people, and its power is constrained by rule of law. An authoritarian state derives its power from a source other than the people, whether it be hereditary or military force. An authoritarian government is also not limited by rule of law, rather it acts in an arbitrary fashion. (1 point)

   (C) It takes time for a democracy to consolidate because former authoritarian leaders tend to not want to give up power. Democratic norms like rule of law, free and fair elections, and protections of civil liberties prevent power from staying in the hands of one group. Groups that are used to wielding power will be reluctant to give it up. Many new democracies backslide into old habits. Only after authoritarian leaders have been voted out of office, is a democracy considered consolidated. (1 point)

   (D) External forces like the UN or the EU can help maintain democratic consolidation by requiring states to protect civil liberties and fair elections if a new democratic state wants to join a supranational group like the EU or face sanctions for human rights violations from the UN. This international pressure helps to constrain potential autocratic leaders. (1 point)

2. (5 points possible)

   (A) There has been a decline in global democratization as over the last 4 years as there has been a decline in free and fair elections and freedom of expression. (1 point)

   (B) A limitation of the data is that although global data is listed, we have no information on specific countries or a quantitative amount of decline for these indicators. (1 point)

   (C) The difference between correlation and causation is how the two variables relate to each other. With a correlation, there is an apparent relationship between two variables. Causation means that one variable had a direct influence on the other. (1 point)

   (D) A political scientist studies global trends to help make comparisons about political systems. Elections, term limits, and freedom of expression are all indicators of regime types and power relationships. (1 point)

   (E) It is easier to report correlations because a person only has to point out an apparent relationship between variables. In the table, for example, all three indicators have declined. It is more difficult to isolate a causal factor. For example, which of these indicators is the main reason for a decline in democracy in the world? (1 point)

3. (5 points possible)

   (A) A regime change is when a political system moves from an authoritarian system to a democratic one. This is a significant change in the entire system and it happens infrequently. A change in government, on the other hand, occurs systematically during elections when the executive can be voted out of office. (1 point).

   (B) In Mexico, a change of government occurred when López Obrador won the presidential election after Peña Nieto had completed his six-year term. The election of 2000 is considered the beginning of a regime change in Mexico, however, because for the first time in 70 years, a non-PRI candidate, Fox, won the presidency. (1 point)

   In Nigeria, a change in government occurred when Buhari defeated Jonathon for the presidency. A regime change occurred in 1999 when the 4th Republic was established after military rule. (1 point)

   (C) In Mexico, regime change reflected the end of the PRI as a dominant party. Even when PRI candidate Peña Nieto won the presidential election, he did not try to reestablish a dominant party. Now one could argue that the PRI provided political stability, but the new democratic regime is consolidating as control of the government switches between parties. (1 point)

In Nigeria, regime change ended a long trend of military coups. The repressive regime may have stabilized the country, but it failed to protect civil liberties. The new 4th Republic has consolidated democratic norms so that even a change in government has not resulted in more coups. (1 point)

4. (5 points possible)

Unitary systems are more efficient in policymaking than federal systems because they centralize sovereignty in the national government. This uniform policymaking increases political efficacy by the voters because they can focus on holding the national government accountable. (1 point)

The UK has a unitary system with efficient policies such as the National Health Service, which provides free, universal health care. The unitary tax system raises the revenue to make sure that all citizens in the UK enjoy this benefit of the welfare state. (1 point)

In addition, the UK has efficiently devolved power to regional governments over certain policy issues. Rather than formally sharing power as in a federal system, the British government has targeted certain areas to efficiently handle specific local issues without giving up national government sovereignty. (1 point)

Efficiency in policymaking is accomplished through a central body making uniform policies for all citizens, which makes it easy for citizens to target that one body to push for change. (1 point)

Critics charge that uniform policymaking is not necessarily efficient if local issues would be better solved by local officials as occurs in a federal system. Federalism means that sovereignty or ultimate authority over the territory is shared between the national and subnational government. In addition, more levels of government with power may actually increase political efficacy as it is easier for voters to speak directly with local officials. Having lots of levels of government and officials can be confusing to voters, however, and difficult to hold accountable, In the end, a unitary system is more efficient. (1 point)

〉 Rapid Review

- To be successful on the AP Comparative Government and Politics exam you must master two things: the comparative method and content vocabulary.
- Comparativists analyze both qualitative (descriptive) and quantitative sources of information.
- One of the most common ways to compare is using a random sample survey.
- A correlation is an apparent association between two variables, while causation is when one variable causes an effect on another.
- Comparativists make both empirical or factual conclusions as well as normative or value-related assertions.
- Politics is "who gets what, when, and how."
- Authority is the right to use power.
- The state is a unified political entity that has a monopoly on the use of force within its borders.
- Sovereignty is a state's ultimate authority over its territory.
- Governments are the individuals who exercise authority for the state.
- A nation is a self-identified group that shares a common culture, ethnicity, language, or religion and aspires for political control.
- Legitimacy is when the people accept the government's authority to make policy.
- A regime is a prevailing pattern of politics in a state over time. Typically, states are characterized as democratic, authoritarian, or transitional.

- Democratic consolidation is a process that occurs over a period of time as a state deepens its commitment to free and fair elections and protecting civil liberties.
- It is important to be able to explain why a state has a particular regime by describing the specific sources of authority for the regime.
- A regime change is when a state moves from being one type of political system to another; for example, moving from authoritarian to democratic. This is different from a change in government, which is a change in leadership of the executive branch.
- Democratization is the process of transitioning from an authoritarian to a democratic state.
- Political stability is a goal of a government as a source of legitimacy. How a government handles conflict often reflects whether the regime is democratic or authoritarian by the amount of force that is used.
- There are three main types of political change: reform, coup, and revolution. Protesting groups are often seeking recognition or representation.
- States differ in the degree to which they centralize authority. A unitary system concentrates power in the central government to maintain uniform control over policymaking. A federal system formally shares power between the national and subnational governments to decentralize policymaking.
- Be sure to be precise in your use of vocabulary.

CHAPTER 7

Political Institutions

IN THIS CHAPTER

Summary: This chapter is a guide to the fundamental government institutions in the AP Comparative Government and Politics course. All states, whether democratic or authoritarian, use some combination of the following institutions to govern a country. Typically, one would first look at a country's constitution to see which combination the state has chosen. Choices are made about the levels of government, the type of legislative-executive relationship, and judicial and bureaucratic systems. Remember that only government institutions make public policy. Legislatures make laws and pass budgets. Executives develop policy, appoint officials, and enforce laws. Bureaucrats write regulations and implement programs. Judges interpret the law.

Key Terms

bicameral legislature	head of government	presidential system
bureaucracy	head of state	prime minister
bureaucrat	impeach	rule of law
cabinet	judicial review	semi-presidential system
code law system	merit	sharia law
common law system	parliamentary system	supranational organization
constitution	patron-client system	unicameral legislature
elite recruitment	president	vote of no confidence

Government Institutions

It is important to understand when studying comparative politics that states have many ways to organize their political institutions. The six case studies will help clarify these differences for you.

Compare Constitutions

One of the first places to look to discern the political choices that a state has made is to review its constitution. To help you do that, check out the website www.constituteproject.org, which was designed to help governments quickly compare already developed constitutions. A **constitution** is a document that describes how the government is to be organized and what the powers of the government are to be. You must be careful, however, to distinguish between a government that has a constitution and one that is constitutional. A constitutional government is one that follows **rule of law** where the formal rules are consistently applied. For example, although Chapter II of the Chinese constitution states that the "Citizens of the People's Republic of China enjoy freedom of speech," one only has to study the career of Nobel Peace Prize winner Liu Xiaobo to understand the inconsistent protection of this right in China.

Compare Types of Legislative-Executive Relationships

There are two basic systems of legislative-executive relationships: presidential and parliamentary. **Presidential systems** are when the chief executive is chosen in separate elections from the legislature for a specific term of office. This is to structurally separate the powers between the two branches. The legislature usually has the power to **impeach** as a further check on executive authority along with its power to approve presidential appointments to the **cabinet**, a group of advisors who help the president develop policy along with directing bureaucratic agencies. **Parliamentary systems** are a fusion of executive and legislative authority. The chief executive is selected by the majority party in the legislature, and the legislature retains the right to a **vote of no confidence** as a way to force him or her from office. Cabinet members are often selected from the majority party in the legislature as well. A **semi-presidential system** is one that has both a president and a prime minister.

- **Head of state:** The ceremonial leader of the state.
- **Head of government:** The chief legislator responsible for proposing legislation.
- **President:** The individual elected separately from the legislature by the people to run the government.
- **Prime minister:** The individual selected by the majority party in a parliament to run the executive branch.
- **Cabinet:** A group of advisors for the chief executive. It provides advice, helps craft legislation, and runs the bureaucratic agencies.
- **Unicameral legislature:** A one-house legislature. An advantage is efficiency in lawmaking because a simple majority can prevail.
- **Bicameral legislature:** A two-house legislature. An advantage is that each house can represent a different constituency. Typically the lower house represents the people by population and the upper house has a geographic component like states. Whether or not the two houses slow the legislative process depends upon whether the houses have symmetric or asymmetric power in the process. For example, in Mexico and Nigeria the legislature is symmetric in that both houses must pass legislation by a majority vote for it to proceed to the president. Great Britain is an example of asymmetric power in that the House of Lords can only vote to delay the passage of legislation approved by the House of Commons.

	CHINA	UNITED KINGDOM	IRAN	MEXICO	NIGERIA	RUSSIA
System Type	Neither— no elections	Parliamentary	semi-presidential theocracy	Presidential	Presidential	Semi-presidential
Head of State	President	Queen	Supreme Leader	President	President	President
Head of Government	Premier	Prime Minister	President	President	President	Prime Minister
Upper House	None	House of Lords	None	Senate	Senate	Federation Council
Lower House asymmetric	National People's Congress	House of Commons	Majlis	Chamber of Deputies	House of Representatives	Duma

Compare the Judiciary

The judicial branch is charged with interpreting the law and adjudicating disputes. A truly independent judicial system is an effective check on executive and legislative power as it has the power to protect the civil liberties and civil rights of individuals in the state by upholding rule of law. Some independent courts have the power of **judicial review**, which is the power of a court to overturn a law or executive action. Courts operate within certain types of legal systems.

- **Common law systems:** Legal system in which the importance of prior judicial decisions takes precedence when a court is making decisions. Found primarily in Great Britain and its former colonies.
- **Code law (civil law) systems:** Legal system that systematically applies the law as written to judicial decisions.
- **Sharia law:** Legal system based on Islamic law.

	CHINA	UNITED KINGDOM	IRAN	MEXICO	NIGERIA	RUSSIA
Type of Law	Code law	Common law	Sharia law	Code law	Common law and Sharia in North	Code law
Judicial Review	No	No Supreme Court of UK can find legislature non-compliant	No Guardian Council can veto law that doesn't follow sharia	Yes Power of Supreme Court	Yes Power of Supreme Court	Yes Advisory power of constitutional court

Compare the Bureaucracy

Legislatures pass laws and budgets to provide services to their constituents. The executive branch is charged with implementing the laws and budgets. **Bureaucrats** are the unelected officials who carry out the laws by writing regulations, enforcing rules, and assigning fines. To accomplish these tasks, bureaucracies are large, complex organizations with hierarchical structures and extensive rules and procedures. Bureaucracies are often characterized by how the bureaucrats are selected. A meritocracy is a **bureaucracy** staffed by subject area experts who are selected in an examination process based on **merit** or expertise. On the other hand, in a **patron-client system** government officials are selected for their party loyalty or loyalty to an elected official and have received a government job in exchange for their political support. Most political systems have elements of both selection systems, but usually one **elite recruitment** process dominates how government officials obtain their jobs. The military is a special case as it has a unique function to protect the state from external enemies. Typically, civilian control of the military is seen as a check on its power.

	CHINA	GREAT BRITAIN	IRAN	MEXICO	NIGERIA	RUSSIA
Elite Recruitment	CCP nomenklatura	Merit Oxbridge	Supreme leader bonyad or cleric	Merit used to be PRI camarilla	Federal Character	Siloviki
Military Controlled by	CCP general secretary heads Central Military Commission	Prime minister exercises the royal prerogative	Supreme leader who also controls Revolutionary Guard	President	President	President

› Review Questions

Multiple Choice

1. Which of the following is characteristic of a parliamentary system?
   - (A) The head of state is selected by the majority party in the legislature.
   - (B) The prime minister can be removed from office by a vote of no confidence by the legislature.
   - (C) The head of government is a ceremonial position with little active involvement in the policy process.
   - (D) Policy gridlock often results when the prime minister and the majority party cannot agree on a policy position.

2. An advantage of a presidential system of government over a parliamentary system of government is that in a presidential system:
   - (A) the national government makes uniform policies for all local governments
   - (B) there is a true separation of power between the executive and legislative branches
   - (C) there is less gridlock during legislative policymaking
   - (D) the Supreme Court has to have judicial review

3. The purpose of the cabinet is to:
   (A) oversee elections for national offices
   (B) advise the judiciary on which cases to review
   (C) prohibit the bureaucracy from implementing the law
   (D) provide political management over bureaucratic agencies

4. Bicameral legislatures are:
   (A) more democratic than unicameral legislatures because a bill must pass both houses to become a law
   (B) more efficient than unicameral legislatures because there are more people to scrutinize legislative proposals
   (C) more likely to gridlock than unicameral legislatures, especially when the bicameral legislature is symmetrically organized
   (D) more likely to have a greater number of women legislators than unicameral legislatures

5. Which of the following is an example of policy-making by a bureaucratic agency?
   (A) European environmental interest groups protest a new climate change treaty.
   (B) The British prime minister proposes to reduce tuition fees at university.
   (C) The chief justice of the Nigerian Supreme Court announces the court's decision about a land dispute.
   (D) A Russian customs official generates a list of guidelines to implement a new travel process.

Free Response

1. (A) Define rule of law.
   (B) Describe the role of the judiciary.
   (C) Explain how the judiciary upholds the rule of law in a democracy.
   (D) Explain how an authoritarian regime controls the judiciary to restrict rule of law.

2. Use the table to complete your answer.

Women in Parliament 20 Years in Review

	WORLD	AMERICAS	AFRICA	EUROPE	MIDDLE EAST	ASIA
1995	11.3%	12.7%	9.8%	13.2%	4.3%	13.2%
2005	15.7%	18.6%	14.8%	18.4%	6.5%	15%
2015	22.1%	26.4%	22.3%	25%	16.1%	18.5%

*regional averages of women in parliament
Source: Inter Parliamentary Union

   (A) Using the data in the table, identify the area of the world with the biggest increase in the percentage of women in parliament from 1995 to 2015.
   (B) Using the data in the table, describe the worldwide trend in the percentage of women serving in parliament.
   (C) Describe the role of a legislature in both democratic and authoritarian regimes.
   (D) Explain why political scientists study the gender composition of a legislature.
   (E) Explain how a change in gender composition of a legislature affects policymaking.

3. Compare the role of cabinets in parliamentary and presidential systems in two different AP Comparative Government and Politics course countries.
   (A) Describe the role of a cabinet.
   (B) Describe the difference in how cabinets are selected in a parliamentary system and a presidential system by using two different AP Comparative Government and Politics course countries.
   (C) Explain how the different methods of selecting cabinets in parliamentary and presidential systems reflect the executive-legislative relationship in each of the course countries in (B).

4. Develop an argument as to whether a presidential or semi-presidential system is more efficient in policy-making.

   Use one or more of the following course concepts in your answer.
   • Sovereignty
   • Political Stability
   • Legitimacy

   In your response, you should do the following:
   • Respond to the prompt with a defensible claim or thesis that establishes a line of reasoning using one or more of the provided course concepts.
   • Support your claim with at least TWO pieces of specific and relevant evidence from one or more course countries. This evidence should be relevant to one or more of the provided course countries.
   • Use reasoning to explain why your evidence supports your claim or thesis, using one or more of the provided course concepts.
   • Respond to an opposing or alternate perspective, using refutation, concession, or rebuttal.

› Answers and Explanations

Multiple Choice

1. **C.** A parliamentary system is a fusion of executive and legislative power. The majority party in the legislature selects the prime minister, who is the head of government. The prime minister selects the cabinet to formulate policy and manage bureaucratic agencies. Since the government controls the majority, policy initiatives become law because a vote of no confidence would force the prime minister and cabinet to step down. The head of state in a parliamentary system serves a ceremonial function.

2. **B.** The major advantage of a presidential system is that there is a true separation of power between the executive and legislative branches due to separate elections. This separation provides a check and a balance in legislative policymaking that often results in gridlock, especially in a divided government. Although many presidential systems have courts with judicial review, it is not a requirement of a presidential system. National government uniformity in policymaking is a characteristic of a unitary system and not an outcome of a presidential system.

3. D. The cabinet is a group of advisors chosen by the executive to help develop policy and manage the bureaucratic agencies in the executive branch. Cabinet positions are patronage jobs, given to party loyalists to help implement policy and provide political management over civil servants.

4. C. Bicameral legislatures are composed of two houses, usually representing two different constituencies such as regional areas in the upper house and the population in the lower house. If symmetrically organized, it is often difficult to obtain the majority vote in both houses needed to pass a law, thereby resulting in gridlock. A unicameral legislature is often more efficient because it has fewer checks on the will of the majority. The party and gender composition of either type of legislature is more a function of election systems than it is of legislative structure.

5. D. A bureaucratic agency is composed of unelected government officials who implement policy, often by writing regulations and then enforcing them.

Free Response

1. (4 points possible)

(A) Rule of law is characterized by the fair and equal administration of legal procedures. Rule of law is often described as "no one is above the law." (1 point)

(B) The judiciary plays an important role in a political system. Its function is to interpret the law and administer justice. (1 point)

(C) The judiciary upholds the rule of law in a democracy by acting as an effective check on any arbitrary use of power by the executive or legislative branches. It can rule on the constitutionality of laws if it has the power of judicial review, and it protects civil liberties of the people from overreach by government officials. (1 point)

(D) Authoritarian regimes control the judiciary in different ways to restrict rule of law. One way is to have judges that are loyal to the government and not independent. Chinese judges, for example, are loyal to the CCP and do not act as independent arbiters. In addition, China has a separate discipline system for party members, which results in an unequal and arbitrary application of justice. (1 point)

2. (5 points possible)

(A) The Americas had the biggest increase in the percentage of women serving in the legislature. (13.7%) (1 point)

(B) The worldwide trend from 1995 to 2015 is an increase in the percentage of women serving in the legislature from a low of 5.3% in Asia to a high of 13.7% in the Americas. (1 point)

(C) The role of a legislature is to represent the people and pass laws and budgets. (1 point)

(D) Gender composition is an important element of descriptive representation. In order to represent a group of people, an argument can be made that the legislature reflect the demographic diversity of the people, including gender. (1 point)

(E) A change in the gender composition of a legislature can change the substance of the laws or budgets passed to better reflect the needs of women. This could include more laws to protect women from violence or more money to support girls' education. (1 point)

3. (5 points possible)

(A) The function of a cabinet is to advise the head of government and to manage the bureaucracy. (1 point)

(B) In a presidential system, the president has the power to select the cabinet, but this choice must be confirmed by the legislature. In Nigeria, the president selects the cabinet and the Senate confirms the choice. (1 point)

In a parliamentary system, the prime minister selects the cabinet from among the members of the prime minister's party serving in the lower house of the legislature. In the UK, the prime minister selects MPs from his or her party in the House of Commons to serve in the cabinet. (1 point)

(C) In a presidential system, this method of cabinet selection reflects the separation of power between the executive and legislative branches. Members of the cabinet cannot also serve in the legislature at the same time. In addition, it reflects a check and a balance between the branches because the legislature must confirm the president's choice. In Nigeria, the president must select one member of his cabinet from each of the 36 states, but the Senate may refuse to confirm the choice. (1 point)

In a parliamentary system, this method of cabinet selection reflects the fusion of power between the executive and legislative branches. All members of the cabinet, an executive branch institution, are also elected MPs in the legislature. This makes policymaking much more efficient because the majority party will support the PM's choice for the cabinet as well as most legislation sponsored by the government. In the UK, the PM selects the cabinet from among the other leaders in the majority party in the House of Commons and keeps them working together with the principle of collective responsibility. (1 point)

4. (5 points possible)

Presidential systems are more efficient at policymaking than semi-presidential systems because of the unity in the executive. Having one decision maker provides clarity to the process and thus political stability, as it is clear to the people who to hold accountable for government actions. When one person exercises sovereignty or ultimate authority over territory, there is less chance of gridlock. (1 point)

Mexican presidents have a long history of efficient policymaking. During the years when the PRI was a dominant party, the president of Mexico was at the top of a large patron-client network that supported his decision making in order to receive benefits. By not sharing executive power, President de la Madrid was able to push through policy, such as structural adjustment programs (SAP), that may have been stalled had he had to share power with a prime minister. (1 point)

Nigeria also has a presidential system that consolidates the head of government and the head of state roles in one person: the president. This makes policymaking more efficient because the prestige of being the ceremonial leader as head of state boosts the legitimacy of the president as the head of government legislative leader. President Buhari, for example, has launched anti-corruption initiatives to try and reduce corruption and provide more political stability. (1 point)

Neither Mexican nor Nigerian presidents have to share the presidency with a prime minister. By combining the roles of head of state and head of government into one office, it is clear to voters who is in charge of the executive branch, and thus voters hold that person or governing party responsible. In Nigeria, President Jonathan was voted out of office, and in Mexico, the PRI is no longer a dominant party. (1 point)

Critics may charge that a semi-presidential system is more efficient because a president and prime minister can split up foreign and domestic policy so that one person is not overwhelmed by the responsibilities of the charge. The efficiency comes from division of labor and the easier removal of an ineffective PM through a vote of no confidence as opposed to the difficult task of impeaching and removing a president. In reality, however, as head of state, the president has the more visible role, which can be used to force action. In Russia's semi-presidential system, President Putin has effectively diminished the role of the prime minister so that it is clear that major lawmaking initiatives come from the president and that legislative compliance by Putin's dominant party, United Russia, is essential to maintain legitimacy and political stability. (1 point)

› Rapid Review

- A constitution is a document that describes how the government is to be organized and what the powers of the government are to be.
- Rule of law exists when the formal rules of government are consistently applied.
- In a presidential system, the chief executive is chosen in separate elections from the legislature, whereas in a parliamentary system, the prime minister is selected by the majority party in the legislature.
- A president is removed through impeachment by the legislature, while a prime minister is removed by a vote of no confidence by the legislature.
- The head of state is the ceremonial leader of the country, and the head of government is the chief legislator responsible for proposing legislation.
- The cabinet is a group of advisors for the chief executive who provide advice, craft legislation, and manage the bureaucratic agencies.
- A unicameral legislature is a one-house legislature where a simple majority can make policy. A bicameral legislature is a two-house legislature where each house represents a different constituency and each house has a role in passing legislation.
- An independent judiciary is an effective check on executive and legislative power by upholding rule of law.
- Judicial review is the power of a court to overturn a law or executive action.
- A common law system emphasizes the importance of precedence in making judicial decisions. Code law systems systematically apply the law as written to judicial decisions. Sharia law is a legal system based on Islamic law.
- Bureaucrats are unelected officials who carry out the law by writing regulations, enforcing rules and assigning fines. They are usually recruited by merit and expertise or through a patron-client system.
- Remember that only government institutions make public policy. Legislatures make laws and pass budgets, while executives develop policy, appoint officials, and enforce laws. Bureaucrats write regulations and implement programs, while the judiciary interprets the law.

Political Culture and Participation

IN THIS CHAPTER

Summary: Political systems are created to manage the people living within the territorial boundaries of the state. Challenges of historical legacy and social cleavages impact the degree to which political conflict has been exacerbated or mitigated by public policymaking. The degree to which the government feels compelled to use coercion or force to maintain control is often a reflection of the country's political culture and prevailing ideology. Public willingness to participate in the political system is a key source of legitimacy for the regime, whether democratic or authoritarian. The responsiveness of the government to the will of the people, however, is perhaps one of the strongest indicators of the type of regime.

Key Terms

civil society	cross-cutting cleavages	social capital
coercion	political culture	social cleavages
coinciding cleavages	political ideology	social movements
cooption	political socialization	

Compare Social Cleavages in Civil Society

Public policy does not occur in a vacuum; rather, it is a government response to the challenges of governing the state with its own combination of demographic and geographical conditions. The social divisions or **cleavages** within society can make governing difficult, especially if they are **coinciding** or reinforcing, because every policy decision often appears to benefit one group more than another, leading to conflict. **Cross-cutting cleavages**, on the other hand, where social divisions are not so stark, are easier to govern because compromise is possible. It is important to note that not all social cleavages cause political conflict. But if they do cause conflict, it can be a formidable challenge for the state to resolve.

Citizens in every type of regime engage in political participation to influence government policymaking. Their effectiveness, however, is often more pronounced in a democratic system where protection of civil liberties allows autonomous organizations to voluntarily form a robust **civil society** where connections between individuals build **social capital**. In addition, democratic regimes generally respond to conventional forms of participation such as voting, contacting a government official, lobbying, and campaigning, because free, fair elections give politicians real incentives to meet popular demands or face electoral retribution, and independent judiciaries are effective at protecting civil liberties. Even in democratic regimes, however, the people may turn to more unconventional forms of participation such as protest or political violence if the government seems unresponsive to conventional forms. In some instances, various groups will band together around a common cause to form a **social movement** to force change.

Compare the major social cleavages in the AP Comparative Government and Politics core countries:

	CHINA	UNITED KINGDOM	IRAN	MEXICO	NIGERIA	RUSSIA
Ethnic Groups	56 groups 92% Han Uighar 11m Tibetan 6m	87% white 84% English 8% Scot	61% Persian 16% Azeri	62% mestizo 28% Amerindian	250 groups 29% Hausa 21% Yoruba 18% Igbo	200 groups 78% Russian
Religious Groups	52% none 18% Buddhist 5% Christian 2% Muslim	60% Christian 4% Muslim	95% Shia	83% Catholic	50% Muslim 40% Christian	20% Russian Orthodox 10% Muslim
Urban/Rural	58% urban	83% urban	74% urban	80% urban	49% urban	74% urban
Regional	30% live on east coast	30% in SE England	16% in Tehran	25% in Mexico City	60% in north	50% in western part
Median Age	37 years Aging	40 years Aging	29 years	28 years	18 years	39 years Aging

Coinciding Cleavages	Urban/rich/ East vs. Rural/poor/ West Han vs. Uighar/Muslim Tibetan/ Buddhist	Irish/Catholic vs. English/ Protestant London/rest	Urban/rich vs. Rural/poor Educated/ Secular vs. traditional	North/ industry vs. South/poor Mestizo vs. Amerindian	North/ Hausa/ Muslim vs. South/ Yoruba and Igbo (Y&I)/ Christian Delta/rest	Ethnic minority/ Muslim/ Rural (Chechnya) vs. Russian/ Orthodox/ Moscow

	CHINA	**UNITED KINGDOM**	**IRAN**	**MEXICO**	**NIGERIA**	**RUSSIA**
Political Participation	Restricted Censorship Vote only in village elections Repress protests	Extensive High civic culture Civil liberties protected	Restricted Censorship Repress protests	Extensive Vote Protest	Extensive but limited by corruption	Restricted State control TV Restrict protest

Source: World CIA Factbook

Compare Political Culture and Socialization

Political culture is the deeply held, shared attitudes of a group of people about their government. These feelings are often part of the historical narrative of the country as individuals began to identify with the state, but they can change over time. In addition, these values are transmitted to future generations through the process of **political socialization**. Agents of socialization, which are typically family, school, peers, and the media, help individuals acquire their attitudes about the government through frequent discussion and exposure.

	CHINA	**UNITED KINGDOM**	**IRAN**	**MEXICO**	**NIGERIA**	**RUSSIA**
Prominent Political Culture	Confusion principles and Middle Kingdom orientation	Tradition	Martyr complex	Support for revolutionary principles	Fragmented— based on ethnic, religious affiliation	Tsarist mentality

Compare Types of Political Ideologies

Political ideology is a coherent set of ideas on what policy actions a government should take. Political ideology is often displayed on a left-right continuum of political attitudes with the left reflecting a more radical attitude to change and the right being more reactionary to change.

- **Communism:** a political and economic system where all property is collectively owned by a classless society.

- **Socialism:** a political and economic system where the means of production are controlled by the state to ensure equal access.
- **Populism:** doctrine committed to the rights of the common people instead of elites.
- **Liberalism:** political doctrine committed to individual freedom and free markets.
- **Neoliberalism:** committed to government policy of privatization, free trade, and deregulation.
- **Individualism:** committed to government protection of individual civil liberties.
- **Conservatism:** political doctrine committed to traditional values and practices.
- **Fascism:** political doctrine committed to the glorification of the state with extreme nationalism.

Compare Types of Media Roles

The media is a powerful linkage institution. In a democratic state, an independent press can serve as an effective watchdog on government activity and can provide citizens with a wide variety of timely, accurate assessments of public policy. Citizen groups can use the media to cover protests and investigate problems to help get issues on the policy agenda of the government. Social media is also widely available for use to gather information and mobilize participation. But even in a democratic state, there may be restrictions on the media to protect national security or the privacy rights of individuals.

In an authoritarian state, the media is controlled by the government to carefully craft a pro-government narrative. Whether the government owns the media or merely controls it through restrictive legislation and intimidation, media outlets present information that will pass government censors. Increasingly, authoritarian states also restrict Internet access to control information or prevent social media from being used to mobilize participation. Constantly changing technology, however, makes it difficult for government officials to keep up. Current rankings by Freedom House are as follows:

	CHINA	UNITED KINGDOM	IRAN	MEXICO	NIGERIA	RUSSIA
Press Freedom	Not free	Free	Not free	Partly free	Partly free	Not free
Internet Penetration	60%	93%	44%	68%	56%	76%

› Review Questions

Multiple Choice

1. Political culture is:
   - (A) the deep, shared attitudes held by citizens about their government
   - (B) the belief that a citizen can actively participate in the political system
   - (C) a coherent set of attitudes about what policies the government should pursue
   - (D) how people acquire their attitudes about government and politics

2. Civil society flourishes when:
   - (A) the government allows only state-controlled NGOs to form to represent specific interests
   - (B) governments establish corporatist relationships with a few peak associations to negotiate public policy
   - (C) governments require foreign NGOs to register in order to ensure that domestic groups are not pressured by external forces
   - (D) governments allow NGOs to freely form autonomously and work to protect freedom of expression

3. Which of the following is the most significant agent of socialization?
   - (A) School
   - (B) Media
   - (C) Church
   - (D) Family

4. Which of the following ideologies is correctly matched with a desired public policy initiative?
   - (A) Communism: Protection of private property in the constitution
   - (B) Neoliberalism: Reduction of tariffs and the privatization of state-owned enterprises
   - (C) Fascism: The rejection of a plan to adopt a national language
   - (D) Populism: The adoption of a regressive tax policy

5. Which of the following coinciding cleavages has caused the most significant political conflict since 2000?
   - (A) The ethnic, religious, and economic cleavage in Nigeria between the Muslim herders and Christian farmers in the Middle Belt
   - (B) The religious and economic cleavage in Northern Ireland between Protestant and Catholic voters
   - (C) The ethnic, economic, and regional cleavage in Mexico between indigenous farmers and industrialists
   - (D) The ethnic, religious, and regional cleavage in Russia between Russians and Muslim Chechens

Free Response

1. (A) Define political socialization.
   (B) Describe how families act as agents of political socialization.
   (C) Explain why governments use public schools as agents of socialization.
   (D) Explain how agents of political socialization transmit political culture to future generations.

2. Use the information in the table to answer the question.

DO YOU SUPPORT/OPPOSE THE BRITISH MONARCHY?	SUPPORT	OPPOSE
Overall	69%	21%
18–24	57%	25%
25–34	61%	23%
35–44	64%	22%
45–54	70%	21%
55+	77%	18%

Don't-knows are not shown.
Source: YouGov Poll May 2018

(A) Using the data in the table, identify the age group that is most supportive of the British monarchy.
(B) Using the data in the table, write an empirical statement about support for the British monarchy.
(C) Define political culture.
(D) Explain why the age group in (A) is more supportive of the British monarchy than the other age groups.
(E) Explain how British political culture can be used to explain support for the British monarchy.

3. Compare the role of the media in an authoritarian and democratic regime in two different AP Comparative Government and Politics countries.
   (A) Define legitimacy.
   (B) Describe the degree of state censorship of the press in two different AP Comparative Government and Politics countries.
   (C) Explain how the degree of state censorship of the press in (B) reflects the legitimacy of the regime in the two different AP Comparative Government and Politics countries.

4. Develop an argument as to which promotes more political stability—a civil society with numerous political ideologies or one where there is one dominant political ideology?

   Use one or more of the following concepts in your answer.
   • Political Culture
   • One-Party State
   • Legitimacy

   In your response, you should do the following:

   • Respond to the prompt with a defensible claim or thesis that establishes a line of reasoning using one or more of the provided course concepts.
   • Support your claim with at least TWO pieces of specific and relevant evidence from one or more course countries. This evidence should be relevant to one or more of the provided course countries.
   • Use reasoning to explain why your evidence supports your claim or thesis, using one or more of the provided course concepts.
   • Respond to an opposing or alternate perspective, using refutation, concession, or rebuttal.

› Answers and Explanations

Multiple Choice

1. **A.** Political means about government, so focus on culture. Culture is a deeply held, shared attitude. Political efficacy is when citizens believe that they can actively participate in a political system. Political ideology is a coherent set of attitudes about government policy whereas political socialization is the process by which people acquire their attitudes about government.

2. **D.** Civil society by definition is composed of autonomous groups free from government control. Therefore, civil society will flourish and grow in a democratic environment where civil liberties are protected.

3. **D.** The most significant agent of socialization in any society is the family, mainly because a child spends the most time with them from an early age and will internalize attitudes about the government based on family experiences and traditions.

4. **B.** Neoliberalism is focused on liberalizing the economy, which would include lowering tariffs and privatizing state-owned industries. Communism as an ideology has the goal of the abolition of private property, so don't confuse the actions of the CCP with the ideology. Fascism has the goal of glorifying the state and so would want to build up national institutions such as a national language. Populism wants to help the poor against elites, and a regressive tax system would disproportionately hurt the poor.

5. **A.** Although all these cleavages are significant, since 2000, the most violent political conflict is occurring in Nigeria's Middle Belt where clashes between the two groups have killed over 10,000 people in the last decade.

Free Response

1. (4 points possible)

   (A) Political socialization is the process of acquiring one's attitudes about government. (1 point)
   (B) Families act as agents of socialization by spending time with children discussing political issues and teaching political traditions. In this way, a child internalizes his or her attitudes about the government. (1 point)
   (C) Governments use public schools as vehicles for political socialization. Through required coursework and textbook choices, a government ensures that a child spends time thinking about and discussing political issues so that the child acquires certain attitudes about the government—how to be patriotic, for example. (1 point)
   (D) Political socialization is a lifetime process. Political culture embodies the deep-set, shared attitudes about a government. Family traditions, school subjects, and media programs all tend to reinforce a common attitude towards the government. These agents of socialization (family, school, media) spend time in both traditional and episodic ways to get citizens to accept these societal attitudes from the time when people are children. (1 point)

2. (5 points possible)

   (A) People aged 55+ are the most supportive of the British monarchy. (1 point)
   (B) A majority of British people supports the British monarchy. (1 point)
   (C) Political culture is the deep-set, shared attitudes about government. (1 point)
   (D) Older people tend to be more conservative and resistant to change; consequently, older British people support a historic institution like the monarchy. (1 point)
   (E) British political culture is characterized by respect for tradition, and the monarchy is a traditional institution. One can conclude that support for the monarchy is based on a deep-set, shared belief in tradition. (1 point)

3. (5 points possible)

(A) Legitimacy occurs when people accept a government's authority. (1 point)

(B) The UK has a long tradition of a free press. Although the BBC is state-owned and funded by a TV-license fee, it enjoys freedom to scrutinize the government. Censorship would be limited for protection of national security but a Freedom of Information Act ensures that government control of the media is limited. (1 point)

Iran does not have a free press. The Supreme Leader appoints the head of the media whose ministry is charged with suppressing information that is critical of the regime. Reporters are imprisoned for writing stories that are critical of the government. (1 point)

(C) The UK is a democracy with a strong tradition of protecting freedom of expression. Having an independent press as a watchdog on government activity is a powerful check on government. People look to the press to investigate government action to hold the government accountable. This boosts legitimacy, or public acceptance, for the democratic regime as one protecting civil liberties with a limited government. (1 point)

The Iranian government represses free expression as is typical of many authoritarian regimes. People resent the intrusion but are fearful of criticizing press restrictions because of the potential reprisals from the government. In this way, state censorship of the press is reflective of the authoritarian regime and people tend to accept the policy as legitimate, but public backlash can also occur when the government goes too far, as it did in 2009. (1 point)

4. (5 points possible)

A civil society with numerous political ideologies that are allowed to coexist and compete for power in a pluralistic environment promotes more political stability as a consolidated democracy than any authoritarian, one ideology state can enforce. A government that is responsive to the public interest and then compromises and reforms is going to be more legitimate and acceptable to the people than a system that is imposed on them. (1 point)

The UK is a consolidated democracy with enviable political stability ever since the Civil War in the 1600s. The British system has evolved with a tradition of increasing democratization and adaptation to changing viewpoints. Even when there is a collective consensus on health care, or one party's ideology is pervasive, as Thatcherism was, the opportunity for dissent is still available. Elections have consequences, and parties adapt their ideologies and policy prescriptions in order to attract votes. Even when violent dissent, such as The Troubles in Northern Ireland, pushes for the government's attention, it has to respond to maintain legitimacy or face being voted out of office. (1 point)

Mexico provides another example of the legitimacy of numerous political ideologies promoting stability. Even when the PRI was the dominant party in Mexico, the people in part accepted the system because alternate ideologies were allowed to exist to provide the illusion of choice. The PAN, a northern conservative party, and later the PRD, a party on the left centered in Mexico City, provided choice to voters and stability to the electoral process. Interestingly, the PRI itself as a party of power had no overwhelming ideology to guide policymaking. This flexibility of views added to its legitimacy. (1 point)

Diverse populations have diverse opinions on what actions a government should take. A diversity of ideologies provides a safety valve for people to express themselves. A pluralistic, democratic regime channels civil society action to allow for recognition and even representation. This promotes a natural political stability based on freedom of expression. (1 point)

Critics will charge that a country like China with the exclusive ideology of the CCP provides more stability because no alternative is allowed. The problem with this type of stability is that it has to be enforced with force, which may be viewed as illegitimate if it is used to excess. For example, the protests in Hong Kong have only increased as the CCP tries to force government policy on a group of people used to more political liberalization as it enjoyed as a British colony. (1 point)

› Rapid Review

- Social cleavages, or divisions within society, can make governing difficult if they are coinciding or reinforcing, because policy decisions often appear to benefit one group more than another, leading to political conflict.
- In civil society, autonomous organizations, such as interest groups and churches, are able to form free from government control. A robust civil society is a strong indicator of a democratic society where political participation, civil liberties, and civil rights are protected by rule of law.
- Political culture is the deeply held, shared attitudes of a group of people about their government, while political socialization is the process by which people acquire their attitudes about government
- Political ideology is a coherent set of ideas on what policy actions a government should take. It is often displayed on a left–right continuum of political attitudes, with the left reflecting a more radical attitude toward change and the right being more reactionary to change.
- An independent media is an important component of a democratic society, as it serves as an effective watchdog on government activity and provides citizens with a wide variety of timely, accurate assessments of public policy.
- In an authoritarian state, the media is controlled by the state to craft a pro-government narrative. In addition, Internet access and social media are censored to restrict anti-government political mobilization.

CHAPTER 9

Party and Electoral Systems and Citizen Organizations

Summary: Political institutions include more than just governmental institutions. They also include those established practices that link the people to the government. These typical processes are referred to as linkage institutions and include elections, political parties, interest groups, and the media. The key to understanding these relationships is to understand that the links work both ways: citizens use the institutions to influence government behavior, and governments use the same institutions to shape citizen input. Obviously, the type of regime that a state has will have a significant impact on the effectiveness of the institutions. In a democratic regime, fair competitive elections, an independent press, and active pressure groups can lead to popular reforms. In contrast, an authoritarian regime can rig elections, censure the media, and create government-sponsored groups to maintain power.

Key Terms

corporatism
dominant party system
general election
majority
multiparty system
one-party system
pluralism
plurality
policy agenda

political ideology
primary election
referendum
single-member district
   system (SMD)
social movements
two-ballot election
two-party system

Compare Election Systems

There are two basic ways for states to organize elections. Election systems have strong effects on the type of party systems that develop. In a **single-member district system,** voters select one person on the ballot to represent them and the candidate with the most votes wins the seat, whereas in a **proportional system,** voters select one party on the ballot to represent them and the party wins seats in the legislature based on the percentage of the votes cast above a certain threshold. Both election systems have advantages and disadvantages, and several countries employ a combination of the two to minimize the disadvantages.

TYPE OF ELECTION SYSTEM	SINGLE-MEMBER DISTRICT (SMD) OR (FPTP)	PROPORTIONAL REPRESENTATION (PR) SYSTEM USES MULTIMEMBER DISTRICTS	MIXED SMDP AND PR
Used in which country?	United Kingdom, Nigeria	Russia 2005–2012	Mexico Russia 1993–2003, 2016–present
Party system relationship	Two-party system	Multiparty system with low threshold Dominant party system with high threshold	Multiparty system
Advantages	Voters are selecting the person to represent them Exaggerates the winning margin of the majority party	Range of parties in legislature to reflect diversity of interests if low threshold Party lists can be required to distribute seats to women to increase the percentage of women in the legislature	Multiple parties in legislature to reflect diverse interests, but major parties have the numbers to direct policy
Disadvantages	Wasted votes Discourages third parties	Difficult to form a majority party Often results in coalition governments that are more unstable Voters select party, not the individual representative	Gridlock if no clear majority

Compare Types of Elections

There are also several distinct types of elections. One key point to remember is that a **plurality** means the most votes, whereas a **majority** means one more than half or greater than 50 percent of votes.

- *Primary elections:* the type of elections where political parties allow voters to select the party's candidate for the general election.
- *General elections:* the type of elections where the voters select the officeholder.
- *Two-ballot elections:* the type of election where if no candidate receives more than 50 percent of the popular vote, a runoff election is scheduled between the top two vote-getters.

- **Referendums:** an election where the government (usually the chief executive) allows the public to vote directly on a policy, thereby circumnavigating the legislature.

	CHINA	GREAT BRITAIN	IRAN	MEXICO	NIGERIA	RUSSIA
How selected?	President	Prime Minister	President	President	President	President
	CCP Standing Committee selects—formal vote by NPC	Majority party in House of Commons votes	Guardian Council vets candidates and then two-ballot election by voters	Party primaries and direct plurality election by voters	Party primaries and **two-ballot system** and must win 25% of votes in 2/3 of states	Two-ballot election
Method of selection?	National People's Congress	House of Commons	Majlis	Legislature Senate and Chamber of Deputies	Legislature Senate and House of Representatives	Duma
	Selected by regional legislatures	FPTP	SMD	mixed	SMDP	mixed
		House of Lords is appointed				Federation Council is appointed
Referendums	NO	YES	YES	NO	NO	YES
Examples		Scottish Parliament and independence Brexit	Vote for Islamic Republic			Ratify new constitution in 1993

Compare Party Systems

Different types of election systems result in distinct types of party systems. Party systems are characterized by how many parties stand a chance to control the legislature.

- **One-party system:** In a one-party system, only one party is allowed to exist by the government.
- **Dominant party system:** In a dominant party system, smaller parties can compete, but because of government-imposed regulations or ballot manipulation, only one party—the dominant party—is assured of a large electoral victory and control of the government.
- **Two-party system:** In a two-party system, smaller parties compete but are unable to win the electoral majorities that the two largest parties can. The use of the single-member district, winner-take-all systems overrepresents the larger parties with a "winner's bonus" and discourages voters from wasting their votes on third parties.

- *Multiparty system:* In a multiparty system, numerous parties compete and win legislative seats. Oftentimes, no party can win a majority and a coalition government must be formed.

	CHINA	GREAT BRITAIN	IRAN	MEXICO	NIGERIA	RUSSIA
Party System	One	Two plus regional	None	Multi	Multi	Dominant

Compare Types of Political Parties

The primary goals of a political party is to win elections and govern. To do so, parties often identify with a specific political ideology to attract voters. Certain demographic groups tend to support specific government policies as well, although it is important to note that dominant parties often are more pragmatic than ideological and offer platforms designed to attract and maintain support rather than focus on ideological purity.

	PARTIES ON THE LEFT	NONIDEOLOGICAL PARTIES	PARTIES ON THE RIGHT
Political Attitudes	Move from center toward radical / Focus on reform	Personality driven / Focus on power	Move from center toward reactionary / Focus on restoration
Political Ideology	Liberalism / Socialism / Communism		Conservativism / Fascism
Role of State	To promote equality	To maintain power	To protect tradition
Economic Policy	Use government programs to expand economic equality	Use government programs to maintain support	Use government programs to protect elite groups
Typical Supporters	Young, urban, educated, minorities	Traditional supporters	Older, rural, business groups, nationalistic
China	CCP		
United Kingdom	Labour, Liberal Democrat		Conservatives, UKIP
Iran	Reformers		Conservatives
Mexico	PRD, MORENA	PRI	PAN
Nigeria		PDP, APC	
Russia	KPRF, Yabloko, A Just Russia	United Russia	Liberal Democrat

Compare Types of Interest-Group Systems

The primary goal of an interest group is to get its issue on the **policy agenda** so that it becomes a focus of government attention. There are two basic approaches to establishing the linkage between interest groups and the government: **pluralism** and **corporatism**.

	# OF GROUPS	RELATIONSHIP TO GOVERNMENT	ACTION	REASON FOR USING
Pluralism	Many	Independent from government Autonomous	Compete for access to promote agenda	Protect individual liberty to form organizations and to petition government
Corporatism	Few peak associations Often tripartite association of business, labor, and government	Appointed by government	Negotiate policy with government	Control the number of state-sanctioned groups to give illusion of citizen input in policymaking

Impact of Social Movements and Interest Groups

The success of an interest group in getting its issue on the policy agenda depends on many factors, including public support for their initiative and the receptiveness of the regime. Even though democracies protect civil liberties, regime type is no guarantee that an interest group will be successful in convincing the government to change a specific policy. Sometimes political participation evolves into a **social movement**, which occurs when large groups of people with a loosely defined organizational structure push for significant political or social change. When nonviolent, social movements are more likely to be perceived as having legitimate grievances against public policy decisions by the government.

› Review Questions

Multiple Choice

Use the following chart for Questions 1 and 2:

CANDIDATE	PERCENTAGE (%) OF POPULAR VOTE
A	41%
B	37%
C	12%
D	10%

1. Using the election results above, in which country would Candidate A become the president for winning a plurality of the popular vote?
   (A) Iran
   (B) Mexico
   (C) Nigeria
   (D) Russia

2. Using the election results above, in which countries would Candidate A and Candidate B be involved in a presidential run-off election?
   (A) Iran, Mexico, and Nigeria
   (B) Nigeria, Russia, and China
   (C) China, Iran, Russia
   (D) Iran, Nigeria, and Russia

3. If political leaders wanted to increase the representation of women in the legislature, which of the following election systems would most quickly increase the percentage of women in the legislature?
   (A) Single-member district (SMD) with a majority vote requirement
   (B) First past the post (FPTP)
   (C) Proportional representation (PR) with a gender party list requirement
   (D) Alternative vote system (AV)

4. Which of the following would be an example of a corporatist system?
   (A) Environmental groups protest loudly as oil companies lobby the government for drilling rights on protected lands.
   (B) Both business and labor groups compete for influence over the drafting of new healthcare regulations.
   (C) Many civil rights groups form coalitions to put public pressure on the legislature to pass antidiscrimination laws.
   (D) Peak associations of business and labor negotiate tax policy with government officials.

5. Which of the following is an advantage of using a single-member district election system?
   (A) The voter has a direct vote on a specific candidate to represent him or her.
   (B) It leads to the creation of a multiparty system to better represent ideological differences.
   (C) There are numerous incentives to create a third party to compete in the election.
   (D) It minimizes the differences between the percentage of the votes won and the actual number of seats won in the legislature.

Free Response

1. (A) Define civil society.
   (B) Describe the major difference between a political party and an interest group.
   (C) Explain why people may choose to form an interest group instead of a political party.
   (D) Explain why authoritarian regimes restrict civil society.

2. Use the information in the following table to answer the question.

PARTY	% OF POPULAR VOTE	# OF SEATS IN THE LEGISLATURE
PARTY A	29%	30
PARTY B	24%	25
PARTY C	19%	20
PARTY D	14%	15
PARTY E	9%	10
PARTY F	5%	0

   (A) Identify the type of election system used to award legislative seats.
   (B) Describe how the election system in (A) allocates legislative seats.
   (C) Define political efficacy.
   (D) Explain why Party F did not receive any seats in the legislature.
   (E) Explain why the type of election system in (A) promotes political efficacy.

3. Compare the role of social movements in two different AP Comparative Government and Politics countries.
   (A) Define social movement.
   (B) Describe a social movement that occurred in two different AP Comparative Government and Politics countries since 1990.
   (C) Explain how the social movements in (B) are similar or different in their effectiveness on reforming the political system of their country.

4. Develop an argument on whether a single-member district (SMD) election system or a mixed election system, with SMD and proportional system elements, is the best system to increase political efficacy.

   Use one or more of the following course concepts in your answer.
   • Legitimacy
   • Party system
   • Gender parity

   In your response, you should do the following:

   • Respond to the prompt with a defensible claim or thesis that establishes a line of reasoning using one or more of the provided course concepts.

   • Support your claim with at least TWO pieces of specific and relevant evidence from one or more course countries. This evidence should be relevant to one or more of the provided course countries.

   • Use reasoning to explain why your evidence supports your claim or thesis, using one or more of the provided course concepts.

   • Respond to an opposing or alternate perspective, using refutation, concession, or rebuttal.

› Answers and Explanations

Multiple Choice

1. **B.** Mexico is the only AP Comparative Government and Politics country with a plurality system for president. The presidents of Iran, Nigeria, and Russia must win a majority of the popular vote. There are no direct elections for president of China.

2. **D.** Iran, Nigeria, and Russia all have a two-ballot system for president. If no candidate receives 50 percent of the popular vote on the first ballot, the top two candidates compete in a run-off election. In addition, a Nigerian president must also win 25 percent of the vote in two-thirds of the states.

3. **C.** PR election systems with gender parity quota requirements are an effective way to quickly increase the number of women in the legislature. All the other systems cannot guarantee gender parity.

4. **D.** Corporatism is a system of a few government-recognized interest groups directly negotiating public policy with government officials. Pluralism, on the other hand, involves many competing interest groups competing for access to work with government officials on policy by using different strategies such as lobbying, protests, and boycotts.

5. **A.** A major advantage of a SMD system is that a voter gets to select a specific individual to represent him or her, unlike in a PR system where a voter only gets to select a party. In addition, according to Duverger's law, SMD plurality systems lead to two-party systems. Other features of the SMD system are the number of wasted votes and the fact that it rewards the majority party with a higher percentage of seats than the percentage of the vote won.

Free Response

1. (4 points possible)
   (A) Civil Society is the space where autonomous groups are allowed to form free from government control. (1 point)
   (B) The major difference between a political party and an interest group is that a political party wants to be the government, as opposed to pressuring the government to adopt a certain policy. To this end, political parties nominate candidates and compete in elections, whereas an interest group may give electioneering support to a party but does not seek to rule the country. (1 point)
   (C) People will choose to form an interest group if it is focused on a single issue. Parties must have policy positions on many of the issues that a government will face. Bringing together people in one interest group allows people to organize solely on that issue to raise awareness and pressure the government to adopt its position. (1 point)
   (D) Authoritarian regimes want to remain in power. To keep power, authoritarian governments are hesitant to allow any political group to organize as it may threaten the regime. If an interest group has a nonpolitical campaign, it may be allowed to exist, but registration requirements and government scrutiny will keep the interest group from getting too much power. (1 point)

2. (5 points possible)
   (A) This is a proportional representation (PR) election system. (1 point)
   (B) A PR system allocates seats based on the % of votes earned in an election. Each party received close to the % of the seats that it won as part of the popular vote. (1 point)
   (C) Political efficacy is the ability of a citizen to understand the political system and to know how to take part in it. (1 point)
   (D) Party F did not receive any seats in the legislature because its 5% of the vote was too low to earn seats. The threshold must be higher than 5%. (1 point)
   (E) A PR system promotes political efficacy because multiple parties win seats in the legislature unlike a SMDP election system that results in a two-party system. Consequently, there are fewer wasted votes in a PR system and more people feel like their vote actually matters, thus raising political efficacy. (1 point)

3. (5 points possible)
   (A) A social movement is when a variety of groups come together for a specific purpose to pressure the government to either reform public policy or allow for more representation. An example of a social movement would be a civil rights movement or one for climate change. (1 point)
   (B) A social movement that occurred in Mexico is one for indigenous rights. Different tribal groups have protested for protection of land rights, education, and culture. Some of the groups have been violent, like the Zapatistas in Chiapas, but others have protested, petitioned, and even formed a National Indigenous Congress to serve as a forum for public action for the movement. (1 point)
   (C) The Russian government has long been pressured by the environmental social movement in that country. Various NGOs work together to force the government to clean up pollution and maintain natural areas. Efforts to protect Lake Baikal, for example, are particularly noteworthy and garner international attention. (1 point)
   (D) The indigenous rights movement in Mexico has had limited effect. Whether the government is controlled by the PRI, the PAN, or Morena, indigenous rights are not the center of any party's platform, often because the indigenous in Mexico are fighting for traditional rights that are often at odds with the government's focus on growing the economy. (1 point)
   (E) Environmentalists in Russia have also had a limited effect. The foreign NGO registration policy and other repressive tactics may diminish the effectiveness of the movement, but the passion of the environmentalists compels them to continue the fight. (1 point)

4. (5 points possible)

The purpose of an election system is to allow voters to select their political leaders. The system needs to appear fair to the voters so that they will view the elections as legitimate and accept the results. So, the best election system is one that best reflects the diverse views of the voters. A mixed election system (SMD and PR) allows voters to both pick an individual to represent them (SMD) and to pick a party. The hope is that the voter will be successful with one of these systems and feel like their vote counts, meaning that they will have political efficacy. (1 point)

Mexico uses a mixed election system. After many years with only SMDP and a dominant party system under the PRI, the Mexican government was forced to democratize by creating an independent election commission and adding PR seats to the legislature so that more parties could win seats. Now that many parties can win seats in the legislature, voters feel that there are less wasted votes and more competition. In addition, their political efficacy has increased, particularly with the introduction of a gender parity law with the PR seats increasing the % of women in the legislature. (1 point)

Russia had a mixed election system, until President Putin made changes to an all-PR system to help consolidate control for his dominant party, United Russia. After the protests of 2011–12, however, the mixed system returned as a way to placate voters. By using the mixed system, voters felt higher political efficacy, although United Russia still dominates the results. (1 point)

The problem with SMD is that although voters pick a person to represent them, there is only one winner and lots of wasted votes in the resulting two-party system. When voters feel like their vote doesn't count, they lose political efficacy and don't participate. The mixed system with PR seats opens up the legislature to more parties winning seats and thus increases descriptive representation. (1 point)

Critics may charge that a SMD election system increases political efficacy and legitimacy because the voters are directly involved in voting for the person that they want to represent them. In a mixed system, the PR seats come from a list that is controlled by the party. In the end, however, in a SMD system lots of voters don't get the candidate of their choice and feel locked out of the election. The mixed system allows the chance to vote SMD but tempers it with a party vote to increase representation in the legislature, which increases voter acceptance and efficacy. (1 point)

› Rapid Review

- Linkage institutions (elections, political parties, interest groups, and the media) link people to the government.
- There are two basic types of election systems: single-member district (SMD) and proportional representation (PR). In an SMD system, the candidate must win a plurality of the votes to win a seat, whereas in a PR system, a party receives a percentage of the seats based on the percentage of the votes that it received. Some countries, like Mexico and Russia, use a mixed system of both types.
- Election systems have strong effects on the party systems. SMD systems lead to two-party systems, whereas the use of PR leads to multiparty systems.
- An advantage of SMD is that voters select the individual that they want to represent them, but this is a disadvantage as well in that there are many wasted votes.
- An advantage of PR is that there are a range of parties for voters to choose between, but this can be a disadvantage if no party is able to form a majority government.
- Primary elections allow voters to select candidates for the general election, while in the general election voters select the officeholder.
- Two-ballot elections occur when a candidate does not win a majority of the vote and so a runoff must occur between the top two vote-getters.
- In a referendum, the government allows the public to vote directly on policy, thereby circumnavigating the legislature.
- In a one-party system, only one party is allowed to exist by the government, whereas in a dominant party system, smaller parties can compete, but the dominant party is assured of electoral victory and control of the government.
- Two-party systems occur when the use of SMD overrepresents the larger parties with a "winner's bonus" and discourages voters from wasting their votes on third parties.
- Multiparty systems occur when numerous parties compete and win legislative seats. Oftentimes, no party can win a majority and a coalition government must be formed.
- Pluralism is the interest group system where many autonomous organizations compete for access to government policymakers, while in corporatism a few peak associations are appointed by the government to negotiate policy.
- Social movements occur when large groups of people with a loosely defined organizational structure push for significant political or social change.

CHAPTER 10

Political and Economic Changes and Development

IN THIS CHAPTER

Summary: The policymaking process is often the government's response to public demands, even if it is to repress those demands. Governments need the legitimacy gained from effective public policies about the economy, social welfare, and the environment. The challenge for the government is to develop policies that address the various social cleavages within the society so as not to exacerbate conflict.

Key Terms

austerity
command economy
debt
deficit
democratization
dependency theory
economic liberalization
foreign direct
   investment (FDI)
Gini index
globalization
Human Development
   Index (HDI)

import substitution
   industrialization (ISI)
Keynesian approach
market economy
multinational corporations
   (MNCs)
nongovernmental
   organizations (NGOs)
political liberalization
privatization
public policy
recession
rentier state

special economic
   zones (SEZs)
state-owned enterprises
   (SOEs)
structural adjustment
   program (SAP)
supranational organization
sustainability
welfare state

Political and Economic Change

There is a French saying, "The more things change, the more they stay the same." This is especially true when you analyze political and economic change for each of the six AP Comparative Government and Politics countries. Although each country has a very individual experience with change, there are two trends that are important to trace: democratization and privatization.

As mentioned previously in Chapter 6, **democratization** is the process of a state transitioning from an authoritarian regime to a democratic one. Also referred to as political liberalization, historical patterns in the twentieth century trended towards democracy as universal suffrage became the norm, colonial powers granted independence, and the Soviet Union collapsed. **Globalization** itself, defined as the increasing interconnectedness of markets and cultures, helped to speed the process along as **multinational corporations (MNCs)** looked for political protection of their foreign investments.

Keep in mind that there are two basic types of economic systems: markets and command. Both are methods that governments use to allocate scarce resources. A **market economy** allocates resources according to the forces of demand and supply, which determine price and quantity. Markets are based on private property and individual choice and, if purely competitive, are the most efficient method. In a **command economy**, the government determines how resources are to be allocated, usually delegating the task to a bureaucratic agency and leading to inefficiency. Most economies are actually mixed systems that combine elements of market principles within a regulated economy where the government provides some public services.

	CHINA	UNITED KINGDOM	IRAN	MEXICO	NIGERIA	RUSSIA
Type of Economic System	Command until 1983—now mixed	Mixed	Mixed	Mixed	Mixed	Command until 1985—now mixed

Economic change is characterized by **economic liberalization** or a freeing of the economy from government control to promote economic growth. The most visible change that a government can make is to undergo a process of **privatization**, which is to sell off **state-owned enterprises (SOEs)** to private investors. Economists believe that competitive industries are more efficient by producing more products at lower prices. Other ways to release market forces would be to reduce tariffs, taxes, and regulations to allow markets to expand using **foreign direct investment (FDI)** and **special economic zones (SEZs)**.

	CHINA	UNITED KINGDOM	IRAN	MEXICO	NIGERIA	RUSSIA
Examples of Privatization	Creation of TVEs Sale of SOEs	Privatize steel, water, rail, telecom	Privatization of industry to public pension funds	Some privatization of PEMEX	Sale of oil leases to foreign firms	Sale of USSR assets to oligarchs Consolidation by Putin

International Trade	Creation of SEZs Allow FDI WTO	EU, WTO	Faces sanctions	NAFTA Maquiladoras WTO	Import refined oil products WTO ECOWAS	WTO Faces sanctions

Globalization has helped to speed both the political and economic liberalization process along as multinational corporations (MNCs) looked for political protection of their foreign investments. In order to facilitate free trade and movement of goods and people, various supranational organizations have been constructed. A **supranational organization** is composed of member states that have agreed to cede some sovereignty to the organization for a specific policy area. States apply for membership in the supranational organization and agree to follow its policies, so that decisions by the supranational organization supersede national policy.

	CHINA	UNITED KINGDOM	IRAN	MEXICO	NIGERIA	RUSSIA
Level of Government	Unitary	Unitary devolved	Unitary	Federal	Federal	Federal
Supranational Organization Membership	WTO	WTO		WTO	ECOWAS WTO	WTO

ECOWAS = Economic Community of West African States
WTO = World Trade Organization

Public Policy

Public policies are decisions made by governments. Sometimes governments are gridlocked and are unable to make decisions, but the most typical policies are:

- Legislative: the legislature passes a new law and it is signed by the executive
- Budgetary: the legislature appropriates the money requested by the executive
- Regulatory: bureaucratic agencies issue regulations to enforce legislation
- Executive action: executive order to a bureaucratic agency or the military
- Court decision: majority ruling by a court

Domestic Factors

Individuals use linkage institutions to get their issues to the attention of government officials. Once on the policy agenda, the policy must be enacted by the legislature or executive and then implemented by the bureaucracy unless challenged by a court. People provide feedback to the government about the impact of the policies, and reforms may be offered. An unresponsive government might find itself facing protests, a coup, or perhaps even a revolution. How a government responds either with reform or repression can then mitigate or exacerbate political conflict.

International Factors

Both international **nongovernmental organizations (NGOs)** and multinational corporations (MNCs) put pressure on governments to adopt public policies that promote protection of civil liberties, private property, and free trade. Supranational organizations like the WTO, EU, or ECOWAS only accept members committed to open global trade. Winning the right to host the Olympics is another goal that requires that countries conform to a global standard. Treaties like NAFTA or the Paris Climate Accords require countries to adjust trade practices. The effectiveness of a global watchdog like Amnesty International has limited effect on authoritarian regimes.

Economic Public Policy

All governments seek the legitimacy that comes from managing a high performing economy. Steady economic growth along with low inflation and unemployment rates can be used to demonstrate competence and support for the government's policies. If a government fails to respond effectively to an economic downturn, that government will struggle politically as well. There are two basic approaches to handling an economic slowdown or **recession**. During a recession, firms lay off workers and output drops, and tax revenues decline but there are increased requests for food assistance and unemployment benefits, so the government faces a **deficit** where spending exceeds revenue.

- **Keynesian approach:** Increase government spending and lower taxes to increase consumer income. This approach will increase the deficit, but supporters believe that it will also increase output levels and restore the economy.
- **Austerity:** The government should take steps to decrease the deficit by reducing spending and increasing taxes. This "tightening of the belt" approach will be difficult in the short run, but supporters of this policy claim that it will lead to a stronger economy in the long run.

In addition, developing countries have the added challenge of increasing a country's standard of living while diversifying the economy to move people out of agricultural jobs to those in manufacturing or services. How to increase economic development depends on what one thinks about the cause of the lack of development. If one ascribes to the **dependency theory**, which asserts that developing countries are being exploited by developed countries, then the solution might be the **import substitution industrialization (ISI)** model. The ISI principle is that countries should raise their tariff walls to protect infant industries, which should also be supported with government subsidies to develop a domestic industrial economy. The problem for followers of ISI is that eventually to continue to grow the economy, new markets need to be found. Particularly in a climate of globalization where there are increasing levels of integration of markets, communication networks, and culture, critics of ISI claim that the better model would be a **structural adjustment program (SAP)**. A SAP policy requires that a government pursue austerity by raising taxes and decreasing spending to control **debt** levels while also reducing tariff levels and allowing an infusion of foreign direct investment (FDI) and privatizing SOEs. Developing countries that need to borrow money from either the World Bank or the International Monetary Fund (IMF) will often be required to adopt SAP policies along with good governance practices.

SAP policies that stress economic liberalization often do result in economic growth and industrial diversification for countries that adopt them. The results of rapid economic development, however, are often uneven and tend to increase income disparity as measured by the **Gini index**. A rising social cleavage between rich and poor, especially if it coincides with an urban/rural divide and/or a regional divide can spark political unrest that will be difficult for the government to resolve.

Another challenge facing developing countries is often an overreliance on the sale of natural resources to generate revenue for the government. A state that gains more than half of its revenue from this practice is called a **rentier state**. By relying on one natural resource for its revenue, a government is susceptible to market price fluctuations and may find it difficult to fund services if the price of the resource drops too low. In addition, this steady stream of income may lead to government corruption instead of incentivizing to modernize the state.

	CHINA	UNITED KINGDOM	IRAN	MEXICO	NIGERIA	RUSSIA
UN Economic Status	Developing Upper middle income	Developed High income	Developing Upper middle income	Developing Upper middle income	Developing Lower middle income	Transition High income
GDP per Capita	$15,400	$42,500	$18,100	$18,900	$5,900	$26,500
International Status	G20	G7 and G20		G20		G20 Kicked out of G7 in 2014
HDI*	High .74 Rank 90	Very High .9 Rank 16	High .77 Rank 69	High .76 Rank 77	Low .52 Rank 152	Very High .8 Rank 49
% Labor Force in Agriculture	28%	1.3%	16%	13%	70%	9%
Rentier State			Yes		Yes	

*HDI is the Human Development Index, which includes GDP per capita, literacy rates, and life expectancy to measure standard of living. It ranks 188 countries.

Source: World CIA Factbook

Social Welfare Policy

The interlocking forces of industrialization, modernization, and globalization resulted in pressure on states to move beyond a night watchman or security model to that of a nanny or **welfare state**. A welfare state is one that seeks to provide a universal safety net for its citizens by providing pensions, unemployment insurance, health care, and poverty programs.

In addition, governments may pursue active policies to deal with issues of population growth or migration. Some countries, like China, have actively restricted the number of children that a couple can have, although China's one-child policy has been recently relaxed to a two-child policy. Russia, on the other hand, is facing a decline in population, so it incentivizes families to have more children, even creating a special award for families with more than seven children.

Environmental Policy

Focusing on environmental policy is considered a characteristic of postmaterialistic society. Many individuals, NGOs, and Green political parties are particularly focused on protecting natural resources with the goal of **sustainability**, by protecting them for future generations. The challenge for developing countries is that the typical path of modernization with industrialization has occurred simultaneously with a dependence on fossil fuels. International agreements like the Paris Climate Accords along with individual countries pursuing renewable energy programs will help, but it is difficult to get countries that depend on revenues from the sale of oil to make significant changes.

› Review Questions

Multiple Choice

1. Which of the following is an example of economic liberalization?
   (A) Increasing tariffs on imported goods
   (B) Increasing state ownership of businesses
   (C) Increasing foreign direct investment (FDI)
   (D) Increasing subsidies for cotton

2. A government pursuing an austerity program would do which of the following to reduce the deficit?
   (A) Increase income taxes
   (B) Increase defense spending
   (C) Increase spending on poverty programs
   (D) Increase subsidies for clean energy

3. Which of the following is an example of a coup?
   (A) Environmentalists protest the building of a government pipeline.
   (B) Citizens reject a referendum on independence.
   (C) Military generals remove the president from office.
   (D) The legislature votes to impeach the president.

4. Federalism is effective at minimizing coinciding cleavages because:
   (A) local governments have the sovereignty to develop local policies
   (B) the national government retains all sovereignty to reduce conflict
   (C) local governments defer all policymaking to the national government
   (D) it offers simple recognition to ethnic or religious groups

5. Which of the following is a sustainability policy?
   (A) The government builds a large dam that will flood farmland.
   (B) The government increases its use of coal-burning plants to generate electricity.
   (C) The government relaxes car emission requirements.
   (D) The government bans the use of gas and diesel cars.

Free Response

1. (A) Define supranational organization.
   (B) Describe the goals of a supranational organization.
   (C) Explain why a state would want to belong to a supranational organization.
   (D) Explain why a state would want to leave a supranational organization.

2. Use the following line graph to answer the question.

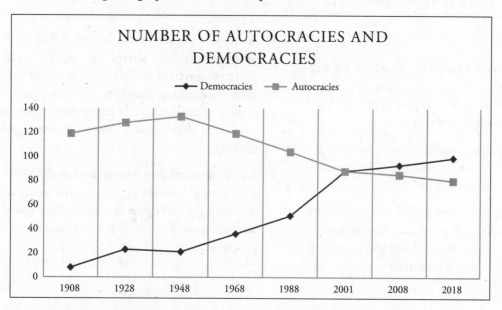

Source: Varieties of Democracies Project

(A) Using the data in the line graph, identify the year that the number of democracies and autocracies was equal.
(B) Using the data in the line graph, describe the trend for the number of autocracies since 1908.
(C) Define democratization.
(D) Explain what a limitation of the data in this line graph is.
(E) Explain how the trend in (B) correlates with the process of democratization.

3. Compare the role of the state in the economy in two different AP Comparative Government and Politics countries.
(A) Define rentier state.
(B) Describe the degree to which the state is in control of the economy in two different AP Comparative Government and Politics countries.
(C) Explain why the countries mentioned in (B) can be defined as rentier states or not as rentier states.

4. Develop an argument whether internal forces or external forces have a greater impact on the democratic consolidation of a state.

Use one or more of the following concepts in your answer.
• Globalization
• Supranational organization
• Civil society

In your response, you should do the following:
• Respond to the prompt with a defensible claim or thesis that establishes a line of reasoning using one or more of the provided course concepts.
• Support your claim with at least TWO pieces of specific and relevant evidence from one or more course countries. This evidence should be relevant to one or more of the provided course countries.
• Use reasoning to explain why your evidence supports your claim or thesis, using one or more of the provided course concepts.
• Respond to an opposing or alternate perspective, using refutation, concession, or rebuttal.

❯ Answers and Explanations

Multiple Choice

1. **C.** Economic liberalization is the act of freeing up market forces. Allowing an increase of FDI accomplishes that goal. All the other policies would reduce economic freedom.

2. **A.** Austerity programs reduce deficits by increasing taxes and reducing spending. All the other policies would increase the deficit.

3. **C.** A coup is when an elite group, often military, seizes control of the government through non-constitutional means. Impeaching and removing a president would not constitute a coup.

4. **A.** The main advantage of federalism is that a local government shares sovereignty with the national government. In that way, the groups with coinciding cleavages feel that they have actual representation because they have power over local affairs and a voice in national policy-making.

5. **D.** A sustainability policy is aimed at protecting natural resources for future generations. Banning gas and diesel cars will reduce smog and air pollution. The other policies would not offer protection.

Free Response

1. (4 points possible)
   (A) A supranational organization is one that member national states apply to join and once they are accepted, the state gives up some sovereignty over a policy area to the supranational organization. An example would be the UK giving up some sovereignty to join the EU. (1 point)
   (B) The goals of supranational organizations are to create policies to govern member states. Most of these organizations, like the EU or the WTO, have a goal of streamlining the movement of goods between member states to increase the benefits of free trade. (1 point)
   (C) A state will want to join a supranational organization if it agrees to the policies and feels that the benefits from the membership (access to free trade) outweigh the costs of giving up some sovereignty. (1 point)
   (D) A state will want to leave the supranational organization if compliance with the policies of the organization is too restrictive or burdensome. The UK, for example, voted to leave the EU to regain control over fishing and immigration. (1 point)

2. (5 points possible)
   (A) The number of democracies and autocracies appears to be equal in 2001. (1 point)
   (B) Since 1908, the number of autocracies in the world has been declining. (1 point)
   (C) Democratization is the process of a state moving from an authoritarian regime to a democratic one. In order to accomplish this, elections would become more free, fair, and competitive; the independence of the press and the judiciary would increase; and the rule of law would be established. (1 point)
   (D) A limitation of this data is that there is no way to determine if one state backslides from democratic to authoritarian as only the total number in the world is shown. (1 point)
   (E) Since the number of autocracies is declining, it appears that more democracies are emerging. This indicates that democratization is occurring. (1 point)

3. (5 points possible)
   (A) A rentier state is one where the government gets the majority of its revenue from the export and sale of natural resources, often oil. (1 point)

(B) Mexico has gone through economic liberalization policies since the 1980s, which has resulted in a diversified economy. The government still controls PEMEX, however, which is the national oil company. (1 point)

Nigeria has also gone through some economic liberalization policies and so the economy has diversified in some areas, although a high percentage of the population is still involved in agriculture. Nigeria also has a national oil company, but it leases the drilling rigs to foreign companies to actually extract the oil. (1 point)

(C) Mexico cannot be defined as a rentier state because the sale of oil is not the major source of revenue for the government. (1 point)

Nigeria, on the other hand, is a rentier state because the government receives the majority of its revenue from the sale of oil to the foreign companies. (1 point)

4. (5 points possible)

Internal forces, such as political parties or social movements, have a greater impact on the democratic consolidation of a state than external forces, such as MNCs or supranational organizations, because it is the citizens of a state who must accept the government as legitimate. Internal sovereignty must occur first before a state will feel compelled to strive to gain international acceptance. (1 point)

The recent Brexit referendum is a case in point. Although British voters agreed on a referendum to join the Common Market in the 1970s, they had never been directly asked again about EU membership. (A vote on the EU Constitution was scheduled but never held.) So, although governments from Thatcher, Major, Blair, and Brown all made deals with the EU, the increasing constraint on British sovereignty angered enough people to force the referendum in 2016. The Leave campaign mobilized voters to put pressure on the government to reform and leave the EU, consolidating power back into the hands of the British voter. (1 point)

Mexico made most of its democratic reforms in response to the rigged election of 1988. Internal protest forced the government to create an independent election commission, add PR seats to the legislature, and reform the Supreme Court. All of these reforms contributed to democratic consolidation much more than the external NAFTA treaty or Mexico's joining of the WTO. It was internal forces that had the more important impact. (1 point)

Governments need the citizens of a state to view them as legitimate and accept their authority. Democratic reforms are often the result of internal pressure for the government to reform, and thus consolidation occurs because of the greater impact of the power of the people in the system. (1 point)

Critics charge, however, that admission to supranational organizations like the WTO or scrutiny by intergovernmental bodies like the UN will compel a country to consolidate democratic reforms to protect property rights of foreign investors. China, for example, has added private property protections to its constitution as it has liberalized economically. So one could argue that outside global forces may make a country conform to international democratic standards. Unfortunately, China is an excellent example of how economic reforms have not led to the political liberalization associated with democratic consolidation. The repression of individual civil liberties in China is an excellent example of how external forces have been able to bring about some reform but not democratic consolidation. (1 point)

> Rapid Review

- The public policymaking process is the government's response to public demands, even if it is to repress those demands. Governments need the legitimacy gained from effective public policies about the economy, social welfare, and the environment.
- Democratization or political liberalization is the process of a state becoming more responsive to the consent of the governed.
- The three types of political change are revolution, coup, and reform.
- In a market economy, goods are allocated according to the forces of demand and supply, while in a command economy, the government determines how resources are allocated.
- Recognition and representation are two common types of reform.
- Economic liberalization is the process of freeing the economy from government control to promote economic growth. This often involves privatization or the sale of state-owned enterprises (SOEs), along with a reduction in taxes and regulations and the promotion of foreign direct investment (FDI) and special economic zones (SEZ).
- Public policies are decisions made by governments. Typical policies are:
  - Legislative: The legislature passes a new law, and it is signed by the executive.
  - Budgetary: The legislature appropriates the money requested by the executive.
  - Regulatory: The bureaucracy issues regulations to enforce or implement legislation.
  - Executive action: An executive order is given to a bureaucratic agency.
  - Court decision: A court makes a majority ruling.
- Individuals use linkage institutions to bring issues to the attention of government officials. Once an issue is on the policy agenda, legislation is enacted and implemented by the bureaucracy unless challenged by a court.
- Governments face both domestic and international pressure to adopt public policies. Nongovernmental organizations (NGOs) and multinational corporations (MNCs) lobby governments to promote protection of civil liberties and private property. Supranational organizations like the EU and WTO only accept members committed to free trade.
- All governments seek the legitimacy that comes from managing a high-performing economy, but officials have different views on how to solve a recession or high deficit.
- Officials also disagree on the efficacy of the import-substitution industrialization (ISI) model or the structural adjustment program (SAP) model to improve economic performance.
- Globalization occurs when increasing levels of integration of markets, communication networks, and culture characterize world trade.
- A welfare state is one that seeks to provide a universal safety net for its citizens.
- Sustainability or the protection of natural resources is an important environmental goal.

CHAPTER 11

United Kingdom

IN THIS CHAPTER

Summary: The United Kingdom is an essential case in the AP Comparative
Government and Politics course because it is the example of a consolidated
liberal democracy with a parliamentary system of government. Despite
its longstanding political stability, the United Kingdom continually faces
challenges to its sovereignty as it seeks to govern multiple nations while
also establishing a new relationship with the European Union after Brexit.
Additional concerns stem from the pressures of an aging population on its
welfare state, the ongoing threat of terrorism, and the ramifications of a
global pandemic.

Key Terms

austerity
civil society
collective responsibility
common law
Confederation of Business
    Industry (CBI)
Conservative Party
corporatism
democratic deficit
devolution
European Union (EU)
first past the post (FPTP)
globalization
head of government
head of state

House of Commons
House of Lords
Liberal Democrats
National Health Service
    (NHS)
New Labour
parliamentary sovereignty
parliamentary system
pluralist
quangos
referendum
single-member district
    system
social capital
supranational organization

Supreme Court of the
    United Kingdom
sustainability
Thatcherism
Third Way
two-plus party system
unitary state
vote of confidence
vote of no confidence
welfare state
Westminster model
World Trade Organization
    (WTO)

The United Kingdom as a Case Study

As you study the United Kingdom, pay careful attention to the discussion of the following concepts as they are the most frequently used in comparing it with other countries on the AP Comparative Government and Politics exam.

CONCEPT	POSSIBLE COMPARISONS/USEFUL EXAMPLES
Democratic regime	Authoritarian regime
Parliamentary system	Presidential system
Bicameral legislature based on class	Bicameral legislature based on regions
Supranational organization	Challenges to sovereignty
Referendum	Scottish parliament, Scottish independence, Brexit
Strong civil society	High rates of political participation
Public policy	Welfare state, NHS, austerity
Colonial legacy	Nigeria
Legitimacy	Traditional, rational-legal

Sovereignty, Authority, and Power

The State

The United Kingdom of Great Britain and Northern Ireland was established through an evolutionary state-building process.

Important dates in its evolutionary process are:

- 1066   Norman invasion by William the Conqueror
- 1542   Wales united with England
- 1707   Act of Union joining England, Wales, and Scotland to form Great Britain
- 1801   Act of Union joining Great Britain and Ireland
- 1922   Partition of Ireland results in creation of the current state

The Nation

The United Kingdom is a multination state with longstanding social cleavages between regional groups. The English are 84 percent of the population and historically have been the dominant power in the union. The Scottish (8 percent), Welsh (5 percent), and Northern Irish (3 percent) have had varying degrees of success in maintaining their national identity within the union. All the countries have their own flags and national symbols, which are often combined when trying to show unity. The Union Jack, for example, which is the official flag of the United Kingdom, is a combination of the cross for the patron saint of each of the four countries. Significantly, however, in recent years, the regional governments have achieved a measure of self-government through devolution **referendums**, yet challenges for the British parliament to govern the unified country continue to exist. Even participation in international sports competition is complicated as to which countries can participate.

OLYMPICS	FIFA WORLD CUP	RUGBY	CRICKET
Team GB	England, Scotland, Wales, Northern Ireland	England, Scotland, Wales, Ireland*	England, Scotland, Ireland*

*Northern Ireland plays with the Republic of Ireland

Legitimacy

Traditional legitimacy is a vital component of the British political system. Longstanding adherence to a common-law tradition has established the formal powers of the Crown as well as provided protections of civil liberties to citizens even in the absence of a codified constitution. Precedence and custom have led to long-established practices and conventions that help people accept the government's authority. The queen herself personifies this relationship, as it is "Her Majesty's Government" and she is the visible symbol of not only the state but also as the head of the Church of England.

Rational-legal legitimacy is also an integral source of authority in the British system as laws and norms are respected. Although it is uncodified, the concept of the British constitution is widely accepted in Great Britain. In addition, adherence to rule of law is a longstanding practice dating back to the limits placed on the king in the Magna Carta of 1215.

Regime

The United Kingdom is a consolidated liberal democracy with a longstanding commitment to the protection of civil liberties and rule of law. Prime Minister Theresa May declared that "this is Great Britain, the country of Magna Carta, parliamentary democracy, and the fairest courts in the world."

Freedom House Ratings: Free (political rights: 39/40, civil liberties: 54/60).

The Economist Intelligence Unit Democracy Index: Full Democracy: 8.10.

- Fair, free competitive elections
- Universal suffrage since 1928
- Independent press and judiciary
- Robust civil society
- Civilian-controlled military

Type of Economic System

The United Kingdom has a mixed economy. Historically an imperial power with extensive colonies, postwar Great Britain actively developed a welfare state complete with universal, state-owned health care (NHS). The economic policies of Margaret Thatcher, otherwise known as Thatcherism, reduced the government's role in the economy in the 1980s through the privatization of several industries. Membership in the WTO commits Great Britain to global free trade, which will require extensive negotiations as the Brexit from the European Union slowly evolves.

Political Culture and Socialization

Tradition is the essential characteristic of British political culture. An island nation, the United Kingdom is insular and seeks a uniquely British approach to public policy. A proud country that once ruled a global empire, Britain retains an interest in influencing global events and still struggles to keep the United Kingdom intact. The Crown remains a unifying symbol as personified by Queen Elizabeth II.

Agents of socialization continue to be the family, schools, peer groups, and the media. Discussions about politics with friends and family, civic education classes, and a vibrant media environment all help the transmission of political attitudes about the government.

Government Institutions

Constitution

The United Kingdom has an uncodified constitution that is often described as an unwritten constitution. This means that there is not a single, authoritative document that establishes the powers and functions of the British government. Instead, the British constitution is a collection of documents, statutes, and political practices that have evolved over time. The advantage to this system is its inherent flexibility. In countries with a single, written constitution, the formal process of amending that document requires much more effort and coordination than simply passing a law. In contrast, Parliament can change the constitutional structure of the political system by passing a law. Under the leadership of Tony Blair, significant constitutional laws were passed in 1998–99 establishing a Scottish Parliament, Welsh Assembly, Northern Ireland Assembly, and elected mayor of London, along with reforms to the House of Lords and the adoption of a Human Rights Act. Yet this flexibility can also be a disadvantage in that there are few checks on the power of the government of the day to make such substantial changes without the input of those from other parties. Because of this threat, various groups over the years have advocated for a written constitution. Currently, a group called Unlock Democracy argues that "the government is too powerful because we don't have a written constitution that sets out what they can and can't do." Many politicians, however, argue that the current system allows them to respond more quickly to changing conditions.

Levels of Government

The United Kingdom is a **unitary state** with all power centralized in the Crown in Parliament. Despite this, there are still numerous levels of subnational governments, however, including local councils and regional assemblies and the trend has been to cede more authority to these bodies through devolution. **Devolution** occurs when a central government transfers power to a lower level of government. It is not the same as federalism in that the central government retains sovereignty, but it does allow for local governments to have a larger role in developing policy for their own area. Interestingly the process of devolution was preceded by a referendum that allowed local voters to determine if they wanted their local government to have this authority. Based on the results of the referendum, Parliament then passed the legislation necessary to grant the power. Technically, as a unitary government, Parliament retains the authority to dissolve these local governments, although realistically it would be difficult given popular support.

Devolution Referendums

England	1998 Greater London Authority (72% yes)
	2004 Northeast England Assembly (78% no)
Scotland	1997 Scottish Parliament (74% yes)
	1997 Scottish Parliament power to tax (64% yes)
	2014 Scottish independence (55% no)
Wales	1997 Welsh Assembly (50% yes)
	2011 Welsh Assembly legislative power (63%)
Northern Ireland	1998 Good Friday (Belfast) Agreement to create Northern Ireland Assembly (72% yes)

The United Kingdom is a member of the World Trade Organization (WTO) and used to be a member of the European Union (EU), both supranational organizations. A **supranational organization** is composed of member states that have agreed to cede some sovereignty to the organization over a specific policy area.

In 1995, Great Britain was one of the founding members of the World Trade Organization (WTO), which evolved from the General Agreement on Tariffs and Trade (GATT). WTO members are committed to free trade and agree to abide by the decision of the WTO in settling trade disputes.

The history of Great Britain's involvement in the European Union (EU) is more complex. Although the Treaty of Rome created the European Economic Community in 1957, Great

Britain did not join this Common Market until 1973. PM Margaret Thatcher reluctantly signed the Single European Act in 1986 because she had become increasingly skeptical about the challenges to British sovereignty from this new European super-state. Her successor, John Major, signed the Maastricht Treaty in 1993, which created the European Union, thereby subjecting Great Britain to compliance with EU rules, regulations, and decisions by the European Court of Justice (ECJ). Great Britain did not join the European Monetary Union, however, and retained control over its own currency, the pound. By 2015, membership in the European Union had become a political issue driven in large part by the rise of the United Kingdom Independence Party (UKIP) and PM David Cameron promised to offer voters a referendum on the European Union to appease the Euroskeptics in the **Conservative Party**. In June of 2016, the referendum was held and 52 percent of the voters chose the leave option, resulting in Cameron resigning his position and new PM Theresa May in charge of a difficult Brexit. After a three-year process and two snap elections later, Prime Minister Boris Johnson celebrated the exit of the United Kingdom from the EU on January 31, 2020. Significant challenges remain, however, as British companies navigate the new complexities of trade between the United Kingdom and the European Union.

Legislative-Executive Relationships

The United Kingdom's Westminster model, called such because Parliament meets in the Palace of Westminster, is the epitome of a parliamentary system with a fusion of executive and legislative authority that evolved over time.

Key developments are listed below.

DATE	EVENT	SIGNIFICANCE
1066	Norman Invasion	William I established feudal councils as advisors.
1215	Magna Carta	Required the king to consult with nobles before taxation, thus limiting the power of the sovereign.
1264	Parliament	First calling of the Commons to include representatives from towns, in addition to the nobility and clergy.
1327–77	Reign of Edward III	Institutionalized lawmaking procedure—must pass both houses of Parliament and be signed by king.
1689	Glorious Revolution	Established parliamentary sovereignty and the creation of a constitutional monarchy.
1721–42	Reign of George I, George II	Robert Walpole is considered the first prime minister to wield significant executive authority.
1832	Great Reform Act	Dissolved "rotten boroughs" to create more uniform districts and extend suffrage.
1911 and 1949	Parliament Acts	Reduced the role of the House of Lords in the legislative process. Can only delay the passage of legislation.
1999	House of Lords Act	Removed all but 92 hereditary peers from the House of Lords.
2011	Fixed Parliament Act	Since 2015, Parliamentary terms have been five years unless there was a vote of no confidence in the government or a 2/3 majority vote to hold a new election.

To understand how the Westminster model works, scholars consult several authoritative texts on the subject. Walter Bagehot's *English Constitution* is regularly cited for how it explains how the three components of the Parliament may be viewed as having two separate functions.

- Dignified: The queen and the **House of Lords** are symbolic of authority and add legitimacy.
- Efficient: The **House of Commons** and the cabinet are charged with making policy and being answerable to the voters.

The Dignified

Queen Elizabeth II is Great Britain's **head of state**, having served as its constitutional monarch for 70 years. Because of her commitment to her symbolic role, the British public favor retaining the monarchy (76 percent) to a republic (17 percent) according to a recent Ipsos MORI poll. The queen has the right "to be informed, to be consulted, to warn, and to encourage." She meets weekly with her prime minister, delivers the queen's speech to open Parliament, and must give the royal assent for a bill to become a law. Her son, Charles, the Prince of Wales, is next in line for the throne.

The House of Lords also provides a mainly symbolic role in that its members can only vote to delay legislation for a year, unless it is a money bill, which they can delay for only one month. But the Lords do play a key role in legitimizing the legislative process. As an appointed, not elected, body, the Lords deliberate and scrutinize legislation from a unique perspective because of their membership. Since 1999, only 92 hereditary peers sit in the House of Lords. They are joined by 687 life peers who are appointed by the prime minister for their contributions to the country and 26 "Lords Spiritual" who are bishops in the Church of England. Because of its inherently undemocratic composition, there are often calls to reform the House of Lords even more by adding a popular election process, but to date no consensus has been reached.

The Efficient

The House of Commons is the premier legislative body in the Westminster model. It enjoys **parliamentary sovereignty** because the only thing that can overturn an act of Parliament is another act of Parliament, which must be passed by the Commons and can only be delayed by the Lords, the queen's assent being automatic. The House of Commons is a representative body because its 650 Members of Parliament (MPs) must win a plurality election to gain their seats. MPs sit in the Commons with members of their political parties and vote for party leaders. The leader of the majority party in the House of Commons is asked by the queen to form a government. If there is no majority party, as there was not in 2010, the queen will ask the leader of the largest party to form a government based on the ability of the leader to form a coalition government as David Cameron of the Conservative Party did with the **Liberal Democrats** in 2010. There can also be a change in prime minister without a popular election being held. There may be an internal party leadership challenge as happened to Margaret Thatcher in 1990, and Theresa May in 2019, or the prime minister may resign as David Cameron did after the Brexit vote in 2016. In both cases, the majority party selected a new leader and that leader was asked to form a government by the queen.

The cabinet, referred to as the government, is headed by the prime minister, who serves as **head of government** or the chief executive in charge of policymaking. The prime minister selects members of her party to serve as ministers of bureaucratic agencies, the most important positions being chancellor of the Exchequer (Treasury), foreign secretary, and home secretary. The recruitment process involves selecting between the other most senior members of her party in parliament to serve in a position of leadership as "frontbenchers." The government, therefore, is composed of MPs who are serving in the executive and legislative branches simultaneously—a fusion of executive and legislative authority. The cabinet then operates under the convention of **collective responsibility** where all members of the government must speak with a unified voice on policy or resign. This also means that if the government loses a **vote of confidence** by the full House of Commons, the entire government must resign and call for a new election.

How a Parliamentary System Differs from a Presidential System

	PARLIAMENTARY SYSTEM	PRESIDENTIAL SYSTEM
Legislative-Executive	Fusion of executive and legislative power	Separation of executive and legislative power
Chief Executive	Prime minister	President
Position	Head of government	Head of state, head of government
Selection	Head of majority party in lower house	Separate election from legislature—usually direct election by people
Cabinet	Selected by prime minister from senior members of party in lower house—retain position as MP	Appointed by president, approved by legislature—do not have to be in legislature—must give up seat if are
Removal	Vote of no confidence by lower house	Impeachment vote by legislature

The prime minister and the cabinet along with significant party leaders, such as the whips, and senior career civil servants develop government policy proposals and oversee implementation through the bureaucracy. Many of the prime minister's powers fall into four main categories:

- Royal Prerogative: to direct actions of the armed forces, sign treaties, execute laws
- Patronage: appoint/remove cabinet ministers, recommend life peerages
- Party leader: using party whips to maintain backbench support
- Media: controlling image, speaking directly to people

The main constraint on the power of the prime minister is maintaining the support of his or her party. Party whips are deployed to keep discipline among the regular party members known as backbenchers. The prime minister faces weekly Prime Minister's Questions (PMQs) where MPs of both parties are permitted to query about government actions. In fact, all party leaders need to perform well during question time to questions from MPs about their policy positions and actions or face public humiliation. Media scandals, cabinet resignations, and backbench revolts can all diminish the power of the prime minister to the point where the party in parliament may change its leader midterm or defeat the government in a **vote of no confidence**.

Judiciaries

The United Kingdom's judicial system has a long tradition of independence and adherence to rule of law and due process. Yet in 2005 a Constitutional Reform Act (CRA) was passed to formalize the independence of the court system by creating the **Supreme Court of the United Kingdom**. To better maintain the appearance of impartiality, the Law Lords were moved out of the House of Lords and across the street to the new location of the Supreme Court where they sit as the court of last resort for British courts and devolution cases. This was a symbolic action in that the Supreme Court was given no new powers. In addition, the CRA created a new system of selecting judges. Judges are selected by a 15-member Judicial Appointment Commission on the basis of merit and formerly appointed by the Lord Chancellor. Because of the principle of parliamentary sovereignty, British courts do not have the power of judicial review to overturn Acts of Parliament, but the courts can find that legislation is "incompatible" with the Human Rights Act of 1998

Common law is an essentially British practice, found primarily in Great Britain and former British colonies such as the United States. It is the practice of "judge-made" law in that prior judicial decisions are considered binding in future cases.

Bureaucracies

The British government bureaucracy is referred to as Whitehall because most of the administrative offices are found along Whitehall Road. Whitehall is staffed by career civil servants selected based on merit after taking exams. Government positions are highly sought after by recent graduates who are willing to put in the time to become experts in their policy field and advance up the career ladder to a senior position. The British civil service prides itself on its neutrality and its willingness to work with whichever political party controls the government of the day. Each ministry is headed by a member of the cabinet who as a political appointee must rely heavily on the expertise of the career civil servants.

A unique feature of the British political system are **quangos** or quasi-autonomous non-governmental organizations, which are independent from direct state control but serve as semi-public regulatory bodies financed by the government. Examples include Ofcom, which regulates communications, and Ofwat, which regulates water. The current trend is to eliminate or consolidate quangos as an unnecessary level of bureaucracy.

Military and Other Coercive Institutions

The British Armed Forces are a highly regarded, professional organization with a worldwide reach because of the Royal Navy and overseas bases. As one of the world's few nuclear powers, Great Britain plays a significant role in the United Nations and NATO as a peacekeeping force. In 1969 the British Army was deployed to Northern Ireland during "The Troubles" to fight the Irish Republican Army (IRA). Although hostilities stopped with the Peace Agreement in 1998, some troops remained until 2007.

Police jurisdictions are managed by local governments, and most police officers do not carry guns. Specially trained and armed units exist, however, for use when needed, and these groups often face criticism by protesters for coercive tactics.

Leadership and Elite Recruitment

The path to political leadership in Great Britain often starts early. Thirty-one percent of MPs attended private secondary schools, and 24 percent went on to earn a degree from Oxford or Cambridge. After a short career in consulting, law, or journalism, potential MPs often stand for office in a district where their party is not strong to get the experience of running. As there is not a residency requirement for parliamentary seats, potential MPs try to be selected by the local party in a safe district to win a seat. After time spent on the backbenches demonstrating party loyalty, MPs may be selected to serve as a junior minister, then minister, before trying for prime minister. Compare the leadership paths of two recent prime ministers.

DAVID CAMERON	GORDON BROWN
• Educated at Eton, Oxford	• Educated at University of Edinburgh
• Consultant	• Lecturer, journalist
• Ran for office and lost 1994–2001	• Ran for office and lost 1979
• MP 2001	• MP 1983
• Shadow minister 2003	• Shadow minister 1987
• Conservative leader 2005–2010	• Chancellor Exchequer 1997–2007
• Conservative prime minister 2010–2016	• Labour prime minister 2007–2010

Linkage Institutions

Elections

There are several types of elections held in the United Kingdom.

TYPE OF ELECTION	FREQUENCY	ELECTION SYSTEM	MOST RECENT EXAMPLE
House of Commons MP	Every 5 years unless vote of no confidence or 2/3 vote in Commons	First past the post	December 2019 called early by PM Johnson and agreed by 2/3 vote of the Commons
Devolved Parliaments	Every 4 years unless vote of no confidence or 2/3 vote in Parliament	Proportional representation	Scotland: 2016 Wales: 2016 Northern Ireland: 2017
Local Councils	Every 4–5 years	First past the post	May 2019
European Union Parliament	Every 5 years	Proportional representation	May 2019
Referendums	Called by prime minister	Majoritarian	Brexit June 2016

Election Systems and Party Systems

Elections for the MPs in the House of Commons are considered the most important elections in Great Britain. The entire United Kingdom is divided into 650 constituencies by the Electoral Commission. England has 533 seats, Scotland has 59, Wales has 40, and Northern Ireland has 18, each consisting of 60,000 to 70,000 constituents.

First Past the Post

All seats are contested using the **single-member district system** or as it is called in Great Britain, **first past the post (FPTP)**. This means that voters select one name from the ballot, and the person with the most votes wins the seat. This type of election system results in a **two-plus party system** with only two large parties (Conservative, Labour) winning enough support to form a government. Significant smaller parties include the Liberal Democrats and regional parties like the Scottish National Party and the Plaid Cymru of Wales. Thus, the British party system displays the classic advantages and disadvantages of using the FPTP model. As a perennial third party, the Liberal Democrats pushed an Alternative Vote referendum in 2011 that failed to win voter support.

FPTP Winner-Take-All Plurality Election System

ADVANTAGES	DISADVANTAGES
• Domination by two parties able to form a majority government • Voters select a specific candidate to hold accountable • Traditional legitimacy because it is a longstanding method of selection • Parties with regional identification win the most votes in that region to ensure geographic representation	• Large parties tend to be overrepresented with a "winner's bonus" • Can result in a "hung parliament" with no majority party • A feeling of "wasted votes" may hurt support for third parties

For comparison purposes, here are the results of the most recent elections for the House of Commons. Reminder: A majority in the House of Commons is 326 seats. All results are from BBC Election Coverage.

Election of 2010

Conservatives form a coalition government with Liberal Democrats—first in 36 years.

PARTY	% OF POPULAR VOTE	NUMBER OF SEATS	NET GAIN/ LOSS	% OF SEATS	PRIME MINISTER
Conservative	36%	307	+97	46%	David Cameron Coalition with LD
Labour	29%	258	−91	39%	
Liberal Democrats	23%	57	−1	8.8%	
Scottish National	1.7%	6	—	1%	
Plaid Cymru	.6%	3	+1	.5%	
Democratic Unionist	.6%	8	−1	1.2%	
Sinn Fein	.6%	5	—	.7%	
Other		6			

Election of 2015

Conservatives win majority. Rise in popularity of UKIP. Stunning win of SNP after independence referendum loss in 2014.

PARTY	% OF POPULAR VOTE	NUMBER OF SEATS	NET GAIN/ LOSS	% OF SEATS	PRIME MINISTER
Conservative	36.9%	331	+24	51%	David Cameron
Labour	30.4%	232	−26	36%	
Liberal Democrats	7.9%	8	−49	1.2%	
Scottish National	4.7%	56	+50	8.6%	
Plaid Cymru	.6%	3	—	.5%	
Democratic Unionist	.6%	8	—	1.2%	
Sinn Fein	.6%	4	−1	.6%	
UKIP	12.6%	1	+1	.15%	
Other		7			

Election of 2017

Snap election called by PM Theresa May. Conservatives form confidence and supply support agreement with DUP.

PARTY	% OF POPULAR VOTE	NUMBER OF SEATS	NET GAIN/ LOSS	% OF SEATS	PRIME MINISTER
Conservative	42.4%	318	−13	48.9%	Theresa May Agreement with DUP
Labour	40%	262	+ 30	40.3%	
Liberal Democrats	7.4%	12	+ 4	1.8%	
Scottish National	3%	35	−21	5.38%	
Plaid Cymru	.5%	4	+1	.6%	
Democratic Unionist	.9%	10	+2	1.54%	
Sinn Fein	.7%	7	+3	1.1%	
UKIP	1.8%	–	−1		
Other		2			

Election of 2019

Snap election called by PM Boris Johnson to increase support for Brexit.

PARTY	% OF POPULAR VOTE	NUMBER OF SEATS	NET GAIN/ LOSS	% OF SEATS	PRIME MINISTER
Conservative	43.6%	365	+48	56.2%	Boris Johnson
Labour	32.2%	203	−60	31.2%	
Liberal Democrats	11.5%	11	−1	1.7%	
Scottish National	3.9%	48	+13	7.4%	
Plaid Cymru	.5%	4	−	.6%	
Democratic Unionist	.8%	8	−2	1.2%	
Sinn Fein	.7%	7	−	1.1%	
Other	6.8%	4	+2	.6%	

Political Parties

The United Kingdom has a longstanding party system with two catch-all parties, Conservatives and Labour, dominating the postwar governments. There are also significant regional parties that win only in their respective countries, such as the Scottish National Party (Scotland), Plaid Cymru (Wales), and the Democratic Unionist and Sinn Fein (Northern Ireland). In addition, the Liberal Democrats had broad appeal through the 2010 election, but have suffered electorally for their participation in the Conservative coalition government of 2010–15. It is important that you have a basic understanding of the ideological and policy positions of the major parties, along with voter demographics.

PARTY	CONSERVATIVE (TORIES)	NEW LABOUR	LIBERAL DEMOCRATS
Current Leader	Boris Johnson May	Keir Starmer	Jo Swinson Farron
Ideological Position	Center-right	Center-left	Social Democrats
Regional Support	England	London, Northern Cities	London
Voter Demographics	Older, retired, professional class, skilled manual workers, less educated	Young, students, unions, semiskilled workers, unemployed, highly educated	25–44, professional, highly educated

PARTY	CONSERVATIVE (TORIES)	NEW LABOUR	LIBERAL DEMOCRATS
Economic Policy Position	• Balance budget with austerity measures • Decrease immigration • Smooth exit from EU	• End austerity • Raise taxes on business and the rich • Nationalize utilities, rail, post, water • Guarantee EU rights	• Hold another referendum on EU to stay • Increase taxes to fund NHS and social care • Support freedom of movement with EU workers
*Social Policy Positions**	• Build more homes • Increase NHS funding	• Abolish university tuition fees • Increase NHS funding	• Increase funding for education • Build more homes
*Foreign Policy Positions**	• Commitment to free trade • Commitment to NATO, WTO, UN, G20, G7	• Commit to spending 2% of GDP on defense	• Commit to spending 2% of GDP on defense

*Party positions are based on 2017 party manifestos

Positions of Other Parties

SCOTTISH NATIONAL PARTY	PLAID CYMRU	DEMOCRATIC UNIONIST PARTY	SINN FEIN	UKIP
• Opposed to Brexit • Wants second independence referendum	• Negotiate Brexit that puts Wales first	• Restore devolution to Stormont • NI Brexit deal	• Special status for NI in EU • Ireland reunification referendum	• Complete Brexit without paying EU

Interest Groups Systems

The United Kingdom is a **pluralist** society with a wide variety of active interest groups that compete for a position on the policy agenda in addition to providing services for their members. This is a change from the 1970s when organizations such as the **Confederation of Business Industry (CBI)** and the Trades Union Congress (TUC) formed a tripartite association with the government. This close partnership of peak groups negotiating with the government is called **corporatism**. Margaret Thatcher dismantled this special relationship during her tenure as prime minister. Today, groups that wish to influence government policy compete for influence with the core executive (prime minister and cabinet) and civil servants in Whitehall as they seek access to provide information in both the development and implementation of policy. In addition, groups compete for influence with devolved parliaments, and for the time being, EU institutions as well.

Interest Groups

The most powerful interest groups in Great Britain are the economic ones because of the importance of their issues for job creation and trade and their ability to pay for professional lobbyists. The two most prominent groups are:

- CBI: the largest business lobby group composed of numerous industries. Closely associated with the Conservative Party, the CBI works to promote policies to increase trade.
- TUC: the largest union organization composed of numerous trade unions. Closely associated with the Labour Party, the TUC works to promote policies to benefit workers.

There are also numerous issue-based groups that focus on supporting causes from civil rights to the environment.

- Issue groups include: Amnesty International, Electoral Reform Society, Campaign for Nuclear Disarmament (CND)
- Environmental groups include: Greenpeace, Campaign to Protect Rural England, Keep Britain Tidy

Citizens, Society, and the State

Social Cleavages

Historically the greatest cleavage in Great Britain was class. The aristocracy, middle class, and working class enjoyed different sports, attended different schools, and read different newspapers. They also supported different political parties. Recent elections, however, have seen a narrowing of class identification with parties, although a tendency remains for the wealthy to support the Conservatives and union workers to support Labour. Now retired, working-class people are among the Conservatives' strongest supporters while highly educated degree holders vote Labour.

Regional cleavages are strongly felt as viewed by growing support for regional parties. The Scottish National Party may have failed to win an independence referendum, but it has markedly increased its power in the Scottish Parliament and in Westminster. Northern Ireland voters only support NI parties with the DUP attracting Protestant voters and Sinn Fein appealing to Catholic voters, revealing that a substantial religious cleavage continues to divide that country.

Religious cleavages also exist among Christian and Muslim voters. As the number of Muslims increases in Great Britain (4 percent of population, second-largest religion), tensions have occurred over Islamophobia and terrorist acts. There is also a coinciding cleavage of ethnicity with Muslim groups in that most are immigrants from former British colonial areas, such as Pakistan, Bangladesh, and Nigeria.

Civil Society and Social Capital

The United Kingdom has a robust **civil society** with many opportunities for citizens to form voluntary, autonomous organizations. Although membership in churches and unions has declined, individuals actively join both nonpolitical groups, such as garden or sports clubs, and political cause groups, such as environmental or civil rights based organizations, thus building **social capital** or networks of trust and cooperation. Trust in political institutions, however, continues to decline from 36 percent to 26 percent in 2017, according to the Edelman Trust Barometer.

Media Roles

Because of freedom of the press protections, the United Kingdom has an active, competitive media environment. Publications ranging from the tabloid press to the prestigious *Financial Times* newspaper and *Economist* magazine are widely circulated. In addition, the BBC, publicly funded by an annual fee charged to all households, is world renowned for independent coverage. Strengthened by the 2000 Freedom of Information Act, the British media are active government watchdogs exposing MP scandals, while also serving as agenda setters in their coverage of government and interest group actions. Media consolidation is a concern, however, as only a few firms own most of the media outlets from newspaper to television to Internet news sites. But on a positive note, 92 percent of the country has Internet and the British government does not censure access.

Political Participation

There is considerable political participation in the United Kingdom, although the nature of that participation is changing. Formal methods of involvement continue to decline as fewer British people join political parties and voter turnout remains below historically high levels. Sixty-five percent of voters participate in the general election for the House of Commons, with lower turnouts for local elections. Recent referendums, however, have garnered higher turnout rates: Brexit (72 percent) and Scottish Independence (84 percent).

On the other hand, informal methods of participation are increasing. Although the British continue to demonstrate and protest, such organizing is made easier with the use of social media tools. One prominent example is the 2010 student protests against an increase in tuition fees that resulted in numerous sit-ins and marches across the United Kingdom. Online activism is also increasing, although the concern is that people are content to simply write a check as a sign of involvement. In addition, the government has tried to use the Internet to increase citizen engagement. One example is the use of e-petitions to bring issues directly to the attention of the MPs.

Unfortunately, the United Kingdom has also faced political violence. Older residents remember the bombing tactics of the IRA during the 1970s, '80s, and '90s. The most serious recent terrorist incident was the 7/7 attack on the subway and bus system by Islamic suicide bombers in 2005. In addition, from March through June of 2017, four separate ISIS-inspired attacks have occurred in Great Britain, including the bombing of an Ariana Grande concert in Manchester.

Social Movements

Social movements are when diverse groups of people with a shared political commitment to a common goal push for change using both formal and informal tactics. A prominent British example would be the women's suffragette movement of the early 1900s. Contemporary examples include a Stop the War movement against the Iraq invasion, the Occupy London movement against the government's austerity program, and the LGBT movement to expand civil rights.

Citizenship and Representation

British citizenship is acquired through birth in the United Kingdom or to a British citizen or through the process of naturalization. Great Britain's participation in the European Union and as a member of the Commonwealth present additional options for people to have the right to settle in the United Kingdom. Consequently, immigration policies are always contentious between groups that want to expand access to the economy and those who want it restricted. The recent vote for Brexit was in large part supported by those individuals who would like to see less immigration to Great Britain.

The 2019 House of Commons has the most diverse collection of MPs ever, although it still lacks descriptive representation in that each of the following demographic groups are smaller than their populations as a whole: 220 women, 65 ethnic minorities, 45 LGBTQ, and 5 disabled. Interestingly, for the first time in history, a majority of Labour and Lib Dem MPs are female. In addition, the devolved parliaments and the use of proportional voting systems to select their members has provided voters with more opportunities for representation at the local level.

Political and Economic Change

Revolution, Coups, and War

Great Britain's approach to political change has been more evolution than revolution as political elites throughout British history gradually chose reform over armed conflict. Since Cromwell's reign as Lord Protector in the 1650s, the dignified members of Parliament (queen, House of Lords) slowly ceded political power to the efficient (prime minister, cabinet, and Commons) where policy control is the hands of the electorate.

Political Change

Great Britain was part of the first wave of democratization in the world as defined by Samuel Huntington, but has continued to further pursue policies of political liberalization. Of note are the constitutional reforms pursued by **New Labour** under Tony Blair to increase opportunities for voters to select local representatives for the devolved parliaments in Scotland, Wales, and Northern Ireland along with increased protection of civil liberties through the Human Rights Act of 1998 and the reduction of hereditary peers in the House of Lords. The increased use of referendums allows for more direct democracy as well. The ramifications from the Brexit referendum, for example, will take more time to take effect as the government continues to struggle with disentangling the United Kingdom from the European Union. In addition, the Johnson government would like to increase devolution to regional governments in an effort to use "leveling up" as a way to decrease regional disparities.

Economic Change

Postwar Great Britain has experienced both the highs and lows of the business cycle. Consensus wartime politics had led to an increased role for the state in the economy through the nationalization of major industries, the creation of the **National Health Service (NHS)**, and a corporatist relationship with major trade groups. The result was that during the 1970s Britain was regarded as "the sick man of Europe" because of a sluggish economy, devalued pound, and an International Monetary Fund (IMF) bailout. Margaret Thatcher's Conservative party won the 1979 election on a promise of economic liberalization. These policies became known as Thatcherism.

- **Thatcherism:** Privatize major industries (examples: British Telecom, British Gas, British Airways), reduce the power of unions by ending corporatism, reduce taxes, sell council housing to residents, maintain high interest rates to reduce inflation.

As Conservatives controlled the economy through the 1980s and '90s, Tony Blair pressed the Labour Party to modernize its approach to the economy. The party agreed to reword Clause 4 of its Manifesto to abandon the goal of renationalizing industry and to reduce the voting power of the TUC. Instead, the newly branded New Labour Party would adopt Blair's "Third Way" economic policy.

- **Third Way:** Between liberal capitalism and democratic socialism. It involves a commitment to markets and social justice to be accomplished through public-private initiatives, low taxes, and efficiently run social programs to provide opportunity.

The Conservative Party came back to govern in 2010 at a time of global recession. David Cameron's response was to pursue a policy of austerity to deal with government deficit spending.

- **Austerity:** Government policy to reduce deficit spending by raising taxes and cutting spending.

These spending cuts were met with widespread protests by Occupy London and student groups protesting increases in tuition fees.

The single biggest change to the British economy, however, during this period was the creation of the European Union in 1992, which created a supranational organization with the authority to mandate changes in British regulations to bring them into compliance with those of the European Union. The freedom of movement of goods and people proved to be a mixed blessing as trade boomed and London became the financial capital of the world, but the working class felt threatened by increased levels of immigrants. The vote for Brexit was driven by those voters who felt that their financial situation has worsened under the European Union. It is still too early to understand the long-term effect that leaving the European Union will have on the British economy. As leaving coincided with the global pandemic, the expected drop in trade with the European Union was larger than expected and hit small businesses in the United Kingdom particularly hard. Implementation of the Northern Ireland Protocol has also been difficult as the system has caused an increase in costs and delays due to the required additional paperwork.

Public Policy

The United Kingdom is a pluralist society with an active civil society where individuals enjoy the freedom to express opinions and mobilize for political reforms. Citizens have access to linkage institutions to help pressure the government to add their initiatives to the policy agenda. The prime minister and cabinet have the challenge to initiate policies that will satisfy their party members and the electorate. These initiatives are first presented as white papers for discussion before being developed into government bills that then face scrutiny in Parliamentary committees, at question time, and during floor debates. Party-line voting ensures that government bills pass the Commons and usually the Lords as well to be given the royal assent by the queen. Cabinet ministers and their career staff in the bureaucracy then implement the policies by drafting regulations and enforcing rules. Courts may intervene if specific cases have standing because the plaintiff has been harmed by government action.

The European Union

Great Britain's involvement in the European Union has been controversial from the start with Margaret Thatcher's Euroskepticism continuing to find support within the Conservative Party. Although membership in this free trade zone had been a way to further the advantages of **globalization** or the economic integration of national economies, it had also meant giving up sovereignty to the ECJ and EU bureaucracy in return for the increased trade. Some British voters felt a **democratic deficit** when it came to the European Union because they only were involved in selecting MEPs for the European Parliament, which is the least powerful branch of EU government. The EU Commission, an appointed body, wields the most authority over EU standards and regulations. Although most young, urban, educated British citizens voted to stay in the European Union, they were defeated by older, rural, working-class voters who wanted to regain British sovereignty and reduce immigration.

The Environment

Many people in Great Britain support a postmaterialistic approach to the environment and support organizations and government policies that promote **sustainability** to avoid the depletion of natural resources. The Green Party has won more electoral support and now has one MP in the Commons, has two in the House of Lords, and had seven in the European Parliament. Other organizations such as Greenpeace and Save the Earth also enjoy support as does the Land Trust. There is wide popular support for policies to combat climate change, to prevent nuclear proliferation, and to prevent fox hunting.

The Welfare State

After World War II, consensus politics led to the expansion of the **welfare state**, which is when a government offers universal benefits to all citizens to protect and promote health and a standard of living. This social safety net includes pensions, unemployment insurance, subsidized council housing, poverty programs, and free universal health care in the form of the National Health Service (NHS). The NHS is the nationalized, state-owned health care provider in Great Britain that is immensely popular and very expensive to run. Politicians of all parties struggle with the increasing cost of running a program for Britain's aging population that continues to require more care.

Terrorism

The United Kingdom has faced domestic terrorism for much of the postwar period. After Irish independence, only Northern Ireland remained in the United Kingdom. The minority Catholic population who wanted Irish reunification (the nationalists) felt discriminated against by the Protestant-dominated government that wanted to stay in the United Kingdom (unionists). Violence broke out between paramilitary groups, most notably the Provisional Irish Republican Army (IRA) and the Ulster Volunteer Force (UVF) during the 1960s with the British Army being deployed to restore order in 1969. Sporadic conflicts continued until the Good Friday Peace Accord of 1998, which established a power-sharing arrangement for the government of Northern Ireland. The devolved legislature of Stormont must be governed by a mandatory coalition of the two largest parties, currently the DUP and Sinn Fein.

More recent terrorist attacks have come from Islamic radicals. The 7/7 subway attack in 2005 was Great Britain's 9/11 moment. The government response to this and later terrorist attacks has been multifaceted. Security precautions have been increased at airports and other public places. There is extensive use of CCTV surveillance cameras in urban areas, and the government has passed the Investigatory Powers Act of 2016 to increase the power of officials to gather data while still protecting privacy rights.

Colonial Legacy

At one point in history, the sun never set on the British Empire. Great Britain retains 14 overseas territories including Gibraltar, the Falklands, and Bermuda, but the rest of its former colonies are fully independent states. Fifty-four countries remain part of the British Commonwealth, an association of countries dedicated to democracy and rule of law. Fourteen of these countries, including Canada and Australia, have Queen Elizabeth II as their head of state. In November 2021, Barbados voted to remove the Queen as their head of state but will stay in the Commonwealth. The domestic legacy of colonialism is the resulting immigration of individuals from former colonies to the United Kingdom. According to the 2011 census, 6.8 percent of the British population is Asian with the largest number identifying as Indian or Pakistani. Three percent are Black with 2 percent claiming African heritage and the other 1 percent identifying as Caribbean. An increasing number of ethnic minorities are involved politically, with a record number of MPs winning in the 2017 election. In addition, the new mayor of London, Sadiq Khan, is the first Muslim and member of an ethnic minority to hold that office. He is a member of the Labour Party and a former MP.

Covid-19

The British government instituted a nationwide lockdown in March 2020 in response to the rapid spread of Covid-19. Parliament also issued emergency powers to the devolved governments to handle the crisis. Consequently, Scotland, Wales, and Northern Ireland pursued different public health restrictions. By late 2021, the Johnson government was facing criticism for its handling of the pandemic, most visibly for holding parties at 10 Downing Street during lockdown.

› Review Questions

Multiple Choice

1. The British legal system is based upon:
   (A) common law
   (B) commonwealth legal principles
   (C) European Union legal principles
   (D) civil law

2. British prime ministers are officially selected and appointed by:
   (A) the chief justice of the Supreme Court
   (B) the speaker of the House of Commons
   (C) the monarch (king or queen)
   (D) the senior member of the House of Lords

3. In the British system, which position or institution is considered to have supreme power?
   (A) The monarch
   (B) The Parliament
   (C) The prime minister
   (D) The cabinet

4. A vote of no confidence is:
   (A) a public statement by the king or queen
   (B) a negative vote in a referendum
   (C) a defeat of the ruling party in an election
   (D) a negative vote on government policy in Parliament

5. Collective responsibility refers to:
   (A) the obligation of the cabinet to support all government policies
   (B) the obligation of civil servants to implement government policy
   (C) the obligation of the House of Lords to protect civil rights
   (D) the obligation of Commonwealth states to come to the aid of other states during war

6. Today, Supreme Court judges:
   (A) must be members of the House of Lords
   (B) must be members of the ruling party
   (C) are selected by committee
   (D) are elected by regional legislatures

7. Devolution refers to:
   (A) redistributing power from the Parliament to the European Union.
   (B) redistributing power from the monarchy to the House of Lords
   (C) redistributing power from the House of Lords to the House of Commons
   (D) redistributing power from the national government to local and regional governments

8. Which of the following combinations correctly identifies Great Britain's election system and party system for Westminster elections?

	Election System	Party System
(A)	Alternative vote	Dominant party
(B)	First past the post	Two-plus party
(C)	Proportional	Multiparty
(D)	Single transferable vote	Two party

9. Which of the following is a policy associated with Thatcherism in Great Britain?
   (A) Privatizing national industries
   (B) Cutting defense spending
   (C) Giving the EU greater powers
   (D) Increasing the power of trade unions

10. When Theresa May became prime minister replacing David Cameron who resigned, there occurred a change in:
    (A) regime
    (B) nation
    (C) government
    (D) culture

Free Response

1. (A) Define referendum.
   (B) Describe a recent referendum.
   (C) Explain why a government would choose to offer a referendum.
   (D) Explain how a referendum can deepen social cleavages.

2. Use the following table to complete your answer.

Life Expectancy in the United Kingdom (UK)

YEAR	LIFE EXPECTANCY
1960	71 years
1980	74 years
2000	78 years
2017	81 years

Source: World Bank

   (A) Using the data in the table, identify the trend in life expectancy in the UK.
   (B) Describe a limitation of the data in the table.
   (C) Define welfare state.
   (D) Explain how the trend in life expectancy in (A) impacts the welfare state in the UK.
   (E) Explain how the British government could use austerity policies to address the impact in (D).

3. Compare how states select dual executives within the political systems in two different AP Comparative Government and Politics course countries. In your response, you should do the following:
   (A) Describe the difference between a head of state and a head of government.
   (B) Describe how dual executives are selected in two different AP Comparative Government and Politics course countries.
   (C) Explain why the purpose for maintaining dual executives for the two different AP Comparative Government and Politics course countries in (B) is similar or different.

4. Develop an argument as to whether the upper house of a legislature should be elected or appointed to enhance political efficacy.

   Use one or more of the following course concepts in your answer.
   • Legislative independence
   • Political culture
   • Political stability

   In your response, you should do the following:

   • Respond to the prompt with a defensible claim or thesis that establishes a line of reasoning using one or more of the provided course concepts.
   • Support your claim with at least TWO pieces of specific and relevant evidence from one or more course countries. This evidence should be relevant to one or more of the provided course concepts.
   • Use reasoning to explain why your evidence supports your claim or thesis, using one or more of the provided course concepts.
   • Respond to an opposing or alternate perspective, using refutation, concession, or rebuttal.

› Answers and Explanations

Multiple Choice

1. **A.** The British legal system is based on common law. Although different types of laws exist (B and C), Great Britain and its former colonies emphasize the importance of taking previous case law into consideration.

2. **C.** Although the British prime minister is the leader of the majority party in the House of Commons, he or she is officially selected and appointed by the monarch.

3. **B.** Although the monarch is a king or queen, and Great Britain is a constitutional monarchy, it is Parliament that is supreme.

4. **D.** A vote of no confidence is when Parliament fails to cast a majority vote for a government bill, thus requiring the government to resign.

5. **A.** Collective responsibility is a unified approach to policy by the members of the cabinet. If cabinet members cannot agree with government policy, they must resign their post.

6. **C.** Unlike in the past when the prime minister selected the Law Lords, recent reforms have the Supreme Court justices selected by committee.

7. **D.** Devolution is the transfer of power from the national government to lower levels of government.

8. **B.** The correct combination of election system and party system for Great Britain is first-past-the-post electoral system and two-plus party system.

9. **A.** One of the characteristics of Thatcherism was privatizing government agencies. It also included increasing defense spending, raising interest rates, and decreasing the power of the unions. In addition, Margaret Thatcher was Euroskeptic of the European Union.

10. **C.** A change in prime ministers is a change in government.

Free Response

1. (4 points possible)
    (A) A referendum is when a government allows voters to directly vote on a public policy. (1 point)
    (B) A recent referendum in the UK was Brexit. UK voters were allowed to vote to stay in or leave the European Union. (1 point)
    (C) Governments choose to offer referendums to enhance the legitimacy of the public policy. Instead of simply having the legislature pass a law, voters have a direct say on the policy issue, which makes them more likely to accept the policy itself. (1 point)
    (D) Referendums can deepen social cleavages, however, if the vote leaves a minority group even more isolated than before. For example, with the UK Brexit referendum, Scottish voters overwhelmingly voted to stay in the EU. Now that the UK has left the EU, Scottish voters feel that the decision by mostly English voters has left them with no alternative but to seek another independence referendum so that Scotland could rejoin the EU. (1 point)

2. (5 points possible)

(A) Life expectancy in the UK has slowly increased between 1960 and 2017, from 71 years in 1960 to 81 years in 2017. (1 point)

(B) A limitation of the data is that it is not broken down between men and women, who typically have differences in life expectancy. (1 point)

(C) A welfare state is one that offers public policies with universal coverage. A welfare state is often called a nanny state because it provides services to protect the health and well-being of all citizens. (1 point)

(D) As people live longer lives in the UK, more pressure will be placed on the National Health Service (NHS) to care for these elderly patients. This increase in patients will increase the costs of the NHS system as facilities need to be expanded to provide services. (1 point)

(E) The increased costs associated with taking care of more elderly patients will cause UK budget spending to increase. This increase in spending will cause budget deficits unless the government engages in austerity measures such as cutting spending in other programs or raising taxes to cover the needed higher health spending. (1 point)

3. (5 points possible)

(A) The difference between a head of state and a head of government is in job responsibilities. A head of state is the ceremonial leader of a country, whereas a head of government is the legislative leader who develops public policies. (1 point)

   In the UK, the head of state is Queen Elizabeth II. She is a hereditary monarch who became queen when her father died. Her son, Charles, will be the next king. The head of government, on the other hand is Prime Minister Boris Johnson. Although he was formally appointed PM by the queen, he actually won the job by being the head of the majority party in the House of Commons. (1 point)

(B) In Russia, the head of state is President Vladimir Putin. He was directly elected by the Russian people. The head of government is Prime Minister Mikhail Mishustin. He was appointed by President Putin and his nomination confirmed by the State Duma. (1 point)

(C) The purpose of maintaining a dual executive in the UK and Russia is similar. By separating the ceremonial and legislative leader roles in both countries, it is easier to replace the legislative leader as a scapegoat if there is a domestic problem, such as a sinking economy. This allows the ceremonial leader to provide political stability as the government of the day scrambles to make policy shifts. In the UK, the queen is politically neutral, serving as a symbol of British unity and stability. Shifting from PM May to PM Johnson allowed the Conservative Party in the House of Commons to make a leadership change to show adaptability. When May could not get a Brexit vote through Parliament, a party change provided a change in leadership, so that the new head of government, Johnson, could get the policy change adopted. (1 point)

   In Russia, President Putin has been a very powerful head of state but even he and his party face challenges. Recent proposed changes to the Russian political system were significant enough that PM Medvedev stepped down, and President Putin appointed new PM Mishustin. In this way, Putin continued as the ceremonial leader promoting stability, but a new PM is a way of sending a message of policy change without upsetting the system too much. (1 point)

4. (5 points possible)

Political efficacy is the ability of voters to understand how a political system works and feel that they have a say in policymaking. If the goal of a society is to have the structure of the legislature enhance political efficacy, it is clear that an elected upper house rather than an appointed upper house is more democratic and thus more legitimate because voters have a direct say in who those legislators are. Legislative independence will be enhanced because the power to pass laws comes from the people and not another source. (1 point)

The Mexican Senate is an elected upper house and not an appointed one. Voters in all 32 states select Senators to serve 6-year terms. To ensure political efficacy, Mexican voters select Senators using a mixed election system of single-member district seats and proportional seats. In this way, even minority party supporters know that their votes are rewarded with seats in the Senate. In fact, gender parity laws increase representation as well. Consequently, legislative independence is increased because Senators know that they will have to answer to the voters and not some other authority for their actions. (1 point)

The Nigerian Senate is also an elected upper house and not an appointed one. Even though Nigeria was a former British colony, when it earned its independence, it did not copy the House of Lords in its new system of government. After trying a parliamentary system, Nigeria adopted a presidential system with a bicameral legislature modeled after the United States. Having an elected upper house with 3 senators per state assured people that the legislature would be responsive to all areas of the country. Political efficacy was enhanced because the voters of each state would have a direct vote in selecting their senators. Again, this process protected legislative independence because a Senator's power comes from the people and not a different authority. (1 point)

It is clear that the ability of voters to feel like a political system is accountable to them is through the use of fair, competitive elections, like those for the Senate in Mexico and Nigeria, enhance political efficacy and legislative independence because the people are the source of authority and not some other entity. (1 point)

Critics may charge that an appointed upper house may in fact enhance political efficacy because it provides political stability. The British House of Lords is considered "the conscience of the nation" because its appointed members do not have to worry about elections, but instead can do what they feel is best for the country. In a political culture that values tradition, like that of the UK, it could be argued that the appointed House of Lords enhances political efficacy because the British people understand how the system works. Yet the traditional stability that it provides is not democratic. Consequently, there are frequent proposals to make it more democratic and responsive. In 2010, for example, the Law Lords were moved out to create the UK Supreme Court. This made the judicial process more transparent by taking it out of the legislative branch. Considering that the House of Lords has been losing power since 1911 (it now can only delay legislation), it is clear that an elected upper house is more legitimate because the people have more direct power to hold it accountable. (1 point)

› Rapid Review

- The United Kingdom of Great Britain and Northern Ireland (Great Britain) is a state that has evolved over time to become a consolidated liberal democracy with a parliamentary system of government.
- The United Kingdom is a multination state with longstanding social cleavages between regional groups (English, Scottish, Welsh, Northern Irish).
- Traditional legitimacy is a vital component of the British political system with strong adherence to common law, precedence, and customs.
- The British constitution is uncodified, but adherence to rule of law provides rational-legal legitimacy. The constitution is a collection of documents, statutes, and political practices that have evolved over time.
- The United Kingdom is a welfare state complete with a universal, state-owned health-care system called the National Health Service (NHS).
- The United Kingdom is a unitary state with all power centralized in the Crown in Parliament. Since 1998, however, Parliament has devolved or transferred power to regional parliaments (Scottish, Welsh, Northern Irish) after voters approved referendums.

- The United Kingdom currently belongs to one supranational governments: the World Trade Organization (WTO). It left the European Union in 2020 after long negotiations after the 2016 Brexit referendum.
- An essential characteristic of the Westminster model is parliamentary sovereignty.
- The British parliament is composed of an appointed House of Lords and an elected House of Commons. Ministers of Parliament (MPs) compete in first-past-the-post elections (FPTP) where the Conservative, Labour, and regional parties dominate. If no party wins a majority of seats, a coalition government is formed (2010).
- The British prime minister is selected by the House of Commons and by convention is the leader of the majority party. The PM selects members of her party to serve as the cabinet. The cabinet retains their seats as MPs but are bound by the principle of collective responsibility. A vote of no confidence requires the government to resign.
- The British legal system is based on common law, and courts have a long history of judicial independence. Because of parliamentary sovereignty, courts do not have judicial review. Judges are selected by commission.
- The British bureaucracy is merit-based, and each ministry is led by a political appointee (cabinet minister) who relies on the expertise of the career officials.
- The United Kingdom moved in the 1970s from corporatism to a more pluralistic system of interest group representation under Margaret Thatcher. Civil society is robust and is enhanced with an active, competitive, independent media.
- Thatcherism was a policy of economic liberalization and included the privatization of industries. Blair's Third Way continued the commitment to markets while boosting social programs. Cameron's austerity program raised taxes and cut programs to reduce deficit spending.

Iran

IN THIS CHAPTER

Summary: Iran is one of the few theocracies in the world, which makes it the most unusual case in the AP Comparative Government and Politics course. Officially named the Islamic Republic of Iran ever since the Revolution of 1979, Iran is a political power in the Middle East. It has, however, significant differences from its neighbors in that Iran is primarily a Persian, Shia state, whereas its rivals, such as Saudi Arabia, are Arab, Sunni states. In addition, Iran faces the challenge of reconciling two competing forces, theocracy and democracy, within its political structure while dealing with the economic pressure of being a rentier state.

Key Terms

Assembly of Experts
Baha'i
Basij
bazaaris
bonyad
chief justice
Constitutional Revolution
   of 1906
corporatist
coup
Expediency Council
Green Movement

Guardian Council
Iran-Iraq War
Iranian Revolution of 1979
Islamic Revolutionary
   Guard Corps (IRGC)
jurist guardianship
Majlis
military coup
multimember district
   election system (MMD)
president of Iran
rentier state

republic
Sharia
sharia law
Shia Islam
single-member district
   (SMD)
supreme leader
theocracy
unitary state
velayat-e faqih
White Revolution

Iran as a Case Study

As you study Iran, pay careful attention to the discussion of the following concepts as they are most frequently used in comparing Iran with other countries on the AP Comparative Government and Politics exam.

CONCEPT	POSSIBLE COMPARISONS/USEFUL EXAMPLES
Theocracy	Democracy
Competitive elections	Vetting by the Guardian Council
Two-ballot election system for president	Parliamentary systems
Religious legitimacy	Rational-legal legitimacy
Regime change	Change in government
Revolution	Coup
Rentier state	Corruption

Sovereignty, Authority, and Power

The State

The Islamic Republic of Iran was established by popular referendum after the Revolution of 1979. Important dates in the development of the Iranian state include:

- 550 B.C.   Persian Empire established by Cyrus the Great with the capital at Persepolis
- 661–750 C.E.   Umayyad Dynasty established Islam in Persia
- 1502–1736   Safavid Dynasty adopted Shiism as state religion
- 1794–1925   Qajar Dynasty faced Constitutional Revolution in 1906—created Majlis
- 1921   Military coup by Reza Khan
- 1925   Majlis appoints Reza Khan Pahlavi as Shah
- 1935   Persia officially known as Iran, this traditional name meaning Land of Aryans
- 1941   Great Britain and Russia force Shah to abdicate in favor of his son
- 1953   Great Britain and the United States help stage a coup to remove PM Mohammad Mosaddeq after he nationalizes oil
- 1963   Shah begins forced modernization process known as the White Revolution
- 1979   Iranian Revolution led by Ayatollah Ruhollah Khomeini

The Nation

Iran is a multination state where ethnicity and religion structure the country's major social cleavages. The majority of people in Iran are of Persian descent (61 percent), speak Farsi, and ascribe to Shia Islam. The second-largest group are the Azeris of Turkic descent (16 percent) who are also Shia. (There are more Azeris living in Iran than nearby Azerbaijan.) Azeris are well integrated into Iranian society. For example, Supreme Leader Khamenei is of Azeri descent as is former Prime Minister Mousavi. The third-largest ethnic group, the Kurds (10 percent), are more problematic for the regime. The Iranian Kurds speak the same language, Sorani, as Iraqi Kurds as well as practicing Sunni Islam. The recent independence referendum by the Iraqi Kurds in 2017 was unsettling for Iran, which has already had to put down Kurdish rebellions in 1946 and 1979. There are also smaller ethnic groups in Iran, including Arabs (2 percent) and small numbers of religious minorities, including Zoroastrians, Jews, and Christians.

Legitimacy

Traditional religious legitimacy is extremely important in the Islamic Republic of Iran. The supreme leader must be a high-ranking cleric, and all judges must be clerics as well because the legal system is based on sharia, or Islamic law. In addition, the supreme leader also appoints the Friday prayer leaders for the capital cities in all 31 provinces to maintain a consistent message to the people.

The Ayatollah Khomeini had charismatic legitimacy as the leader of the Iranian Revolution in 1979 as his followers were devoted to him and to his belief in *velayat-e faqih,* or clerical rule. His challenge was to use this support to institutionalize his philosophy in the new system of government.

Looking to reinforce the legitimacy of the revolution, Supreme Leader Khamenei issued "The Second Phase of the Revolution" in February 2019 to mark the 40th anniversary. He specifically urged the next generation of young people to help Iran continue to reach its revolutionary goals.

Rational-legal legitimacy is also important in Iran. Voters overwhelmingly approved a referendum in 1979 to establish the Islamic Republic of Iran and later approved a referendum adopting the current constitution, which institutionalized the theory of jurist guardianship or clerical rule through the creation of the position of supreme leader. To fulfill the designation of a republic, voters can select the president, the Majlis (legislature), and the members of the Assembly of Experts. To ensure that all political candidates are acceptable to the regime, the Guardian Council is given the job of vetting them before their names can be placed on the ballot. Elections have been held consistently in Iran at intervals called for in the constitution.

Regime

Iran is a **theocracy**, or a government run by religious leaders. It is an authoritarian regime based on **sharia law**, or Islamic law, which treats men and women differently, effectively undermining rule of law in Iran. Although competitive elections are held, all candidates for national office must be vetted by the Guardian Council, thereby denying voters a true choice. Neither the judiciary nor the press are independent bodies, and although the government has separation of powers, there is no effective check on the power of the supreme leader.

Freedom House Ratings: Not Free (political rights: 6/40, civil liberties: 10/60)

The Economist Intelligence Unit's Democracy Index: 1.95 (authoritarian)

Type of Economic System

Iran has a mixed economy with a long tradition of the bazaar or marketplace, now dwarfed by state-run enterprises. The state has a wide variety of ways of controlling the economy, from direct ownership to those sectors controlled by the Islamic Revolutionary Guard Corps (said to control one-third of the economy), to **bonyads**, which are public welfare organizations controlled directly by the supreme leader. In addition, Iran is a **rentier state** because the National Iranian Oil Company (NIOC) supplies 60 percent of government revenues through the export of oil and gas.

Political Culture and Socialization

Political culture in Iran is strongly nationalistic with pride in belonging to an ancient civilization. In addition, there is a strong theme of martyrdom, drawn primarily from the tenets of **Shia Islam**. The Shia or followers of Ali trace their origins back to the dispute over the Prophet Mohammad's successor upon his death in 632. The Shia believe that Mohammad's successor should have been Ali, the Prophet's cousin and son-in-law, but the first caliph, Abu Bakr, was chosen instead. Although Ali was eventually selected as the fourth caliph, he was assassinated, becoming the first martyr. His son, Husayn, attempted to regain the title of caliph but was martyred during the Battle of Karbala, effectively causing a split between Sunni and Shia that lasts to this day. The Iranian government emphasized reverence for martyrs by claiming that all soldiers killed in the Iran-Iraq war were martyrs and providing special benefits for their families from bonyads like the Martyrs Foundation.

Agents of socialization are the family, mosques, schools, and the state-run media. The supreme leader appoints all the leaders of Friday prayers and the head of the radio and television to control the government's message and maintain public support for the regime. There is vigorous censorship of the Internet, books, and movies to limit dissent. School curriculum and textbooks are crafted to support the regime. Families who have been repressed by officials, however, provide a different view of the government to their children. In addition, a highly educated, urban population with access to satellite TV and foreign vacations is difficult to control.

Government Institutions

Constitution

The Constitution of Iran was approved by referendum on December 3, 1979. It was designed by the Ayatollah Khomeini to enshrine his view of **jurist guardianship** or clerical rule, primarily through the role of the leader. Though the constitution initially included roles for both a president and a prime minister, Khomeini amended the document in 1989 to remove the role of prime minister. This was done to strengthen the role of the Expediency Council and to reduce the religious qualifications needed by the next leader. The constitution allows for direct election by the voters for president, the Majlis, and the Assembly of Experts to ensure that the government is a **republic**, a government where the voters select the officials who make public policy. The Guardian Council, however, is composed of Islamic clerics and lawyers who ensure that all public policies are acceptable to the leader.

Levels of Government

Iran is a **unitary state** with all sovereignty centralized in the national government. In addition to voting for president, Majlis, and Assembly of Experts, the people of Iran were given the opportunity to vote in city and village elections for council members in 1999. Although local elections were listed in the constitution, it was not until the reform period under President Khatami 20 years later that they were instituted, opening 200,000 seats across the country. In the most recent local elections in 2017, reformers won decisively across the country, as well as increasing the number of women holding these posts. Local councils are charged with selecting a mayor and managing the municipality.

The Leader or Leadership Council

Chapter 8 of the Iranian constitution establishes the position of the leader, separate from the executive branch, which is in Chapter 9. The **supreme leader** is the most powerful figure in the Iranian political system with the power to overrule every other institution. There have only been two supreme leaders in the history of the Islamic Republic of Iran; its founder, Ayatollah Khomeini, and its current office holder, Ayatollah Khamenei. Both men were selected by the directly elected **Assembly of Experts**, a body of clerics and religious experts who serve eight-year terms, and whose power is to select and/or dismiss the supreme leader. The Ayatollah Khomeini was the undisputed senior cleric in Iran, renowned for his intellect and the development of his theory of jurist guardianship. The Ayatollah Khamenei, on the other hand, "overcame being a junior cleric by becoming an institution builder," according to Iranian scholar Mehrzad Boroujerdi. Boroujerdi's research shows that the majority of the current Assembly of Experts have been or are Friday prayer leaders appointed by Khamenei and will be primed to appoint his chosen successor when he dies. (Khamenei is 80.) Many texts classify the supreme leader as Iran's head of state, but others recognize the unique status of the office. Khamenei is certainly not a traditional head of state in that he has not left Iran since becoming supreme leader, instead letting the Iranian president travel to represent Iran. The powers of the supreme leader are extensive.

The Powers of the Supreme Leader

- Determine overall policies of the Islamic Republic of Iran after consultation with the Expediency Council
- Supervise implementation of general policies and coordinate relationships between the three branches of government
- Issue referendums
- Commander of armed forces
    - Appoint head of military
    - Appoint head of Islamic Revolutionary Guard Corps
- Declare war, peace, and mobilize forces
- Issue appointments, dismissals of:
    - Six Clerics to Guardian Council
    - Chief justice (cleric)
    - President of mass media (TV and radio)
    - Friday prayer leaders
    - Members of Expediency Council
- Sign appointment of president after election by the people (and vetting by Guardian Council)
- Dismiss president if either convicted by Supreme Court or impeached by Majlis
- Pardon
- Control bonyads (massive and wealthy parastatal welfare organizations) (informal power—not in Constitution)

The Executive

The **president of Iran** is elected directly by the people in a two-ballot system; if no candidate wins 50 percent of the vote during the first round, then the top two candidates face off in a runoff election. The only runoff, however, was in 2005 between former President Rafsanjani and Tehran Mayor Ahmadinejad. Presidents serve four-year terms and can serve two terms consecutively. Presidents select members of the cabinet, who then must be approved by the Majlis. The government is charged with proposing the budget and other necessary legislation. The president also signs the bills that are approved by the Majlis, but he cannot veto a bill (the Guardian Council has that power). The president appoints ambassadors, signs treaties, and in general sees that laws are carried out. Most of the presidents of Iran have been clerics, except most recently, Ahmadinejad, including the current President Raisi, who was elected in 2020.

The Legislature

The Islamic Consultative Assembly or **Majlis** is the unicameral legislative body in Iran. Composed of 285 directly elected members and 5 appointed members representing Zoroastrians (1 seat), Jews (1 seat), and Christian (3 seats), they all serve four-year terms. In the parliamentary elections in 2016, 17 women were elected to the Majlis, the highest number ever. The women outnumbered the clerics for the first time because there were only 16 clerics elected. This was the lowest number of clerics ever elected.

The Majlis has the responsibility of giving a vote of confidence on the selection of the cabinet, as well as passing legislation initiated by the government and ratifying treaties.

The **Guardian Council** is an assembly formed to protect the commands of Islam. The Supreme Leader appoints six clerics to the body. The other six members are lawyers selected by the chief justice and approved of by the Majlis. All serve six-year terms. The Guardian Council oversees elections and is charged with vetting all candidates for national political office to make sure that they loyal to the regime. In addition, the Guardian Council must review all legislation passed by the Majlis for its compatibility with Islamic law and the constitution. The Council can veto legislation and return it to the Majlis. If the Majlis refuses to make the required changes, then the **Expediency Council** reviews the legislation and makes the final decision. The Expediency Council is appointed by the supreme leader for the purpose of advising him on major policy decisions.

The Judiciary

The most powerful judge in Iran is the **chief justice** who is appointed by the supreme leader for a five-year term. The chief justice selects the rest of the judges. Because the legal code is **sharia,** or Islamic law, all judges, including the chief justice, are clerics. The highest court in Iran is the Supreme Court, and there are lower-level civil and criminal courts, along with revolutionary courts to deal with those deemed a threat to the regime. There are also special courts just for clerics. Penalties for crimes can be severe in Iran. Iran is only second to China in the number of executions per year. There were more than 500 in 2017.

The Bureaucracy

The bureaucracy in Iran is massive as the state controls 60 percent of the economy, so many Iranians work for the state in some capacity. Although Iran has a highly educated population, the public sector is not a meritocracy; instead, the bureaucracy is characterized by cronyism and corruption. In 2016, in an episode called "Payslip-gate" by the Iranian press, the exorbitant salaries of top officials were leaked, causing public outrage.

Military and Other Coercive Institutions

Iran has a parallel structure to its armed forces. The traditional armed forces were supplemented in 1979 by the **Islamic Revolutionary Guard Corps (IRGC)**, which were designed to help the supreme leader protect the revolutionary ideals of the regime. Since that time, the IRGC has accumulated much more power than the traditional forces, particularly in the economic sector. It is estimated that the IRGC owns up to one-third of the Iranian economy, including control of several wealthy bonyads. The IRGC also controls the **Basij**, a paramilitary group that is used to repress public protests. Supreme Leader Khamenei expanded the IRGC to include the Quds force, which deals with international conflict in Syria, Iraq, and Lebanon.

Leadership and Elite Recruitment

In a theocracy, the path to political leadership is obviously open to religious leaders. Iranian clerics, therefore, have positions as judges and high-ranking officials, including the position of supreme leader, Guardian Council, and Assembly of Experts. The Iranian people, however, have not continued to support clerics for positions in the Majlis. Although clerics dominated the legislature after the revolution, their percentage has decreased to less than 20% since 2000.

Linkage Institutions

Elections

Several types of elections are held in Iran.

TYPE OF ELECTION	FREQUENCY	ELECTION SYSTEM	MOST RECENT EXAMPLE
President of Iran	Every 4 years	2-ballot system	June 2021 Raisi elected on first round with 62% of vote.
Majlis	Every 4 years	SMD and MMD	February 2020
Assembly of Experts	Every 8 years	SMD and MMD	February 2016
Local and Village Councils	Every 4 years	MMD	June 2021
Referendums	Called by supreme leader	Majority vote	1989 to ratify changes to Constitution—won at 97%

Election System and Party Systems

The first step for a national office candidate in Iran is to file an application to run for that office with the Guardian Council, which vets candidates to determine their loyalty to the supreme leader. In the most recent election for the Majlis, 16,000 people filed to run, and the Guardian Council rejected 9,000 of them. For the Assembly of Experts, 800 applied and 500 were invited to take the religious test, including 10 women. In the end, only 166 men could compete in the election (no women have ever served). For the presidency, 592 applied, including 40 women; the Guardian Council rejected all (including former President Ahmadinejad) except 7 male candidates.

All seats contested using **single-member district (SMD)** or **multimember district election systems (MMD)** have different requirements to win the seat. The Iranian parliament recently approved a reduction in vote thresholds for the 2020 election. In a SMD election, the winner must win the most votes and at least 20 percent (down from 25 percent) of the vote to win in the first round, or the top two candidates compete in a runoff. For MMD election, the voters cast as many votes as there are seats; candidates who receive 20 percent of the vote win on the first round, and the rest are in a runoff. Iranian presidents must win 50% of the vote. If no candidate wins a majority, then a runoff election is held between the top two candidates.

The traditional relationship between election systems and party systems does not occur in Iran, simply because there is no stable party system in Iran. What does exist is a shifting alliance of factions usually divided between a reformist camp that would like to see some political and economic liberalization in Iran and a conservative camp that prefers a more statist approach. In the 2020 Majlis election, the Guardian Council disqualified many reformist candidates, including eighty incumbent legislators. Voter turnout dropped to a historic low of 43%. Conservatives, also known as principalists, won 220 seats, more than doubling the 83 seats won in 2016 because of a lack of competition in many constituencies.

CONSERVA-TIVES	REFORMERS	INDEPENDENTS	RELIGIOUS MINORITIES
221	20	38	5

Source: IranSource

Presidential elections are the most prominent elections in Iran. After the first two presidents (Banisadr was impeached in 1981, and his successor Rajai was assassinated in 1981), Iranian presidents have served for two terms after being reelected.

Iranian Presidential Election Results

PRESIDENT	DATES	TERM I ROUND I	ROUND 2	TERM 2 ROUND 1	ROUND 2
Ali Khamenei	1981–1989	95%		88%	
Akbar Hashemi Rafsanjani	1989–1997	94%		64%	
Mohammad Khatami	1997–2005	69%		77%	
Mahmoud Ahmadinejad	2005–2013	19%	62%	63%	
Hassan Rouhani	2013–2021	50.71%		57%	
Ebrahim Raisi	2021–present	62%			

Interest Group Systems

Given the authoritarian nature of the political system in Iran, a **corporatist** system exists in Iran in that certain groups have strong ties to the state and can negotiate public policy. The IRCG has strong influence at all levels of government. In addition, bonyads such as the Martyr's Foundation have substantial resources to engage in clientelism. The political system in Iran is supported by a web of patron-client relationships. Government officials trade jobs and contracts in exchange for loyalty. In addition, all political groups must seek permission to form from the Interior Ministry, meaning that reformist groups have a more challenging time organizing.

Interest Groups

Some of the interest groups are political in nature. The Society for Combatant Clergy, for example, is a political association of elites who become active around election time. The government encourages the development of Islamic societies in workplaces and universities to speak for workers and students. Economic groups, like the **bazaaris** (bazaar merchants), also form to protect their interests. During the administration of President Khatami, more autonomous groups formed in response to a freeing up of civil society. One notable example would be the work of Shirin Ebadi, who mobilized lawyers in support of the rights of women and children for which she won a Nobel Prize in 2003. A crackdown on dissent after the 2009 election, however, has limited the ability of individuals to form political associations.

Citizens, Society, and the State

Social Cleavages

The main social cleavage in Iran mirrors the two political election camps, reformers and principlists, although many Iranians would label themselves moderate. These two camps are a result of several coinciding cleavages; for example, reformists tend to be highly educated, urban, middle-class Iranians who would prefer better relationships with the West and more political and economic liberalization, particularly in women's rights. Principlists, on the other hand, tend to be more religious traditionalists, rural, and poor and embrace the role of the clerics in government. What both groups support, however, is the Islamic Republic of Iran. The division is more about how to balance the two competing influences of theocracy and democracy.

Civil Society and Social Capital

Civil society is constrained in Iran. Public morality laws, aimed in large part at women, are restrictive. Women who fail to wear proper hijab or have on too much makeup are subject to arrest. Gender segregation is also evident at large sporting events. Iranian women were furious when they were not allowed into the stadium to watch the Iran-Syria World Cup qualifier in 2017, although Syrian women were. But women flourish at university, and a majority of students are women, although they are still restricted from certain majors and jobs. In addition, Iranians have strong family and social networks that provide many opportunities to connect with others and build social capital. It's just that more of this occurs out of the public eye when the government cracks down on civil society.

Perhaps the most repressed group in Iran are the **Baha'i**. As Iran's second-largest religious group, it is not given the constitutional protection that the Zoroastrian, Jewish, and Christian faiths are, primarily because these religions preceded Islam and their followers are considered "People of the Book." The Baha'i trace their faith to the preaching of a merchant in Shiraz, Iran, in 1844 who was executed for his beliefs about a new interpretation of Shia Islam. Subsequently, the Baha'i are prohibited from attending university or holding certain jobs and often face assault and vandalism of their property.

Media Roles

State-owned TV and radio networks are supervised by an official directly appointed by the supreme leader. This serves to control the government's message to the people. Iranians get around this limitation by installing illegal satellite dishes and then replacing them after the government seizes one. During the Khatami thaw, more independent newspapers and journals were published, but they were closed after his administration ended. The Internet has allowed for more freedom of expression, if one knows how to access a virtual private network (VPN) that the government hasn't blocked yet. Consequently, as the government tries to control the Internet and social media, enterprising individuals develop new apps and ways of circumnavigating government control. There is even an app to help avoid the morality police. Journalists face numerous redlines in trying to report about the government, and often face arbitrary arrest for publishing stories critical of the regime. These journalists are also frequently denied due process and tried in revolutionary courts, reports Freedom House, which scores Iran Press Freedom as Not Free (90/100 with 100 being the most repressive).

Political Participation

As in most countries, the number one form of participation is voting in presidential elections at a rate of 65 percent. Women are allowed to vote but are restricted from holding any office that requires the officeholder to be a cleric, as Shia clerics are only male. Many individuals also seek political office, including women, but they often face being disqualified by the Guardian Council. Although many voters are tempted to boycott elections when reform candidates are not allowed on the ballot, Iranian election results are not predetermined by the Supreme Leader, thereby incentivizing voters to participate. In 2016, for example, Supreme Leader Khamenei supported Ebrahim Raisi for the presidency, yet incumbent President Rouhani was able to win reelection with 57% of the vote. In addition, a strong culture of government corruption frustrates those who contact government officials directly or try to form reformist groups. Given these repressive practices, many individuals, especially university students, turn to public protest as a way to express grievances. Notably in both 1999 and 2003, protests that began at Tehran University spread to other cities but were both put down by the Basij.

Social Movements

Although protests in Iran tend to be focused on the grievances of specific groups such as workers or students, there are examples of social movements such as the one for women's rights. The best example of a recent social movement in Iran, however, is the **Green Movement**, which formed in response to the 2009 presidential election between the conservative President Ahmadinejad and former Prime Minister Mousavi who called for major reforms to the political system. Protests spontaneously formed after it was clear that the election had been rigged for Ahmadinejad to win in the first round. Those protesting represented a wide range of society, including millions of students, workers, professionals, and families, rich and poor. Although Ahmadinejad arranged counterprotests, the situation was dire, for these were the largest protests since the Revolution in 1979. The government's response was a massive crackdown with numerous arrests, beatings, and 110 killed. Mousavi and his wife were put under house arrest and remain there in 2019.

Citizenship and Representation

Citizenship in Iran is granted to children whose father is Iranian (not mother). The only children who gain citizenship from being born in Iran are children born to unknown parents or who are born to noncitizens of whom one parent was born in Iran. Women marrying an Iranian man gain citizenship. Everyone else must be naturalized.

Representation in Iran is limited. No women serve in the Assembly of Experts, Guardian Council, or judicial branch, and only 17 women serve in the Majlis. Some religious minorities have guaranteed seats in the Majlis in order to give that institution legitimacy in that all other legislators must be Muslim, but others like the Baha'i are prohibited from holding political office.

Political and Economic Change

Revolution, Coups, and War

Iran has experienced revolution, coups, and war in the modern era. Although the Shah had been pressured to accept limits on his authority during the **Constitutional Revolution of 1906** with the creation of the Majlis, imperial conflict among foreign powers in Iran during World War I constrained Persian rule. In 1921, a **military coup** led by Reza Khan was supported by the British, and by 1925 Reza Shah Pahlavi had been installed as the Shah by the Majlis. The new Shah began a process of top-down forced modernization of the economy and culture, even banning the wearing of the hijab. His support of Hitler in World War II caused Great Britain and Russia to invade and force the Shah to abdicate in favor of his son. The new Shah, Mohammad Reza Pahlavi, was unable to stop a revitalized Majlis that under the direction of Prime Minister, Mohammad Mosaddeq, nationalized the oil industry in 1951. The British and American governments responded with financing a **coup** of the Shah's supporters to overthrow Mosaddeq. The Shah then continued his father's modernization program, naming it the **White Revolution**, and sought to bring land reform, infrastructure, industry, and education to Iran, along with a substantial military expansion. But as scholar Ervand Abrahamian explains, "The White Revolution had been designed to preempt a Red Revolution. Instead, it paved the way for an Islamic Revolution." Although the Shah's plan did bring prosperity to some sectors of the Iranian economy, it was uneven, with a disproportionate amount of wealth and property going to the Shah's families and friends, thereby bypassing the traditional bazaar merchants. Some reforms, such as giving the right to vote to women and increasing educational opportunities, challenged the power of the clerics. Repression of civil society groups and the use of SAVAK, the secret police, to put down dissent infuriated elites. The scene was set for revolution.

The **Iranian Revolution of 1979** was an uprising of many sectors of society. Ironically, the Shah's attempt at some political liberalization loosened dissenting voices. Marxists wanted a communist regime, others wanted a pluralist democracy, and followers of the Grand Ayatollah Khomeini wanted an Islamic state governed by jurist guardianship. Khomeini had been exiled to Iraq years earlier but still was a prominent voice in the debate. A series of protests began to escalate, especially against symbols of westernization. Then SAVAK was blamed for the deaths of over 400 people in the burning of the Cinema Rex, and the protests grew across the country. The Shah declared martial law and the conflict escalated.

Hoping to reduce Khomeini's influence, the Shah pressured Iraq to expel him, and Khomeini traveled to France where the international media made him the face of the Revolution as he organized with the National Front to propose a new Islamic Republic. In December of 1978, millions of Iranians participated in antigovernment protests, and the military became increasingly reluctant to intervene. The Shah tried to restore civilian rule with a new prime minister and a promise to leave the country. As soon as the Shah left, however, Khomeini returned to Iran at the invitation of the new prime minister, who thought that it would reassure the protesters. Instead Khomeini set about installing his own provisional government in opposition. Within 10 days, the revolutionary forces were in control, and now it was time for Khomeini to consolidate his power. A referendum was offered to the people about the establishment of an Islamic Republic, which passed by 98 percent. A constitution was then formalized with the role of supreme leader and passed by the people in another referendum, helped by public support for the seizure of the American Embassy, which sidelined many of the moderate leaders who wanted the hostages released.

Over the next few years, Khomeini took advantage of the eight-year **Iran-Iraq War** to help consolidate his rule. After Saddam Hussein invaded Iran in 1980 to try to seize territory, Khomeini mobilized a patriotic force of Basij (mostly young men) to fight like "martyrs" alongside the Revolutionary Guards. (Khomeini had executed senior generals and forcibly retired many of the skilled military forces.) As years passed, the conventional forces were built up again, but they were unsuccessful at stopping Iraqi bombing raids on major cities. Finally, Iraq's use of poison gas against civilians pressured Iran to accept a ceasefire. The war was over, and in addition, the Ayatollah Khomeini had systematically eliminated his domestic opposition through imprisonment and execution.

Political Change

The one constant in Iranian politics since 1989 has been the Supreme Leader Ayatollah Khamenei, but even under his leadership, there have been subtle changes in public policy. Most notably would be the reformist pressure that accompanied the presidency of Mohammad Khatami. Yet even with the support of a reformist Majlis, Khatami was not able to enact many of his proposed reforms because of the power of the Guardian Council and the supreme leader. On the other hand, conservative President Ahmadinejad was also unable to make sweeping reforms, although the power of the IRGC rose during his presidency. In the end, political change has been gradual, characterized by a period of reform followed by a tightening of the rules.

Economic Change

Iran's economy is dominated by state-run enterprises and a dependence on the exportation of oil. Crippled by international economic sanctions for its nuclear weapons program, Iran has a high unemployment rate, especially among its youth and its female population, resulting in a significant "brain drain" as people leave to find better opportunities. Iran is a **rentier state**, with the government receiving most of its revenue from the export and sale of oil. It is also a member of the OPEC cartel and collaborates on setting production limits to affect world oil prices.

Many economists argue that to improve its economy, Iran must work to privatize firms, allow foreign direct investment to help diversify the economy, and reduce subsidies to individuals. The challenge remains, however, that economic control over the economy is tied to the legitimacy and stability of the regime. Upsetting the economic balance can lead to instability. These fears were realized in November 2019 when a policy to reduce gasoline subsidies was implemented. Public reaction was swift, with massive protests throughout the country. The Iranian government cracked down on this dissent with physical force, along with shutting down the Internet. Consequently, as many state actors have incentives to maintain their positions of wealth and influence, substantive economic change appears to be limited.

Public Policy

Public policy in Iran is driven by competing influences. Reformists seek to enact political and economic liberalization policies but are often defeated by conservative forces that are focused on retaining power over existing political and economic structures. The president and cabinet are charged with initiating policy to the Majlis where it is debated and voted on before being sent to the Guardian Council. The Guardian Council has the power to veto the bill and send it back to the Majlis for changes. If the two bodies cannot resolve their differences, the Expediency Council and the supreme leader make the final decision. Given that the state controls much of the economy and jobs, along with the revenue from the export of oil, an elaborate patron-client system has developed where jobs, contracts, and other benefits are exchanged for political loyalty. The corruption inherent in the system discourages citizens from affecting change, although a majority will vote in elections because even though the Guardian Council disqualifies many candidates, often there is some competition among those whose names remain on the ballot.

Foreign Policy

Iran has a very aggressive foreign policy, complete with the long-term goal of producing a nuclear weapon. To try to pressure Iran to not become a nuclear power, international sanctions have hobbled the Iranian economy. To remove these sanctions, Iran agreed in 2015 to abide by an agreement with the United States, United Kingdom, Russia, China, France, and Germany to reduce its stockpiles of uranium and to have its facilities inspected by the International Atomic Energy Agency (IAEA) to ensure compliance. In 2018, however, President Trump withdrew the United States from this agreement and imposed stricter economic sanctions on Iran. Tension between the two countries intensified over Iran's funding of terrorist groups in proxy wars in Syria and Yemen. After the killing of IRGC Major General Qassim Soleimani by the United States in January of 2020, Iran announced that it was no longer going to restrict the production of nuclear fuel. It remains to be seen how this issue will impact the legitimacy and stability of the regime.

Population Growth

The Ayatollah Khomeini hoped that his vision of an Islamic state would spread across the Middle East. In addition, he wanted the Iranian population to grow as well. So, laws were passed to encourage families to have more children. These programs were so successful that the population growth rate rose to 3 percent and government officials were concerned about Iran's ability to provide for so many people. In 1989, the government changed its policy to recommending that families have only two children, and to help incentivize this initiative, the government provided free contraceptives and required a family-planning class before a couple could get married. This program was also very successful, and the population growth rate dropped to 1.2 percent. (The U.S. rate is .7 percent.) President Ahmadinejad, however, wanted this policy reversed and for women to have more children. So the policy has been changed again, with cuts to family-planning budgets and increasing benefits to parents, but this time the growth rate has stayed steady at 1.2 percent. Critics charge that Iran's high unemployment rates, particularly for the young, would suggest that having more children is not the problem, and many families facing high inflation simply choose not to have more children. The rise in the number of women seeking higher education is also a factor. Typically, as a female population becomes more educated, the birth rate drops.

Drugs and Addiction

According to the UN Office of Drugs and Crime, Iran has the highest proportion of opiate addicts in the world. One cause is proximity, as 90 percent of opium is produced in next-door Afghanistan, making Iran a hub in the drug's journey to the West. Another cause is the high levels of unemployment is Iran, especially among the youth, who turn to drugs out of boredom and frustration. The drug of choice is heroin, although the use of crystal meth is increasing. The government has reacted to the epidemic in two ways: it has expanded the number of methadone clinics to treat addiction, and it has increased the punishment for drug crimes and hanged hundreds of smugglers.

The Environment

Iran has four of the most polluted cities in the world, according to a report by the World Health Organization. These cities, which include Tehran, have poor air quality especially in the winter months. One environmentalist is quoted as saying, "Air pollution is reaching a point where it is noticeable as a social or political demand. If the people were crying 'where is my vote' in 2009, their demand in 2014 will be, 'where is my breathable air?'" One cause of the pollution is domestically refined gasoline, which was used extensively because of trade sanctions. With the nuclear deal, the Iranian government has hoped to be able to import cleaner fuel while constructing a new oil refinery. Another cause is simply the number of cars on the road, helped along by government subsidies to keep fuel prices low. Requiring higher emission standards for new cars and reducing fuel subsidies will also help solve the problem, except that Iranians expect cheap fuel from the government. A final cause is lack of public awareness of the need to conserve energy and recycle. So the government has launched a public information campaign (billboards, TV ads) to increase support for environmental protection.

Covid-19

The handling of the Covid-19 pandemic in Iran has been characterized as government mismanagement. Supreme Leader Khamenei publicly claimed that U.S. and UK vaccines were untrustworthy and prohibited their use. As Iran was slow to manufacture a domestic vaccine, Iran's rate of vaccination remains the lowest in the region and its death rate the highest.

› Review Questions

Multiple Choice

1. Which of the following Iranian institutions are directly elected by the voters?
   (A) Supreme leader
   (B) Assembly of Experts
   (C) Guardian Council
   (D) Expediency Council

2. A theocracy is:
   (A) a government based on religious principles
   (B) a government with a state religion
   (C) a government with a monarch who is the head of the church
   (D) a government ruled by religious officials

3. Which of the following actions by the Shah of Iran, Mohammad Reza Pahlavi best explains why the people of Iran pursued a revolution in 1979 instead of simply advocating for reform?
   (A) The Shah's use of secret police to intimidate the population
   (B) The Shah's granting the right to vote to women
   (C) The Shah's exile of the Ayatollah Khomeini
   (D) The Shah's investment in transportation options, such as rail and air

4. Which of the following bodies has the power to vet potential candidates and veto legislation?
   (A) Assembly of Experts
   (B) Majlis
   (C) President
   (D) Guardian Council

5. The Green Movement in 2009 was caused by:
   (A) public outrage over Ahmadinejad's rigged first-round reelection
   (B) a new environmental campaign sponsored by the government
   (C) Ahmadinejad's reduction of gas subsidies in urban areas
   (D) a series of protests against Iran's nuclear weapons program

Free Response

(A) Define rentier state.
(B) Describe an environmental problem that often occurs in rentier states.
(C) Explain why the problem identified in (B) often occurs in rentier states.
(D) Explain why rentier states are often reluctant to pursue sustainability policies.

Use the following chart to complete your answer.

CANDIDATE	FIRST ROUND 6/17/2005	SECOND ROUND 6/24/2005
Mahmoud Ahmadinejad	19.43%	61.69%
Akbar Hashemi Rafsanjani	21.13%	35.93%
Mehdi Karroubi	17.24%	
Mohammad Bagher Ghalibaf	13.93%	
Mostafa Moin	13.89%	
Ali Larijani	5.93%	
Mohsen Mehralizadeh	4.38%	

Source: Iran Data Portal

(A) Using the data in the chart, identify the winning candidate in the 2005 Iranian presidential election.
(B) Using the data in the chart, describe why two rounds of voting were necessary in the 2005 Iranian presidential election.
(C) Describe legitimacy.
(D) Explain how a two-round election system for president provides legitimacy for an election system.
(E) Explain why authoritarian systems use elections for legitimacy.

3. Compare how states integrate religion within their political systems in two different AP Comparative Government and Politics course countries. In your response, you should do the following:
(A) Define theocracy.
(B) Explain how states integrate religion within their political systems in two different AP Comparative Government and Politics course countries.
(C) Explain why or why not each of the two AP Comparative Government and Politics course countries described in (B) can be described as theocracies.

4. Develop an argument as to whether the use of coercion by an authoritarian state is effective or not effective at maintaining stability.

Use one or more of the following course concepts in your response.
• Sovereignty
• Political Culture
• Political Participation

In your response, you should do the following:
• Respond to the prompt with a defensible claim or thesis that establishes a line of reasoning using one or more of the provided course concepts.
• Support your claim with at least TWO pieces of specific and relevant evidence from one or more course countries. This evidence should be relevant to one or more of the provided course concepts.
• Use reasoning to explain why your evidence supports your claim or thesis, using one or more of the provided course concepts.
• Respond to an opposing or alternate perspective, using refutation, concession, or rebuttal.

› Answers and Explanations

Multiple Choice

1. **B.** The Assembly of Experts is directly elected by the voters as are the president and the Majlis.

2. **D.** A theocracy is a government ruled by religious officials, just as a monarchy is a government ruled by a king.

3. **A.** The Shah's internal improvements were not the cause of the Iranian Revolution. His use of the secret police, SAVAK, was arbitrary and cruel and one of the people's chief complaints along with his corruption and extravagance. The Shah's exile of Khomeini angered his followers, who called for his return to Iran. His granting of the right to vote to women angered some of the clergy who preferred to maintain a traditional role for women.

4. **D.** The Guardian Council has the power to vet candidates and veto legislation. The Assembly of Experts selects the supreme leader. The president and cabinet propose laws to be passed by the Majlis.

5. **A.** The Green Movement was caused by public outrage over the rigged presidential election in 2009.

Free Response

1. (4 points possible)
   (A) A rentier state is one in which the government receives most of its revenue from the sale and export of a natural resource like oil. (1 point)
   (B) One environmental problem that occurs in rentier states is air pollution. In Iran, for example, antiquated refineries pollute the air. (1 point)
   (C) Air pollution often occurs in rentier states because government officials want to maximize revenue for themselves instead of investing in new, cleaner equipment. (1 point)
   (D) Sustainability policies would mean diversifying the economy and pursing alternative, renewable energy sources. Corrupt politicians are not incentivized to move the economy away from the government's main source of revenue. (1 point)

2. (5 points possible)
   (A) The winning candidate is Mahmoud Ahmadinejad. (1 point)
   (B) Two rounds of elections were necessary because no candidate received a majority of the ballots cast. A runoff was held between the top two candidates so that a majority could be earned. (1 point)
   (C) Legitimacy is when the people of a state accept the right of the government to rule. (1 point)
   (D) A two-round election system provides legitimacy for an election system by providing the winning candidate with a clear mandate from the voters. The people are more likely to accept the right of the government to rule when a clear majority of the voters voted for that candidate. (1 point)
   (E) Authoritarian systems need legitimacy. The Islamic Republic of Iran must have democratic features to its election system to be a republic. Iran has a two-ballot system to provide voters with a clear winner. To maintain control of the election, however, the Guardian Council vets candidates who are acceptable to the regime. Therefore, elections are held for legitimacy but vetted to maintain authoritarian control. (1 point)

3. (5 points possible)
   (A) Theocracy is a government run by religious leaders. (1 point)
   (B) The Islamic Republic of Iran has integrated religion within its political system. The Supreme Leader of Iran must be a high-ranking Shia cleric, the judges must be clerics, and sharia is the foundation of the legal system. (1 point) The UK has a state-sponsored religion, the Church of England. The queen is the head of the Church of England. (1 points)
   (C) Iran can be considered a theocracy because the Supreme Leader and judges are clerics. Consequently, Iran is governed by religious leaders even though it has non-cleric leaders as well. The UK, on the other hand, is not a theocracy. Although the queen is the head of state and the head of the Church of England, she is not a member of the clergy. The source of her authority is hereditary and not theological. (2 point)

4. (5 points possible)

   The use of coercion by an authoritarian state is effective at maintaining stability because the use of force allows the government to maintain its sovereignty, or ultimate authority, over its territory. Any nonconventional political participation, like protests, can be effectively dispersed using force and therefore maintain political stability for the regime. (1 point)

   Iran is an authoritarian state that effectively uses coercion to maintain stability. During recent protests in November 2019 over a decrease in fuel subsidies, the Iranian government shut down the Internet and jailed protestors to end the protests and maintain stability. (1 point)

   This crackdown on political participation is a common response by the Iranian government. During the 2009 Green Movement, people protesting the rigged presidential election were violently repressed by government forces in the name of restoring order and stability. (1 point)

   These two incidents reflect the effectiveness of a coercive strategy. The Iranian government is willing to use force to put down dissent to maintain its ultimate control over Iranian society. Coercion was an effective strategy for the Iranian government to use to stabilize the political system. (1 point)

   Critics will charge that the use of excessive force is not effective at maintaining long-term regime stability. Resentment about the abuse of civil liberties can ultimately undermine the legitimacy of a regime and lead to revolution, as happened in Iran in 1979 as numerous repressed groups in Iranian civil society rose to overthrow the Shah in large part because of his coercive policies. Ultimately, however, revolutions are rare, and coercion is an effective technique for authoritarian regimes to use to maintain stability. (1 point)

❯ Rapid Review

- The Islamic Republic of Iran (Iran) is a theocracy or government run by religious leaders with a legal system based on sharia, or Islamic law. It has republican elements as well with an elected president and legislature, the Majlis.
- The Islamic Republic was established by referendum after the Iranian Revolution led by the Ayatollah Khomeini ousted the dictatorial Shah Mohammad Reza Pahlavi in 1979.
- The Iranian constitution enshrines Khomeini's view of jurist guardianship or clerical rule, most significantly in the position of supreme leader who has the power to overrule every other institution. Khomeini was the first supreme leader, followed by Ali Khamenei. The supreme leader is chosen by the directly elected Assembly of Experts.
- To compete in elections, candidates must be vetted by the appointed Guardian Council.
- Voters elect members of the Assembly of Experts, the Majlis (legislature), and the president. The president must win a majority of the vote to take office. President Rouhani won his second term in the first round in 2017.
- There is no stable party system in Iran; instead, what does exist is a shifting alliance of factions divided between reformists and principalists.
- Iran has a traditional military that is overshadowed by the powerful Islamic Revolutionary Guard Corps (IRGC).
- Iran is a multination state where the majority of the population identifies as Persian and as adherents to Shia Islam.
- Civil society is restricted in Iran with public morality laws, Internet censorship, and repression of public protest. State-controlled media is prominent and nonconforming journalists face arrest.
- Iran is a rentier state because a majority of government revenues come from the sale of oil by the National Iranian Oil Company (NIOC).
- Iran has a very aggressive foreign policy, complete with the long-term goal of producing a nuclear weapon. President Rouhani agreed to restrict development of a weapon, however, in return for the lifting of economic sanctions.

CHAPTER 13

Russia

IN THIS CHAPTER

Summary: Russia is a challenging case to master in the AP Comparative Government and Politics course because it has gone through so many transitions in the modern era. To understand the Russian Federation of today, you must first reflect on the rise and fall of the Soviet Union and the tumultuous Yeltsin years before you focus on President Putin's consolidation of authority. But even though Putin is extremely powerful, he faces many challenges both domestically and in foreign affairs. Domestically, an educated, urban middle class chafes under civil society restrictions while falling oil prices and a stagnant economy produce economic unrest. Internationally, Putin's seizure of the Crimea and intervention in Ukraine resulted in sanctions that have caused more economic distress, and in early 2022, Putin seems poised to invade Ukraine again. Yet Putin's control over Russia continues because in 2020, constitutional amendments were passed that would allow him to remain as president until 2036.

Key Terms

Chechen Republic
civil society
code law
Communist Party of the
   Russian Federation (KPRF)
Constitutional Court
corporatist
coup
demokratizatsiya
dominant party
dual executive
federal
Federal Assembly
federal districts
Federation Council

glasnost
head of government
head of state
A Just Russia
Kremlin
Liberal Democrats (LD)
"loan-for-shares"
   privatization program
NGOs
nomenklatura
oligarch
perestroika
Public Chamber
proportional representation
   (PR) model

Roskomnadzor
RT
semi-presidential system
shock therapy
siloviki
State Council
State Duma
super-governors
Supreme Court
tsar
two-ballot format
United Russia
USSR
Yabloko

Russia as a Case Study

As you study Russia, pay careful attention to the discussion of the following concepts as they are the most frequently used in comparing Russia with other countries on the AP Comparative Government and Politics exam.

CONCEPT	POSSIBLE COMPARISONS/USEFUL EXAMPLES
Authoritarian regime	Hybrid/transitional regime
Semi-presidential system	Parliamentary and/or presidential system
Asymmetrical bicameral legislature	Symmetrical bicameral legislature
Dominant party system	One-, two-, and multiparty systems
PR election system with high threshold	Mixed electoral system
Transition command to market economy	Economic liberalization and consolidation
Rentier state	Diversified economy

Sovereignty, Authority, and Power

The State

The Russian Federation is a young state with a constitution ratified by a referendum in 1993. Yet its president, Vladimir Putin, is often characterized as a **tsar**, a reference to Russia's autocratic past that stretches back to Ivan IV's territorial consolidation in the 1550s. In fact, acquiring territory and protecting itself from invasion has been a constant theme in Russian history as first the tsars, then the Soviets, and now Putin have moved to consolidate control over neighbors for protection from invasion. Analyzing the challenge of creating and maintaining state control over so much territory and its diverse peoples is an effective strategy for comparing the various regimes of the Russian state.

TIME PERIOD	NAME	REGIME TYPE	EXECUTIVE
1550–1917	Russian Empire	Authoritarian	Tsar

- Ivan IV, first *Tsar of All the Russians*: Consolidated Russian empire
- Peter the Great: Campaign to westernize and modernize Russia
- Alexander II: Reformer—emancipated serfs in 1861 and created local councils (*zemstvo*)
- Nicholas II: Responded to Revolution of 1905 with October Manifesto creating State Duma

TIME PERIOD	NAME	REGIME TYPE	EXECUTIVE
1922–1991	Soviet Union	Authoritarian	General secretary

- Stalin: Created command economy with collectivization of farms and rapid industrial five-year plans
- Khrushchev: Destalinization; Cuban Missile Crisis
- Brezhnev: Economic stagnation; détente with United States
- Gorbachev: Glasnost; perestroika; democratization

TIME PERIOD	NAME	REGIME TYPE	EXECUTIVE
1991–present	Russian Federation	Transitional-authoritarian	President

- Yeltsin: Constitutional referendum; shock therapy
- Putin: Creation of dominant party, United Russia

The Nation

Russia is a multination state with longstanding social cleavages between regional groups. Russians are the largest group at 78 percent of the population, but over 200 different ethnicities are recorded in the census such as Tartars (3.7 percent), Ukrainians (1.4 percent), and Chechens (1 percent). Ethnic minorities are concentrated in the state's 22 republics where they can officially recognize their own language in addition to Russian. Many of the ethnic minorities are also religious minorities, for although years of Soviet rule diminished religious identity, groups like the Chechens maintained their Muslim faith. Since the fall of the Soviet Union, more people (15 to 20 percent) of the population are now identifying as Russian Orthodox, while 10 to 15 percent are Muslim.

Legitimacy

Traditional legitimacy in Russia has frequently been found in the support for a strong leader. Consistently in Levada-Center polls, Russians select Stalin and Putin as the most outstanding people in world history, followed by Pushkin and Lenin. In addition, Putin has closely associated himself with Russian Orthodox Patriarch Kirill to gain national legitimacy and, in a sense, to develop a charismatic cult of personality about his leadership.

Putin also relies on rational-legal legitimacy as the constitutionally elected president of Russia. He even abided by its two-term limit by becoming prime minister from 2008 to 2012. The fact that Putin retained his control on power even when he was not president, however, is reflective of the arbitrary nature of his regime.

Regime

Russia is an authoritarian regime. Although the fall of the Soviet Union provided a democratic opportunity, scholar William Zimmerman states that "in the period between the 1996 Yeltsin electoral victory and 2008 when Vladimir Putin selected Dmitri Medvedev as his replacement as president, presidential elections became decreasingly open, decreasingly competitive, and increasingly meaningless." Some actions of the current regime have been:

- Manipulation of elections and suppression of the opposition
- State control of the media, which serves as a propaganda mouthpiece for government
- Restriction of NGOs as "foreign agents"

Freedom House Ratings: Not Free (political rights: 5; civil liberties: 5)
Economist Democracy Index 3.24 (authoritarian)

Type of Economic System

Russia has a mixed economy. During the years as the **USSR**, the Soviets ran a command economy with the bureaucratic agency, Gosplan, managing five-year economic plans. Gorbachev introduced some economic reforms, known as perestroika, under his administration, but it was Yeltsin's adoption of "shock therapy" that led to the rapid dismantling of a state-run economy to one based on market principles. The results of shock therapy included hyperinflation and the growth of a class of powerful oligarchs who quickly amassed control over former state-run businesses. Vladimir Putin reasserted government control over the powerful energy sector of the economy, utilizing high gas and oil prices to fund his government. Currently Russian state-owned enterprises (SOEs) comprise about 30 percent of Russian firms and employ 40 percent of the labor force.

Political Culture and Socialization

The study of Russia most often involves the scrutiny of one strong leader from Ivan IV, the first Tsar of All the Russians, to today's President Vladimir Putin. Across the centuries political observers have noted a tsarist mentality that pervades Russian politics. Even Alexis de Tocqueville noted in *Democracy in America* in 1835 that "the Russian centers all the authority of society in a single arm."

Agents of socialization are the family, schools, the media, and peer groups. The Putin administration has gained control over most media outlets, especially television, and uses these resources to propagandize the public. School textbooks are revised to reflect the Kremlin's position.

Government Institutions

Constitution

The formal political structure of the Russian Federation was approved by referendum on December 12, 1993. After forcibly dissolving the Congress of People's Deputies in September of 1993, Boris Yeltsin, elected president of the Russian Federation, convened an assembly to write a new constitution that would enhance the power of the presidency. Adapting the French Fifth Republic model devised by Charles de Gaulle, Yeltsin submitted a plan to the voters while also simultaneously holding elections for the new legislative body, the Federal Assembly. After an initial two-year transition period, both presidential and legislative elections have been held in Russia at regularly scheduled intervals.

Levels of Government

The Russian Federation is formally a **federal** republic with a variety of types of subnational governments, each type having different amounts of power over its own affairs. The 22 republics have the most sovereignty with the right to have their own constitution and official language in addition to Russian. This institutional structure provides representation for the non-Russian ethnic minorities who compose the majority population of many of the republics. Other subnational units such as oblasts, krays, okrugs, and federal cities have varying amounts of power resulting in a system of asymmetrical federalism, although all have two seats in the Federation

Council. Initially, the Russian Constitution of 1993 called for each subnational unit to hold elections for its chief executive and legislature. But to consolidate power in the presidency, Putin in 2004 pushed through legislation that abolished direct elections of governors and mayors and made them appointed presidential positions. In response to the parliamentary protests of 2011, however, these positions have been made elected again, although candidates must clear a "municipal filter" or approval of other elected officials. The result has been that many of the "appointed" officeholders have easily won elections as representatives of United Russia, as Moscow Mayor Sergey Sobyanin has done.

In an earlier push to reduce the independence of the subnational units, President Putin in 2000 created seven new **federal districts** (now eight with the addition of Crimea) with appointed **super-governors** to oversee the regional governments and bring their laws into compliance. But not all the local governments willingly complied with directives from Moscow. The **Chechen Republic** engaged in a civil war with Yeltsin first in 1994–96 over independence and then later in 1999–2000 with Prime Minister/Acting President Putin. A 2003 referendum in Chechnya, orchestrated by the Russian government, passed with voters agreeing that Chechnya should stay part of the Russian Federation. Since that time, Chechnya has been controlled by pro-Putin associates. For example, in 2007, Putin nominated Ramzan Kadyrov to be the president of Chechnya and he was approved by the legislature. In 2016, he stood for elections and won 98 percent of the vote despite allegations of substantial human rights abuses. Given the dominance of pro-Putin-elected officeholders across Russia, federalism is a merely a formality.

Russia joined the WTO in 2011 after 18 years of negotiations and actively engages in its trade-disputing function, including asking the WTO to investigate Ukrainian sanctions against Russia. Russia has also had to deal with rulings against its actions when the WTO ruled that Russia had improperly banned pork products from Europe.

Executive Branch

The executive branch is a **semi-presidential system** with a **dual executive** consisting of a president who serves as **head of state** and a prime minister who serves as **head of government**. Presidents are elected for a six-year term (changed from a four-year term in 2008) using a two-ballot majority system, although Yeltsin's 1996 election is the only one to date that has required a second round. Presidents can serve two consecutive terms. Despite the existence of two executive offices, the presidency is clearly designed to be the most powerful branch with its extensive list of formal powers, although when Vladimir Putin was prime minister from 2008 to 2012, he was clearly in charge to the point that many scholars were calling the relationship a tandemocracy. In his annual address in 2020, however, Putin proposed constitutional changes that would restructure the executive branch to reinforce the need for "a strong presidential republic." These amendments were offered as a nationwide vote (not a referendum) to the Russian people in June of 2020 and were approved overwhelmingly with 78% voting yes. Turnout was high at 68% according to the Russian Central Election Commission. Technically, the vote was not necessary, because the formal process to amend the constitution is a two-thirds majority vote in the national legislature and ratification by two-thirds of regional parliaments. Putin, however, wanted the legitimacy of a mandate from the voters, as one of the amendments resets the limits on presidential terms so that he could run again in 2024 and 2030. Going forward, presidents will only be allowed to serve two terms in total.

Powers of the President

- Appoint the prime minister—subject to approval by the State Duma (if the State Duma rejects the same candidate three times, the president must dissolve the Duma and call for new elections)
- Appoint judges to the Constitutional Court and the Supreme Court, subject to approval by the Federation Council
- Appoint members of the Security Council: Minister of Defense, Minister of Foreign Affairs, Director of Federal Security Service (FSB)
- Issue decrees, which have the force of laws, if they are not in violation of existing laws
- Propose bills to the State Duma and implement laws
- Veto bills passed by the State Duma—to be overridden would require two-thirds vote by both the State Duma and the Federation Council
- Commander in chief of the armed forces and in charge of foreign policy
- Pardon
- 2001: Appoint super-governors to supervise newly created seven federal super districts
- 2004: Appoint regional governors (Putin restored gubernatorial elections in 2012)

Powers of the Prime Minister

- Propose the budget and oversee economic policy
- Appoint other members of the cabinet (Unlike a traditional parliamentary system, the prime minister and cabinet members do not have to be members of the State Duma nor belong to a political party, although currently most are associated with United Russia.)
- Serve as acting president if the current president dies, resigns, or is removed from office

Legislative Branch

The **Federal Assembly** is an asymmetrical bicameral body with the **State Duma** wielding more power than the **Federation Council**. Reflecting the federal structure of the Russian Federation, the Federation Council (upper house) is designed to provide equal representation (two seats) to the 85 various subnational divisions, including republics, oblasts, territories, and federal cities. It has always been an appointed body, although initially regional leaders themselves would sit in the chamber. One of President Putin's first reforms was to forbid dual offices so now regional governors and the heads of local legislatures have the power to appoint the members of the Federation Council, although as most of these officials are members of United Russia, President Putin has an enormous influence over the Chamber. There is no fixed term of office for the Federation Council, as its 170 members serve according to local selection. In addition, to allow regional leaders to continue to have a role in the national government, Putin created the **State Council** so that all the governors and presidents of the subnational governments could have an advisory role in policymaking. One of his proposed amendments in 2020 is to make the State Council a formal constitutional body.

Powers of the Federation Council

- Approve presidential nominations to the Constitutional Court, the Supreme Court, and the Prosecutor General
- Approve bills passed by the State Duma (Although, if the Federation Council rejects a bill, the State Duma can override it with a two-thirds vote.)
- Approve declarations of war
- Approve treaties
- Two-thirds vote to override a presidential veto (along with two-thirds vote in State Duma)
- Two-thirds vote to impeach the president (along with two-thirds vote in State Duma and approval of both high courts)
- Three-quarters vote to amend the constitution (along with three-quarters vote in State Duma)

Powers of the State Duma

- Approve the president's appointment of the prime minister (If State Duma rejects the same choice three times in a row, then the president must dissolve the Duma and call for new elections.)
- Call for a vote of no confidence in the prime minister (The president can ignore the first vote, but after a second consecutive vote of no confidence, the president must recall the prime minister or dissolve the Duma and call for new elections.)
- Make laws (Bill must originate in State Duma. If it receives a majority vote, then it is sent to the Federation Council. If the Federation Council rejects it, a committee is formed to reach a compromise, and if the Federation Council still rejects it, the State Duma can override it with a two-thirds vote and send the bill to the president for his signature.)
- Two-thirds vote to override presidential veto (along with two-thirds vote in Federation Council)
- Two-thirds vote to impeach the president
- Three-quarters vote to amend the constitution

The State Duma is the lower house of the Federal Assembly and is designed to be the more powerful of the two houses, as it represents the people of the Russian Federation. There are 450 members who serve five-year terms (changed from four-year terms in 2008). Currently members are selected under the original 1993 Constitution election system, which means that 225 seats are elected using the single-member district plurality (SMDP) model and the other 225 seats are elected using the **proportional representation (PR) model** with a 5 percent threshold. (From 2003 to 2011, all State Duma seats were elected using PR with a 7 percent threshold to help consolidate power for United Russia as a dominant party.) After the 2016 legislative elections, United Russia holds a supermajority of the seats (343/450), enabling President Putin to push through any needed constitutional amendments.

Judicial Branch

The Russian judicial system is based on a **code law**, inquisitorial model with significant changes since 1993 to make the system more adversarial with the addition of jury trials and defense attorneys to challenge the power of the prosecutors. Despite these reforms, however, the system remains corrupt with only 22 percent of Russians saying that they believed in the court system according to a 2016 Levada-Center poll. It is clear with such high-profile cases such as Mikhail Khodorkovsky in 2003 and Pussy Riot in 2012 that the court system is used to legitimize state action against political opponents. The system has two high courts, the **Constitutional Court** and the **Supreme Court**, whose members are appointed by the president and approved by the Federation Council.

The Powers of the Constitutional Court

- Issue advisory opinions on the constitutionality of issues, including impeachment of the president
- Judicial review on a specific case—most willing to overturn a regional law that violates the constitution

---

The Powers of the Supreme Court

- Final court for civil and criminal cases

The Bureaucracy

The bureaucracy of the Soviet Union was immense, buttressed by a system of **nomenklatura** that ensured that party loyalty was the key to advancement in the system as opposed to merit and efficiency. Despite the creation of a new regime in 1991, elite recruitment in Russia is still predominantly a patron-client system with those with ties to the security forces having an advantage. These **siloviki** have a disproportionate amount of influence, particularly in the higher offices of government, which are appointed by Putin. In addition, individuals with close ties to the president are also put in charge of semiprivate or state-controlled businesses such as the energy company Gazprom.

Military and Other Coercive Institutions

The Russian military is smaller than it was during Soviet times, but still retains an extensive arsenal of nuclear weapons and a large fighting force. Morale in the ranks is low, however, due to the uneven enforcement of the military draft law and allegations of hazing. Despite these problems, President Putin has aggressively used the military in occupying areas of South Ossetia, the Crimea, and parts of Eastern Ukraine. In addition, he has supplied Russian troops to support the Assad regime in Syria.

To better control internal divisions in Russia, President Putin issued a decree in April of 2016 creating the National Guard of Russia. This fighting force will be charged with fighting terrorism and protecting public order with the authority to fire into crowds to prevent riots.

Leadership and Elite Recruitment

Vladimir Putin has topped the Forbes list of most powerful people in the world since 2013. This "vertical of power" as he terms it means that access to leadership in Russia is dependent on association with Putin. Consequently, elite recruitment is primarily from the security forces, the siloviki, whom Putin entrusts with both political and economic positions. An example of this would be the career of Igor Sechin, the current CEO of Rosneft, the state-owned oil company that controls the assets of the former Yukos firm of Mikhail Khodorkovsky. Sechin is a former KGB agent, like Putin, who served Putin when he was deputy mayor of St. Petersburg and then moved with him to Moscow, eventually rising to the position of deputy prime minister before being named as the head of Rosneft in 2012 when Putin returned to the presidency.

Linkage Institutions

Elections

Elections are used in Russia to enhance the legitimacy of the regime. Voters enjoy universal suffrage and a variety of types of elections to take part in, including national, regional, local, and referendums. The problem is that elections systems have been manipulated in Russia to ensure a pro-Putin outcome for the dominant party, United Russia. Freedom House, which ranks the political rights of a country, has consistently downgraded Russian political rights from a high of 4 in 1998 to a worst-case level of 7 in 2017, due in large part to the flawed parliamentary elections of 2016 that saw the further exclusion of opposition forces from effective political participation through manipulation of registration requirements, media manipulation, voter intimidation, and ballot stuffing.

The most important election in Russia is for the presidency. Voters directly elect the president in a **two-ballot format**. If a candidate does not win 50 percent of the popular vote in the first round, then the top two candidates compete in a runoff election. The only candidate to not win 50 percent of the vote in the first round was Boris Yeltsin in his 1996 reelection campaign. His second-round win over Communist Party Leader Zyuganov was orchestrated by media oligarchs fearful of losing power. As there is no vice president in the Russian system, when the president resigns, as Yeltsin did on December 31, 1999, the prime minister becomes acting president until elections can be held three months later. Acting President Putin made it clear that he wanted a first-round victory, and he accomplished his goal with 53 percent of the vote. In the election of 2004 it was so clear that Putin was going to win that his perennial challengers did not even compete, instead running others in their place.

The Russian constitution limits the president to two consecutive terms, so in 2008 Putin selected Dmitri Medvedev to be his successor and he became prime minister instead. While prime minister, Putin had the presidential term of office extended from four to six years and then announced in 2011 that he and Medvedev were going to change places, with Putin running for president for a third term and Medvedev becoming prime minister. Many young, urban Russians were dismayed by this announcement and voted against United Russia in the parliamentary elections held in December of 2011, but Putin's party won a majority of the seats in the Duma in a blatantly rigged election. Large protests followed the election and were suppressed for fear of them leading to an Arab Spring–like event. Putin easily won reelection in 2012 and put in place heavy fines for unauthorized protests, but he also restored some democratic features to the system, including direct election of regional leaders and a mixed election system for the Duma.

Putin was reelected in 2018 as well. Interestingly, he chose to run as an independent as opposed to the nominee for United Russia. He was endorsed, however, by United Russia, A Just Russia, and several other parties. Communist Party leader Zyuganov managed the campaign for Pavel Grudinin who won 11 percent of the vote. TV journalist Ksenia Sobchak ran as the nominee for the Civic Initiative Party and won almost 2% of the vote. Activist Alexei Navalny was prevented from being on the ballot because of a prior conviction. He urged his followers to boycott the election. Voter turnout was 68%.

PRESIDENTIAL CANDIDATES	1996 RESULTS	2000 RESULTS	2004 RESULTS	2008 RESULTS	2012 RESULTS	2018 RESULTS
Yeltsin	36%/54%					
Putin		53%	71%		64%	77%
Medvedev				70%		
Zyuganov	33%/41%	29%		18%	17%	
Zhirinovsky	6%	3%		9%	6%	6%
Yavlinsky	7%	6%				1%

*Other candidates competed in these elections—this chart is to show perennial challengers.
**Only in 1996 did a presidential candidate fail to win 50 percent on the first round and require a second round.
***In 2004, the KPRF and LD ran candidates other than Zyuganov and Zhirinovsky.

Election Systems and Party Systems

It is important to understand how United Russia became a dominant party in Russia. The 1993 Constitution guarantees the right to a multiparty system, and early elections in the Russian Federation involved over 100 different parties often organized to support specific individuals. Boris Yeltsin was not able to generate majority support for his policies in the State Duma because of party fragmentation. In the elections of 1993, 1995, and 1999, more than 10 separate parties won seats in the State Duma along with over 100 individuals winning SMDP seats. In addition, the party coalitions continued to shift with only a few strong parties competing across elections. These parties were the **Communist Party of the Russian Federation (KPRF)** headed by Gennady Zyuganov, the **Liberal Democrats (LD)** headed by Vladimir Zhirinovsky, and **Yabloko** headed by Grigory Yavlinsky.

The parliamentary elections of 1999 first saw the creation of a nonideological pro-Putin party called Unity. Putin's strong handling of the Second Chechen War and his position as acting president in 2000 after the resignation of Boris Yeltsin also solidified his credentials. Once president, Putin pushed through increased regulations making it more difficult to qualify as a national political party and as a candidate. But the major electoral changes came in response to the terrorist attack on a school in Beslan after which Putin centralized control by ending the direct election of regional leaders and eliminating the SMDP seats for the State Duma, replacing it with a multimember PR list with a 7 percent threshold in the 2007 election. This election system change resulted in United Russia winning a majority of the seats in the Duma, the first party to do so.

United Russia easily took a dominant role in the legislature but saw a loss of seats in 2011 because of public protest over the Putin-Medvedev executive switch. In response to this public protest, changes were made to reinstate the original 1993 mixed election system for the 2016 Duma elections along with renewing direct elections for regional leaders. But the damage had been done to opposition parties; only pro-Kremlin parties won seats in 2016 and 2021, with United Russia easily dominating elections at all levels.

STATE DUMA	1999 SEATS		2003 SEATS		2007 SEATS		2011 SEATS	2016 SEATS		
	PR	SMD	PR	SMD	PR	%	PR	PR	SMD	TOTAL
KPRF	67	46	40	12	57	12%	92	20%	35	7	42
Unity ('99) United Russia	64	9	120	102	315	64%	238	53%	140	203	343
LD	17	0	36	0	40	9%	56	12%	34	5	39
Yabloko	16	4		4	0	2%	0	3%			
Other parties	61	52	29	39	Fair Russia 38	8%	Fair Russia 64	14%	A Just Russia 16	7	23
									Other	2	2
Individuals *no party	114		68						1	1	

Russian Duma Elections September 2021

PARTY	PR	SMD	TOTAL
United Russia	126	198	324
KPRF	48	9	57
LD	19	2	21
A Just Russia	19	8	27
New People (a new party)	13	—	13
Other	—	3	3
Independent	—	5	5
Totals	225	225	500

The Parties

United Russia is a **dominant party**—a nonideological party of power designed to mobilize support for Vladimir Putin. To accomplish this, a national political machine has been created to generate loyal candidates for national and local offices across the country as well as leadership positions in state-controlled businesses. Voters are attracted by the call for national pride, restoration of Russia's place in the world, along with economic development and conservative values. United Russia polls well with younger voters, state employees, and the military.

The **Communist Party of the Russian Federation (KPRF)** was established after Boris Yeltsin outlawed the Communist Party of the Soviet Union, and it has consistently been the second largest political party in Russia. The party maintains close ties to its Soviet past and ideology but is losing its most loyal supporters as its elderly voters decline in number. It still enjoys support from those voters who wish to protest United Russia's economic policies that have led to income inequality.

The **Liberal Democrats** are neither liberal nor democratic but rather are a far-right, nationalistic party with a bombastic leader. Fascistic in ideology, Zhirinovsky attracts alienated young men who are anti-immigrant, anti-Semitic, and supportive of military intervention.

A Just Russia (also called Fair Russia) was founded in 2006 to provide an outlet for anti-Putin voters who would like to see a more traditional Western-style multiparty system. After the electoral failures of the Yabloko, a pro-western, free-market party, smaller parties banded together to provide a choice for urban, educated voters who wanted more social justice. Critics charge that this party is a manufactured pro-Kremlin party designed to provide voters with the illusion of choice.

Interest Groups

The 1993 Russian constitution provides for freedom of speech and assembly. Ever since the introduction of glasnost by Gorbachev, Russians have been able to form civil society groups to pursue their interests. Groups that do not challenge the regime are left alone. Pro-Kremlin groups have flourished and are often manufactured to create support. The pro-Putin youth group Nashi was one such group created to generate support for United Russia during the 2008 election.

Following the creation of the **Public Chamber** in 2005, it is clear that Russia has adopted a **corporatist** approach to managing interest groups. For the Public Chamber, President Putin selects interest groups to represent various aspects of civil society and the Chamber in turn has an advisory role in reviewing legislation at both the national and regional levels. The chamber is a parallel institution to the State Duma with the role of representing the various interests of civil society and providing them with an opportunity to comment on government policy. In addition, nongovernmental organizations (**NGOs**) increasingly face restrictions on their activities, including a new law in 2006 that requires registration with the government and intense financial scrutiny. The government, fearful of potential unrest, is hypervigilant against any outside foreign influence. In 2016, for example, the independent polling organization, the Levada-Center, was labeled a foreign agent, which limits its abilities to act. In addition, in large part in response to public protest over the 2011 parliamentary elections, the State Duma has passed anti-extremism legislation designed to shut down critical websites, restrict protests, and quiet critics. For those who persist at protesting the government, harsher actions are taken. Opposition leader Boris Nemstov was assassinated in 2015 not far from the **Kremlin**. Parliamentary protest organizer Alexei Navalny was convicted of embezzlement, yet that didn't stop him from organizing massive anticorruption protests against Prime Minister Medvedev in March 2016. Even being poisoned and evacuated in 2020 did not stop Navalny from his campaign. He returned to Russia and was imprisoned for breaking his parole. His allies actively tried to influence the results of the 2021 Duma election by encouraging their supporters to use the Smart Voting app to coordinate votes for non–United Russia candidates. The Kremlin pressured Apple and Google to remove the app from their platforms. In January 2022, the Russian government put Navalny on its registry of terrorists and extremists to continue trying to repress his activism.

Citizens, Society, and the State

Social Cleavages

As the largest country in the world, Russia is home to a diverse population with numerous social cleavages. Coinciding cleavages exist primarily in the remote regions of the country where ethnic minorities are also religious minorities. One such example would be the

Chechens, who are Muslims living in the Caucasus region of Russia. After fighting for independence in 1994–96 and then in 1999–2000 against the Russian government, Chechen terrorists continued to act by seizing a Moscow theater in 2002 and a school in Beslan in 2004, both events ending tragically with deaths of innocent victims. Putin responded by cracking down on terrorism and installing a pro-Kremlin government in Chechnya.

There is also a significant urban/rural divide in Russia, with 70 percent of the population being urbanized and 12 million of the 142 million Russian population living in Moscow. Most of the economic reforms have bolstered an urban middle class, with remote areas of Russia being left behind unless they have large gas and oil fields.

In addition, Moscow's location in the western part of the country highlights a perennial division within Russian society whether to pursue a more western-style manner of living or to retain a traditional Russian culture. Many young, highly educated urbanites would prefer that Russia become socially liberal with equal rights for women and homosexuals, less restrictions on civil society, and more democratic political institutions along with market reforms. In contrast, traditional Russians support antigay legislation, restrictions on nontraditional religions such as Jehovah's Witnesses, and the decriminalization of domestic violence, yet would prefer that the guaranteed employment and public services of the Soviet Union, especially those of the elderly, would be returned.

Civil Society and Social Capital

Russia has a limited **civil society** in that voluntary, autonomous organizations are not allowed to form outside government control. Since 2006, all nongovernmental organizations (NGOs) must register with the government and be approved to operate under close scrutiny, especially their finances, to limit foreign influence. Organizations that have a nonpolitical purpose will have more discretion in their operations than a politically focused group, unless their presence is deemed a threat to a traditional institution. For example, in 2017 Jehovah's Witnesses were labeled an extremist group in Russia and its activities, such as preaching, were made criminal acts. In contrast, however, unlike under the Soviet Union when all religious groups were banned, currently the Russian government is very supportive of the Russian Orthodox church.

The Media

Independent media outlets in Russia face a challenging task. After the days of media oligarch barons like Boris Berezovsky who helped Boris Yeltsin win his second term in office, the Russian media under Vladimir Putin has become state controlled, often as subsidiaries of energy companies like Gazprom. Russian television serves as a major propaganda mouthpiece for pro-Putin nationalistic rhetoric and fails to cover alternative voices, even during elections. For a long time, small independent newspapers and radio stations could operate, but increasingly since the 2011 protests, even these news outlets are being silenced. Russian journalists face intimidation tactics, and 92 journalists have been killed during Putin's time in office.

In addition, new extremism laws allow government officials to target the Internet and shut down critical blogs while requiring that all Russians store their data on Russian servers. The government created a new Internet censoring agency, **Roskomnadzor**, or the Federal Service for Supervision of Communications, Information Technology and Mass Media, with the power to make web content, such as memes, illegal if they harm the honor or dignity of the public official.

In addition, the Russian government has extended its media reach by establishing an international network, **RT**, which broadcasts worldwide, including RT America. Critics charge that RT spreads misinformation.

Political Participation

There is limited political participation in Russia as citizens have low political efficacy in their ability to remove elected officials by voting. In the December 2016 Duma elections, voter turnout was 47 percent, down from an average of 65 percent. As elites enable a corrupt patron-client system of governance, average Russians often do not participate politically. The government mobilizes pro-government rallies and organizes pro-government youth groups to present the illusion of a participatory democracy. Anti-government protests are well-organized by using social media tools, but activists such as blogger Alexei Navalny and his Anti-Corruption Foundation face arrest and repression. A campaign in March of 2017 by Navalny to attack the corruption of Prime Minister Medvedev with a YouTube video resulted in mass protests across Russia, the largest since the election protests of 2011–12. Many of the participants were under 25, and many were arrested. These protests are put down with force. In 2019, police used force and detained over 1,400 protestors in Moscow who were demonstrating against the rejection by government authorities of opposition candidates for local city elections.

Social Movements

Civil society restrictions make social movements in Russia difficult to coordinate, but organizers persist in the face of discrimination. In response to gay propaganda laws, LGBTQ activists have taken a number of steps including holding gay pride parades (denied permits), protest marches (repressed), Internet memes (images of Putin as a gay clown were banned in 2017), and litigation at the European Court of Human Rights, which ruled that the gay propaganda laws were discriminatory. Women's rights groups work to improve protections against domestic violence and improve working conditions and salaries.

Citizenship and Representation

Russian citizenship is acquired through birth in the Russian Federation or to a Russian citizen or through the process of naturalization. As Russia's population growth rate is declining, the economy relies heavily on migrant labor from former Soviet states such as Tajikistan, Kyrgyzstan, and Kazakhstan. Many Russians resent these immigrants, however, and a Levada-Center poll recorded 66 percent of Russians wanting tighter visa controls. The government's response has been limited because of the economic necessity of hiring migrant workers in many industries.

Regional representation in the government is found in the Federation Council with each subnational government unit granted two seats. The mixed election system for the Duma results in opportunities for voters to select an individual to represent them as well as to vote for a political party. Both legislative bodies lack descriptive representation, especially for gender. Both the Duma and Federation Council are only 17 percent female.

Political and Economic Change

Revolution, Coups, and War

The Russian Revolution in 1917 was one of the most pivotal moments in world history. The introduction of Marxist-Leninist doctrine as the governing ideology of the state 100 years ago still impacts Russian politics today. In particular, Stalin's legacy of five-year plans and democratic centralism, rapid industrialization and collectivization, and victory in World War II resonates Russians with nationalistic pride as opposed to memories of gulags, show trials, and starvation. Stalin's Soviet system of Communist Party rule utilized the top-down control of the general secretary and Politburo over a patron-client network staffed using *nomenklatura* to direct an economy that generated a military superpower to rival the United States.

By 1985, however, Mikhail Gorbachev, the new general secretary of the CPSU (Communist Party of the Soviet Union), faced a stagnant economy with a shortage of consumer goods and an impossible arms race with Ronald Reagan. Seeking to strengthen both the party and the economy, Gorbachev instituted several reforms, including **glasnost** or an opening up of civil society, **perestroika** or economic restructuring, and **demokratizatsiya** or the introduction of a new legislative chamber, the Congress of People's Deputies, whose members would be selected by voters. Quickly the reforms had the effect of marginalizing Communist party leaders as satellite states declared their independence and the Soviet Union itself began to disintegrate. In August of 1991, conservative members of the government staged a **coup** to remove Gorbachev from office. The coup failed, however, because of a resistance movement headed by Russian President Boris Yeltsin, as he convinced tank commanders to join with the protestors. Gorbachev returned to Moscow to find that although he was the de facto head of the USSR, Yeltsin was effectively in charge. Gorbachev presided over the dissolution of the Soviet Union in December of 1991.

Political Change

After the fall of the Soviet Union, Boris Yeltsin governed the Russian Federation primarily by decree with the support of the Congress of People's Deputies. He lost that support, however, as his shock therapy reforms resulted in hyperinflation and economic collapse. Yeltsin's response was to dissolve the legislature by force and call for a new constitution to be voted on by referendum in 1993. The new constitution established a semi-presidential system with a bicameral legislature that Yeltsin had a challenging time controlling, particularly as his economic reforms had resulted in the growth of a class of **oligarchs** with immense wealth and power. Facing public outrage over the level of corruption among the political elites in his administration and barely escaping impeachment by the State Duma, Yeltsin resigned his office on December 31, 1999, in favor of his popular prime minister, Vladimir Putin.

In his 20 years in executive power as president or prime minister, Putin has effectively implemented reforms to consolidate his authority. He created regional governments with appointed super-governors to reduce the sovereignty of subnational governments. He gained control over media outlets to effectively control citizen access to information. For example, state television does not broadcast scenes of public protest. He manipulated election systems to create his dominant party, United Russia. He reasserted state control over valuable oil and gas reserves to fund his government. And he accomplished all of this while retaining high public approval ratings. It remains to be seen what the constitutional amendments will actually do, but most scholars conclude that they will be structured to retain Putin's control over the political system for a long time to come.

Economic Change

The Soviet Union's command economy was effective at producing military weapons and a space program. It was not efficient at providing quality consumer goods, with stores having chronic shortages and few options. Gorbachev's perestroika reforms allowed for some market reforms such as allowing McDonald's to open in Moscow in 1990. (It was the first fast-food restaurant in Russia and served 30,000 people on the first day it opened.) But it was Yeltsin's **shock therapy** changes that significantly altered the Russia economy from a command to a market-based economy. American advisors suggested that Yeltsin quickly remove price controls and cut subsidies to encourage the production of more goods; the result, however, was hyperinflation of 2,500 percent and the loss of most Russian's savings. A **"loan-for-shares" privatization program** followed that, instead of distributing ownership among many Russians, ended up consolidating wealth, ownership, and political power in the hands of a few oligarchs.

Once president, Putin quickly moved to control the oligarchs. Those like Mikhail Khodorkovsky, the owner of Yukos, who would not submit to Putin's rules, Putin had arrested, tried, and imprisoned for tax evasion and renationalized their companies. The Russian government now controls the Russian gas and oil industry through stock ownership and Putin's appointment of former KGB associates to run the firms. Putin used high oil prices to raise revenue to support his government programs. He also used the oil and gas as a foreign policy tool by cutting off supply to Ukraine and Europe in order to gain concessions from those countries. Putin has been stymied, however, in his efforts to tap the oil and gas reserves in the Artic Circle by U.S. and European sanctions against him because of his invasion of Crimea. Membership in the WTO as well has been a mixed blessing as it provides Putin with a legitimate way to challenge sanctions against Russia, but the WTO court has also issued rulings against Russia.

Public Policy

Russia is an authoritarian state with a power vertical centered on Vladimir Putin. Putin uses formal constitutional procedures to develop public policy as a way to legitimize his regime. The dual executives, president and prime minister, along with the cabinet, propose legislation to the State Duma, which scrutinizes and debates the bills in committees and on the floor before holding a vote. Once a bill passes the Duma, it is sent to the Federation Council for debate and a vote. The bill is then presented to the president for his signature. Now constitutionally, the Duma could reject the bill as could the Federation Council, and Putin could veto it. Currently, this doesn't happen because Putin's dominant party, United Russia, controls both chambers and supports his proposals. Putin even has the three-quarters majority needed in both chambers to pass constitutional amendments like extending the presidential term to six years. The courts are not independent either, often serving as arms of the executive to punish critics of the president.

President Putin, however, realizes that his legitimacy rests upon a popular public image, so he works relentlessly to be seen as a physically strong leader, whether that be standing in front of the world at the Sochi Olympics or wrestling a tiger. Although he represses public protests, he also counters them with pro-government rallies and minor reforms, such as restoring the mixed election system for the Duma.

Foreign Policy

Vladimir Putin looks to restore Russia to the superpower status of the Soviet Union. He views the Yeltsin years as the "Time of Troubles" and seeks to regain international respect. Although he is viewed as the most powerful leader in the world, his country is not the most powerful country. So Putin has taken various steps to consolidate territory and take advantage of international crises. Russian invasions of Georgia and South Ossetia in 2008 and the Crimea and Ukraine in 2014 were undertaken to control territory and to send a message to the West to not interfere in the Russian sphere of influence, even though it cost Russia its seat on the G8. Russian military support for the Assad regime in Syria is to assert a strong presence in the Middle East under the auspices of fighting ISIS. Interference in elections in the United States is in retaliation for supposed U.S. interference in the 2011 Duma elections. All of these actions appeal to the patriotic nationalism of the Russian people and help Putin maintain his high approval ratings.

The Environment

Grassroots activism to protect forests from road construction or to protect Lake Baikal from environmental hazards has had some effects. Putin signed a law to restrict development along Lake Baikal after UNESCO threatened to remove it from a list of World Heritage Sites. But the Russian economy is still heavily dependent on the sale of natural gas and oil, and so although Russia is part of the Paris Agreement on climate change, critics are skeptical about a real commitment to less reliance on fossil fuels.

Population Growth

The Russian population peaked at the end of the Soviet Union and had been steadily falling until 2009, but experts still predict that this is a temporary uptick problem. Causes include a declining life expectancy for males partly due to alcoholism, high rates of abortion, and low immigration rates. President Putin has had the Russian government offer financial incentives for families to have more than one child and awards "Order of Parental Glory" medals to families that have more than seven children.

Covid-19

The Russian government was quick to claim credit for producing the world's first vaccine for Covid-19, named Sputnik V. Despite this achievement, vaccine hesitancy remained high in Russia and recorded deaths were the fourth highest in the world at the beginning of 2022. Early in the pandemic, President Putin donned a yellow hazmat suit and visited a hospital managing the outbreak. As the pandemic progressed, however, more power was devolved to regional leaders to institute Covid protocols, even as Putin touted the ability of a strong state to handle the crisis better than Western democracies.

› Review Questions

Multiple Choice

1. The Russian legal system is formally based upon:
   (A) common law
   (B) code law
   (C) European Union legal principles
   (D) Communist Party law

2. The Russian prime minister is appointed by:
   (A) the president
   (B) the cabinet
   (C) the Duma
   (D) the Federation Council

3. In the Russian system, which position, or institution is designed to have the most power?
   (A) The chief justice of the Constitutional Court
   (B) The general secretary of the Communist Party of the Russian Federation
   (C) The president
   (D) The cabinet

4. In the Russian system, who calls for a vote of no confidence?
   (A) The president
   (B) The prime minister
   (C) The State Duma
   (D) The Federation Council

5. Which of the following changes resulted in only four parties winning seats in the 2007 Duma elections?
   (A) The use of a proportional election system with a 5 percent threshold
   (B) The use of a proportional election system with a 7 percent threshold
   (C) The use of a mixed SMD and proportional election system
   (D) The use of a two-ballot system

6. Federalism in Russia is constrained by which of the following elements of the political system?
   (A) The use of direct elections for local leaders
   (B) The allocation of two seats in the Federation Council to each subnational unit
   (C) The creation of eight regional districts with appointed super-governors
   (D) The creation of the State Council to serve as an advisory body for the president

7. Which of the following actions the most significant attempt by President Putin to repress social media use by Russians?
   (A) The creation of the Public Chamber to represent interest groups
   (B) The creation of the National Guard to combat extremism
   (C) The creation of the agency, Roskomnadzor, to monitor activity
   (D) The creation of an NGO registration system

8. Elite recruitment in Russia is primarily from:
   (A) the nomenklatura of the Communist Party
   (B) the siloviki or intelligence community
   (C) the generals in the Russian military
   (D) the wealthy media oligarchs

9. What kind of change was it when Boris Yeltsin replaced Mikhail Gorbachev?
   (A) State building
   (B) Regime change
   (C) Nation building
   (D) Change in government

10. Which of the following is an accurate statement about the Russian oil and gas industry?
    (A) The Russian government has a controlling interest in energy giants Rosneft and Gazprom.
    (B) Russia is a member of OPEC.
    (C) The oil and gas industry does not export its product outside of Russia.
    (D) The oil and gas industry provide only a small revenue stream to the Russian government.

Free Response

1. (A) Define pluralism.
   (B) Describe how interest groups engage in political participation in a pluralistic system.
   (C) Explain how democratic regimes restrict political participation by interest groups.
   (D) Explain why authoritarian regimes restrict pluralism.

2. Use the following pie chart to complete your answer.

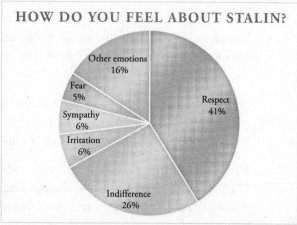

HOW DO YOU FEEL ABOUT STALIN?

Other emotions 16%
Fear 5%
Sympathy 6%
Irritation 6%
Indifference 26%
Respect 41%

Source: Levada Center

   (A) Using the data in the pie chart, identify the strongest reaction to Stalin.
   (B) Using the data in the pie chart, describe an empirical statement about the results of the Stalin poll.
   (C) Define political culture.
   (D) Explain why political scientists would survey a population about their feelings for a former leader.
   (E) Explain how your empirical statement in (B) is a reflection of Russian political culture.

3. Compare methods to select prime ministers in two different AP Comparative Government and Politics course countries. In your response, you should do the following:
   (A) Describe the role of a prime minister.
   (B) Describe the methods to select prime ministers in two different AP Comparative Government and Politics course countries.
   (C) Explain how the method of selecting prime ministers in (B) reflects legislative–executive relationships in the two AP Comparative Government and Politics course countries.

4. Develop an argument as to whether a bicameral or unicameral legislature offers more protection for legislative independence.

   Use one or more of the following course concepts in your response.
   • Legitimacy
   • Federalism
   • Social Cleavages
   In your response, you should do the following:

   • Respond to the prompt with a defensible claim or thesis that establishes a line of reasoning using one or more of the provided course concepts.
   • Support your claim with at least TWO pieces of specific and relevant evidence from one or more course countries. This evidence should be relevant to one or more of the provided course concepts.
   • Use reasoning to explain why your evidence supports your claim or thesis, using one or more the provided course concepts.
   • Respond to an opposing or alternate perspective, using refutation, concession, or rebuttal.

› Answers and Explanations

Multiple Choice

1. **B.** The Russian legal system is a code law system.

2. **A.** The Russian prime minister is appointed by the president and confirmed by the Duma. If the Duma rejects the same candidate three times, the president must dissolve the Duma and call for new elections.

3. **C.** The Russian semi-presidential system is based on the French Fifth Republic model devised by Charles de Gaulle. The presidency is designed to be the most powerful position.

4. **C.** The State Duma has the ability to call for a vote of no confidence in the prime minister. The president can ignore the first vote of no confidence, but after a second consecutive vote of no confidence, the president must recall the prime minister or dissolve the Duma and call for new elections.

5. **B.** The exclusive use of a proportional election system with a high 7 percent threshold eliminated minor parties and independents from the State Duma.

6. **C.** The creation of eight regional districts run by Putin-appointed super-governors essentially minimized the effect of a truly federal system because these super-governors, authority superseded that of local leaders.

7. **C.** Roskomnadozor is the agency empowered to ban websites and monitor social media activity on the Internet. The other policies also restrict civil society.

8. **B.** The siloviki or members of the intelligence community have been awarded high political and economic positions by President Putin.

9. **B.** When Boris Yeltsin replaced Mikhail Gorbachev, it was a regime change from the authoritarian Soviet Union to a transitional Russian Federation.

10. **A.** The Russian government does have a controlling interest in energy giants Rosneft and Gazprom that provides extensive revenues to the government because of the value of these exports.

Free Response

1. (4 points possible)
   (A) Pluralism is a method of organizing interest group behavior in a society. In a pluralist society, autonomous interest groups are free to form and compete for access to influence government policymaking. (1 point)
   (B) Interest groups are free to compete for influence in a pluralistic system. Typically, these interest groups engage in activities to pressure government officials to take action on a public policy. Some interest groups might electioneer a member of the legislature, petition the president, or file a lawsuit with the courts to participate conventionally. Others may participate unconventionally through protest. Either way, competing groups are allowed to form and simultaneously pressure the government to take action. (1 point)
   (C) Democratic regimes restrict interest group activity to maintain order and prevent corruption. Time, manner, place restrictions on public events, limits on campaign contributions, and restrictions on hate speech are common policies in democracies as well as authoritarian regimes. (1 point)
   (D) Authoritarian regimes restrict pluralism because leaders want more direct control over civil society. In Russia, for example, new laws to require NGO registration are specifically aimed at reducing opposition groups. The Public Chamber was created by Putin to be a government-controlled body to specifically negotiate policy with interest groups, a form of corporatism. (1 point)

2. (5 points possible)
   (A) Forty-one percent of those polled respect Stalin, which is higher than the 26% who were indifferent. (1 point)
   (B) An empirical statement is a factual statement. According to this Levada Center, 41% of Russians polled in 2019 selected respect as the emotion they felt about Stalin. (1 point)
   (C) Political culture is the deep-set, enduring attitudes that people have about their government. (1 point)
   (D) Political scientists will survey a population about their feelings for a former leader in order to track changes in perceptions about a political system. Stalin, for instance, was a brutal dictator who has enjoyed a recent surge in popularity. (1 point)
   (E) If 41% of Russians respect Stalin, it supports the assertion that Russian political culture favors a strong leader. Despite his brutal tactics, Russians are characterized as having a tsarist mentality that respects an authoritarian figure. This is reflected in Russian government propaganda to restore support for Stalin to boost legitimacy for the Putin regime. (1 point)

3. (5 points possible)
   (A) A prime minister is typically considered the head of government. This means the prime minister works with the cabinet to develop policy, often introducing legislation to the legislature and then overseeing its implementation by the bureaucracy. (1 point)
   (B) In the UK, the prime minister is chosen by the majority party MPs in the House of Commons. (1 point) In Russia, the prime minister is appointed by the president, but must be approved of by the State Duma. (1 point)
   (C) In the UK, the method of selecting the PM reflects the fusion of executive–legislative power in a parliamentary system. The PM and the cabinet are all MPs as well as members of the government. This makes lawmaking more efficient if the majority party sticks together as it controls the legislative and executive branch. (1 point)

   In Russia, the method of selecting the PM reflects the dual executive of a semi-parliamentary system. The president of Russia is elected in a separate election from the State Duma, thereby separating legislative and executive power. Consequently, the prime minister serves as a bridge between the two branches of government, answerable to both the president and the Duma, potentially providing an opportunity for each branch to check the other. (Something that doesn't happen given the dominant party status of United Russia and the power of Vladimir Putin.) (1 point)

4. (5 points possible)

A bicameral legislature is more likely to protect legislative independence because it is more difficult for another political institution to gain control over two different houses than simply one. Oftentimes, a bicameral legislature reflects different populations within a state, thereby increasing the legitimacy of the system and the acceptance of legislative authority. (1 point)

In the UK, the House of Lords provides a temporary check on the government. As the upper house in the bicameral legislature, it can only delay legislation for a year. But even this small delay protects legislative independence in that the government has to answer to a body that it does not directly control. (1 point)

In Nigeria, the Senate reflects the federal structure of the political system. While the House of Representatives is divided by population, each state in Nigeria is entitled to three senators. As Nigeria created more states to give more ethnic groups representation, it mitigated conflicts caused by coinciding cleavages. Small-population states have the opportunity for more political power than in the House. A bicameral legislature increases the legitimacy of the system and makes it more difficult for a president to push through his agenda. (1 point)

Legislative independence is protected when a legislature cannot be constrained by other institutions. Therefore, a two-house legislature like Parliament in the UK and Congress in Nigeria provides an intra-branch check that makes it difficult for the executive branch to efficiently impose its will on the legislature. (1 point)

It could be argued, however, that a bicameral legislature often ends in gridlock and therefore displays no legislative independence because it doesn't legislate, rather leaving decision making up to an executive. Theoretically, a unicameral legislature with a simple majority principle would be more efficient and decisive and consequently more legislatively independent. Problematically, however, the two comparative countries with unicameral legislatures—the Majlis and the National People's Congress—are not effective examples of legislative independence as they defer to the wishes of the supreme leader and CCP, respectively. Bicameralism, however, is also no guarantee of legislative independence as President Putin has effectively neutered the Federation Council in Russia. But even Putin continues to tinker with a bicameral legislature to bring it under his control. Certainly, the perception of a bicameral legislature, with different ways to represent people and regions, protects its legitimacy and the façade of its independence. (1 point)

› Rapid Review

- The Russian Federation (Russia) is an authoritarian regime that has gone through significant transitions since the end of the Soviet Union in 1991.
- Political culture and traditional legitimacy in Russia reflect support for a strong leader or tsar. Russians select Stalin and Putin as the most outstanding leaders in world history.
- Russia is a multination state with long-standing cleavages between regional groups. Ethnic minorities, which are often religious minorities as well, are concentrated in 22 republics.
- Russia has a mixed economy. Yeltsin's policy of "shock therapy" transformed Russia from a Soviet command economy to one based on market principles, although quickly dominated by a class of oligarchs. Putin reasserted control over the energy sector to use the sale of natural gas and oil as a source of revenue and international pressure.
- The Russian constitution was approved by referendum in 1993. It established a federal republic with a semi-presidential system, a bicameral legislature, a Supreme Court, and a Constitutional Court.
- Russian presidents are directly elected by the people in two-ballot elections. Voters also elect members of the lower house, the State Duma, in a mixed system: 225 seats are SMD and 225 seats are PR with a 5 percent threshold.
- As head of state, the president appoints the prime minister (head of government), subject to the approval of the State Duma. The prime minister selects the cabinet.
- The president appoints judges to the Constitutional Court and the Supreme Court, subject to the approval of the upper appointed house, the Federation Council.
- President Putin made significant constitutional changes to consolidate his authority, including the creation of eight federal super-governors to oversee the 85 regional bodies.
- Although the Duma can pass a law without the approval of the Federation Council, all constitutional amendments must have a three-quarters vote approval from both bodies.
- President Putin created a dominant party, United Russia, in part by changing election laws in the State Duma to an all PR system with a 7 percent threshold in 2003 and by appointing regional governors in 2004. These changes were reversed in 2012 to appease the protestors of the Putin-Medvedev position switch in the 2011–12 elections.
- The Russian judicial system is based on code law with the Supreme Court serving as the final court for civil and criminal cases. The Constitutional Court has advisory judicial review on the constitutionality of issues. The court system is not independent and is often used to legitimize state action against political opponents.
- Russian bureaucracy is controlled by a patron-client system dominated by security forces known as siloviki and is characterized by corruption. The Russian military has been used aggressively to occupy territory, including the Crimea and parts of Eastern Ukraine.
- Civil society in Russia is restricted with state-controlled media, a requirement that NGOs must register with the government, the creation of the corporatist Public Chamber, and new extremism laws to target critics and censor the Internet.

CHAPTER 14

China

IN THIS CHAPTER

Summary: President Xi Jinping of the People's Republic of China has an ambitious agenda for his party and his country. His vision of "Socialism with Chinese Characteristics for a New Era" marks a notable change in the political status quo in China. Through the creation of several powerful leading policymaking groups and an intense anti-corruption campaign, Xi seeks to restore the authority of the CCP over Chinese society. His Belt and Road Initiative and global leadership on green technology, combined with increased military spending are indicative of his goal of the "Chinese Dream" to restore China's greatness on the world stage. Consequently, this is a fascinating time to study China as the country transitions from an economic giant to a global political player.

Key Terms

'89 Democracy Movement
All-China Women's Federation (ACWF)
A New Socialist Countryside
Ai Weiwei
Asian Infrastructure Investment Bank
Beautiful China Initiative
Belt and Road Initiative (BRI)
Central Commission for Discipline Inspection (CCDI)
Central Leading Group on Judicial Reform

Central Military Commission of the Communist Party of China
charismatic legitimacy
Charter 08
Chiang Kai-shek
Chinese Communist Party (CCP)
Chinese Communist Revolution of 1949
Chinese Democratic Party (CDP)
Chinese Dream
Communist Youth League
Confucius
cult of personality

Cultural Revolution
Democracy Wall
democratic centralism
Deng Xiaoping
foreign direct investment (FDI)
GONGOs
Great Firewall
Great Leap Forward
Great Proletarian Cultural Revolution
guanxi
Han Chinese
harmonious society
head of state
Hong Kong

hukou system
Hundred Flowers Campaign
Jasmine Revolution
June Fourth Incident
Kuomintang (KMT)
leading small groups
Liu Xiaobo
Long March
Macau
Mao Zedong
mass incidents
mass line
May Fourth Movement
model of sustainable
  development
National People's
  Congress (NPC)
National Supervision
  Commission
Nationalist Party
nomenklatura
one country, two systems

One-Child Policy
one-party state
Paramount leader
People's Armed Police
  Force (PAPF)
People's Liberation Army
  (PLA)
People's Republic of China
  (PRC)
presidential government
princeling
rational-legal legitimacy
Red Guards
red lines
Reform and Opening Up
Republic of China (ROC)
Sinicize religion
Socialism with Chinese
  Characteristics
special economic zones
  (SEZs)

Standing Committee of
  the NPC (NPCSC)
State Council
state-owned enterprises
  (SOEs)
Sun Yat-sen
Supreme People's Court
  (SPC)
Tiananmen Square
toilet revolution
township and village
  enterprises (TVEs)
traditional legitimacy
Uighurs
women hold up half the
  sky
World Trade Organization
  (WTO)
xinfang
Xinhai Revolution of 1911
Young Pioneers

China as a Case Study

As you study China, pay careful attention to the discussion of the following concepts as they are the most frequently used in comparing China with other countries on the AP Comparative Government and Politics exam.

CONCEPT	POSSIBLE COMPARISON/USEFUL EXAMPLES
Chinese Communism	Marxism-Leninism, Soviet Union
Revolution	Mexico, Russia, Iran
Command economy	Economic liberalization
	Economic growth
	Economic development
Authoritarian regime	Democracy
One-party state	Dominant party
Democratic centralism	Political liberalization
Censorship	Independent press

Sovereignty, Authority, and Power

The State

Chinese civilization stretches back 5,000 years. As the oldest continuous civilization in the world, China was ruled by emperors from 246 B.C. to 1911 C.E. These emperors built dynasties that occurred in cycles; as one would weaken, someone would lead a rebellion and seize power and secure the Mandate of Heaven. Each emperor would sit atop a social caste system of imperial elites, landowners, and peasants. Supporting the ruler was a bureaucracy of scholar-officials who gained their position by taking an exam on Confucian principles. However, by the middle of the nineteenth century, this system began to show cracks in its foundation as the Qing dynasty, founded in 1644, was already weak when it lost the Opium War in 1842. The Treaty of Nanking ceded Hong Kong to the victorious British, but the rest of China was never colonized; rather it was split into spheres of influence by foreign powers.

The last Emperor was deposed by the revolutionary followers of **Sun Yat-sen** in 1911. The Chinese Republic, however, quickly became a battleground among competing warlords. Sun Yat-sen strove for unification by creating the **Kuomintang (KMT)**, or **Nationalist Party** of China, which together with the newly formed **Chinese Communist Party (CCP)** and the help of the Soviet Union finally established control over the country in 1927. The new leader of the Kuomintang, **Chiang Kai-shek**, however, quickly turned on the Communists, and a civil war began, ultimately resulting in the **Long March** (1934–35) where **Mao Zedong** solidified his command over the CCP and the Red Army by leading them on a perilous journey to the far northern province of Yan'an. Ensconced in a cave, Mao refined his message and trained his troops. Renamed the **People's Liberation Army (PLA)**, Mao rejoined forces with the KMT during World War II to fight the Japanese. Once that war was over, the civil war began again, but this time the Communists drove the Nationalists off the mainland to the island of Taiwan.

Mao proudly proclaimed the creation of the **People's Republic of China (PRC)**, celebrating the event in **Tiananmen Square** on October 1, 1949. Mao forcibly imposed his vision for China by using many mass campaigns to change behavior. Both the **Great Leap Forward** (1958–61), designed to quickly industrialize China, and the **Cultural Revolution** (1966–76), structured to revitalize revolutionary fervor, were devastating to society. Millions died during both campaigns. It was not until after Mao's death in 1976 that China began to become the modern state known today.

By winning the struggle for leadership, **Deng Xiaoping** became the second **Paramount leader** and instituted a series of reforms, including the creation of a constitution and a plan to gradually liberalize the economy. China's GDP grew at an astounding rate of over 10 percent from 1978 to 2014. China now has the second-largest economy in the world. Under the leadership of its current President and CCP General Secretary Xi Jinping, China is confidently expanding its political, economic, and military power on the world stage as a global superpower.

The Nation

China has the largest population in the world at 1.4 billion. It is a remarkably homogeneous population with 92 percent identifying as **Han Chinese**. The Chinese government, however, recognizes 56 other ethnic groups, including Tibetan, Uighur, Manchu, and Mongol. Most ethnic groups disproportionately reside on the outer fringes of the Chinese state, while the vast bulk of the Han population resides in the eastern region, with the highest density along the coast. The official language of China is Standard Chinese or Mandarin, which is spoken by about 70 percent of the population, especially in the northern region around Beijing or in international transactions. Cantonese, on the other hand, is the official language of Hong Kong and Macau and is widely spoken in the southeastern part of China. Ethnic groups in autonomous regions can keep their own language, religion, and traditions, along with having a measure of self-government. Unusually for a developing country, China has a median age of 37 and faces the challenge of an aging population. For this reason, the one-child policy was relaxed in 2015 to allow couples to have two children, although ethnic minorities are not subject to this population growth policy.

Legitimacy

As the leader of the Chinese Revolution in 1949, Mao Zedong had **charismatic legitimacy**, meaning that he enjoyed unparalleled support, an almost religious-like zeal from his followers. This was later cultivated into a **cult of personality** with reverence for his words in the *Little Red Book* and the vast propaganda posters of his likeness. The challenge for any state, however, is how to institutionalize the charisma of a revolutionary founder.

China accomplished this transition through the adoption of a party constitution and a state constitution to provide **rational-legal legitimacy**. The current state constitution was adopted in 1982 and establishes a unitary, "socialist state under the people's democratic dictatorship" based on **democratic centralism**, where the **National People's Congress (NPC)** is the formal source of all authority. Borrowed from the Soviet Union, this means that all government decisions are made by the leadership of the CCP. Consequently, the party constitution is also an important document in China. This was highlighted in a meeting of the National Party Congress of the CCP that was held in October 2017, when "Xi Jinping Thought on Socialism with Chinese Characteristics for a New Era" was unanimously added to the constitution. The only other leaders mentioned by name in the party constitution are Mao and Deng, and only Mao's name was added while he was alive. This level of support gives Xi a very powerful mandate of support, and it is fully expected that he will be selected for a third term as the General Secretary of the CCP in November 2022.

In addition, Xi Jinping is also striving to strengthen his position with **traditional legitimacy** by reviving respect for ancient traditions and philosophers, especially **Confucius**. Xi was the first party leader to attend a birthday party for Confucius in 2015, the sage's 2,565th birthday, and he frequently speaks about a return to the precepts of discipline, respect for authority, and moral behavior that Confucius espoused.

Regime

China is an authoritarian one-party state. The true power in the political system is found in the positions of the general secretary and the standing committee of the Politburo of the CCP. These seven men not only direct the activities of the 89 million members of the CCP, but they also hold significant government positions as well. Xi Jinping, for example, is general secretary of the CCP and president of China, whereas Li Keqiang is the premier of the State Council. Chinese leadership has allowed economic liberalization since the 1980s but has resisted political liberalization. There is no independent court system, and there is a restricted civil society and a high degree of censorship.

Freedom House: Not Free (political rights: −2/40, civil liberties: 11/60)

Economist Intelligence Unit Democracy Index: authoritarian regime: 2.21

Economic System

China has been famously pursuing economic liberalization policies since the 1980s as the government adopted Deng Xiaoping's reform programs. Creating **special economic zones (SEZs)** that would allow **foreign direct investment (FDI)**, promoting **township and village enterprises (TVEs)**, and privatizing industries were all free market policies designed to help modernize China and grow the economy. The progress was such that China joined the **World Trade Organization (WTO)** in 2001 because the country was on its way to becoming a market economy. The initial agreement was that China would receive "full market economy status" in 15 years. Well, 20 years have gone by, and China wants to retain its "developing economy" status due to lingering poverty in certain areas, as this allows them to liberalize the economy at a slower pace. The United States and the European Union continue to claim that China has not truly opened its economy to free trade, but rather forces foreign companies to form joint ventures with local **state-owned enterprises (SOEs)** and requires the foreign firms to share technology. In addition, ever since the 2008 financial crisis, the number of SOEs in China has increased slightly, although there is a current tendency for these firms to merge in hopes of achieving some economies of scale. Currently, over 40 million people work for Chinese SOEs, of which 10 million of these are members of the CCP. Although most economists recommend that the SOEs be made more efficient by privatizing them or laying off workers, the CCP worries about the social unrest that would be caused by a rise in unemployment. Xi Jinping remains committed, however, to free trade. In January of 2017, Xi was the first Chinese president to travel to the World Economic Forum in Davos, Switzerland, where he spoke positively about the role of globalization and committed that "China will keep its door wide open and not close it." Despite this pledge, however, it would still be more accurate to describe China as a mixed economy rather than a market one.

Political Culture and Socialization

Chinese political culture is strongly nationalistic. Even describing China as "on the socialist road with Chinese characteristics" is indicative of a uniquely Chinese approach to economic development. Collective pride in being part of a such a long-lasting civilization is evident in events like the 2008 Summer and 2022 Winter Olympics held in Beijing.

As in any society, the family is the primary agent of socialization, but the CCP takes an active role in using publicity (propaganda) to deliver the government's message. Xi Jinping has been promoting the concept of the "**Chinese Dream**" ever since he became general secretary. This follows the years of "**harmonious society**" under Hu Jintao. These and other slogans are found on posters, billboards, and in government rhetoric. The government also has strict control over school textbooks to help socialize the young, along with state-run media to frame public issues.

Political Institutions

Constitution

The Chinese constitution was adopted in 1982 as part of Deng Xiaoping's modernization program. To open the economy, clarifications needed to be made with regard to the status of public ownership. Article 6, for example, asserts that "the system of socialist public ownership supersedes the system of exploitation of man by man." It goes on to say, however, "in the primary stage of socialism, the State upholds the basic economic system in which the public ownership is dominant and diverse forms of ownership develop side by side," or in other words, although SOEs will continue, private firms will be allowed. In addition, Article 8 reinforces the role of "rural collective economic organizations" but states that "working people who are members of rural economic collectives have the right, within limits prescribed by law, to farm plots of cropland and hilly land allotted for their private use, engage in household sideline production, and raise privately owned livestock," a remarkable concession in a system that had previously banned private property. It is important to note, however, that land is still collectively owned.

The constitution also establishes the structure of the government. The National People's Congress is "the highest organ of state power." In addition, the document enumerates the "fundamental rights and duties of citizens," which include "freedom of speech, of the press, of assembly, of association, of procession and of demonstration." In reality, however, the Chinese people do not have these rights, making China an example of a country with a constitution, but not a constitutional government. The arbitrary nature of an authoritarian regime does not uphold rule of law.

But a growing middle class and a global economic community resulted in two important amendments to the document in 2004, passed with an almost unanimous vote by the NPC. The first amendment guarantees that "legally obtained private property of the citizens should not be violated," and the second that "the State respects and protects human rights." Both of these sent a message to citizens and foreign investors alike that there is a new emphasis on individual rights, at least in principle. As one NPC deputy stated, "We write all these things into amendments, so all Chinese officials realize they have to do it. When we write it into the constitution, we are changing an era."

Levels of Government

China is a unitary government with all formal power vested in the National People's Congress. In reality, however, China is a one-party state that has organized itself to oversee all government offices. Chinese governance occurs at the national, provincial, city, town, and village levels. A party committee exists alongside the government unit to provide direction and personnel to formulate and implement policymaking decisions.

In addition, there are five autonomous regions in China with a high population of a minority group that is granted specific rights to retain its language, religion, and traditional culture, along with the ability to make some policies. The five are Xinjiang (Uighur), Tibet (Tibetan), Inner Mongolia (Mongol), Ningxia (Hui), and Guangxi (Zhuang). The constitutional right to autonomy, however, has not held up in practice.

There also two special administrative regions (SARs) in China: **Hong Kong** and **Macau**. Hong Kong was a British colony until 1997 when it was returned to China. Macau was a Portuguese colony until 1987. Both of these former colonies had well-developed market-based economies and legal systems, so a new policy was adopted to incorporate them into the Chinese system. The policy "**one country, two systems**" allowed Hong Kong and Macau to operate outside the Chinese socialist system; in fact both are separate members of the WTO. A new national security law, however, significantly reduces Hong Kong's autonomy. In addition, President Xi has called for reunification with Taiwan despite that country's assertions that Taiwan is a sovereign state.

President

Although China has a president, it is not a presidential government. A **presidential government** is defined as one in which the president and the legislature are chosen in separate elections. In the Chinese system, the president and the chairman of the Central Military Commission are formally selected by the National People's Congress (NPC) for a five-year term (a previous two-term limit was rescinded by the NPC in 2018). Yet since the 1990s, the general secretary of the CCP is the person that is "selected" for both of these roles. For although the president has the formal power to select the premier and other high-ranking ministers to be approved by the NPC, in reality, these decisions are made by the Politburo. In addition, the president implements laws, confers medals, pardons, proclaims war and states of emergency, receives ambassadors, and makes treaties. The president's constitutional powers were designed to be primarily ceremonial as **head of state**. The writers of the 1982 constitution were trying to diffuse power between different people to promote more collective decision making with the hopes of preventing another cult of personality like the one that had supported Mao. After the protests at Tiananmen Square in 1989, however, power was reconsolidated in the hands of one leader, although Deng Xiaoping retained his position informally until his death. Today, President Xi's real power comes from his party position as general secretary, and perhaps, even more importantly, from his position as the head of the CCP's Central Military Commission (CMC), which controls the PLA. In addition, Xi has also been extremely successful at consolidating his power over both the CCP and the

Chinese government. *Xi Jinping Thought* has been added as a guiding principle to both the party constitution and the national constitution. Term limits for position of general secretary and president of China have also been eliminated.

DATES	LEADERSHIP GENERATION	PARAMOUNT LEADER	HEAD OF CMC	CCP CHAIRMAN/ GENERAL SECRETARY	PRESIDENT OF PRC
1949–76	First	Mao Zedong	1954–76	Chairman 1945–76	1954–59
1976–78	Second	Hua Guofeng	1976–81	Chairman 76–78	
1978–92	Second	Deng Xiaoping	1981–89		
1992–2002	Third	Jiang Zemin	1989–2002	GS 1989–2002	1993–2003
2002–2012	Fourth	Hu Jintao	2002–2012	GS 2002–2012	2003–13
2012–present	Fifth	Xi Jinping	2012–present	GS 2012–present	2013–present

Legislature

The National People's Congress (NPC) is a unicameral body established by the constitution as the source of all authority in the national government, being charged with selecting the president of the PRC, the president of the Supreme People's Court, and the chairman of the Central Military Commission, along with approving the choice of premier (head of government) and ministers, and having the power to remove these officials. The NPC is given the authority to supervise the enforcement of the constitution, as well as amending it, examining the actions of the Standing Committee of the NPC, and deciding on questions of war and peace. Yet this body of 3,000 delegates, serving a five-year term, only meets ceremonially for two weeks a year, so obviously the real legislative work is done elsewhere. The annual meeting is a significant event as it serves as a forum for discussion and debate, although the final votes are nearly always unanimous. Membership is drawn from all regions of the country to include ethnic minorities, and there are separate delegations from Hong Kong, Macau, Taiwan, and the PLA. It is important to note that only about 70 percent of the delegates to the NPC are members of the CCP.

The **Standing Committee of the NPC (NPCSC)** is a group of 150 delegates selected to act as a more continuous body to perform legislative functions. Of note, it is often the NPCSC that is called upon to interpret the constitution if there is a legal dispute.

Judiciary

According to the constitution, the **Supreme People's Court (SPC)** is the highest appellate court in China. There are lower courts at the provincial, municipal, and town levels. In addition, there are special courts for the military and the CCP. The president (chief judge) of the SPC is formally chosen by the NPC but is really selected by the CCP; in fact all judges are selected with local party officials' approval. In addition, the entire legal system is overseen by political and legal committees that "coordinate the work of the police, prosecutors and judiciary at every level."

Part of Deng Xiaoping's "reform and opening up" system required judicial reform. For China to attract foreign direct investment and entrepreneurs, laws protecting private property and contracts needed to be enacted, along with more transparent procedures for adjudication. The challenge for the CCP was how to strengthen the judicial system without reducing party control. A series of reforms have attempted to create a judicial system independent of corruption, but not independent of the Party. These reforms are the work of the CCP's **Central Leading Group on Judicial Reform**, headed by Xi Jinping. One reform has been to increase the professionalization of judges. In a five-year training plan for Party cadres (judges), emphasis is placed on legal university training and the use of "active and practical methods" to handle more complex cases, although training must also include ideological training. Other reforms include improving the criminal procedure system to reduce coerced confessions and reducing local government interference in judicial decision making. One solution has been to introduce circuit courts that are above local courts and allow the people to directly petition the court about unfair judgments (*xinfang*) without traveling to Beijing. Problems remain, however, with the arbitrary use of the law to control dissent. An example of this is the arrest of human-rights lawyers on charges of subversion. Another tactic is the suspension of law licenses as happened to defense lawyer Zhu Shengwu for defending a social media user who used the illegal phrase "Steamed Buns Xi" on social media. The blogger received two years in jail, but the lawyer lost his license for "endangering national security."

Bureaucracy

According to the constitution, the **State Council** is "the highest organ of State Administration" and is charged with implementing policies passed by the NPC. Headed by the premier, the State Council oversees the bureaucracy.

The bureaucracy of the China is immense. Forty-seven million people work in government positions throughout the country, but only 10 million are civil servants or "cadres." According to a new Civil Service Law in 2006, administrative or leadership positions (including the president and premier) are referred to as civil servants and all other positions are "personnel." Civil servants are selected by exam and a "hearing from the masses," which is a "democratic" recommendation from the appropriate level party committee. Most people working for the government are not members of the CCP, but 95 percent of those holding leadership positions are party members. These leadership positions are therefore controlled by the CCP's system of **nomenklatura**, which is a list of important positions by seniority. The goal of a CCP member is to move up this list to attain more senior positions of power. The way to accomplish this is be to show ideological loyalty, performance-based merit, and some **guanxi** or personal connections, such as a mentor or family member. Performance-based merit, however, has increased in importance in a data-driven world where increasingly the party is looking to professionalize the bureaucracy to manage a globalized economy and aging workforce.

Military and Other Coercive Institutions

The **People's Liberation Army (PLA)** celebrated its ninetieth anniversary in August of 2017 with an enormous military parade. Formed to fight the Kuomintang, the PLA has always been an integral part of the CCP's power base. President Xi reinforced this relationship by stating "our army will remain the army of the party and the people." But Xi also sent a clear message regarding necessary reforms by explaining, "The army should increase its political awareness . . . and carry forward and implement the Party's absolute leadership." This comment references the fact that over 100 military officers have been convicted in a recent anti-corruption campaign. Because although the PLA was forced to give up its economic enterprises under Jiang Zemin in the 1990s, opportunities for personal enrichment still exist. In addition, Xi has overseen a complete restructuring of military divisions from 5 to 15 to break up old power structures.

Xi has made other reforms to modernize the PLA into a worldwide fighting force. This means celebrating the launching of China's first aircraft carrier and the production of new fighter jets and intercontinental missiles. In addition, China recently established its first overseas military base at Djibouti and regularly supplies UN peacekeeping forces. It has also acted aggressively to militarize islands in the South China Sea. The PLA consists of 2 million personnel serving in the army, navy, and air force. The Rocket Force manages an arsenal of more than 100 nuclear weapons.

The governance of the PLA is reflective of dual party-state organizations. The **Central Military Commission of the Communist Party of China** is in direct control of the military, with Xi Jinping serving as chairman along with several high-ranking military officers. These same names are then submitted to the NPC so that they can be elected to the Central Military Commission of the People's Republic of China. In that way, the CCP's military is also the Chinese military. Consequently, Xi Jinping's power comes from being general secretary of the Communist Party, commander in chief of the PLA, and president of China.

Another significant coercive force in China is the **People's Armed Police Force (PAPF)**, which is charged with maintaining social stability and national security. This internal security force of 600,000 is the world's largest and is organized to deal with emergencies ranging from riot control to disaster relief missions. After the PLA was used to disperse the "Democratic Movement" in Tiananmen Square in 1989, the CMC determined that the PAPF would now be the first force mobilized to deal with domestic unrest. Amid allegations of misuse of the force, however, in 2009 a law was passed to prevent local authorities from having the power to summon the armed police. Criticism of the PAPF continues, however, as the number of mass incidents in China increasingly bring more citizens into conflict with the police and their use of excessive force.

Leadership and Elite Recruitment

In a one-party state like China, it is obvious that the way to political leadership is through the CCP. Starting with membership in the **Young Pioneers**, and then **Communist Youth League**, young Chinese are socialized with ideological rhetoric. Recently, however, President Xi has criticized the League for "chanting empty slogans" and for failing to connect with young people because "how can it talk about uniting all our young people? . . . it can't even keep up with them!" Xi's goal is to transform the League back to an organization that can mobilize the masses by reducing the central leadership of the organization and putting it more closely under party control. This is to reduce the influence of the "Youth League Faction" of the party from reaching high political positions.

This shake-up of the Communist Youth League is another indication of how the CCP evolves to maintain its legitimacy. Probably the most significant example of this was the 2001 change in the party's constitution to allow private business owners, capitalists, into the CCP. As one expert explained, "If these entrepreneurs are not included inside the party, they will be inclined to develop organizations and channels outside the party, and they will have ample resources to do so." And why would capitalists want to get into the CCP? Because being in the CCP will provide access to government contracts, privatization opportunities, favorable regulations, and bank loans.

The CCP today has 88 million members and a long history of developing the talents of China's best and brightest. Academically talented students in college are invited to join the party, while others can be nominated by current party members. An applicant must be a Chinese national and at least 18 years old. The process involves taking party courses and written tests, along with interviews. It is difficult to get into the party. In 2011, 22 million people applied and only 3 million were accepted. Once accepted, a person seeking political power will first start in a regional government, earning a strong reputation for handling local problems. It helps to have a mentor who has the guanxi to help one climb the nomenklatura ladder. It also helps to have revolutionary ties.

The career of President Xi Jinping is a good example of how the system works. President Xi is a "**princeling**" because of his father's position in the first generation of Chinese leadership. During the Cultural Revolution, when his father was denounced and jailed, Xi was sent to work in the countryside. He joined the Communist Youth League in 1971 and the CCP in 1974. After earning a degree in chemical engineering at Tsinghua University, he served as aide to the Central Military Commission before being sent to be a deputy Party secretary in Hebei in 1982. He was promoted to secretary in 1983. In 2000, he became governor of Fujian, and in 2002 Xi was made provincial party chief and a full member of the Central Committee. He was transferred in 2007 to become party chief in Shanghai to clean up after a corruption scandal. Also in this year, Xi was appointed to the Politburo Standing Committee, and in 2008 he became the vice president of the PRC and in 2012 the general secretary of the CCP.

Linkage Institutions

Elections

The Chinese constitution relies on **democratic centralism** as an organizing principle. This means that the legislative bodies, representing the people, select the members of the executive and judicial branches. This provides for a separation of functions, but not a true separation of powers. Chinese citizens have the right to vote for members of the local people's congresses, whose members then select the city and provincial level congresses, who then select the NPC. The CCP creates the ballots, making it virtually impossible for an independent candidate to get his or her name on the ballot. There is choice on some of the ballots: for example for the NPC ballot, there are 10 percent more names on the ballot than available seats. Above the NPC level, however, the choice decreases. For example, when the NPC voted to make Xi Jinping the president of the PRC, only his name was on the ballot, and only one person out of 3,000 voted no.

Besides local party congresses, only village chiefs are directly elected. As there are over 600,000 villages in China, this is not an insubstantial number of votes. Deng Xiaoping made this reform of village elections in an attempt to have local residents help keep local party officials in line. As a Chinese proverb states, "Heaven is high, and the emperor is far away," so even the powerful CCP has a challenging time getting local authorities to follow party guidelines; therefore, villagers were given a role in helping keep local officials accountable.

Election System and Party Systems

China refers to itself as a multiparty state under the leadership of the CCP. In reality, the CCP governs as a **one-party state** without an extensive election system. There are eight minor parties that are allowed to exist and hold seats in the NPC, but their power is negligible. The largest of these is the China Democratic League with 274,000 members, and the smallest is the Taiwan Democratic Self-Government League with 3,000 members.

Efforts to create true opposition parties have ended in failure. For example, the Chinese Democratic Party was formed in 1998 by former Tiananmen Square student activists. The leaders were all arrested after trying to register the party and sentenced to 11 to 13 years in prison for subversion.

The Party

The Chinese Communist Party (CCP) was founded in 1921 upon Marxist-Leninist principles. After an initial period of working with Sun Yat-sen's KMT party, the new leader of the Nationalists, Chiang Kai-shek, tried to destroy the Communists. In 1927, the Communists created the Red Army to fight the KMT but were forced to retreat on the Long March to Yan'an where Mao Zedong took leadership of the party.

After World War II and the Chinese Revolution, the CCP established the PRC in 1949. The CCP relies on the following ideology as stated in the party's constitution.

Marxism	• Revolution is inevitable • Revolutionary force is workers in an industrialized economy
Leninism	• Revolutionary force is the party vanguard • Use democratic centralism to govern transition
Mao Zedong Thought	• Revolutionary force is the peasants • Mass line: "from the masses, to the masses"
Deng Xiaoping Theory	• Socialism with Chinese characteristics • Four Modernizations: agriculture, industry, defense, and science • Seek truth from facts
The Theory of the Three Represents	• Articulated by Jiang Zemin • Peasants, workers, and capitalists form the party
The Scientific Outlook on Development	• Articulated by Hu Jintao • Goal is to promote a Harmonious Socialist Society
Xi Jinping Thought	• Socialism with Chinese Characteristics for a New Era • "Chinese Dream"—restore China to greatness

The CCP is organized in a hierarchical manner in tandem to state government offices. There is considerable overlap between the members of the highest party organizations and government offices.

PARTY ORGANIZATIONS	STATE GOVERNMENT OFFICES
General Secretary of CCP	President of PRC
Standing Committee of Politburo	Premier of PRC
Politburo	State Council
Central Committee	Standing Committee of NPC
National Party Congress	National People's Congress
Provincial/City/Town/Village Committees	Provincial/City/Town/Village People's Congress

The National Party Congress meets once every five years to select the leadership for the next five years. At the 19th Party Congress in October of 2017, President Xi was reelected to his position as general secretary and his ideological contributions were added to the Party's constitution as Xi Jinping Thought, an acknowledgment only previously given to Mao. His goal is to restore discipline to the CCP because the "government, military, society and schools, north, south, east and west—the party is the leader of all." In this way, the CCP will be able to stay in power, unlike the Communist Party of the Soviet Union. Xi has begun this process by convicting prominent officials and military officers of corruption. He mandated that party officials stop their extravagant lifestyles by limiting themselves to meals with "four dishes and soup." To enforce this anti-corruption program, Xi has created a government agency, the National Supervision Commission (NSC), which expands the reach of the party-controlled Central Commission for Disciplinary Inspection (CCDI). Unlike the CCDI which only had authority over CCP members, the new NSC will formally work with the CCDI to oversee all public employees, including those at universities and SOEs.

Interest Groups

Civil society is constrained in China, but interest group politics are still significant. Some interest groups have a great deal of influence on public policy, while others play a limited role. Influence is determined by how the group is organized, but also how well the group utilizes social media opportunities. The largest effect on interest group development in China has been the movement to a market economy. Not only have private businesses developed their own interests, but the widening gap between rich and poor has led to social unrest. Consequently, the CCP has dual strategy regarding interest groups or social organizations. Those that have a nonpolitical purpose (providing services to schools, the elderly, or the poor) can register; those that are political are targeted and repressed.

There are several distinct types of interest groups. There are the **GONGOs** (government organized NGOs), which can raise money. Examples would be the China Youth Development Foundation or the China Foundation for Poverty Alleviation. There are mass organizations organized by the party, including the Trade Union, the All-China Women's Federation, and the Youth League. There are also professional associations, charitable organizations, and churches. In addition, there are more than 7,000 foreign NGOs in China.

Xi Jinping's administration has been cracking down on NGOs that threaten social stability. In January of 2017 a new law was passed that requires foreign NGOs to find government sponsors, register with the police, and submit annual reports on their financing. In addition, domestic NGOs cannot accept funding from unregistered foreign groups. Some environmental groups wonder how they can survive without funding and are considering becoming for-profit environmental firms that also do advocacy to get around the new rules. The challenge that remains for all groups is how to keep the government from seeing their organization as a threat to national security. The fear is that this new law will have the same effect as Putin's 2012 NGO law that has forced many of the foreign NGOs in Russia to shut down. In fact, many dissidents and human rights lawyers and activists have been arrested in recent years.

Citizens, Society, and the State

Social Cleavages

One of the most significant cleavages in China is the social division between urban and rural areas. This cleavage coincides with differences in income and geographic location as well. Because the developments of special economic zones were in coastal regions in China, the policies of economic liberalization during the 1980s and 1990s brought prosperity to the urban centers of the eastern part of China. This widened income inequality with the more rural, agricultural regions of western China. This cleavage is only exacerbated by the **hukou system** of birthplace registration. Rural residents are not permitted to simply move their families to urban areas. An urban hukou is needed to access education and health services. So many rural migrants leave their children in the countryside with grandparents as they travel to urban areas looking for work. Although some municipalities have adopted a points-based merit system for rural residents to obtain urban hukou, first-tier cities like Beijing and Shanghai have not done so. In addition, rural farmers are often pushed off their land by local governments seeking to develop the property. Each year there are thousands of "mass incidents" in the countryside because of unfair conditions.

The Chinese government has made changes to improve rural life to restore social stability and to maintain food production, because as many as 200 million farmers have migrated to the cities in the last 25 years. Hu Jintao introduced "**A New Socialist Countryside**" plan in 2006 of greater investment in rural areas along with increased agricultural subsidies. Most significantly, the centuries-old agricultural tax was eliminated, and the government pledged to provide free textbooks for rural students and more spending on health cooperatives. Early results of the program are positive. In 2010, rural incomes rose faster than urban incomes, but the disparity is still great. Urban net disposable income is still three times greater than in rural areas. Xi Jinping has continued to focus on improving conditions in the countryside. One popular policy has been "the **toilet revolution**" to upgrade sanitation in rural areas, not only for residents but for the growing domestic tourism industry.

Another significant cleavage in China is between the majority Han population and ethnic minorities. This is also a coinciding cleavage because many of the ethnic minorities are located in the western borders of China and have different religious and cultural traditions. A prominent example of such a group would be the **Uighurs** of the autonomous region of Xinjiang, located on the far western border of China next to Kazakhstan, Kyrgyzstan, and Afghanistan. Uighurs are Muslim, speak a Turkic language, and for many years dominated the population of Xinjiang. Recently, however, the Chinese government has increased investment in the region, motivating more Han to move west to live in the region. In addition, Chinese troops are stationed in the area because of violent separatist incidents led by the East Turkestan Islamic Movement (ETIM). There have been reports of repression of religious and cultural activities by the Chinese government. Old historic Uighur neighborhoods are bulldozed; mosques are closed; strict controls are placed on religious schools and bans on fasting during Ramadan have led to numerous protests. Violent terrorist attacks have killed hundreds. The Chinese government has stepped up digital surveillance of the Uighur population, monitoring movements and conversations, and uses detention camps for suspected terrorists. These detention camps are styled as "re-education centers" and imprison an estimated million Muslims because, as released CCP documents claim, those detained have "been infected by unhealthy thoughts." Both the Trump and Biden administrations have labeled Chinese government actions against the Uighurs as genocide.

Civil Society

Civil society is constrained in China: citizens cannot form new political parties; there are restrictions on the formation of interest groups; the media and Internet are censored, and recently, President Xi also spoke out against religious groups. His goal is to "**Sinicize religion**" or make it more Chinese. Xi wants the CCP to "guide religions to adapt to the socialist society," although he reiterated that all members of the CCP "should be firm Marxist atheists and must never find their values and beliefs in any religion." Consequently, there has been an increase in religious persecution, especially against Buddhist separatists in Tibet and Uighurs in Xinjiang. In addition, crosses on top of Christian churches were demolished and more religious activities were pushed into underground churches. The Falun Gong, a social-religious movement that mobilized in large numbers in the 1990s, is still banned.

In contrast with this repression, nonpolitical activity in urban areas is diverse with a wide range of shops and entertainment opportunities. Yet even here, the CCP wants to make its mark, warning media companies "not to express overt admiration for Western lifestyles" and that movies "need to be more centered on the people, guided by core socialist values."

The Media

The media is heavily regulated in China. CCP mouthpieces *People's Daily*, Xinhua news organization, and China Central Television (CCTV) are required "to show absolute loyalty to the Party." President Xi recently admonished them to craft "more dynamic, technologically sophisticated media products that would shape public opinion." Independent media outlets must also be careful not to cross "**red lines**," which are unspoken understandings against criticizing the government or the party. Journalists that attempt to cover stories on forbidden areas such as Tibet and Xinjiang end up in jail for subversion. In fact, a law prohibiting any independent news gathering was issued by the Cyberspace Administration of China (CAC) to control social media and Internet providers from producing or disseminating any original content that had not been provided by approved sources.

Other laws and regulations on social media include that mobile companies store user data so that officials can collect and use private data, including texts, pictures, and video sharing, to be used to convict people. This is in addition to the censorship capabilities of the "**Great Firewall**" that regularly block content concerning events like the Tiananmen Square massacre and websites like Facebook and Twitter. The new challenge for the Ministry of Industry and Information Technology is streaming sites with more interesting content than state TV. Initially with the advent of 4G services in 2016, there seemed to be an opportunity for the growth of new video platforms, helped along by firms like Tencent and Alibaba facilitating electronic payments. But government censors are now constraining these ventures as well. CCP propaganda movies highlighting the "Chinese Dream" must be shown before other movies, and those movies cannot show Western values, celebrity gossip, pornography, or LGBTQ content.

Political Participation

One of the main reasons for the Chinese government's crackdown on social media is its ability to mobilize the public. Shutting down WeChat is an effortless way to try to stymie protest. Because it is difficult to get permission to hold rallies, most demonstrations are illegal and are broken up by police. Estimates are that over 100,000 "**mass incidents**" occur yearly in China. These include rural farmers protesting a land grab by local government officials, to urban workers striking over unpaid wages, to homeowners trying to prevent their older homes from being bulldozed, to environmental activists trying to stop polluters. Most of these protests are aimed at local officials and local businesses. Often, the organizers of such events end up jailed for subversion.

The number of people who take part in these demonstrations, however, is small. Few Chinese join associations, unless it is politically expedient such as belonging to the All-China Women's Federation. Less than 7 percent of the population belongs to the CCP. Voting in local elections is perfunctory. Political participation in China is risky and therefore avoided by most people.

Social Movements

The CCP has a deep distrust of any groups that organize and coordinate without state approval. Therefore, social movements often face government repression, yet sometimes also gain some government responsiveness to the cause. One example would be the women's rights movement in China. Mao Zedong proclaimed that "**women hold up half the sky**" and crafted policies to integrate them into the labor force. The **All-China Women's Federation (ACWF)** was founded in 1949 to help the CCP mobilize women.

Over the years, the focus of ACWF has been on gender equality and less on mass political campaigns. Currently the organization serves as a sponsor of many other NGOs that are focused on women's issues. It also publishes newspaper and magazines focused on women's issues. Critics charge, however, that the ACWF is "part of the bureaucracy and has to compromise as a women's organization." So other women stage public demonstrations, such as taking over the men's section of a public toilet to protest inequality or marching in white bridal gowns covered in red paint to protest domestic violence. These women are often detained by police. In 2015, five women were arrested for planning a march on International Women's Day. Social media quickly spread the news across the world. "Free the five" became a hashtag even though Twitter is banned in China. Eventually the women were released in large part to international pressure, and the Chinese government passed its first law against domestic violence.

Democracy movements also have a long history in China. Beginning with the **May Fourth Movement**, scholars proposed that the China Republic should pursue a "new culture" that would promote Western values on democracy and science and abandon Confucian hierarchy and obedience. The movement got its name from a mass student protest over the Treaty of Versailles in 1919 that quickly spread across the country. The failure of Chinese diplomacy over the treaty, however, led some intellectuals like Chen Duxiu to move toward Marxism, and consequently he and Li Dazhao created the Chinese Communist Party in 1921. In 1978, the **Democracy Wall**, a long brick wall along a busy Beijing street, was the location for large, handwritten character posters detailing individual suffering under Mao. Deng Xiaoping allowed the posters to stay as a way to consolidate his authority, until Wei Jingsheng put one up advocating for a "Fifth Modernization"—democracy. Wei was arrested, and the movement was over.

The **'89 Democracy Movement** or the **June Fourth Incident** is perhaps the best known of all. Given the economic liberalization policies of the 1980s, student groups began to call for their constitutional rights of freedom of speech and press, along with rule of law. General Secretary Hu Yaobang sympathized with the students and was forced to resign. When he died on April 15, 1989, students gathered in Tiananmen Square to mourn him. The students drew up a list of "Seven Demands" that included "Affirm as correct Hu Yaobang's views on democracy and freedom," "allow privately run newspapers and stop press censorship," and "end restrictions on demonstrations in Beijing." When no party leader would speak to the students, they organized class boycotts and further demonstrations. The official Party newspaper, *People's Daily*, published an editorial that branded the students as anti-party and anti-government. In response thousands of students marched to Tiananmen Square on April 27 promoting a "pro-party" message of "anti-corruption and anti-cronyism." General Secretary Zhao Ziyang acknowledged that the student movement was patriotic and that their concerns were legitimate. As many students began to lose interest, student leaders scheduled a hunger strike on May 13, right before a state visit by Mikhail Gorbachev, who had overseen both glasnost and perestroika in the Soviet Union. Thousands of students arrived in the square and refused to leave. So, the first Sino-Soviet summit in 30 years took place amidst the chaos, embarrassing the CCP as foreign journalists extensively covered the protests. May 17–18 attracted even more students, along with Youth League organizations and even some party leaders to the square and to rallies across China. On May 19, Zhao went to the square to ask the students to end the hunger strike. Although he had advocated rescinding the editorial in the *People's Daily*, Deng had rejected that idea. Zhao was forced to resign his position and was placed under house arrest until his death in 2005. Deng declared martial law on May 20, and troops were sent to clear the square. Thousands of protestors blocked the military vehicles from entering the area, and the army retreated on May 24. The CCP leadership began to refer to the protestors as terrorists and counterrevolutionaries sponsored by the United States. The order was given on June 3 to clear the square. This time as troops entered the area, they shot at protestors trying to block their path. Students in the square resolved to be nonviolent but were beaten as the soldiers cleared the area. The government says that 241 people were killed, including 23 soldiers, and 7,000 were injured. Other sources put the death toll from 300 to 1,000. Many students were arrested and served time in prison.

The events in Tiananmen Square have not dissuaded democracy advocates. During the "Beijing Spring" from 1997 to 1998, after the death of Deng Xiaoping, former student activists formed the **Chinese Democratic Party (CDP)** and announced its creation during a state visit by President Bill Clinton. Waiting until after Clinton left, the government tried several ways to dissuade the party leaders from continuing. Finally, it sentenced all seven leaders to long prison sentences. In 2008, **Charter 08** was published by 300 intellectuals, calling for democratic reforms like "an independent judiciary, election of public officials, freedom of expression, and a federated republic." One of the authors, **Liu Xiaobo**, who was awarded the Nobel Peace Prize in 2010, was arrested and imprisoned for subversion. He died in jail in 2017. In 2011, a **Jasmine Revolution** took place in 12 cities across China. Slogans included "We want fairness, we want justice!" and "Lift restrictions, free the press!" Using social media, protesters were urged to simply "stroll" as a nonviolent way to participate. Police reacted by beating students and foreign journalists covering the events. The word "jasmine" was blocked on social media, and jasmine flowers were banned from being sold. Many participants were arrested, including prominent artist **Ai Weiwei**, to show how seriously the government took the threat.

Citizenship and Representation

Chinese citizenship is granted to those who have at least one parent of Chinese nationality, or through naturalization. The challenge becomes if a child is eligible for hukou, or household registration, which depends on whether the birth was approved by the National Population and Family Planning Commission. In addition, children born in Hong Kong, Macau, and Taiwan to parents of Chinese descent are considered Chinese nationals.

Although Mao insisted that women "hold up half the sky," representation in China is far from that ideal. Only 20 percent of the NPC is female. In the CCP, only 25 percent of the 88 million members are female. No woman serves on the Standing Committee of the Politburo, although there is one woman, Sun Chunlan, in the Politburo itself. Only 5 percent of the Central Committee is female. This contrasts with both Hong Kong and Taiwan, which have female executives, President Tsai Ing-wen of Taiwan, and Chief Executive Carrie Lam of Hong Kong. Reasons for this disparity include the fact that women are required to retire at 55, 10 years earlier than men, to take care of elderly parents and grandchildren. Women are faring better as business executives and academics.

Ethnic minorities have special representation rights. Most groups, such as the Uighurs and Tibetans, live in autonomous zones where their religious, language, and cultural rights are nominally protected. Each autonomous zone also has seats in the NPC. In addition, each ethnic minority is guaranteed to have at least one member of the NPC. In this way, the CCP retains its legitimacy as a protector of all the people. There are currently 400 ethnic minority deputies out of 3,000 in the NPC.

Political and Economic Change

Revolutions, Coups, and War

The **Xinhai Revolution of 1911** marked the end of the Chinese empire, establishing the **Republic of China (ROC)**. The Revolution was supported by many distinct groups: students, intellectuals, and members of the political, business, and military elite against the weak Qing dynasty, which was not able to compete against foreign domination. Sun Yat-sen formed a United League to fight for independence. After many "uprisings," Sun was named the first president of the Republic. He was forced to turn power over to warlord Yuan Shikai, who forced the abdication of Emperor Puyi (age six). Sun Yat-sen regained power through the formation of the Nationalist Party or Kuomintang (KMT). Interestingly, both the KMT (Taiwan) and CCP (PRC) recognize Sun as the "Father of the Nation" for his defeat of the Qing.

The **Chinese Communist Revolution of 1949** established the **People's Republic of China**. Led by Mao Zedong and his People's Liberation Army, the KMT under Chiang Kai-shek was forced to the island of Formosa (Taiwan) after a civil war for control of China. Both armies had fought the Japanese during World War II, but they turned on each other in 1945. For many years the world community recognized the Republic of China as the "real China." The PRC was not given the permanent seat on the UN Security Council until 1971. This was followed by a visit to the PRC by President Richard Nixon as part of his détente strategy, and American recognition of the PRC was given by President Carter on January 1, 1979. All attempts to get the Republic of China recognized by the UN have been defeated. The PRC maintains that the island of Taiwan is part of China.

The victory of the CCP over the KMT led to the establishment of a system of democratic centralism as the Chinese political structure, modeled after the Soviet Union.

Political Change

The establishment of the People's Republic of China under the leadership of the Chinese Communist Party was a radical change for China as Mao was determined to remake China through mass campaigns. Mao Zedong Thought articulated that the communist revolutionary force was the peasants, but there was still a need for the Lenin-inspired party vanguard to lead them. Mao relied on the **mass line** as a technique to ensure that party cadres were effectively leading the people. The phrase "from the masses, to the masses" reflects the role of the party to listen to the peasants "speak bitterness," come up with a solution, and communicate it to the masses as proper "red" or revolutionary thought.

One of the first mass campaigns was that of land reform. The peasants were encouraged to overthrow and kill the landowners. Next came the campaign to suppress counterrevolutionaries resulting in mass trials and executions. The **Hundred Flowers Campaign** in 1956 encouraged people to offer criticism to the Party so that it could improve but was quickly followed by an anti-rightist movement to get rid of the critics. The most disastrous mass campaign, however, was the **Great Proletarian Cultural Revolution** of 1966–76. Mao's goal was to restore the revolutionary spirit to the CCP by ridding it of bourgeoisie capitalism. Part of this campaign was to rid China of "old customs, old culture, old habits, and old ideas." Young student **Red Guards** were encouraged to "bombard the command post" and take down any "experts" such as teachers, party leaders, or professionals, along with destroying ancient artifacts, paintings, and books. It is estimated that more than a million people were killed, and a whole generation lost access to education. When the Red Guards became too difficult to control, Mao instituted a "Down to the Countryside Movement" to have the students be sent to the countryside to be reeducated by the peasants. The Cultural Revolution did not end until Mao's death in 1976.

Most modern mass campaigns have focused on economic reforms, but anti-corruption efforts are still pervasive. Whether party cadres are forced into ideology classes or disciplined by the CCP's own **Central Commission for Discipline Inspection (CCDI)**, party leaders know that charges of corruption damage the image of the CCP. There has been no inclination by the party, however, to use the regular court system for party members even though that would strengthen rule of law. In fact, in October 2017, President Xi Jinping oversaw the creation of a new **National Supervision Commission** that expanded the CCDI's powers over any state employee, not just party members. This gives the party more power over lower-level officials than it previously had and expands enforcement efforts by having the party and state work together. Already President Xi has overseen one of the most dramatic anti-corruption campaigns ever as high-ranking government officials, party leaders, and generals have been sent to jail. Combined with increased restrictions on NGOs and social media, China is becoming more politically authoritarian.

Economic Change

At the beginning of the People's Republic of China, Mao relied heavily on suggestions about economic development from the Soviet Union. The USSR under Stalin had focused on industrialization and collectivization of farms to boost economic growth using a command economy managed by five-year plans. Mao's first five-year plan concentrated on eliminating private property in the countryside and building farming cooperatives. By 1958, Mao was ready to launch the **Great Leap Forward**, his plan to catch China up to the West. Rural peasants were forced onto large communal farms and given unrealistic grain targets. The state then commandeered the grain that was produced, and the people were left to starve. Those who resisted were often killed. Recent estimates are that 45 million people died between 1958 and 1962. The party quietly allowed the de-collectivization of the communes back to village committees. Any economic recovery, however, was eliminated during the height of the Cultural Revolution, which saw the shutdown of schools, hospitals, and workplaces. Finally, with the death of Mao in 1976, China was ready for a different kind of economic reform.

Deng Xiaoping announced his **Reform and Opening Up** program, also known as **Socialism with Chinese Characteristics** in 1978. The program was rolled out gradually, as Deng put it, "crossing the river by feeling the stones." It was also a switch in emphasis for the CCP. In the classic "red" versus "expert" debate between ideological factions in the party, Deng preferred a reliance on technical expertise.

Components of Deng's reforms included:

REFORM	ACTION	RESULT
Household-Responsibility System	Decollectivize agriculture into private plots	Farmers produce more because of the incentive to sell the extra
Special Economic Zones (SEZs)	Open certain areas along the coast to foreign direct investment	Rapid increase in private firms and investment
Privatization of State-Owned Enterprises (SOEs)	Sell off companies	Large layoffs of workers = social unrest
Township and Village Enterprises (TVEs)	Allow local governments to sponsor firms	Increase in economic growth

Overall the result of these policies, combined with an increase in contract law and the reopening of the stock market in Shanghai, has led to impressive economic growth, averaging 10 percent from 1978 to 2014. It is projected that the size of the Chinese economy will surpass that of the United States. All incomes, urban and rural, rose, although urban incomes rose at a much faster rate. In addition, the gap between rich and poor rose, with a GINI index of .45, which is like that of the United States. Under Presidents Jiang and Hu,

China continued to privatize some firms and emphasize exports. To join the World Trade Organization (WTO), reforms were made to banking laws and other services.

President Xi has worked to assert CCP control over much of Chinese society, but he has ambitious plans for China's future on the world stage. The best example of this is his **Belt and Road Initiative (BRI)**, which was enshrined in the party's constitution in October of 2017. Designed to be a modern Silk Road, the plan involves building land and sea transport routes to 60 countries, from Europe to Africa. The Northern Belt will go to Russia and Europe. The Central Belt will go through Asia to the Mediterranean and the South Belt to Pakistan and the Indian Ocean. Most of this will be financed by the new **Asian Infrastructure Investment Bank** started by China as an alternative to the UN's World Bank and IMF. Already freight trains make the journey from the Chinese port city of Yiwu to London, England. The 8,000-mile journey goes through China, Kazakhstan, Russia, Belarus, Poland, Germany, Belgium, and France in 18 days.

Public Policy

Despite being a one-party state, policymaking in China is far from quick and efficient. There are many factions within the party itself and many layers of party committees and levels of government offices to coordinate. Even at the higher levels of the party, where the overlap with government offices is most obvious, there is always conflict over policy formulation and implementation. The most significant policymaking bodies are the **leading small groups** of the CCP. These panels are composed of various leaders and experts who tackle issues from economic reform to propaganda. Often the party adopts the policy suggested by the leading group, leaving the state ministry to implement it. Just recently, President Xi has created two more groups, which he plans to chair. These are the "Leading Small Group for the Comprehensive Deepening of Reform" and the "National Security Commission." These policy groups allow the party's Secretariat to conduct the daily affairs of the party, as well as allowing President Xi to put his allies in positions of importance. In addition, the CCP faces the difficulty of getting its policies followed across the country. Party officials and local officials must work together on issues, but power is fragmented, and confusion occurs about who to be responsive to and when. One official explained that it is like "they have too many mothers-in-law." President Xi is reinforcing that the CCP is the main authority with his creation of the National Supervision Commission. Because the CCDI is the most feared body in China, local officials are quicker to toe the party line or face detention by the party.

Population Growth Policy

After the formation of the PRC, Mao's official policy was to encourage families to have more children to provide workers. After the Great Leap Forward and Cultural Revolution, however, concerns over feeding the population were prominent. In addition, Deng Xiaoping knew that a fast-growing population would slow economic growth in that GDP per capita would not rise as quickly. So in 1979, the **One-Child Policy** was enacted, limiting Han couples to just one child or they would face penalties. Ethnic minorities were not limited under this policy because of their small numbers. Exceptions were also made for rural families if the first child was not a son. Local administration of this policy widely varied, with some officials forcing women to have abortions and sterilization, while other families faced no access to health care or schooling for a second child. The results were dramatic as the population growth rate dropped significantly. Unintended consequences of the policy were a gender imbalance because of families preferring sons, often leading to abortions or infanticide, and an aging population with fewer children to take care of the elderly.

These problems led to an easing of the policy in 2015 to allow families to have two children. The government hoped that this policy would lead to an increase in births of 20 million, but the growth was only 8 percent or 18 million, resulting in a birth rate that is still below replacement levels. Part of this dynamic is that urban couples have already adapted to a one-child culture given the expense of raising a child. In addition, a more educated, urban, female workforce tends to have less children anyway. Parents cite a lack of affordable housing, daycare, and parental leave as obstacles to having more children. Some even blame urban air pollution. Although some scholars recommend lifting all limits on family size, in 2021 the government formally revised the law to allow couples to have up to three children and pledged to provide more support for parental leave and childcare.

Environmental Policy

President Xi reaffirmed his commitment to green development in his speech to the 19th National Party Congress in October of 2017. He stated that "taking a driving seat in international cooperation, China has become an important participant, contributor, and torchbearer in the global endeavor for ecological civilization." To accomplish this, Xi explained that "we must realize that lucid waters and lush mountains are invaluable assets . . . we must pursue a **model of sustainable development** featuring increased production, higher living standards, and healthy ecosystems. We must continue the **Beautiful China Initiative** to create good working and living environments for our people and play our part in ensuring global ecological security."

The reason for so much emphasis on the environment is that China has significant problems from its rapid industrialization programs. Most major cities are shrouded in smog, especially in the wintertime, and activists estimate that more than two-thirds of the rivers are too toxic for even agricultural use. This has led to an increase in social unrest. Many "mass incidents" are aimed at local polluters. The government responded with the creation of a new Ministry of Environment, but local officials remained targeted on production quotas rather than pollution limits. President Xi hopes that by increasing the reach of the Discipline Committee to all state officials, he can force compliance with environmental policy. In addition, Chinese state media focuses on positive environment stories, often covering examples of national officials forcing local authorities to shut down polluting factories. Xi has also instituted a "river chief system" mandating that local officials are responsible for the water quality in their region. A national park system is being piloted. Yet critics are skeptical about real change as the Chinese government censors documentaries like *Under the Dome* and *Plastic China* and resists infiltration of foreign NGOs with environmental mandates. This means that the average person in China has very little understanding of the scope of the problem, except when their workplace is shut down for polluting, or their car driving is restricted for some international event like the Olympics or G-20 Economic Summit. Many hope that an increased focus in schools will help educate children and their families about the need to recycle and conserve.

Covid-19

After initially trying to cover up reports of a new virus outbreak in Wuhan, Chinese officials moved to lock down the city in January 2020. Strict travel protocols, aggressive testing measures, and quarantine centers were used throughout the country to control outbreaks. By effectively controlling the virus, President Xi and the CCP are touting the virtues of a one-party state in handling the crisis, and there is a sense of national pride in how Chinese society endured the lockdowns.

❯ Review Questions

Multiple Choice

1. What does Mao Zedong Thought add to Marxism-Leninism?
   (A) The concept of class struggle
   (B) The concept of a party vanguard
   (C) The concept of the inevitability of revolution
   (D) The concept of peasants as the revolutionary force

2. Who did the PLA overthrow in the Chinese Revolution of 1949?
   (A) The Japanese
   (B) The Qing Emperor
   (C) The Kuomintang
   (D) The Soviet Union

3. Which of the following demographics about China is correct?
   (A) China's population of 1.4 billion is the largest in the world.
   (B) China's GDP per capita of $8,123 is the second largest in the world.
   (C) China's population is 75 percent Han Chinese.
   (D) China's population has a median age of 18.

4. Deng Xiaoping's Reform and Opening Up policy included which of the following?
   (A) Creation of special economic zones (SEZs)
   (B) Decreasing the amount of foreign direct investment
   (C) Increasing the nationalization of private industries
   (D) Dismantling of Town and Village Enterprises (TVEs)

5. The Chinese policy "One country, two systems" refers to:
   (A) allowing Hong Kong and Macau to retain independent legal systems and police forces
   (B) allowing ethnic minorities to live in autonomous zones
   (C) utilizing a dual party-state model to govern the country
   (D) allowing Tibetans to continue to practice the Buddhist faith

6. Which institution has the most formal authority in the Chinese system?
   (A) Central Committee of the CCP
   (B) National People's Congress of the PRC
   (C) Standing Committee of the NPC
   (D) President of PRC

7. Nomenklatura is:
   (A) a personal connection to a mentor
   (B) the household responsibility system
   (C) the process of appealing for justice
   (D) the recruitment system used by the CCP

8. Which of the following country groups use a presidential system of government?
   (A) China, Russia, Mexico
   (B) Russia, Mexico, Nigeria
   (C) Mexico, Nigeria, Great Britain
   (D) China, Iran, Nigeria

9. Which of the following mass campaigns was led by the Red Guards bombarding the command post?
   (A) Great Leap Forward
   (B) Hundred Flowers Campaign
   (C) Cultural Revolution
   (D) Reform and Opening Up

10. Which of the following Chinese political institutions is the most powerful?
    (A) State Council of the PRC
    (B) Standing Committee of the NPC
    (C) Standing Committee of the Politburo
    (D) Central Committee of the CCP

Free Response

1. (A) Define economic development.
   (B) Describe why governments pursue economic development policies.
   (C) Explain why the economic development policies in (B) often lead to environmental problems.
   (D) Explain how states implement sustainable development policies.

2. Use the graph to complete your answer.

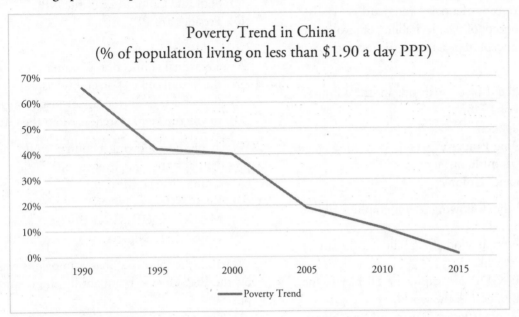

Poverty Trend in China
(% of population living on less than $1.90 a day PPP)

Source: World Bank

   (A) Using the data in the graph, identify the percentage of the Chinese population living on less than $1.90 a day in 2008.
   (B) Using the data in the graph, describe a trend in the percentage of the Chinese population living in poverty since 1990.
   (C) Define economic liberalization.
   (E) Explain how the adoption of economic liberalization policies in China reduced poverty in China.
   (D) Explain why authoritarian regimes adopt economic liberalization policies while resisting political liberalization.

3. Compare how states employ party systems within their political systems in two different AP Comparative Government and Politics course countries. In your response, you should do the following:
   (A) Describe the difference between a one-party system and a dominant party system.
   (B) Describe how two different authoritarian AP Comparative Government and Politics course countries established a one-party system or a dominant party system.
   (C) Explain how the decision to maintain a one-party system or a dominant party system in the two different AP Comparative Government and Politics course countries described in (B) strengthened the authoritarian regime in that country.

4. Develop an argument as to whether authoritarian regimes should use a merit-based or a patronage system to staff the bureaucracy of a state.

   Use one or more of the following course concepts in your answer.
   • Cooption
   • Coercion
   • Legitimacy

In your response, you should do the following:
- Respond to the prompt with a defensible claim or thesis that establishes a line of reasoning using one or more of the provided course concepts.
- Support your claim with at least TWO pieces of specific and relevant evidence from one or more course countries. This evidence should be relevant to one or more of the provided course countries.
- Use reasoning to explain why your evidence supports your claim or thesis, using one or more of the provided course concepts.
- Respond to an opposing or alternate perspective, using refutation, concession, or rebuttal.

〉 Answers and Explanations

Multiple Choice

1. **D.** The most significant difference between Mao Zedong Thought and Marxism-Leninism is Mao's concept of the peasants as a revolutionary force. Marx thought that because of class struggle, industrial workers would lead the inevitable revolution. Lenin decided to give history a nudge and use a party vanguard to lead the peasants to revolution with democratic centralism to guide the dictatorship of the proletariat.

2. **C.** The People's Liberation Army fought the Kuomintang or Nationalists following World War II. Both armies had presented a united front to fight the Japanese. The Qing Emperor had been overthrown in the Xinhai Revolution of 1911.

3. **A.** China has the largest population in the world, followed by India. Its overall GDP is the second largest in the world, but its GDP per capita marks it as a middle-income country. The Chinese population is 92 percent Han and has a median age of 37. Although China is officially atheist, 18 percent of the population identifies as Buddhist, 5 percent Christian, 2 percent Muslim, and 22 percent folk religion.

4. **A.** Deng's Reform and Opening Up policy was about economic liberalization. This meant that state-owned firms would have been privatized. The creation of SEZs, TVEs and the addition of foreign direct investment are consistent with the policy.

5. **A.** The "One country, two systems" model was adopted to accommodate the former British colony of Hong Kong and the Portuguese colony of Macau.

6. **B.** According to the Chinese constitution, the NPC is the most powerful body in the PRC as it selects the executive and judicial branches. Because it is such a large body that only meets for two weeks a year, it is not the real source of power in the political system.

7. **D.** *Nomenklatura* is a term used by the CPSU and adopted by the CCP to describe the recruitment system for cadres. The nomenklatura is a list of senior party positions used to incentivize party members.

8. **B.** A presidential system of government requires separate elections for president and the legislature as occurs in Russia, Mexico, and Nigeria, In China the legislature formally selects the head of state and the head of government. In Great Britain, the legislature formally selects the head of government.

9. **C.** The Cultural Revolution was the mass campaign led by the Red Guards to destroy the expert class in China. The Great Leap Forward was Mao's attempt to rapidly industrialize China. Both the Hundred Flowers Campaign and the Democracy Wall were periods of criticism of the CCP. Reform and Opening Up was the name given to Deng's economic plan.

10. **C.** The most powerful political institution in China is the Standing Committee of the Politburo. These seven men are the premier elite of the CCP. Both the Politburo and State Council and the Central Committee and Standing Committee of the NPC are further down the party-state hierarchy.

Free Response

1. (4 points possible)
   (A) Economic development is the process of moving more of a population in a state into more industrialized and service-level occupations. For example, China predominately had an agricultural economy with most of the population working as farmers, until Deng's policies moved more individuals into manufacturing jobs. (1 point)
   (B) Governments pursue economic development policies to boost economic growth and raise a country's standard of living. Economic success helps support the legitimacy of the regime. People are more likely to accept governmental authority when the economy is doing well. (1 point).
   (C) Rapid industrialization is the most common way for a state to pursue economic development. This often relies on coal-burning plants and the use of fossil fuels for energy. Pollution is a negative externality that is ignored in the quest for increased capacity. For example, in China, Deng's Reform and Opening Up policy caused substantial air and water pollution. (1 point)
   (D) States implement sustainable development policies by prioritizing them and ensuring that they are enforced. In China, President Xi has created a "Beautiful China" initiative to clean up waters and limit smog. A ministry of environment has been created to enforce pollution standards and shut down firms that do not comply with the regulations. (1 point)

2. (5 points possible)
   (A) Approximately 15% of the Chinese population was living on less than $1.90 a day in 2008. (1 point)
   (B) The percentage of the Chinese population living in poverty has declined since 1990, from a high of 66% in 1990 to less than 1% in 2015. (1 point)
   (C) Economic liberalization is the process of moving an economy to a free market. This is accomplished by reducing tariffs, privatizing state-owned industries, and promoting free trade. (1 point)
   (D) The adoption of economic liberalization policies by the Chinese government led to sustained rates of economic growth. Increased output meant more jobs and wages for many people, thus decreasing the percent of the population earning less than $1.90 a day. (1 point)
   (E) Authoritarian regimes, like China, do not want to cede political control to the people and risk losing power, so they do not engage in political liberalization policies such as increasing the freedom of expression or suffrage. But authoritarian regimes need the legitimacy of a growing economy to provide jobs and wages to their citizens. Economic liberalization policies lead to rapid economic growth and a rising standard of living, which placates the people facing political restrictions. (1 point)

3. (5 points possible)
   (A) The difference between a one-party system and a dominant party system is the number of parties that can successfully participate politically. In a one-party state, by law only one party can govern. Whereas in a dominant party system, several parties can participate in the political process, but the system is rigged to ensure that only the dominant party governs. (1 point)
   (B) China is a one-party state where only the CCP can govern. Although several other parties exist because of their formation before the Chinese Revolution, they do not exert any political power. The formation of new political parties is forbidden. Limited elections are controlled by the CCP. (1 point) Russia is a state with a dominant party system. Putin's United Russia Party wins elections by controlling ballot access and intimidation, but other parties can form and compete in elections. These parties include the Communist Party of the Russian Federation and the Liberal Democrats. These other parties win seats in the legislature but not enough to be close to a ruling majority. (1 point)
   (C) Authoritarian regimes restrict the political process so that they do not lose power. But they also must be legitimate so that the people will accept their authority. The Chinese CCP employs the principle of democratic centralism to justify the guiding role of the party over the government. A one-party state is legitimized with the mass line. The party speaks for the people. Since the 1949 Chinese Revolution, the CCP has used the one-party system to establish and maintain its control over China.

(1 point) Putin's challenge in consolidating authoritarian control in Russia was that the Soviet Union's one-party state under the CPSU had been overthrown by the Russian people. Consequently, the creation of a dominant party system under United Russia was a more legitimate strategy to strengthen an authoritarian regime. By allowing other parties to compete in elections, like the CPRF for example, Putin could allow the façade of electoral competition to make the dominance of United Russia more palatable. By manipulating election systems and intimidation, United Russia is clearly the dominant party in Russia, and its existence has strengthened Putin's authoritarian regime. (1 point)

4. (5 points possible)

The most important goal of an authoritarian regime is to remain in power. This requires a bureaucracy that is loyal to the regime. Consequently, authoritarian regimes should use a patronage system to staff its bureaucracy because then the political leaders can be assured that the unelected government officials are loyal to the ruling government. This loyalty is assured because bureaucrats are appointed to their positions primarily for their relationship with the regime leaders as opposed to a merit-based system where unelected officials are selected for their expertise in an area and not their political affiliation. (1 point)

The CCP uses an elaborate system of nomenklatura to staff many high-level bureaucratic positions in the Chinese government. Nomenklatura is a recruitment strategy for the CCP. Party members are ranked on a list of seniority and matched with appropriate-level jobs. Getting a position with more power requires that a party member be loyal to the party in order to move up the bureaucratic ladder. This cooption strategy is successful because it motivates party members to support the regime to further their own ambitions. (1 point)

In addition, a loyal bureaucracy is more likely to follow the dictates of the authoritarian regime without question. To remain in power oftentimes requires coercion or a forceful response to dissent. A patronage-based system of appointed government officials, whose power comes from regime leaders, is more likely to enforce unpopular policies. In China, for example, Chinese government officials have implemented coercive policies such as the establishment of reeducation camps for Uighurs. These government officials are more worried about being disciplined by the CCP than they are about violating civil rights. (1 point)

All authoritarian regimes must get the power to govern from something other than the people. China's system of democratic centralism is structured to ensure that the CCP remains in power. The party's legitimacy to govern is based on its ability to staff the enormous Chinese bureaucracy. Through nomenklatura, the CCP's system of patronage is then used to assert the authority of the government in coercive actions against dissent. (1 point)

On the other hand, because the unelected officials of a country's bureaucracy are often the members of a regime that the people in a country come in contact with the most, it could be argued that the political leaders of any regime would want these appointed individuals to be able to do the job with professionalism. A merit-based system, therefore, where bureaucrats are selected for their skills as opposed to their loyalty would seem the obvious choice for even an authoritarian government to ensure that it could deliver needed government services. Unfortunately, however, most often authoritarian regimes prioritize loyalty to maintain power. (1 point)

❯ Rapid Review

- The People's Republic of China (China) is an authoritarian, one-party state.
- China has the oldest continuous civilization in the world along with the world's largest population (92 percent of its people identify as Han Chinese). Political culture is strongly nationalistic, and social cleavages exist with ethnic minorities such as the Uighurs.
- China is a unitary government with many territorial challenges like Hong and Taiwan.
- China is governed by the Chinese Communist Party (CCP), which won control of the country from the Kuomintang or Nationalist Party during the Revolution (1945–1949).
- Mao Zedong was the charismatic leader of the CCP who adapted Marxist-Leninist philosophy to enshrine the peasants as the revolutionary force. He adopted the Soviet model of democratic centralism in creating the current Chinese political system.
- The CCP is organized in a hierarchical manner in tandem to state government offices, with considerable overlap between the members of the highest party organizations and government offices. President Xi Jinping epitomizes this system by holding the highest party position (General Secretary of the CCP), along with the highest political position (President of the PRC) and military position (Chairman of the Central Military Commission).
- The 1982 constitution states that the National People's Congress (NPC) is "the highest organ of state power." Therefore, formally, the NPC selects the president and approves his selection of the premier and State Council (cabinet). In reality, the NPC approves the decisions already made by the powerful members of the CCP's Politburo.
- The CCP today has 88 million members and maintains an elaborate system of recruitment. Since 2001, entrepreneurs have been allowed to join the party. Party members are managed through a system of nomenklatura (party list of positions).
- The People's Liberation Army (PLA) has always been an integral part of the CCP's power base. The People's Armed Police Force is used as a domestic coercive force.
- After the destruction of Mao's Cultural Revolution (1966–1976), Deng Xiaoping's Reform and Opening Up program in 1978 led to a gradual reshaping of the Chinese economy from a command system to one based more on market principles. Policies such as the creation of special economic zones for foreign direct investment and the privatization of some state-owned enterprises resulted in rapid economic growth and development.
- To support this growth, laws protecting private property and contracts needed to be enacted along with judicial reform to professionalize judges without losing party control.
- Rapid growth has led to income inequality between urban centers and rural regions of China. Despite policies to improve rural conditions, mass incidents regularly occur.
- Civil society is constrained in China. The media is heavily regulated, and officials censor the Internet. Interest group formation is restricted, and social movements are repressed.
- Rapid industrialization has created significant environmental problems like air and water pollution. Sustainable development goals include the use of more green technology.

CHAPTER 15

Mexico

IN THIS CHAPTER

Summary: Mexico is a country of contrasts. Formerly authoritarian, it is now an electoral democracy. At one time a state with nationalized industries and a high tariff wall, it now has one of the most open economies in the world. Consequently, to study Mexico in the context of the AP Comparative Government and Politics course is to study both political and economic transitions from a Spanish colony to a member of the G20. Challenges still face Mexico, however, as high levels of poverty, corruption, and drug-related violence plague policymakers as they seek to further consolidate Mexico's political and economic liberalization reforms.

Key Terms

Amerindian
Article 27
camarilla
Chamber of Deputies
clientelism
Confederation of Mexican
　Workers (CTM)
Confederation of Popular
　Organizations (CNOP)
corporatist system
democradura
direct plurality vote
ejido
el dedazo
Federal Electoral Institute
　(IFE)

foreign direct investment
　(FDI)
gender parity law
hacienda
import-substitution
　industrialization (ISI)
Institutional Revolutionary
　Party (PRI)
maquiladora
mestizo
Mexican Revolution of 1910
National Action Party
　(PAN)
National Confederation of
　Popular Organizations
　(CNOP)

National Congress
National Electoral Institute
　(INE)
National Indigenous
　Congress
National Liberation Army
　(EZLN)
National Peasant
　Confederation (CNC)
National Regeneration
　Movement (MORENA)
non-reelection principle
North American Free Trade
　Agreement (NAFTA)
Pact for Mexico

Party for the Democratic
  Revolution (PRD)
PEMEX
Porfiriato
primary system
Prospera
sexenio

structural adjustment
  programs
  (SAPs)
Televisa
Telmex
Tlatelolco massacre

United States Mexico
  Canada Agreement
  (USMCA)
War on Drugs
Yo Soy 132
Zapatistas

Mexico as a Case Study

As you study Mexico, pay careful attention to the discussion of the following concepts as they are the most frequently used in comparing Mexico with other countries on the AP Comparative Government and Politics exam.

CONCEPT	POSSIBLE COMPARISONS/USEFUL EXAMPLES
Colonial legacy	Nigeria
Revolution	Russia, China, Iran
Dominant party	United Russia
Mixed election system	Advantages/disadvantages of SMD and PR
Non-reelection principle	Term limits
Political liberalization	Democratic dictatorship
Economic development	ISI and SAP strategies
State-controlled oil sector	Russia, Iran, Nigeria
Ethnic conflict	Government responses
Anticlerical tendencies	Religious legitimacy

Sovereignty, Authority, and Power

The State

Mexico has had a long and tumultuous history. A country ruled by emperors and presidents, Mexico was colonized by Spain in 1519. The Spanish retained control of the former Aztec Empire through an elaborate caste system and land division, called the encomienda. After declaring independence in 1821, Mexico endured a chaotic 50 years with 52 different presidents. Santa Ana alone was president 11 times. Following the temporary reign of French-installed Emperor Maximilian, Mexico next endured the 34-year Porfiriato of President Diaz, who ruthlessly attempted to modernize the economy and was finally driven from power by the Revolution of 1910. Seven years of conflict followed as military generals and campesinos like Emiliano Zapata fought for control. The formation of a constitution in 1917, however, failed to stop the assassination of revolutionary leaders. Finally, the bloodshed led political elites to agree to a power-sharing agreement around the formation of a political party, known today as the Institutional Revolutionary Party (PRI) in 1929. The PRI would control Mexico as a dominant party until 2000. Your study of the Mexican state should focus on how the PRI maintained its dominant party status for 70 years and then lost it in 2000 as Mexico became an electoral democracy.

The Nation

A country with 129 million people, the Mexican population reflects both its indigenous and Spanish past. The largest percentage of the population are **mestizo** at 62 percent, which is a mix of indigenous and Spanish heritage. Thirty percent of the population still identifies as **Amerindian**, concentrated in the southern, rural region of the country. Eighty-three percent of the country is Catholic as Church missionaries were instrumental in helping the Spanish government control the colony. Eighty percent of Mexicans live in urban areas, with 25 percent of the population living in Mexico City. The result is a coinciding cleavage between an urbanized, educated middle class and a poor, rural, indigenous one.

Legitimacy

The Constitution of 1917 is the source of rational-legal legitimacy in Mexico. As a product of the Mexican Revolution, its non-reelection principle and emphasis on national land rights, along with its anticlerical provisions, still resonate with Mexicans today.

Reverence for the Revolution is reflected in how the political parties try to claim their allegiance to its goals. The **Institutional Revolutionary Party**, or **PRI**, has the strongest ties given its longevity and its association with the national colors of red, white, and green. The **Party of the Democratic Revolution**, or **PRD**, was formed by former *priístas* in 1988 who felt that the PRI had strayed from its revolutionary roots. The **National Action Party**, or **PAN**, was founded in 1939 as an opposition to the extremes of the Revolution, including those seen as anti–property rights or anticlerical. Part of the PAN's success has been its willingness to associate itself with the image of Our Lady of Guadalupe, the Catholic patron saint of the Americas, thereby absorbing some traditional legitimacy. In addition, revolutionary heroes such as Emiliano Zapata still resonate today as is seen with the name of the Zapatistas of Chiapas.

Regime

Until 2000, Mexico was an authoritarian state governed by a dominant party. Known today as the PRI, the party was established in 1929 by Plutarco Calles to establish a presidential succession process without all the bloodshed that had characterized leadership battles since 1910. Often referred to as a *democradura*, or democratic dictatorship, the PRI had the trappings of democracy with multiple parties allowed to compete for places in the legislature, an independent press not owned by the government, and vibrant civil society complete with trade unions and interest groups. On closer examination, however, it was obvious to the Mexican people that no party except the PRI would control the presidency, the legislature, and the governorships, that the media was controlled through revenues from the PRI, and that the corporatist arrangement with trade unions and interest groups was to maintain support for the PRI.

The election of 2000 was a watershed moment for Mexico. For the first time, the PRI candidate lost the presidency to PAN candidate, Vicente Fox. Obviously, the groundwork for this historic win was laid in the 1980s, but Mexico has maintained fair, competitive elections since that date. Even the return of the PRI to the presidency in 2014 has not caused a regression. The current Mexican regime, therefore, can be characterized as an electoral democracy.

Problems remain in Mexico, however, particularly with press freedom. Journalists face deadly violence from the drug cartels that dominate Mexico, and the state's failure to protect them has resulted in a "Not Free" Press Freedom rating from Freedom House.

Freedom House: Partly Free (political rights: 27/40, civil liberties: 34/60)

Economist Intelligence Unit Democracy Index: Hybrid 5.57 (Hybrid falls between flawed democracy and authoritarian.)

Economic Systems

Mexico has a mixed economy with elements of both market and command economies. Particularly since the 1980s when presidents de la Madrid and Salinas pursued **structural adjustment programs (SAPs)** of economic liberalization, Mexico has become a global player in manufacturing. Joining the NAFTA treaty with Canada and the United States opened Mexico to trade opportunities as **maquiladoras**, factories, were built in northern Mexico to take advantage of free trade. Unfortunately, however, although these trade policies have led to economic growth and rising GDP per capita, they have also widened the gap between rich and poor. This large gap in income equality is measured with a .48 GINI index.

In addition, the Mexican government also retains ownership of industries, most prominently the oil giant **PEMEX**. Because of constitutional protections of natural resources, PEMEX remains state-owned and is notoriously inefficient. Recently, however, although President Peña Nieto was able to get legislation passed to allow some foreign direct investment in the industry with hopes of improving the sector, President Lopez Obrador was elected on a platform to restrict such joint ventures.

Political Culture and Socialization

Mexican political culture is strongly nationalistic with proud references to the Mexican Revolution. It is a very traditional society with an element of machismo. As a majority Catholic country, many Mexicans tend to be socially conservative. Indigenous traditions are also a powerful element of political culture, where politicians will refer to themselves as Amerindian or indigenous to show solidarity.

Family is the most important agent of socialization in Mexico as traditional family ties are strongly supported. The government maintains an intrinsic role in socialization through control of textbooks in schools. Increasingly, however, social media may be supplanting the role of established institutions like the Catholic Church as young people acclimate quickly to a globalized world.

Political Institutions

Constitution

Mexico has had several constitutions, starting with one following independence from Spain in 1821. The Constitution of 1917, however, is the foundation of the modern political system and shares many of the same elements as the U.S. Constitution. Interestingly, Mexico moved from an authoritarian regime to a democratic regime without writing a new constitution. This is a classic example of the difference between a country having a constitution and being a constitutional government. During the 71-year reign of the PRI, the Madisonian model elements of separation of powers, checks and balances, and federalism did not limit the arbitrary power of the government. It was only after the stolen presidential election of 1988 that the PRI was pressured to introduce reforms like the independent Federal Election Institute to make elections fair and competitive.

Levels of Government

Mexico is a federal state. Consisting of 32 states, the constitution stipulates that sovereignty is shared between the two levels of government. During the 71-year reign of the PRI, the president of Mexico was so powerful that the individual states were merely prizes for his most loyal supporters. Truly competitive elections have changed that relationship. In fact, the PRI's weakness was first exposed when PAN candidates won governorships in 1989. Now Mexico's governors tend to reflect the regional strength of a political party with the

PAN winning northern states and the PRI southern states, with the PRD capturing Mexico City. The dominance of the MORENA party since the 2018 election cycle, however, is challenging the electoral status and relevance of the PRI, PAN, and PRD.

Although the governors' elections are more competitive and powers over utilities and education have been devolved to municipalities, Mexico's federal states are still very dependent upon the national government for revenue. The situation is better than it was when the PRI president used the national treasury to reward supporters, but the difficulty that states have in raising their own revenue still puts them in an inferior power relationship with the national government. Recent reforms have seen national revenue transfers to the states increase from 25 percent to 38 percent, but fiscal reform is still needed.

At the supranational level, Mexico is a member of the World Trade Organization, WTO.

President

Mexico has a presidential system of government. During the years that the PRI was the dominant party in Mexico, it was the president who controlled the party apparatus with the power to appoint members of his **camarilla**, or patron-client network, to be the party candidates for judicial, legislative, and gubernatorial seats. The **non-reelection principle**, which limits a Mexican president to one term, meant that everyone frequently needed a new job, and the Mexican president had the power to nominate candidates and appoint bureaucrats, along with control of the national government budget to dispense funds to his supporters through grants and contracts.

One of the most important powers that a PRI president had, however, was the power to appoint his successor. Called *el dedazo*, presidents were able to command the loyalty of their supporters by being able to offer the prospect of being handed the most powerful position in Mexico. So it was a significant reform when President Zedillo refused to use the *dedazo* in 2000 to select a successor. For that election, the PRI held its first presidential primary, further solidifying the transition to democracy. Zedillo also significantly reformed the judicial appointment process by replacing the informal tradition of judges resigning their lifetime seats with each presidential election to a fixed 15-year term, with the president selecting judges from a list prepared by a nonpartisan commission. This helped strengthen the independence of the judiciary, another important democratic step.

Although the Mexican presidency has lost some of its PRI-associated powers, it still is the most powerful institution in the political system. Limited to one 6-year term, called the *sexenio*, Mexican presidents have extensive powers.

POWERS OF THE PRESIDENT	CHECKS
• Propose legislation/budget	
• Commander in chief	
• Pardon	
• Appoint cabinet, ambassadors	• Confirmed by Senate
• Appoint judges from list	• Confirmed by Senate
• Sign/veto bills	• Legislature can override with 2/3 vote
• Make treaties	• Ratified by Senate

Legislature

The **National Congress** of Mexico is a symmetrical bicameral legislature. The Senate, or upper house, is designed to represent the Mexican states with 128 members. Each of the 32 states has 3 senators in addition to 32 proportional seats. The **Chamber of Deputies**, or lower house, has 500 members based on population, with the 300 single-member district seats divided among the states and 200 proportional seats. The senators serve six-year terms, while the deputies serve three-year terms. The 2018 elections were be the first ones that members of the National Assembly could stand for reelection. Now senators are be able to serve two terms and deputies four terms.

When the PRI was the dominant party in Mexico, the legislature simply existed to serve the president. As former President Fox recalls in his autobiography, "Until 2000 the Mexican Congress was not so much a legislative body as it was a lifestyle. Congressmen had no power; they just rubber-stamped the decisions of the executive, . . . to discuss a bill's flaws would have been heresy, and anyway it would have made them late for their three-tequila lunches." Unfortunately for Fox, however, the Mexican legislature awoke during his presidency to defeat much of his legislative agenda. Gridlock between Mexican presidents and the legislature continued through the Calderon administration as well. President Peña Nieto fared better because of a pre-election agreement between the main three parties on a legislative agenda to improve the Mexican economy.

JOINT LEGISLATIVE POWERS	ONLY CHAMBER OF DEPUTIES POWERS	ONLY SENATE POWERS
• Representation	• Introduce revenue bills	• Impeachment trial
• Pass legislation	• Impeach	• Confirm appointments
• Pass the budget	• Verify outcomes of elections	• Ratify treaties
• Legislative oversight		

Bureaucracy

Historically, the Mexican bureaucracy has been viewed as corrupt and inefficient. As part of the PRI's elaborate patron-client network, a president's camarillo would expect jobs and government contracts in return for their electoral support. Because of the non-reelection principle, political elites always needed new jobs, and a cabinet position would provide opportunities for personal enrichment, jobs, and government contracts for that leader's supporters. As the economy was liberalized and more state-run companies became privatized, there were fewer jobs for supporters and less government revenue to share, helping to lessen the power of the PRI.

Since 2000, the Mexican bureaucracy has not completely recovered from its earlier traditions. Although more bureaucrats obtain jobs through a merit process based on expertise, there are still problem areas. Security forces, for example, are under incredible stress from the fight with the drug cartels, and often succumb to pressure from drug lords to cooperate. The government is also involved in perennial battles with the teacher's union over pay and benefits. In addition, slow government response to earthquakes and hurricanes has angered the public.

Military and Other Coercive Institutions

The Mexican military has a long history of mixed results. Certainly, the loss of an enormous amount of territory to the United States in the Mexican-American War and the establishment of the French-installed Emperor Maximilian were not high points in Mexican military history. But the troops responded under General Juárez to regain control of the government and later were used effectively to enforce the Porfiriato of President

Diaz. The Mexican Revolution, however, was in many ways a series of coups between military generals, both traditional forces and the indigenous followers of Emiliano Zapata and Pancho Villa. The power-sharing agreement among political elites that formed the PRI finally moved the troops back to the barracks, where they have remained under civilian control.

Currently, the Mexican military is in one of its low points. Used against the indigenous EZLN army of the **Zapatistas** in 1994, they were never able to eradicate the rebels from Chiapas where they remain to this day in gated compounds. In 2006, President Calderon decided on a military response to drive the drug cartels out of their area of control in northern Mexico, but the troops have been ineffective at stopping the violence. Even working in conjunction with U.S. law enforcement has not been able to reduce the threat to the area.

Leadership and Elite Recruitment

When the PRI was the dominant party in Mexico, leadership and elite recruitment was straightforward. After attending university and earning a technical degree, one joined a patron's camarilla and worked their way up the job ladder by supplying electoral support to the patron. Today, with a multiparty system and a truly federal system of government, there are more available paths to leadership, especially for women. It still helps to have a university degree, but some individuals find success by moving toward a governorship of a state, while others begin at the national level in a bureaucratic post. As recent reforms have removed the non-reelection principle for legislative elections, it will be interesting to see what happens as members do not have to switch jobs as frequently.

Linkage Institutions

Elections

The most important election in Mexico has always been the one for president. Even when he had dictatorial authority in Mexico, Diaz still stood for elections, which he made sure that he won. The Mexican Revolution began when Diaz decided to run one more time after promising to finally step down. When the PRI was the dominant party, its candidates competed for office with the three other parties that were allowed on the ballot, but the PRI nominee would win as presidential elections simply required a plurality vote, not a majority. The election of 1976 was worrisome, however, because no party ran a candidate against PRI nominee José López Portillo, which upset the illusion of democracy cultivated by the PRI. Election reforms were made in 1977 to add proportional seats to both the Senate and Chamber of Deputies to ensure that more parties would form and run for office as a sign of democratic legitimacy.

Then the presidential election of 1988 changed everything. Cuauhtémoc Cárdenas, son of PRI hero Lázaro Cárdenas, bolted the PRI and formed the Party of the Democratic Revolution (PRD). Cárdenas had the name recognition and support to be a strong candidate against Carlos Salinas, who had received the dedazo from President Miguel de la Madrid. In addition, the National Action Party (PAN) also ran a formidable candidate in Manuel Clouthier, who had staunch support in the northern states. Famously remembered as "the night the lights went out in Mexico City," election officials did not announce the winner until the next day because of a power outage. Salinas had won with 50.7 percent of the vote even though most people felt that Cardenas earned more votes. Chaos ensued as people protested across the country. Even in the National Congress, opposition legislators tried to nullify the results by bringing in boxes of forged ballots, but the PRI prevailed for the last time. To pacify the protestors, reforms were made that would pave the way for an opposition victory in 2000.

Elections reforms included the creation of an independent **Federal Electoral Institute (IFE)** to oversee elections. This would be a multiparty commission to oversee fair elections by having election observers, transparent ballot boxes, and voter ID cards. The media would be required to give all parties free coverage, and national parties would receive public financing. But these legislative changes were also followed by changes in PRI rituals. In 2000, PRI President Ernesto Zedillo refused to point the dedazo and name a successor. The PRI instead turned to a **primary system** to select its presidential candidate, thereby breaking decades of tradition and enshrining a democratic practice that gave power to the voters instead of party leaders.

Since 2000, elections have been fair and competitive. A remaining challenge for Mexican presidents, however, is the **direct plurality vote**. For example, in 2006, PAN candidate Felipe Calderón (35.98 percent) beat PRD candidate Andrés Manuel López Obrador (AMLO) (35.31 percent) by only 200,000 votes. After the IFE recounted ballots and announced Calderón as winner, AMLO turned to the Electoral Tribunal of the Federal Judiciary to nullify the results. Losing his case, AMLO and his supporters set up camp in the Zócalo or main square of Mexico City where they stayed for 47 days blocking traffic and setting up a shadow government. The election of 2012 had a similar result with AMLO winning 31.59 percent for the PRD but losing this time to PRI candidate Enrique Peña Nieto, who earned 38.2 percent. Again, AMLO questioned the results but to no avail. Critics of a single round plurality vote suggest that Mexico would be better served with a dual ballot system to ensure that the president has secured at least 50 percent of the popular vote to show a clear mandate from the voters. President Calderón proposed a switch to the two-ballot system in 2009, but it stalled in the legislature. In 2014, however, President Pena Nieto was able to restructure the IFE into a truly national authority, the **National Electoral Institute (INE),** with the power to not only organize federal elections, but to also coordinate local elections as well in an effort to strengthen democracy by overseeing party activity at all levels of government.

The 2018 presidential elections were historic. After narrowly losing elections in 2006 and 2012 as the PRD candidate, Andres Manuel Lopez Obrador (AMLO) formed a new political party, the **National Regeneration Movement,** or **MORENA,** party in 2014. The party secured 35 seats in the Chamber of Deputies in 2015. In 2018, AMLO formed a coalition *Juntos Haremos Historia* (*Together We Will Make History*) with the left-wing Labor Party and the right-wing Social Encounter Party. This coalition won the first absolute majority in a presidential election since 1988 and legislative majorities in both the Senate and the Chamber of Deputies. Election turnout was 63 percent.

Presidential Election Results

ELECTION YEAR	PRI	PAN	PRD	OTHER PARTIES
1976	**José López Portillo: 100%**			
1982	**Miguel de la Madrid: 74.3%**	Pablo Emilio Madero: 16.8%		5

1988	**Carlos Salinas de Gortari: 50.7%**	Manuel Clouthier: 16.8%	Cuauhtémoc Cárdenas: 31.1%	2
1994	**Ernesto Zedillo: 48.69%**	Diego Fernández de Cevallos: 25.92%	Cuauhtémoc Cárdenas: 16.59%	6
2000	Francisco Labastida: 36.11%	**Vicente Fox: 42.52%**	Cuauhtémoc Cárdenas: 16.64%	3
2006	Roberto Madrazo: 22.26%	**Felipe Calderón: 35.89%**	Andrés Manuel López Obrador: 35.31%	2
2012	**Enrique Peña Nieto: 38.2%**	Josefina Vázquez Mota: 25.41%	Andrés Manuel López Obrador: 31.59%	1
2018	Jose Antonio Meade 16.41%	Ricardo Anaya 22.28%	**MORENA Andrés Manuel López Obrador: 53.19%**	2

Source: Mexico INE

Election Systems and Party Systems

The initial election system enshrined in the Mexican Constitution of 1917 was all single-member district (SMD) seats for the Senate and the Chamber of Deputies. PRI hegemony, however, prevented a classic two-party system from being established. It was only after the 1976 presidential election that PRI leaders felt it necessary to change election rules to encourage the formation of more opposition parties to legitimatize the election process. So in 1977 the rules to form a political party were eased and 100 seats were added to the Chamber of Deputies to be allocated to minority parties using proportional representation (PR). Further changes occurred in 1986, 1993, and 1996 as the PRI tried to increase electoral competition without giving up control of the National Congress by manipulating the number of SMD versus PR seats, while adding governability formulas to try to control outcomes. For example, the PAN did not win any seats in the Senate until 1994. Eventually the rise of opposition forces overcame the attempts of the PRI to control the results.

Currently, a mixed election system is used for both the Senate and the Chamber of Deputies, and the result is an expected multiparty system. In addition, all elections, including presidential, are publicly funded, with strict limits on campaigning and the use of private funds. All parties are also guaranteed free airtime on TV and radio stations, and they are prohibited from buying ads. A major change in 2018 was that members of the National Assembly could run for reelection. Deputies may now serve for 4 terms and Senators for 2 terms. (The non-reelection principle still applies to governors and the president.)

Allocating Seats in the Senate

Last Election: July 2018   Next Election: July 2024

128 seats		
96 SMD plurality	64 First Majority: Parties run pairs of candidates. The pair that receives plurality wins 2 Senate seats.	32 Relative Minority: One candidate (preselected by party) of the pair that came in second gets 1 Senate seat.
32 PR	2% party threshold of closed party list 50% gender quota	
Quick Calculations	• Majority = 65 seats	• 2/3 to Amend = 86 seats

LXIV Senate by Party (Election July 2018)

PARTY	FIRST MAJORITY	RELATIVE MINORITY	PR ALLOCATION	TOTAL	CHANGE OF SEATS
MORENA	38	4	13	55	+55
PAN	7	10	6	23	−15
PRI	1	6	6	13	−39
PRD	1	5	2	8	−14
PVEM (Green)	1	4	2	7	−2
PT (Labor)	5	0	1	6	+1
Other Parties	11	3	2	16	
Totals	64	32	32	128	

Source: Mexican INE

Allocating Seats in the Chamber of Deputies

Last election: June 2021   Next Election: July 2024

500 SEATS	PROVISIONS	EXAMPLES
300 SMD plurality	Based on population—each state must have at least 2 seats	Federal District has 24 State of Mexico has 41
200 PR	2% party threshold of closed party list 50% gender quota	Parties supply 5 regional lists of 40 seats each
Governability Rules	• No party can have more than 300 seats • No party can have more than 8% of the seats over its national vote count	• Party wins 35% of vote—cannot have more than 43% of 500 seats (215 seat max)
Quick Calculations	• Majority = 251 seats	• 2/3 to Amend = 335

LXV Chamber of Deputies by Party (Election June 2021)

PARTY	SMD PLURALITY	PR	TOTAL	GAIN/LOSS SEATS
MORENA	125	77	202	+10
PVEM (Green)	30	12	71	+26
PT (Labor)	26	7	33	−27
MORENA-PVEM-PT COALITION			306 short of 2/3 needed for constitutional amendments	2018 MORENA and allies had 334 seats = loss of 28
PAN	73	40	113	+31
PRI	31	40	71	+26
PRD	8	8	16	−5
PAN-PRI-PRD COALITION			200	New coalition formed to counter MORENA
Citizen's Movement	7	16	23	−11

The Parties

PRI

For 70 years, the PRI established what has been referred to "the perfect dictatorship," a democratic dictatorship run by a dominant party with revolutionary roots. Formed in 1929 by Plutarco Calles, the Revolutionary National Party (PNR) was a power-sharing arrangement among political elites over presidential succession so that they would stop assassinating each other. Calles miscalculated, however, when he selected Lázaro Cárdenas to be president in 1934, as Cárdenas had him exiled. Cárdenas also changed the name of the party to the Party of the Mexican Revolution (PRM) as he worked to enact the 1917 constitutional principles of land reform by nationalizing the oil industry to form PEMEX and reestablishing the **ejido** system of communal farms. The modern PRI is the result of the final renaming/reorganization by President Camacho in 1946 to form the Institutional Revolution Party.

The PRI is a centrist party, much more of a party of power than one of ideology. As its adoption of the tricolor (red, white, green) of Mexico indicates, the PRI's legitimacy rests on its roots in the Mexican Revolution. By creating a **corporatist system** of peasant and workers groups, the PRI delivered resources to its supporters (seed and fertilizer to farmers, job to workers) in return for political support. The PRI also maintained a veneer of democratic legitimacy by holding regular elections against opposition parties, and by abiding by the non-reelection principle, the people in political office were constantly changing. Eventually, however, the corruption linked with clientelism and the stresses of economic liberalization caused the PRI to make electoral changes that reduced their control over elections.

The PRI suffered major electoral defeats in 2018 and 2021. In 2018, it lost large numbers of seats in the national and state legislatures and the presidency. In 2021, it lost 8 governorships. For the first time since 1929, the PRI does not dominate state leadership. Its strongest supporters remain in the countryside where local leaders are still able to use traditional tricks of persuasion, like giving grocery store debit cards in return for votes. Therefore, the PRI voters of today tend to be older, less educated, rural, or still associated with state-run industries.

PRD

The Party of the Democratic Revolution was founded in 1988 by Cuauhtémoc Cárdenas, the son of legendary PRI leader Lázaro Cárdenas, because he felt that the structural adjustment policies of economic liberalization were widening income inequality. The PRD quickly found its strongest support among those on the left, such as urban workers, the poor, and students. In fact, a PRD candidate has held the position of head of government of the Federal District, often referred as the mayor of Mexico City, ever since it became a directly elected position in 1997. (Prior to 1997, the position was filled by presidential appointment.) Cuauhtémoc Cárdenas was the first holder of this elected office, and all five mayors since have belonged to the PRD. After losing three presidential elections, Cárdenas stepped down from party leadership and was replaced by Mexico City Mayor Andrés Manuel López Obrador, known as AMLO. AMLO went on to fight two closely contested presidential contests in 2006 and 2012, disputing the results of both, even going as far to set up a shadow protest government in 2006 while his followers called him the legitimate president of Mexico. After losing in 2012, AMLO has started a new party, the National Regeneration Movement, or MORENA, based on a civic association that he had started to help his election campaign. Competing in elections in 2015 and 2016, MORENA won seats at the municipal and legislative levels, although no governorships. It will be interesting to see if MORENA displaces the PRD as the main party on the left. The PRD continues to contest elections, however, as not all members left to join AMLO. But the party has lost control of Mexico City as its current mayor, Claudia Sheinbaum, is a member of the MORENA party. Operating as part of a PAN-PRI-PRD coalition in 2021, however, the party was able to win back the western districts of Mexico City from MORENA.

PAN

The National Action Party, or PAN, was founded in 1939 as an opposition party to the PRI. Much of its support came from devout Catholics in northern states who had fought against the government in the Cristero Rebellion of 1926–29. By the 1980s, the PAN was a pro-business, pro-Catholic party with its strongest support in the north. Taking advantage of the PRI's reputation for corruption and the unfavorable economic conditions, the PAN was well positioned to gain support, first starting at the governorship level. But PAN leaders needed to find candidates to run for office. Manuel Clouthier personally took on the task of recruiting Vicente Fox in 1988 to run for the Chamber of Deputies. Fox's family did not want him to run because of potential PRI retaliation against the family business. Fox decided to run anyway, and the PRI retaliated by revoking their business license, shutting down their vegetable plant, and calling in their bank loans. Fox recalls that "ironically, the government had given me the two things I really needed: the time to campaign and the anger to do it right." After his stint in the Chamber of Deputies, Fox ran for governor and then became the PAN presidential candidate in 2000. He won that election with a coalition of businessmen, middle-class consumers, and Catholics.

The PAN party of today continues to be the second-largest electoral winner in Mexico, holding 11 governorships along with its seats in the legislature. Electorally strong in northern Mexico and in wealthy urban areas, the PAN is Mexico's party of the right, advocating for free market principles and socially conservative policies. Notably, it was the PAN that nominated the first female major party presidential candidate in 2012, Josephina Vázquez Mota, who suffered more at the polls in an anti-PAN backlash as opposed to a lack of qualifications.

MORENA

The MORENA party is the new party which had spectacular success in the 2018 elections because of its alliance with the Labor and the Social Encounter parties. Based on its roots in the PRD, MORENA is a left-wing party that emphasizes protection from neo-liberal economic policies such as the privatization of PEMEX, protection of civil liberties, including the rights of indigenous groups, and reduction of government corruption. The challenge for the party is that it is mostly based on support for its charismatic leader, AMLO. He won the presidential vote in 31 of 32 states and in Mexico City. MORENA candidates won as the mayor of Mexico City (urban district), as the governor of Chiapas (southern agricultural state), and as the governor of Baja California (northern industrial state). In 2021, MORENA exceeded expectations by capturing 10 additional governorships, up to 16. The results in the legislative midterms, however, were disappointing. AMLO was hoping to have a two-thirds majority in the Chamber of Deputies in order to push through progressive constitutional changes. A coalition of the PAN-PRD-PRI was able to win enough seats to deny the MORENA alliance with PVEM and PT a supermajority, although it has an absolute majority.

Interest Groups

One of the primary ways that the PRI maintained control for 70 years was the elaborate **corporatist system** that it built to co-opt civil society. In fact, a large part of the Lázaro Cárdenas party reorganization was the creation of two large peak associations to represent the interests of the poor. One was the **National Peasant Confederation**, or **CNC**, and the other was the **Confederation of Mexican Workers**, or **CTM**. A third sector would be formed in 1943, to organize the "popular" or middle class, called the **National Confederation of Popular Organizations**, or **CNOP**. In true corporatist fashion, these three sectors of society negotiated benefits and services directly with the government for their members, and in return the organizations delivered the votes. This practice of receiving services for votes is called **clientelism**. Peasants working on communally owned ejidos were dependent on the government for seed, fertilizer, roads, and other services. State-owned industries provided jobs for union workers. All the local bosses required were the people's votes on election day.

This arrangement began to unravel during the neoliberal economic reforms of the 1980s. As presidents pursued structural adjustment programs, the agricultural subsidies dried up. Privatized industries meant fewer government jobs. Falling oil prices meant less government revenue. High inflation, a devalued peso, and rising unemployment unraveled the former corporatist contract. By 2000, the CNC had dissolved; the CTM had joined the independent Union of Workers, and in a more pluralistic environment, independent interest groups have been established.

Today in Mexico, interest groups have formed around various causes, in addition to professional and economic organizations. Some groups have a very limited focus, such as the Center for Worker's Support, which advocates for female workers' rights in maquiladoras, while others like Pronatura México take on environmental issues throughout Mexico, and finally, many organizations are associated with international bodies, such as the U.S.-Mexico Chamber of Commerce, which concentrates on bilateral trade agreements.

Citizens, Society, and the State

Social Cleavages

Although Mexico is predominantly mestizo and Catholic with a growing middle class, there are significant social divisions between northern and southern Mexico, between urban and rural areas, and between rich and poor. A growing coinciding cleavage is the one between the increasingly industrialized, urbanized north and the rural, agrarian south. This cleavage is exacerbated by the fact that the poorest regions in southern Mexico are also dominated by indigenous Amerindian groups fighting to retain their traditional culture and language in an increasingly globalized world. This conflict is still best exemplified by the example of the **National Liberation Army (EZLN)**, who first came to world attention on January 1, 1994, when they seized territory in Chiapas to highlight their demands. Decades later after fighting Mexican troops, marching to Mexico City, rejecting a weak Indigenous Bill of Rights, and resisting government intervention programs, the Zapatistas remain in isolated compounds cultivating a communal life. Yet in an important development, and making a statement on the violence plaguing Mexico, the Zapatistas announced that "taking up arms is out of the question," and instead they supported the 2018 independent presidential candidacy of María de Jesús Patricio Martínez of the **National Indigenous Congress**, a body representing all Amerindian groups in Mexico. Although AMLO won 1.5 million votes in the state of Chiapas, the Zapatistas remain skeptical about his commitment to protecting indigenous rights.

Civil Society

After enduring years of a corporatist culture and an anticlerical government, civil society has been slow to adapt to an environment where people are free to form autonomous organizations. According to the World Values Survey, 80 percent of Mexicans are still not inclined to join either art, environmental, charitable, or professional organizations. The only type of organization that a majority of Mexicans would agree that they were an active/inactive member of were religious organizations.

Media

Control of the media was one of the PRI's most effective ways of maintaining its position as a dominant party. Determined to keep up the facade of a democracy, however, the PRI had ingenious ways to maintain control. For example, the state did not own newspapers or journals; they were privately owned. What the government did have was a state-owned monopoly on newsprint. Want access to the newsprint at a low cost? Cover the PRI government in a favorable light. Journalists were also part of the clientelism system by getting paid for positive stories. Television coverage was dominated by the independent **Televisa** Network and a small state-owned network. President Salinas privatized the state-owned network in the 1990s by selling it to billionaire Ricardo Salinas (no relation) who renamed it Azteca. Today, Televisa and Azteca control the Mexican television market and fight for viewers. For example, during the 2012 presidential election, Ricardo Salinas decided that his network would cover a quarter final football (soccer) match in the Mexican Primero Division instead of the debate. He tweeted, "If you want to see the debate, watch it on Televisa; if not, watch the game on TV Azteca."

The power of the government over the media, however, is still strong. Recent election reforms to require the TV stations to provide free air time to all qualified political candidates, along with the ban of private political advertising, is a loss of a revenue stream that did not please the networks, especially given the competition with social media. The social media market, however, is dominated by billionaire Carlos Slim, who purchased **Telmex** from the Mexican government during the privatization of the 1990s and then turned this monopoly on landlines into the spin-off Telcel, which controls 65 percent of the Mexican cell phone market.

Recently, concerns have been raised about AMLO's media practices. As president, he has held a daily press conference which is live-streamed on several channels. A Mexican fact-checking organization, Verificado, states that "45% of the verifiable messages affirmed in the morning have been true, 28% correspond to half-truths or taken out of context, 25% are determined as lies and 2% have their opinion pending." The editor of the newpaper *El Financiero* states that these briefings have become "the centerpiece of the government's propaganda strategy as they allow him to be part of the public agenda in a systematic and permanent way." Given AMLO's 64 percent approval rating and his MORENA party's electoral dominance, it is up to an independent media to counter this practice with some effective watchdog analysis.

Political Participation

As a federal state, Mexicans face numerous elections. The only activity that a majority of Mexicans participate politically in would be voting in presidential elections at a rate of 63 percent. Few Mexicans sign petitions, join boycotts, or attend peaceful demonstrations. In fact, according to the World Values Survey, a majority of Mexicans surveyed said specifically that they would never do any of those activities.

Social Movements

Mexico has a young population as the median age is 28. Significantly, it has been social movements led by students that have had significant impact on the public consciousness. The most notable of these movements was the Mexico 68, a series of student protests against the PRI and the lack of democratic reforms. These protests were timed right before the Olympics took place in Mexico City to garner international attention. On October 2, 1968, troops fired on a group of student protestors in an event called the **Tlatelolco massacre**. Thousands of students were jailed, and the PRI-led government resisted calls for a formal investigation. It wasn't until the Fox Administration in 2001 reopened the case that former President Luis Echeverría was questioned about his role in Tlatelolco and in another attack on students in 1971 referred to as the Corpus Christi massacre. Attempts to charge Echeverría with genocide failed, but both incidents still resonate with the Mexican population today as examples some of the worst atrocities of an authoritarian regime.

A contemporary student movement was the **Yo Soy 132** social media campaign during the 2012 presidential election. PRI candidate Peña Nieto faced protestors at an event at Ibero-American University, and he later claimed that these protestors were not real students. In response, 131 students posted a YouTube video of each of them showing their student IDs. "I am 132" refers to solidarity with the students and their concerns about the lack of democracy in Mexico.

Other social movement are focused on human rights. For example, the Zapatistas of Chiapas have now been working to protect indigenous rights since 1994. In cooperation with the National Indigenous Congress (CNI), the two groups backed a presidential candidate to bring attention to the need for autonomy for indigenous groups along with economic, educational, and health services to help the rates of extreme poverty.

Citizenship and Representation

There are two ways to be a natural-born Mexican citizen. One is to be born on Mexican soil (jus soli) and the other is to be born to a Mexican citizen (jus sanguinis). All others interested in becoming citizens must go through the naturalization process. It is important to note, however, that being a naturalized citizen prohibits one from holding most government positions including president, governor, legislator, or mayor. Initially, Article 82 even required that to be president, both of a candidate's parents had to have been born in Mexico. A 1993 amendment changed the requirement to that a president only had to have one parent born in Mexico, thereby making Vicente Fox, whose mother was born in Spain, eligible to run for the office in 2000.

Women have made significant gains in the electoral arena in recent years. The number of women representatives has increased because of a election reform **gender parity law** that requires political parties to field 50 percent female candidates. In addition, parties cannot only run women in districts where party support is weak, and if a female legislator is replaced, it must be by another female. Currently, the National Congress is 50 percent female in the lower house and 49 percent female in the upper house, compared with 27 percent in the U.S. House of Representatives and 24 percent in the U.S. Senate. It has proven more difficult, however, for women to reach the highest office levels. Only two woman serve as governor, and no woman has won the presidency. In addition, few women are CEOs of corporations in Mexico, although the exclusive Mexican Council of Businessmen changed its name to the Mexican Business Council when it inducted its first female member in 2015.

Political and Economic Change

Revolution, Coups, and War

The **Mexican Revolution of 1910** was the first major revolution of the twentieth century, galvanized by the dictatorship of Porfirio Díaz. Although Mexicans appreciated the political stability of his regime after the chaotic times since the War of Independence 100 years earlier, they resented Díaz's top-down modernization efforts and his repression of dissent. Campesinos, or peasant farmers, were mobilized by Emiliano Zapata to fight for land reform because Diaz had ceded large tracts of land to hacienda owners and foreign corporations. The middle class sought democratic reforms to reduce the power of an autocratic state and highly influential Catholic Church. Fighting between various groups continued even beyond 1917, the year that the Constitution was written, as various leaders would seize control and then be assassinated.

The Constitution of 1917, however, reflected the ideals of the revolution. One essential element would be the non-reelection principle so that no one holding political office could control the country as long as Díaz had. To limit the power of the president, federalism was established to force the national government to share power with the states. **Article 27** famously enshrined land reform by stating that all land and water belongs to the nation and called for return of communal land to indigenous groups. Anticlerical measures included a prohibition on public religious services and parochial schools, and restrictions on the clergy's right to vote.

Despite the new Constitution, however, presidential succession was still characterized by assassination. Finally, in 1929, Plutarco Calles orchestrated the formation of a political party to help stabilize the process of leadership transfer by establishing a power-sharing system among elites to stop the violence. The PRI would then go on to rule Mexico for 70 years.

Political Change

Political change in Mexico can best be explained through the process of political liberalization that Mexico has undergone since 1977. At that time, the PRI was at the height of its power as a dominant party and enjoyed widespread support, buttressed with a corporatist system of peak associations that translated that support into votes. And if the vote count was threatened, the PRI was not above conjuring some electoral alchemy to generate the needed votes. Typical tactics included moving polling stations or handing out "vote tortillas" with one ballot wrapped around forged ones or stuffing the ballot boxes before the election even began. But maintaining a veneer of democracy was important to the party's legitimacy as a product of the Revolution, so when no opposition party produced a presidential candidate to challenge PRI in 1976, the PRI devised a plan to increase competition while still maintaining control over the state. Then, in response to democratic pressures over the next 20 years, the PRI politically liberalized the Mexican political system by making the following reforms.

YEAR	POLITICAL CHANGE	RESULT
1977–1996	Moving from a SMD electoral system to a mixed SMD/PR electoral system for both the Senate and the Chamber of Deputies.	Increase in the number of political parties in the legislature = multiparty system.
1990	Creation of an independent Federal Election Institute (IFE) to manage elections.	Increase in voter identification systems = less duplicate voting.
		Elections not controlled by PRI-led government.
1994	Judicial reform to limit judges to 15-year term, and president selects judges from a list prepared by a nonpartisan commission. Strengthened power of judicial review.	Creates greater judicial independence at Supreme Court level to serve as an effective check on the other branches.
1996	Increase public funding for elections. Reduce private contributions to 10%. Increase free media access to all registered parties.	Level the playing field to increase competition in elections.
1997	Moving from a presidential dedazo to primaries for selecting candidates.	Increase voter input in selection of candidates = weakens party leaders.
2008	Gradual shift of judicial system from an inquisitorial model to an adversarial model with emphasis on procedural due process rights for the accused.	"Oral trials" will increase transparency of the process and judicial accountability.
2014	Reform the non-reelection principle for seats in the Chamber of Deputies (can serve four 3-year terms and the Senate can serve two 6-year terms). Starts with July 2018 election.	Allowing legislators to be reelected will increase the level of expertise in the National Congress and hold legislators accountable for long-term policymaking.
2014	Reform of gender parity law requiring political parties to run women as candidates on 50% of legislative seats. Started with June 2015 election in Chamber of Deputies.	Increase female representation in National Congress = increase in descriptive representation.
2014	Transform IFE to the **National Electoral Institute (INE)** to ensure fair elections at all levels of government by maintaining a voter list and registering political parties and monitoring access to public funds and free media access.	Continue to improve Mexican status as an electoral democracy by bringing election reform to all levels of government = increased attempt to reduce corruption in rural areas.

The result of all these political changes is that Mexico is an electoral democracy with competitive, fair elections where control of the government shifts between political parties. Problems, however, remain in that a corrupt, inefficient bureaucracy and security forces fail to provide adequate services and protection to all segments of the Mexican population. Reform is still necessary to move Mexico to consolidated democracy status.

One positive development that led to the 2014 electoral reforms was President Pena Nieto's **Pact for Mexico**, which was developed in concert with party leaders from the PAN and PRD. Devised to break the gridlock in the National Assembly, this agreement combined the priorities of all three parties for political and economic reform. The more than 90 proposals included plans to modernize PEMEX, reform the education system, expand the social welfare safety net, create a national police force, and establish an Anti-Corruption Commission. Although not all the provisions became legislation, it set an important precedent that opposition parties could work together to find common ground.

AMLO is pushing for a Fourth Transformation (4T) of the Mexican political system. Citing 1821 Independence, Juarez reforms in the nineteenth century, and the 1910 Revolution as the earlier transformations, AMLO wants to strengthen rule of law in Mexico by reforming the Constitution so that there would be a public consultation vote on the president after three years in office, along with a cut in high government salaries and improved infrastructure, health care, and pensions for the poor.

Economic Change

The Mexican Constitution of 1917 has several important economic provisions. Article 27 enshrined the land and mineral rights of the people, while Article 123 guaranteed workers the right to organize and strike. In this way, two groups of revolutionaries were protected—both the peasant farmer and the urban worker. True land reform, however, did not come until the presidency of Lázaro Cárdenas, who moved to reestablish the ejido, or communal farm, for rural farmers by breaking up **haciendas**, or large private farms. In addition, Cárdenas began to nationalize industries to reduce the power of foreign companies in Mexico. The 1938 nationalization of the oil industry to form PEMEX as a state-owned company was highly popular in Mexico, and the Mexican government would come to rely heavily on revenues from the sale and export of oil. Current estimates have oil revenue making up 30 percent of the Mexican budget, not enough to be classified as a rentier state, but still a significant source of income for the government.

The 1940s through the 1970s were the years of the "Mexican Miracle" as the government embraced the **import-substitution industrialization (ISI)** model of economic development. To incentive the growth of local industry, subsidies were provided and tariffs on imports were increased. Large infrastructure projects were commissioned to modernize transportation networks. The economy grew steadily with low inflation rates. Discovery of vast reserves of offshore oil in the early 1970s further expanded the economy as Mexico began to export oil and use the revenue to increase spending on development projects. Strong economic performance also persuaded the government to borrow heavily from international banks to finance programs.

A drop in oil prices and high interest rates characterized the 1980s in Mexico, known as "the lost decade." President Portillo reacted to the crisis by devaluing the peso and nationalizing the banking industry. People lost the value of their savings, the unemployment rate increased, and inflation soared to over 100 percent. The next two presidents, however, were *tecnicos*, with degrees in public administration from Harvard, who were committed to neoliberal reforms. Both Miguel de la Madrid and Carlos Salinas embraced the structural adjustment programs (SAPs) required by the International Monetary Fund (IMF) and the World Bank to restructure the debt and open the economy. Tariffs were decreased, and austerity policies were introduced to raise taxes and cut spending on subsidies. Industries, including banking but not PEMEX, were privatized. Adoption of these policies allowed Mexico to join the General Agreement on Tariffs and Trade (GATT), which evolved into the World Trade Organization (WTO) in 1995. In addition, Mexico joined with the United States and Canada to form the **North American Free Trade Agreement**, or **NAFTA**, to reduce trade barriers between the three countries to spur exports and encourage an increase in **foreign direct investment (FDI)** in Mexico.

The economic results of these neoliberal reforms were dramatic as Mexican GDP grew significantly. With a trillion-dollar economy, Mexico ranks as the fifteenth largest in world and is a member of the G20. It has also been hailed as one of the MINT economies to watch with Indonesia, Nigeria, and Turkey. But significant challenges remain. As is characteristic of most economic liberalization policies, income growth is uneven, widening the gap between rich and poor. This has become a coinciding cleavage because disproportionately, the more urbanized, educated, northern states are outperforming the rural, indigenous, agricultural states in the south. Migration from the south to the north reflects this problem. The Zapatista rebellion in Chiapas in 1994 was an early indicator of the problems that opening the economy would pose for small subsistence farmers who would have to compete with the large industrial farms in the United States. Industrial centers were primarily centered in northern states where maquiladoras already existed to take advantage of the proximity to the United States. But proximity to the United States has also caused problems for Mexico with not only immigration and drug crime, but any fluctuations in the U.S. economy, like the 2009 recession, also impact the Mexican economy. Few of these problems, however, will be mitigated by a new trade agreement, the **USMCA (United States, Mexico, Canada Agreement)** negotiated by President Donald Trump to modernize NAFTA by updating protections for intellectual property and protections for labor and the environment.

One of the largest problems facing the Mexican economy is the lack of investment in PEMEX. The oil giant desperately needs an infusion of funds to expand into deep sea oil fields and improve production, but there was deep resistance from the Mexican people to privatize the company. As part of the Pact for Mexico, President Peña Nieto managed to craft a constitutional amendment that was passed allowing oil, gas, and electricity monopolies to form joint ventures with foreign corporations while maintaining state ownership. It seemed to be working. In November of 2017, it was announced that the largest discovery of oil in 15 years was found off the coast of Veracruz. But the election of AMLO has reversed the government's position on private investment in PEMEX so uncertainty continues. Also, part of the Pact for Mexico was antitrust legislation to reduce telecommunication monopolies in Mexico by creating a Federal Telecommunications Institute to oversee the industry. A prime target was Carlos Slim's control of Telmex, a company that he bought when it was privatized by the Mexican government and whose ownership has ranked him as one of the richest men in the world. Now with competition from firms like AT&T, Mexican consumers have more choices and lower prices. But income disparity and poverty remain high in Mexico, prompting calls for more economic change.

Public Policy

Increasingly, Mexican public policy is formed according to constitutional principles. As a federal republic, state governors have more control over state resources and budgets than during the years under PRI domination. The national government, however, still controls the purse strings by gathering in most of the revenue and then distributing it to the states. But after years of gridlock between the Mexican president and the National Congress,

President Peña Nieto was able to cross party lines to develop a legislative agenda that passed by the two-thirds vote necessary in both chambers to amend the Constitution; a significant achievement given that no one party has even a majority in either chamber. In addition, judicial reforms are a welcome initiative in a country where local judges and police officers are viewed as corrupt, and drug violence impacts entire communities. Only time will tell if the MORENA party under AMLO's leadership will be able to use its political majorities to implement reform that will be able to surmount the corruption and income disparity facing contemporary Mexico.

Poverty

Forty-six percent of Mexicans live below the poverty line, and the gap between rich and poor as measured by the GINI index is the largest of any OECD (Organization for Economic Co-operation and Development) country. People living in poverty are most likely to be rural farm workers or those living in urban areas but working in the informal economy without steady wages and benefits. Social inclusion programs were first aimed at the rural poor in 1997 with the *Progresa* program. President Fox expanded it to urban areas while renaming it *Oportunidades* in 2002, and it was most recently updated in 2014 as the ***Prospera*** program. *Prospera* is a cash transfer program where a poor family receives payments for making sure that their children attend school and receive regular health checkups. The payments are paid directly to the mother of the family to ensure the money is spent appropriately, and payments increase for older girls as an incentive to keep them in school. Estimates are that 25 percent of the Mexican population are receiving these benefits. The government has also instituted reforms to give incentives to more employers to participate in the formal economy, but plans to create a national unemployment insurance plan and universal pension system are stalled in the legislature. Educational reforms have also been made to professionalize the teaching profession, although clashes with powerful teachers' unions slow progress. In all, however, these efforts to improve human capital and reduce poverty in Mexico are promising.

Crime and Corruption

Violent crime in Mexico is at a 20-year high according to a recent study, and the government's attempts to curb the violence have had negligible effect. Much of the crime is associated with the drug cartels operating in Mexico that supply the U.S. market with cocaine, cannabis, and heroin. The official **War on Drugs** began when President Calderón sent troops to fight the cartels in 2006. Since that time, even the help of the U.S. government has not been able to stop the violence, or the corruption associated with local officials and police who cooperate with the cartels. Many Mexicans living in poverty are also willing to work with the cartels for financial advantages. Others are simply intimidated by the gruesome tactics used by the cartels to silence opposition, such as murdering journalists and mutilating corpses. It is no wonder that Mexicans have lost faith in their government to keep them safe. Compounding the problem are incidents like the kidnapping and murder of 43 college students in 2014, which involved the local mayor, police, and a gang. Efforts to restore confidence in the legal system have included a move to an adversarial legal system with "oral trials" to ensure transparency and accountability. A new national police force with military training has been proposed to try to professionalize the force and reduce corruption by using these new officers to replace the military troops who are often accused of human rights abuses. But Mexicans are skeptical of the government's ability to stop the violence by the cartels. Unfortunately, AMLO has not been able to stop the violence despite campaign pledges to do just that. Programs like crop substitution, replacing poppies with corn, or legalizing opium for medicinal use are attempts at improving farmers' income, but does little to stop the actions of the cartels.

Immigration

Immigration challenges the Mexican government from two angles. One is the confrontation with the United States over the 6 million Mexicans who live in the United States without documentation. Although Mexican migration to the United States has declined since 2007, the increase in deportations under the Obama and Trump administrations has put stress on towns where individuals and their families must be reintegrated into society. But currently more non-Mexicans are stopped at the U.S.-Mexican border than Mexicans. These immigrants are typically from Guatemala, Honduras, and El Salvador and are fleeing the violence in their countries, but first they travel through Mexico on their way to the United States. This is the second challenge for the Mexican government—how to secure its own southern border. Increased security at the border has stopped the people who used to ride the trains north, but other methods of transportation are less secure as migrants bribe policemen to let them continue their journey.

In addition, remittances sent by Mexicans living in the United States to their families back home is at its highest levels ever, over $2.5 billion a year. Usually sent as a wire transfer of $300, these remittances provide valuable income for poor families and contribute about 2 percent to Mexican GDP.

Environment

Mexico City is one of the most polluted cities in the world. The rest of the country faces the challenges of deforestation, water contamination, and overfishing. The Mexican government is working with NGOs and the World Bank to develop a Green Plan that will lead to sustainable development. For example, in Mexico City, as the government spends money on revamping public transportation, drivers must have their cars pass emission tests. In addition, public campaigns such as "Hoy No Circula" ("Today, Don't Drive") encourage drivers to walk or bike to work.

Covid 19

The Covid-19 pandemic has hit Mexico hard with over 300,000 deaths by the end of 2021. Only the United States, Brazil, India, and Russia report more deaths. Although President has encouraged people to get vaccinated, he has typically resisted wearing a mask, not instituted many mandates, and tested positive twice. Cuts to public health spending have also limited responses to the pandemic with low levels of testing. Due to a lack of a comprehensive federal approach, some states have implemented their own health measures.

› Review Questions

Multiple Choice

1. Mexico was a colony of which of the following countries?
   (A) Spain
   (B) Portugal
   (C) France
   (D) England

2. Which of the following revolutionary leaders championed the rights of indigenous farmers?
   (A) Álvaro Obregón
   (B) Victoriano Huerta
   (C) Francisco Madero
   (D) Emiliano Zapata

3. From left to right ideologically, classify the three major political parties in Mexico.
   (A) PAN, PRD, PRI
   (B) PAN, PRI, PRD
   (C) PRI, PRD, PAN
   (D) PRD, PRI, PAN

4. How did the PRI manage to control Mexico for over 70 years?
   (A) Continuous violent repression of the civil liberties and political rights of the Mexican people to scare the people into voting for the PRI
   (B) Legislation passed allowing only the PRI to form as a one-party state
   (C) Effective manipulation of the electoral system to run the PRI as a dominant party
   (D) Extensive use of the military to terrorize Mexican citizens into supporting the PRI

5. PEMEX is the name of:
   (A) a drug cartel in northern Mexico
   (B) the state-owned oil company in Mexico
   (C) a multinational manufacturing corporation in Mexico
   (D) a social welfare program in Mexico

6. Which of the following is the most significant political liberalization reform that helped transform Mexico into an electoral democracy?
   (A) The creation of the Federal Election Institute (IFE)
   (B) The addition of PR seats in both the Senate and Chamber of Deputies
   (C) A provision to provide free media coverage for all registered political parties

   (D) The establishment of governability rules limiting one party to 300 seats in the Chamber of Deputies

7. Which of the following economic policies would be used with the adoption of an import-substitution industrialization (ISI) program?
   (A) Lowering tariffs
   (B) Increasing subsidies to domestic businesses
   (C) Reducing spending on infrastructure
   (D) Privatizing state-owned businesses

8. Why did the PRI employ corporatism as a strategy to help it maintain its control of the Mexican government?
   (A) By creating a few peak associations of farmers and workers, the PRI co-opted their electoral support in return for services.
   (B) By allowing many groups to compete for services, the PRI encouraged all groups to support the party.
   (C) By refusing to grant contracts to multinational corporations (MNCs), the PRI gained support from domestic manufacturers.
   (D) The PRI nationalized all major industries to form government-owned corporations.

9. The Pact for Mexico was an ambitious attempt by President Peña Nieto to break legislative gridlock. Which of the following was an important an element of the plan?
   (A) An electoral reform to change the National Congress back to all SMD seats
   (B) An electoral reform to change the non-reelection principle for legislators
   (C) An economic reform to completely privatize PEMEX
   (D) A social reform to improve the education system by reestablishing religious schools

10. Why was press freedom limited in Mexico in 2017?
    (A) The PRI controls the monopoly on newsprint and only sells it to news networks that provide favorable coverage of the party.
    (B) The state-run news networks refuse to criticize the government.
    (C) The drug cartels target journalists and the government has failed to keep them from being murdered.
    (D) Monopoly control of the television networks prevents opposition parties from getting any news coverage.

Free-Response Review Questions

1. (A) Define dominant party.
   (B) Describe the political ideology of a dominant party.
   (C) Explain how the party that you identified in (B) was able to establish itself as a dominant party.
   (D) Explain why a state controlled by a dominant party may be perceived as more legitimate than a one-party state.

2. Use the chart to complete your answer.

MEXICO 2019	FREEDOM RATING
Freedom House: Aggregate Freedom	Partly Free
Freedom House: Political Rights	Partly Free
Freedom House: Civil Liberties	Partly Free
Freedom House: Press Freedom	Partly Free

   Freedom House ranks indicators as Free, Partly Free, and Not Free

   (A) Using the data in the chart, identify the status of press freedom in Mexico.
   (B) Using the data in the chart, describe what a rating of "partly free" indicates about democracy in Mexico.
   (C) Describe the role of an independent press in a democracy.
   (D) Explain why a democracy may limit press freedom.
   (E) Explain how an authoritarian state limits press freedom.

3. Compare how states choose to limit or not limit the number of terms that a member of the legislature can serve in two different AP Comparative Government and Politics course countries. In your response, you should do the following:
   (A) Define electoral competition.
   (B) Explain how states choose to limit or not limit the number of terms that a member of the legislature can serve in two different AP Comparative Government and Politics course countries.
   (C) Explain how the decision to limit or not limit the number of terms in the legislature affects electoral competition in each of the two AP Comparative Government and Politics course countries described in (B).

4. Develop an argument as to whether the adoption of import substitution industrialization policies (ISIs) or structural adjustment policies (SAPs) lead to more political stability.

   Use one or more of the following course concepts in your response.
   - Legitimacy
   - Income inequality
   - Economic growth

   In your response, you should do the following:
   - Respond to the prompt with a defensible claim or thesis that establishes a line of reasoning using one or more of the provided course concepts.
   - Support your claim with at least TWO pieces of specific and relevant evidence from one or more course countries. This evidence should be relevant to one or more of the provided course concepts.
   - Use reasoning to explain why your evidence supports your claim or thesis, using one or more of the provided course concepts.
   - Respond to an opposing or alternate perspective, using refutation, concession, or rebuttal.

› Answers and Explanations

Multiple Choice

1. **A.** Mexico was a Spanish colony until it gained its independence in 1821.

2. **D.** Emiliano Zapata was the revolutionary leader who fought for land reform for the indigenous peasant farmers of southern Mexico. The Zapatistas of Chiapas adopted his name for their movement.

3. **D.** The PRD is the party of the left, while the PAN is the party of the right. The PRI is a centrist party of power.

4. **C.** The PRI manipulated the election system to establish itself as a dominant party by allowing opposition parties to compete, but not win, because the PRI had the corporatist support of member organizations.

5. **B.** PEMEX is the state-owned oil company in Mexico. PEMEX is a shortened version of Petróleos Mexicanos.

6. **A.** Political liberalization reforms in Mexico include the creation of a Federal Election Institute (IFE) to oversee elections and ensure that all registered parties receive public funding and free media access. Measures were also put in place to increase competition in the legislature by adding PR seats and governability rules.

7. **B.** Import-substitution industrialization programs are designed to build infant domestic industries by subsidizing them and restricting foreign ownership. Some countries choose to nationalize these industries while also raising tariffs, increasing spending on infrastructure, and reducing tax burdens.

8. **A.** The PRI used corporatism to gain support from its own membership organizations created to provide votes in return for services. The three main groups were the CNC for farmers, CTM for workers, and CNOP for the "popular class."

9. **B.** The Pact for Mexico was an agreement by PRI, PAN, and PRD leaders to legislate electoral and economic reform for Mexico by creating the INE and establishing term limits for the legislature along with improving the education system and allowing joint ventures to invest in PEMEX. There was no attempt to change the election system for the National Congress.

10. **C.** Freedom House labels Mexican press freedom as "not free" because the government is incapable of protecting investigative journalists from being targeted by the drug cartels. Constitutional protections and a competitive news environment are not useful when journalists are being murdered for their stories.

Free Response

1. (4 points possible)
   (A) A dominant party is one that faces such weak opposition that it is inevitable that the party will win the election and control both the executive and legislative branches. Often the dominant party has the power to manipulate elections to ensure victory. (1 point)
   (B) A dominant party rarely has a specific political ideology. Instead, the focus of the party is to be a party of power. The PRI in Mexico identified itself as the party of the Mexican Revolution and sought to gain support for its regime. It maintained its position as a moderate party between the left PRD and conservative PAN. (1 point)
   (C) The PRI used several strategies to establish itself as a dominant party. One was to give the Mexican president the power of patronage to select office holders and bureaucrats for numerous offices. By providing jobs for his camarilla, the president was able to maintain support as his closest rivals hoped to win the dedazo or appointment as the presidential successor. In addition, the PRI created a corporatist system of membership organizations that supplied votes in return for farming supplies and/or jobs. Finally, the PRI was willing to resort to electoral alchemy to manufacture any needed votes. (1 point)

(D) A dominant party model allows limited electoral competition. This illusion of choice legitimizes the election more than a one-party state would. The dominant party ensures that there is a limited opportunity for a voter to make a choice, thereby making it more likely that the voter will accept the authority of the government. In a one-party state, only 1 party governs; there is no freedom to form an opposition. (1 point)

2. (5 points possible)

(A) Press freedom in Mexico is not free. (1 point)

(B) A "partly free" ranking in political rights and civil liberties reflects that Mexico is a transitional democracy. It has the characteristics of a democratic state, with fair, competitive elections, a government committed to protecting voting rights, freedom of expression, and rule of law. The problem remains that those rights have not been consolidated. Police corruption, drug cartel violence, and media monopolization continue to plague the political system. (1 point)

(C) An independent press serves an important role in a democracy. Most significantly, it serves as a watchdog to investigate government policymaking and report abuses and corruption. Combined with governmental transparency, investigative reporting with protection of whistle-blowers is a critical check on political power. The press informs the public who are then better able to hold their elected officials accountable for their actions. (1 point)

(D) A democratic government may limit press freedom in order to protect national security or individual privacy. Or in the case of Mexico, the government has limited press freedom by failing to protect journalists from the drug cartels. (1 point)

(E) An authoritarian government has less hesitation in restricting press freedom than a democracy. Implementing a state-run television or newspaper system and restricting independent publications is a classic arrangement to allow the government to control its message. Imprisoning political activists and investigating reporters is also an effective technique to discourage negative coverage. (1 point)

3. (5 points possible)

(A) Electoral competition exists when voters have a true choice of candidates. One of the hallmarks of a democratic regime, electoral competition ensures that voters hold governments accountable for policymaking because leaders can always be voted out and replaced with a viable alternative. (1 point)

(B) For decades, Mexico had a non-reelection principle where no office holder could repeat being in an office. Designed to prevent an elected dictatorship like that of Porfirio Diaz, the Mexican Constitution prevented members of the legislature from serving consecutive terms. So deputies could serve a 3-year term and senators could serve a 6-year term, and then they had to seek a different position. (1 point)

In contrast, the UK has no limits on the number of terms that a member of the legislature can serve. A member of the House of Commons can stand for election as many times as the party nominates the MP for the seat. A life peer in the House of Lords serves for life if so desired. (1 point)

(C) The Mexican non-reelection principle hindered electoral competition for many years as the PRI took advantage of office holders' frequent need for new jobs by developing an elaborate patron–client system. This camarilla system gave party leaders the opportunity to provide jobs in either elected positions or the bureaucracy to members of their network. The president of Mexico had the most power to select judges, governors, and even his successor. By employing this patron–client system, the PRI was able to maintain its position as a dominant party and restrict electoral competition. More recently, however, the non-reelection principle has seemed to be too disruptive to electoral competition in Mexico. Therefore a 4-term limit for the Chamber of Deputies and a 2-term limit for the Senate have been enacted to allow for the development of some experience for incumbents. (1 point)

Conversely, the UK is a long-established, consolidated democracy with fair, competitive elections, so at first glance, one might assume that no term limits can promote electoral competition, at least in the House of Commons. On a whole, that is true, as the British government has changed hands between the Conservative and Labour parties on a consistent basis. Upon closer examination, however, many of the seats in the House of Commons are safe seats where the incumbent is easily reelected. Therefore, the incumbency advantage of no term limits could decrease electoral competition because it discourages challengers. This is mitigated, however, by strong political parties that drop new candidates into these safe seats to challenge the incumbent despite the probability that the challenger will lose. And because voter turnout in the UK remains fairly high, a lack of term limits seems to help support electoral competition because the incentive to win a seat and hold it is high. (1 point)

4. (5 points possible)

Import substitution industrialization (ISI) programs are more effective at maintaining political stability because they put the government in more direct control of the economy than a structural adjustment program (SAP) does. ISI is designed to help develop domestic manufacturing firms by making foreign products more expensive with higher tariffs. Under ISI, a government may nationalize firms and provide extensive subsidies to reduce production costs. Consequently, the government is more directly involved in controlling economic outcomes within the country. As long as these efforts are successful, the political system should remain stable, as the government is ensuring that domestic production is robust. This provides jobs and support for the political system and ensures the legitimacy of the regime. (1 point)

The "Mexican Miracle" is an example of a country pursing an ISI strategy and benefiting from the public support for the system. Mexico nationalized its oil industry, raised tariffs, and subsidized domestic production to develop its economy. Economic growth was the result as more production meant more jobs and incomes rose. (1 point)

In addition, the Mexican government was able to use its control over the economy to support its dominant party, the PRI. Using a corporatist model, the PRI created organizations of workers and farmers who then received jobs and benefits directly from the party. In this way, political stability was maintained, as an effective patron–client relationship ensured that access to economic resources was tied to support for the dominant party. (1 point)

Thus, political stability was assured because the government was actively subsidizing domestic industries to economically develop without the fear of predatory international competitors. As the number of jobs increased, so did incomes, and Mexicans' standard of living. Workers and farmers both benefited from government policies and PRI attention to their needs. Stability was maintained, however, at the expense of political and economic freedom. (1 point)

The limitations of the ISI model eventually will be reflected in political discontent in that an economy can only grow so much before it bumps up against the limitations of its production possibilities. Critics of the ISI model promoting stability will point out that as economic growth slows, and a dominant party cannot provide the benefits that it had done before, people become disenchanted with the system and may become politically violent. A switch to a SAP model, however, doesn't necessarily provide political stability. SAP policies promote economic liberalization: lowering tariffs, privatizing firms, reducing subsidies—all actions that benefit many people but that also cause income inequality to rise, causing urban/rural cleavages that cause political conflict, like the Zapatista Rebellion in Mexico. In the end, ISI policies empower the government to maintain more control over the economy and thus maintain stability. (1 point)

› Rapid Review

- The United Mexican States (Mexico) is a federal republic that has transitioned from an authoritarian to a democratic regime.
- Mexico's population reflects its indigenous and Spanish past with 62 percent of the population identifying as mestizo and 30 percent as Amerindian. Eighty-three percent of Mexicans are Catholic.
- The 1917 constitution was written to reflect the ideals of the 1910 Mexican Revolution. Essential elements include the non-reelection principle, federalism, and land reform.
- The national government, based on the U.S. model, is a presidential system that consists of a directly elected president who serves one 6-year term (*sexenio*), a bicameral legislature, and a Supreme Court. There are 31 states and a federal district.
- For 70 years, Mexico was governed by the Institutional Revolution Party (PRI), a dominant party that maintained control with an elaborate patron-client network and a corporatist system of peasant and worker groups. It was called "the perfect dictatorship."
- The PRI began a process of political liberalization in 1977 to maintain legitimacy as a product of the Revolution. Over time, changes included the introduction of a mixed election system and the creation of an independent National Election Institute (INE).
- Mexico today has a multiparty system with four major parties: PRI, PAN, PRD, and MORENA.
- The 2000 presidential election is significant because PAN candidate Vicente Fox became the first non-PRI president since the creation of the PRI. The PAN also won in 2006.
- Recent presidential elections in Mexico have been contentious because a candidate only has to win a plurality. In 2012, PRI President Enrique Peña Nieto won with 38.2 percent of the vote. Significantly, AMLO won a majority of the vote in 2018.
- No party currently has a majority of the seats in either the Senate or the Chamber of Deputies, although MORENA has the largest number of seats.
- The judiciary was reformed by limiting judges to 15-year terms and requiring that the president appoint judges from a list prepared by a nonpartisan commission.
- The Mexican media is independent but dominated by a few major players. The government mandates free airtime to all qualified political candidates. Journalists face deadly violence from drug cartels, and the state's failure to protect them has resulted in a "Not Free" Press Freedom rating from Freedom House.
- Mexico has a mixed economy. The oil giant PEMEX is still owned by the government, but 1980s structural adjustment policies privatized other industries and opened Mexico up to trade, significantly with NAFTA. Mexico has the 15th-largest economy in the world.
- Economic growth has led to income inequality. It is a coinciding cleavage in that more urban, educated northern states are outperforming the rural, indigenous, agricultural states in the south, and this leads to conflict like the Zapatista Rebellion in Chiapas.
- Forty-six percent of Mexicans live in poverty. *Prospera* is a government program to improve the education and health of rural families by giving families cash transfers.
- Crime and corruption is at a 20-year high, with local officials often cooperating with the drug cartels. Efforts to restore confidence in the legal system include more transparency with oral trials and a new national professional police force with military training.

CHAPTER 16

Nigeria

IN THIS CHAPTER

Summary: As the newest state in the AP Comparative Government and Politics course, Nigeria has the youngest, fastest-growing population of the six countries on the exam. Dealing with a legacy of military coups and corruption, the Nigerian government faces the coinciding cleavages of ethnicity, religion, and region along with the terrorist activities of Boko Haram. As a rentier state, the Nigerian economy relies too much on exporting oil and must restructure its economy to provide more job opportunities in the future.

Key Terms

All Progressives Congress (APC)
Boko Haram
bold type
bunkering
civil war
coinciding cleavages
constitutional government
corruption
coup
Economic and Financial Crimes Commission
Economic Growth and Recovery Plan
ECOWAS (Economic Community of West African States)

Federal Capital Territory
federal character
federal state
flaring
foreign direct investment (FDI)
Fourth Republic
Hausa-Fulani
Igbo
import substitution industrialization (ISI)
Independent National Election Commission (INEC)
Indigenous People of Biafra Movement (IPOB)

Ken Saro-Wiwa
LEEDS
Movement for the Actualization of the Sovereign State of Biafra (MASSOB)
Movement for the Survival of the Ogoni People (MOSOP)
Movement to Emancipate the Niger Delta (MEND)
multinational corporations (MNCs)
National Economic Empowerment and Development Strategies (NEEDS)

Niger Delta Avengers
Nigerian Industrial
    Revolution Plan
    (NIRP)
Nigerian National
    Petroleum Corporation
    (NNPC)
Nollywood
OPEC
patrimonialism

People's Democratic Party
    (PDP)
prebendalism
presidential system
rentier state
resource curse
SEEDS
single-member district
    election

special economic zones
    (SEZs)
structural adjustment
    program (SAP)
Westminster model
Westminster parliamentary
    system
Yoruba

Nigeria as a Case Study

As you study Nigeria, pay careful attention to the discussion of the following concepts as they are the most frequently used in comparing Nigeria with other countries on the AP Comparative Government and Politics exam.

CONCEPT	POSSIBLE COMPARISONS/USEFUL EXAMPLES
Less-developed country	Highly developed country
Rentier state	Diversified economy
Coup	Revolution, reform
Presidential system	Parliamentary system
Federal government	Unitary government
Terrorism	Methods of handling
Coinciding cleavages	Methods of dealing with conflict
Colonialism	Impacts on society

Sovereignty, Authority, and Power

The State

The Federal Republic of Nigeria has a complex history of colonialism, military rule, and democratic transitions. Although the Portuguese landed in present-day Lagos in 1472, the British colonized it in 1861 as part of their effort to end the African slave trade. Granted a West African sphere of influence at the Berlin Conference of 1885, Great Britain expanded the territory under its control, formally colonizing Nigeria in 1914. The colony was split with only the coastal areas under direct control, while the northern, Muslim area was governed indirectly through local leaders who were allowed to maintain sharia, or Islamic law. After World War II, calls for independence for African states increased with Great Britain granting Nigerian independence in 1960.

Since gaining independence, Nigeria has alternated between periods of democratic governments and military rule. After the first military coup in 1966, attempts to establish the Second and Third Republics were not successful as the military seized power. Since 1999, however, the Fourth Republic has maintained democratic elections and transfers of power, while the military has remained in the barracks.

NIGERIAN GOVERNMENTS	YEARS	TYPE OF GOVERNMENT	EVENTS
First Republic	1963–66	Westminster model: parliamentary system	• 3 regions North, East, West • Parliament dominated by northerners
Military Rule	1966–79		• 1966 military coup • Creation of 12 states instead of regions • 1967–70 Biafran secession and civil war • 1976 Created 7 more states
Second Republic	1979–83	Presidential system	• Transition overseen by General Olusegun Obasanjo
Military Rule	1983–93		• 1983 military coup led by General Muhammadu Buhari • 1985 military coup led by General Ibrahim Babangida • 1987 created 2 more states • 1991 moved capital from Lagos to Abuja • 1991 created 9 more states
Third Republic	1993	Presidential system	• Presidential election results annulled • Military coup by Sani Abacha
Military Rule	1993–99		• 1996 created 6 more states • Noted for human rights violations—assassination of Ogoni activist Ken Saro-Wiwa
Fourth Republic	1999–	Presidential system	• President Obasanjo (1999–2007) • President Yar'Adua (2007–2010) • President Jonathan (2010–2015) • President Buhari (2015–)

Nation

As a state whose boundaries were arbitrarily drawn by a colonial power, Nigeria is home to over 250 different ethnic groups. For the AP Comparative Government and Politics exam, you should focus on the three largest groups: **Igbo** (15 percent), **Yoruba** (20 percent), and **Hausa-Fulani** (27 percent). The Igbo are concentrated in the lower southeastern portion of Nigeria and are primarily Christian. Igbo leaders created the Republic of Biafra in 1967, and a group called MASSOB (Movement for the Actualization of the Sovereign State of Biafra) still agitates for independence today. The Yoruba are primarily located in central and southwestern Nigeria, including Lagos, and its members are both Christian and Muslim. Both the Yoruba and Igbo were directly ruled by Great Britain during colonial times. The Hausa-Fulani homeland is in northern Nigeria and was governed by indirect British rule. Local emirs were allowed to maintain local control and the Islamic faith, although the British abolished the Sokoto Caliphate. Currently, the Nigerian population is almost evenly split between Muslims and Christians with a great deal of conflict between the groups occurring in the Middle Belt region of the country where the two religious traditions overlap. All tribes maintain their own language, although English is the official language of the state. Because of its colonial legacy, it has been difficult for Nigeria to establish itself as a nation-state.

One of the few national unifying symbols is that of the Nigerian National Football Team, the Super Eagles, who were the first African team to qualify for the 2018 World Cup in Russia.

Legitimacy

As a state that has endured significant regime change since 1960, the 1999 Constitution of the Fourth Republic is the most significant document supporting rational-legal legitimacy in Nigeria. For example, although President Obasanjo wanted the constitution amended in 2006 to allow him to run for a third term, when the Senate failed to pass the amendment by the required two-thirds margin, the former general did not stage a coup, but rather peacefully passed power to the newly elected Yar'Adua. In addition, when President Goodluck Jonathan won his 2011 election without winning 25 percent of the vote in any northern state (he did win the required 25 percent in two-thirds of the states), he served for four years, stepping down when he lost the 2015 election. The 2015 election cycle is notable in that it marked a peaceful transition of power between two political parties, from Jonathan's PDP to Buhari's APC.

Traditional legitimacy also plays a role in Nigeria. Allowing the northern Islamic states to adopt sharia as part of their legal code shows how Nigeria has tried to minimize religious conflict by allowing Islamic law to coexist with common law. A different accommodation that deals with the traditional north-south division in Nigeria is the informal agreement among political elites to alternate northern and southern presidents. For example, southerner Obasanjo was followed by northerner Yar'Adua.

Regime

Nigeria has experienced the most regime change of any country in the AP Comparative Government and Politics course by alternating between democratic and military rule between 1960 and 1999. Since 1999, however, the Fourth Republic has held as a democratic republic with competitive elections and civil society protections. High levels of government corruption and election violence, however, keep Nigeria from being a full consolidated liberal democracy.

Freedom House Ratings: Partly Free (political rights: 21/40, civil liberties: 24/60)

The Economist Intelligence Unit's Democracy Index: Hybrid 4.1 (Hybrid is between an authoritarian regime and a flawed democracy.)

Type of Economic System

Nigeria has a mixed economy with elements of markets and a command economy. Nigeria's main export is oil by the state-owned **Nigerian National Petroleum Corporation (NNPC)**, which relies on **multinational corporations (MNCs)** like Shell and Exxon-Mobile to form joint ventures to do the extraction. Because the Nigerian national government gets two-thirds of its revenue from the export and sale of oil, Nigeria is considered a **rentier state**. Nigeria nationalized the oil industry in 1971 to join **OPEC**. Although the government relies on oil revenue, oil only constitutes 9 percent of Nigerian GDP. The largest component of GDP is household consumption at 80 percent with many Nigerians still involved in subsistence agriculture and the informal economy. According to the World Bank, 60 percent of Nigerians officially live on less than $2 a day.

Political Culture and Socialization

Corruption, the misuse of official authority, is a consistent theme in Nigerian political culture. Scholar Daniel Jordan Smith refers to it as "a culture of corruption" in that "Nigerian notions of corruption encompass everything from government bribery and graft, rigged elections, and fraudulent business deals, to the diabolical abuse of occult powers, medical quackery, cheating in school, and even deceiving a lover." Smith states that Nigerians use the phrase "it's 419" to describe how the state or a businessman or anyone tries to deceive someone else. 419 is the number of an antifraud statute which has become a "universal metaphor for deception." This lack of trust caused by corruption is only exacerbated by the strong ethnic and religious coinciding cleavages that exist in Nigeria. Smith cites an African proverb, "Whoever does not rob the state robs his kith and kin," to explain how strong patron–client solidarity networks reinforce the message that to get ahead in Nigeria, a person's "group" also needs to get ahead. Consequently, the primary agent of socialization in Nigeria is the family, and often the family's political experiences will have the greatest impact on the development of one's attitudes toward government.

Government Institutions

The Constitution

The 1999 Constitution of the Fourth Federal Republic of Nigeria is based primarily on that of the Second Republic. Although leaders of the First Republic established a **Westminster parliamentary system** in 1963, by 1979 Nigerian military leaders felt that a switch to an American **presidential system** would be a more effective way to for them to transition to civilian rule in the Second Republic. Unfortunately, Nigeria experienced military rule again until 1999 except for the very brief Third Republic.

A transition to the Fourth Republic was overseen by General Abubakar after the sudden death of the dictator, General Sani Abacha, in 1998. An **Independent National Election Commission (INEC)** was created to oversee national, state, and local elections for the new regime. The institutions of the Second Republic were maintained: a directly elected bicameral legislature, a directly elected president, and an appointed Supreme Court. Another important carryover was the "**federal character**" concept in that the president's cabinet would have to have one member from each of the 36 states.

Levels of Government

Nigeria is a **federal state** where sovereignty is formally shared between the national and state governments, as delineated in the constitution. A federal system was established in response to the ethnic diversity in Nigeria as a way to establish local governments with the authority to deal with local problems. Northern states, for example, were allowed to adopt sharia, or Islamic law, in addition to common law as part of their legal code. After splitting the three British regions into 12 states in 1966, additional states were added to increase the legitimacy of the national government by sharing power with different regional groups. Each Nigerian state is guaranteed a cabinet seat, three Senate seats, and a population-appropriate number of House of Representatives seats. The **Federal Capital Territory** of Abuja, which elects one senator and two members of the House, was established in the center of the country to be another symbol of unity. The 36 states vary tremendously, however, in their level of economic development as the oil revenues earned by the national government are rarely used for capital improvements or infrastructure, instead being used to enrich the political elite. Social movements, particularly in the Niger Delta region, can erupt as local residents turn to violence to force the national government to share the oil wealth with the region where the oil is located.

Nigeria belongs to two supranational organizations. After joining GATT (General Agreement on Tariffs and Trade) in 1960, Nigeria was included as a founding member of the World Trade Organization (WTO), which was established in 1995. As a member of the WTO, Nigeria agrees to abide by its trade rules and dispute settlement process. In addition, Nigeria is a founding member of **ECOWAS (Economic Community of West African States)**, which is a

15-member regional group committed to free trade among the states. ECOWAS has an executive Commission, a legislative Community Parliament, and a Community Court of Justice. Future plans for ECOWAS include a common currency and an elected parliament.

Legislative-Executive Relationships

The Nigerian political system is based on the U.S. presidential system, so if you remember how the U.S. government is formally organized in the Constitution, for the most part, the Nigerian system works the same way. In the following charts, the major differences between the two systems are in **bold type**.

If you are also taking the AP U.S. Government and Politics exam, this is an excellent time to reflect on the elements of the U.S. political system that allow it to operate as a consolidated democracy, while Nigeria struggles to do so. The key to understanding the difference is to remember that a government with a constitution does not ensure that it is a **constitutional government**, or one based on rule of law. The United States and Nigeria have the same formal institutions, but Nigeria's culture of corruption means that government officials often use their positions to enrich themselves and their friends, along with applying power in an arbitrary manner to punish enemies. This is not to say that that the U.S. system is perfect, but a merit-based bureaucracy, a truly independent judiciary, and a transparent budgetary process enable Americans to protect their political rights and civil liberties in ways that Nigerians cannot.

Executive Branch

	UNITED STATES	NIGERIA
Presidential Election	• Win a majority of electoral college • Separate from legislative elections • 4-year term—2-term limit • Presidential candidate selects vice-presidential candidate	• **2-ballot system—must win 50% on first round or face a runoff** • **Also, must win 25% of vote in 2/3 states** • Separate from legislative elections • 4-year term—2-term limit • Presidential candidate selects vice-presidential candidate
Formal Role of President	• Head of state • Head of government	• Head of state • Head of government
Cabinet Selection	• President appoints • Senate confirms • No dual offices • Advise president • Manage bureaucratic agencies	• **President must appoint one cabinet member from each of 36 states** • Senate confirms • No dual offices • Advise president • Manage bureaucratic agencies
Powers of the President	• Commander in chief • Propose laws • Sign/veto laws • Make treaties (Senate ratifies) • Appoint ambassadors (Senate confirms) • Receive ambassadors • Appoints judges (Senate confirms) • Pardon	• Commander in chief • Propose laws • Sign/veto laws • Make treaties (Senate ratifies) • Appoint ambassadors (Senate confirm) • Receive ambassadors • Appoints judges (Senate confirms) • Pardon • **Call for national referendums**
Residence of the President	• White House, Washington, D.C.	• Aso Rock Presidential Villa, • Abuja, F.C.T.

Legislative Branch

	U.S. CONGRESS	NIGERIAN FEDERAL ASSEMBLY
Senate (Upper House) Elections	• 2 senators per state • Direct election since 17th Amendment • SMD plurality	• **3 senators per state** • **1 senator for Federal Capital Territory** • Direct election • **Multimember plurality**
Senate Membership and Term	• 100 members • 6-year terms	• **109 members** • **4-year terms**
Senate-Only Powers:	• Confirm presidential appointments • Ratify treaties • Hold impeachment trial	• Confirm presidential appointments • Ratify treaties • Hold impeachment trial
House of Representatives (Lower House) Elections	• Based on population • Direct election • SMD plurality	• Based on population • Direct election • SMD plurality
House Membership and Term	• 435 members • 2-year terms	• **360 members** • **4-year terms**
House-Only Powers:	• Introduce revenue bills • Impeach	• Introduce revenue bills • Impeach
Legislative Process	• Use committees to scrutinize bill • Bill must pass majority of both houses and be signed by the president • If president vetoes, both houses must override by 2/3 vote • Constitutional amendments require 2/3 vote in both houses to be proposed—then ratified by 3/4 state legislatures	• Use committees to scrutinize bill • Bill must pass majority of both houses and be signed by the president • If president vetoes, both houses must override by 2/3 vote • Constitutional amendments require 2/3 vote in both houses to be proposed—then **ratified by 2/3 state assemblies**

Judicial Branch

The Nigerian judicial system is also similar to the U.S. system in its organization. Because of its federal structure, Nigeria has a dual court system with state and national level courts. The national courts are the Supreme Court, which is the highest court in the system, a federal appeals court, and a federal high court. The Supreme Court has appellate jurisdiction from lower courts and original jurisdiction for a state vs. state or state vs. national government case. As an independent court, it also has the power of judicial review and can overturn laws and executive actions. States have a high court, an appeals court, and lower courts, including sharia courts in 11 northern states. Nigerian law is based on British common law, although this is supplemented by sharia law in states with sharia courts.

Bureaucracy

The bureaucracy in Nigeria is large and corrupt. Nigerians commonly have to pay a bribe for common government services such as getting a license or often must offer a "dash" (gratuity) for others, like to a policeman at a checkpoint. Transparency International's Corruption Perception Index ranks Nigeria as 136th out of 176 countries in the world with a score of 28/100. The level of corruption is so endemic that it is called **prebendalism,** which is an extreme form of patron-clientelism where officeholders feel justified to use their position to enrich themselves and members of their tribe. This informal relationship is only strengthened by the "federal character" conditions in the constitution. Requiring that the president must appoint a member of each state to a cabinet position reinforces the perception that working for the government is about getting a share of the revenue. Nigerian novelist Adaobi Tricia Nwaubani illustrates this point by explaining that "Political office confers 'a knife with which to cut the national cake.'"

Military and Other Coercive Institutions

The Nigerian military is the largest fighting force in Africa and frequently has been used as a peacekeeping force by the UN, ECOWAS, and the African Union. But the military also ruled Nigeria for 29 of the first 39 years of independence from Great Britain, a concern that has led presidents of the **Fourth Republic** to deal strategically with the military for the last 18 years to prevent a coup. One way to maintain support was to not stop the corrupt practices of the military elite. Because the Nigerian defense budget is not published, fraudulent arms contracts were an effortless way to amass wealth. Officers also maintain "ghost soldiers" on their rosters in order to collect extra pay. The result is that the Nigerian fighting force on paper looks more impressive than it actually is. Recent attempts to fight the terrorist group **Boko Haram** in northern Nigeria have brought this problem to the attention of the world press, as Nigerian soldiers complain of having no bullets with which to fight the terrorists. Human rights activists charge that the military and other security forces, such as the Nigerian police, engage in arbitrary arrests and torture. President Buhari, a former general, has pledged to fight this corruption.

Leadership and Elite Recruitment

Political recruitment in Nigeria is primarily an elaborate system of patron–client relationships. A traditional source of recruitment came from military service as both President Obasanjo and President Buhari are former generals. More recently leaders have come from state-level offices. For example, both President Yar'Adua and President Jonathan were state governors. Prebendalism manifests itself in recruitment as many people obtain government positions through family and kinship ties. Finally, attaining an advanced degree is often a prerequisite to higher office, as many current officials began their careers as lecturers at Nigerian universities.

Linkage Institutions

Elections

Presidential elections are the most important elections in Nigeria and have the highest turnout rates, although this rate has been declining from an average of 50 percent to a low of 35 percent in 2019. Because of the visibility of the office, it was important to design an election process that would give the office legitimacy because of a clear mandate from the electorate. Consequently, the winning presidential candidate must win 50 percent of the direct popular vote or face a runoff with the second-place finisher. In addition, the winner needs to show wide regional support by attaining at least 25 percent of the vote in two-thirds of the states.

The presidential elections of 2015 marked an important milestone for Nigeria as the opposition leader, Muhammadu Buhari, won the election and incumbent Goodluck Jonathan stepped down. This peaceful transfer of power was reflective of the advances that Nigeria has made in ensuring fair, competitive elections for the Fourth Republic. The Independent National Election Commission (INEC) was credited for conducting a fair election with the introduction of new permanent voter cards and updated equipment. Yet problems still existed in that the elections were postponed for six weeks because of a threat by Boko Haram. The number of election-associated deaths was much smaller, however, than it had been in 2011. Election violence, however, increased during the 2019 election in which President Buhari was reelected with 56 percent of the vote.

The presidential elections of 2011 were marred by violence. After President Goodluck Jonathan managed to win the majority of the popular vote and 25 percent of the vote in two-thirds of the states needed to be reelected, northerners were quick to notice that he had accomplished his victory without winning any northern states. Riots escalated and protesters targeted Christians and southerners. Christians retaliated by attacking Muslims. Particularly in the Middle Belt, where religious and ethnic groups overlap, the burning and looting of buildings displaced thousands from their homes. Human Rights Watch calculates that over 800 died and many more were injured.

Unfortunately, violence is not new to Nigerian elections and can be found at all levels of government. Throughout the Fourth Republic, armed gangs have been known to intimidate voters, steal or stuff ballot boxes, and rig elections, especially in contested areas like the Niger Delta. Corrupt election officials and security forces have been known to manufacture results in the past. Hopefully, moving forward, elections will continue to improve.

Presidential Election Results

ELECTION YEAR	CANDIDATE	PARTY	RESULTS
1999	• **Olusegun Obasanjo** • Olu Falae	• People's Democratic Party (PDP) • Alliance for Democracy (AD)	• 63% • 37%
2003	• **Olusegun Obasanjo** • Muhammadu Buhari • 18 other candidates	• PDP • All Nigeria People's Party (ANPP)	• 62% • 37%
2007	• **Umara Yar'Adua** • Muhammadu Buhari • 16 other candidates	• PDP • ANPP	• 70% • 19%
2011	• **Goodluck Jonathan** • Muhammadu Buhari • 18 other candidates	• PDP • Congress for Progressive Change	• 59% • 32%
2015	• Goodluck Jonathan • **Muhammadu Buhari** • 12 other candidates	• PDP • Al Progressives Congress (APC)	• 45% • 54%
2019	• **Muhammadu Buhari** • Atiku Abubakar • 14 other candidates	• APC • PDP	• 56% • 41%

Source: Nigerian IEC

Election Systems and Party Systems

Given its British colonial past and its adoption of the U.S. presidential model, it is not surprising that Nigeria would also adopt a **single-member district election system** (also known as first past the post). Each state is allocated seats in the House of Representatives based on population, from 2 for the Federal Capital Territory to 24 for Lagos. The state is divided into the appropriate number of districts, and voters select the person that they want to represent them. All seats in the House of Representatives are awarded to the winner of the most votes (plurality). For the Senate, each state is divided into three districts and candidates compete to win a plurality of votes in that district.

Typically, the use of a single-member district system results in a two-party system, unless there are significant regional parties. Since 1999, Nigeria's party system has been characterized by numerous small, personalized factions and the **People's Democratic Party (PDP)**, which has dominated elections. With the success of the **All Progressives Congress (APC)** party in 2015, however, the current National Assembly has only a few seats that are not held by either the APC or the PDP. Consequently, the political party system appears to be maturing into a two-party system from a multi-party system.

National Assembly Election Results

ELECTION YEAR	POLITICAL PARTIES	HOUSE # OF SEATS MAJORITY: 181	SENATE # OF SEATS MAJORITY: 55
1999	• **People's Democratic Party (PDP)**	• **206**	• **59**
	• All People's Party (APP)	• 74	• 29
	• Alliance for Democracy (AD)	• 68	• 20
	• Others	• 12	• 1
2003	• **PDP**	• **223**	• **76**
	• All Nigeria People's Party (ANPP)	• 96	• 27
	• AD	• 34	• 6
	• Others	• 7	
2007	• **PDP**	• **263**	• **87**
	• ANPP	• 63	• 14
	• Action Congress (AC)	• 30	• 6
	• Others	• 4	
2011	• **PDP**	• **203**	• **71**
	• Action Congress of Nigeria (CAN)	• 69	• 18
	• ANPP	• 28	• 7
	• Congress for Progressive Change (CPC)	• 38	• 7
	• Others	• 22	• 6
2015	• **All Progressives Congress (APC)**	• **225**	• **60**
	• PDP	• 125	• 48
	• Others	• 10	• 1
2019	• **APC**	• **217**	• **64**
	• PDP	• 115	• 45
	• Others	• 28	• 1

Source: Nigerian IEC

The Parties

Until the 2015 election cycle, the People's Democratic Party, or PDP, was the dominant party in Nigeria, controlling the presidency, the National Assembly, and most of the state governorships. One of only three parties approved to nominate candidates in 1999, the PDP quickly became the most popular vehicle for the political elite to rally around, notably in support of former General Obasanjo who enjoyed public support for his turnover of military rule to the Second Republic. In addition, his imprisonment under General Sani Abacha solidified his credentials. To ensure power-sharing stability, the PDP made an informal agreement among elites, which was to switch between southern and northern candidates for president. After Obasanjo's two terms, the party selected Umara Yar'Adua, a little-known governor from a northern state. Yar'Adua died in office, however, leaving southerner Vice President Goodluck Jonathan in charge. After Jonathan's slim margin win in 2011, many defected from the party.

The PDP is a center-right party, committed to economic liberalization by privatizing state-owned industries, but also supportive of social programs like increasing access to education and health care. The party is socially conservative as well, voting to punish homosexual conduct. PDP strongholds continue to be the states of the Niger Delta and the eastern side of the Middle Belt. But many Nigerians were disillusioned by the PDP's failure to improve conditions in Nigeria after being in power for 15 years, a common explanation is that the PDP is the "poverty development party." Nobel Prize winner Wole Soyinka has expressed that the "PDP is a coalition of the blind, corrupt, and immoral."

The new strongest party in Nigeria is the All Progressives Congress, or APC, a coalition of three opposition parties: Action Congress for Nigeria, Congress for Progressive Change, and the All Nigeria People's Party. Founded specifically to win the 2015 election cycle, rival leaders put aside their differences to beat the PDP. To determine the party's first presidential candidate, a primary was held and won by Muhammadu Buhari. During the 2019 election, the APC looked to expand its success in northern and southwestern Nigeria to the southeast by reaching out to the Igbo with a continuation of the informal north-south agreement. A party spokesman recently said "the shortest distance to Igbo presidency is APC. By 2023, a northerner, President Buhari, will have completed his eight years and an Igbo man will easily come in." This effort was not successful as the Igbo states remained loyal to the PDP in 2019 although President Buhari increased the number of votes he won in the Igbo states of Abia, Ebonyi, Enugu, and Imo. The APC is a center-left party economically, favoring government regulation, but because of its strong base of support in northern Nigeria, it is also a very socially conservative party.

Interest Groups

Since the end of military rule in 1999, interest groups in Nigeria have flourished. Numerous professional organizations, student associations, cause groups, and trade unions exist across the country, suggesting a pluralistic environment. Their effectiveness at influencing public policy, however, is difficult to measure in a political environment of prebendalism. Certainly, the frequent use of protests and strikes by many groups would indicate the difficulty of using conventional forms of political participation to affect change. The most successful interest groups are those that represent ethnic groups. These include: Arewa Consultative Forum (Hausa-Fulani), Ohanaeze Ndigbo (Igbo), Afenifere (Yoruba), the Middle Belt Forum, and the Ijaw Youth Council. The two dominant religious associations are the Christian Association of Nigeria (CAN) and the Nigerian Supreme Council for Islamic Affairs (NSCIA). Many women's groups, like the African Women Power Network and She Leads Africa, concentrate on entrepreneurship, but the Nigerian Women's Trust Fund is focused on increasing the number of women in elected office. The Nigerian Conservation Fund and Friends of the Environment are prominent environmental groups.

Citizens, Society, and the State

Social Cleavages

The Nigerian state confronts powerful **coinciding cleavages**, salient social divisions that cause conflict. The three most powerful social divisions are ethnicity, religion, and geographical region.

ETHNIC GROUP	GEOGRAPHICAL LOCATION	PRIMARY RELIGION
Hausa-Fulani	Northern Nigeria	Islam
Yoruba	Southwestern Nigeria	Christian
Igbo	Southeastern Nigeria	Christian

These cleavages were exploited during colonial times by the British in a typical "divide and conquer" strategy to maintain control. The British directly ruled the southern regions and allowed indirect rule by local Muslim leaders in the north. The British legacy left the south with better educational institutions and infrastructure, particularly around Lagos. Current economic conditions have only exacerbated the conflict. The five wealthiest states in Nigeria are all found in the south as is the oil that supplies so much of government revenue. The poorest states, where over 70 percent of the population live in poverty, are found in the north. Institutional structures such as federalism and election requirements have not been able to surmount the problem of prebendalism, leading to a zero-sum game approach to politics where if one group wins, the rest must lose.

Civil Society

Nigeria has a vibrant civil society where many Nigerians are able to build social capital through family, tribal, and religious activities. Artistic endeavors abound from groups preserving cultural traditions to **Nollywood**, the fast-growing cinema industry. Other groups form to improve societal conditions such as the Wellbeing Foundation with its #Maternal-Monday campaign to improve healthcare access for mothers and children.

The Media

According to the BBC, "the media scene in Nigeria is one of the liveliest." Although there are state-run television and radio stations, these are supplemented by numerous daily newspapers, commercial TV and radio stations, and access to satellite and cable stations. The government does not censor the Internet, and estimates are that 92 million Nigerians have regular access to the Internet. Social media is also popular, with many Nigerians using the Facebook platform. Freedom House, however, ranks Nigerian press freedom as only partly free (scoring 51 out of 100 points). The biggest concern is about government secrecy and treatment of journalists. Although Nigeria passed a Freedom of Information Act in 2011, it is still difficult to obtain accurate government records. In addition, journalists have experienced harassment and imprisonment for reporting on government corruption and military abuses. Boko Haram has also threatened journalists.

Political Participation

Political participation in Nigeria is widespread but follows a typical pattern in that only 50 percent of Nigerians feel that knowledge of politics is important. According to the World Values Survey, Nigerians strongly support democracy and want the government to take more responsibility. They feel that journalists fairly cover elections, but only 52 percent believe that the votes are counted fairly. On the other hand, most people have never signed a petition, joined a demonstration, or gone on strike. The one thing that a majority of Nigerians do is vote in presidential elections.

Social Movements

For certain groups in Nigeria, traditional methods of political participation do not result in the desired public policy, so they form social movements to pressure the government to make changes. Groups in the Niger Delta region, in particular, are notorious for selecting this method. **Ken Saro-Wiwa** famously led a nonviolent group called **Movement for the Survival of the Ogoni People (MOSOP)** to end the environmental degradation of the Ogoni homelands. He was executed by General Sani Abacha in 1995. Nonviolent Niger Delta groups today are often overshadowed by those willing to use violence. The **Movement to Emancipate the Niger Delta (MEND)** was an attempt by young militants to bring economic justice to the region. Often engaged in kidnapping oil workers for ransom, most members accepted amnesty from the government in 2009 to cease its activities. The most recent group calls itself the **Niger Delta Avengers** and since 2016 has engaged in blowing up pipelines to demand more government resources for the region.

Biafran independence is another longstanding goal for social movements in Nigeria. Currently two prominent groups are calling for a referendum to establish Biafran independence. The **Indigenous People of Biafra Movement (IPOB)** and the **Movement for the Actualization of the Sovereign State of Biafra (MASSOB)** are primarily composed of Igbo supporters who still resent the treatment of the region in the civil war of 1967–70. The Nigerian government has recently named IPOB as a terrorist organization and is actively trying to stop its operations.

Citizenship and Representation

Nigerian citizenship is granted to a child by descent if at least one parent is Nigerian. Being born on Nigerian soil does not grant citizenship. Citizenship may be gained through a registration process if a woman marries a Nigerian man, if a child is adopted, or if one's grandparents were Nigerian. All others must be naturalized.

Representation in the Nigerian government is adequate for prominent ethnic groups, as the 36 states correspond to their geographic location. The structure of the National Assembly with the representation of states in the Senate and population in the House reflects this division. The federal character principle ensures that each state has a member of the cabinet in the executive branch and the informal north-south agreement among political elites seems to reduce conflict. The group that is most underrepresented in the political system, however, is women. In the 2015 election, 15 women won seats in the House of Representatives (10 PDP, 5 APC) and 8 in the Senate (5 PDP, 3 APC). The first female candidate for president, Comfort Oluremi Sonaiya of the KOWA party, won few votes, and no woman became a governorship, although 4 female deputy governors won their elections. The 2019 election marked a setback for women with only 11 women winning seats in the House and 7 in the Senate. Women's groups have called for a gender equity law to be passed.

Political and Economic Change

Revolution, Coups, and War

Nigeria, a colony since 1914, did not have to resort to revolution to gain its independence; instead, the British granted it in 1960 as part of the second wave of democracy after World War II. Fairly quickly, Nigeria faced both coups and civil war, mainly caused by tensions between the three main ethnic groups. A **coup** is a quick overthrow of the government by force, usually done by the military. Nigeria experienced both a coup and a counter-coup in 1967 by rival military forces, the latter putting northerner Colonel Yakubu Gowan in charge. Attempts to reorganize Nigeria as a confederation failed, and easterners under the leadership of Colonel Ojukwu seceded to form the Republic of Biafra. For the next two years, Nigeria was engaged in a **civil war,** or war between citizens of the same country. The Nigerian military attacked the area and effectively blockaded the region, causing millions of civilians to die from starvation. After the war, military rule continued in Nigeria because attempts to establish democracy under the Second and Third Republics both ended with military coups. Since the establishment of the Fourth Republic in 1999, however, the military has stayed in its barracks and Nigeria has had an elected, civilian government for 18 years, the longest regime since winning independence.

Political Change

Given its British colonial history, Nigeria established the **Westminster model** of parliamentary government for the First Republic. After a period of military rule, however, Nigeria transitioned to a **presidential system** of government in 1979 with hopes that direct election of the executive would provide a strong unifying force to stabilize the country. The **federal character** principle was also introduced to ensure that the government's legitimacy as a truly national institution would be established. All political parties had to have members from at least two-thirds of the states to compete in national elections and a representative from each state had to be appointed to the cabinet. Subsequent military coups in 1983, 1985, and 1993 continued to thwart the democratic process with the installation of autocratic military dictators who often styled themselves as president and maintained support through sharing oil revenues in a patron–client system often referred to as **patrimonialism**. It should be noted, however, that the military coup leaders always seized power with a promise to transition to democracy when the government was stabilized. The military instigated return to civilian rule for the Second, Third, and Fourth Republics, with some leaders intending to continue to rule as a civilian president, although that never happened. Instead after the death of the ruthless Abacha, Nigerian elites rallied around the presidential candidacy of former General Obasanjo, a southern Yoruba Christian, who as the leader of the People's Democratic Party (PDP) could unify the country, with the understanding that the presidency would alternate to a northerner in 2007.

Since the inception of the Fourth Republic of Nigeria in 1999, there has not been the dramatic political change of earlier years. The Nigerian government has focused primarily on reforms to improve the democratic credentials of the regime. One such reform has been the efforts of the Independent National Election Commission (INEC) to prevent people from voting multiple times in one election by issuing permanent voter ID cards to all eligible citizens. International observers say that the 2015 presidential election was fairly conducted and historic, being the first time that the opposition gained power through elections. In addition, President Buhari has had some success in his anti-corruption efforts by restructuring the state-run oil company and recovering billions in stolen assets.

On the other hand, the actions of Boko Haram, a radical terrorist group operating in northeastern Nigeria, are a true threat to Nigerian sovereignty. Boko Haram, whose name translates from Hausa as "Western education is forbidden," wants to establish an Islamic caliphate in Nigeria. Their methods to achieve this goal are systematic terror and violence by using suicide bombing, kidnapping of girls from school, and guerilla warfare tactics to seize territory, primarily in the northern state of Borno. In 2012, the Nigerian government declared a state of emergency in the area and sent in troops to stop the group. Ten years later and with the help of international forces, Boko Haram has lost territory but still engages in terrorist activities such as using children as suicide bombers to blow up marketplaces and mosques. The Nigerian government's inability to stop Boko Haram using military force is eroding trust and leading to calls for political change.

The #EndSARS movement against police violence reflects an additional call for political change in Nigeria. The Special Anti-Robbery Squad (SARS) was notorious for committing acts of torture, kidnapping, and executions. Organized on social media after a viral video, large public demonstrations began in Lagos and spread. Protesters were killed in October 2020, and the military was deployed to stop the demonstrations. In response to public pressure, the Buhari government disbanded the SARS unit and reassigned its members, promising police reform. The public remains skeptical and demonstrations have been banned in the city of Lagos.

Economic Change

At the time of independence, Nigeria was an agricultural exporter of palm oil and groundnuts. Anxious to develop the economy, Nigeria's political elites (civilian and military) pursued a policy of **import substitution industrialization (ISI)** by raising tariff walls, nationalization, and subsidizing infant industries. Very quickly, however, the high oil prices in the 1970s and the creation of the state-owned **Nigerian National Petroleum Corporation (NNPC)** led to the development of a **rentier state**, or a government that relies primarily on the export and sale of a natural resource for revenues. During the 1980s when the price of oil dropped, government debt loads quickly increased, prompting a bailout from the World Bank and International Monetary Fund. These Bretton Woods agencies required Nigeria to undergo a **structural adjustment program (SAP)** to reduce government intervention in the economy by privatizing industries, lowering tariffs, and raising taxes. Often, however, the privatization schemes only served to reward the president's supporters and the problems associated with a **resource curse**—less economic growth and weak democratic institutions—continue to plague Nigeria.

Today, the NNPC oversees joint ventures with foreign multinational corporations (MNCs) such as Shell and Exxon-Mobile, which conduct the exploration and extraction of the oil and gas. The Nigerian government receives 80 percent of its revenues from the sale and export of oil, but because this money has enriched corrupt officials and not been reinvested in refineries, Nigeria must import gasoline. In addition, the economy is too reliant on the price of oil. In 2017, Nigeria just came out of an economic recession caused by low oil prices and the disruption of production in the Niger Delta by the militant groups. Other problems include **bunkering**, which is when local residents tap into the pipelines to siphon off the fuel to sell it illegally, and **flaring**, which is allowing flammable gas to burn off during oil extraction, which damages the environment.

Recent presidents have called for more diversification of the Nigerian economy. Goodluck Jonathan started the **Nigerian Industrial Revolution Plan (NIRP)** to increase incentives for local manufacturing. Initiatives have begun to capture the natural gas instead of flaring it and use it to provide electricity, which is unreliable in Nigeria. President Buhari has enacted an **Economic Growth and Recovery Plan** that pledges the national government to work with the states to improve infrastructure and manufacturing so that Nigeria can reduce its dependency on imports. Buhari explained recently, "We must become a nation where we grow what we eat and consume what we produce." To bring millions of people out of poverty, however, more than slogans will be needed. Even when the Nigerian government created **special economic zones (SEZs)**, a typically successful form of economic liberalization, most of them have not attracted **foreign direct investment (FDI)**, mainly because of inadequate infrastructure and bureaucratic delays.

Public Policy

Although Nigeria is a federal republic, political power is very much centralized in the national government because oil revenues are funneled directly to the political elite in the capital city of Abuja. Members of the National Assembly are thought to be the highest-paid legislators in the world. Only recently has the legislature responded to pressure and published a budget with line item breakdowns so that the public can review expenditures. Formally the budget process is similar to the regular lawmaking process with the government proposing a budget that has to be passed by both houses and then signed by the president. Unfortunately, a culture of corruption and a lack of accountability make it possible for phantom contracts and ghost workers to earn money for those who can access this system of prebendalism. President Buhari has had some success in his anti-corruption efforts, empowering the **Economic and Financial Crimes Commission** to arrest prominent members of the government on corruption charges. Critics charge, however, that this commission has mostly been used to target political opponents.

Religious Conflict

Nigeria is almost evenly split between Christians and Muslims, exacerbating the coinciding cleavages of ethnicity and geography. To mitigate problems, the government has formally allowed northern states to adopt sharia and the informal north-south agreement by political parties for presidential candidates also includes religion. President Buhari is a northern Fulani Muslim, while Vice President Osinbajo is a southwestern Yoruba Christian. Conflict between the two groups most often erupts in violence in the Middle Belt region where all the groups overlap. For example, Hausa herdsmen often find themselves in conflict with Christian farmers. But violence in the region can often occur in response to outside events, like the riots in Kaduna in 2002 over the Miss World contest, or the 2006 riots over the Danish publication of cartoons about the Prophet Muhammad. It is the systematic terror inflicted by Boko Haram, however, that has truly challenged the government. The smaller riots in the Middle Belt are brought under control within a few days by security forces. It has taken the Nigerian military and its allies, on the other hand, several years to regain territory captured by Boko Haram, and the terrorist group is still successfully employing suicide bombers.

Population Growth

Nigeria has the largest population in Africa at 204 million, but it is an extremely young population with a median age of 18 and life expectancy of 54. With a total fertility rate of 5.5 children per woman, Nigeria's population is expected to exceed that of the United States by 2050 at 440 million. It has already grown by 300 percent since independence in 1960, when the population was only 45 million. The government, however, does not have a family-planning public policy, primarily for both cultural and religious reasons. Researchers note, however, that contraceptive use is higher among educated, urban women living in the southwest at 38 percent. Women living in the northern states have a contraceptive use of less than 2 percent and average 7 to 10 children. The challenge for the government, obviously, is how to educate all of these young people and grow the economy to provide them with jobs.

Improvements in education and job training are a necessity. The literacy rate in Nigeria is 60 percent and lower for women. The Buhari government has increased spending to improve access to education for all children. Partnering with the UN, USAID, and NGOs, specific programs have been introduced to increase opportunities for girls. But this is tempered by Boko Haram's specifically targeting girls and kidnapping them. In addition, improvements need to be made to the university-level education system as well. Many Nigerian students choose to study in Great Britain, the United States, and Indonesia and then decide to stay and pursue careers abroad as well, leading to a potential brain drain. In addition, Nigeria faces multiple health problems. For example, Nigeria has the second-largest HIV population globally, requiring international intervention to provide treatment for victims and support for orphans. It also faces significant outbreaks of tuberculosis and malaria, along with malnutrition. The Nigerian government has been following the **National Economic Empowerment and Development Strategies (NEEDS)** to try to improve access to medical care and education to rural regions. There are also **SEEDS** and **LEEDS** to help at the state and local levels, respectively.

The Environment

Nigeria faces significant environmental problems. Those in the Niger Delta are well documented as oil spills and gas flares contaminate the air, the water, and every living thing, leading to both a public health and economic crisis, compounded by the violence of militant groups. Growing urbanization has led to deforestation and flooding problems. In addition, climate change has led to desertification in northern Nigeria as the Sahara slowly expands south. The Ministry of the Environment is charged with dealing with these problems but faces chronic budget shortages. Nigeria's oldest environmental NGO, the Nigerian Conservation Foundation, however, has praised the Nigerian government's commitment to the Pan-African Great Green Wall Project. Nigeria has pledged to plant a 10-mile band of trees across 1,000 miles of northern Nigeria by employing and training local youth.

Covid-19

Nigeria's fragile health system found it difficult to respond to the global pandemic. Notoriously underfunded, rural hospitals struggled to provide care. Lack of infrastructure, ventilators, and health care workers was common in a country that already faces high HIV and infant mortality rates. Government restrictions on large gatherings and school closures were tolerated at the beginning of the pandemic but resisted as time progressed. Surprisingly, the death toll at the end of 2021 was reported at 3,031. It is not clear at this time whether the low mortality rate is due to the relative young median age of Nigerians or lack of adequate testing or reporting.

> Review Questions

Multiple Choice

1. A coup is:
   (A) a grassroots mobilization of public protestors
   (B) a quick overthrow of a government by military officers
   (C) a violent uprising by multiple segments of society
   (D) a petition calling for reform of the military

2. Which of the following political reforms is LEAST likely to promote national unity?
   (A) Political parties must have registered members in two-thirds of the states.
   (B) Presidential candidates must win 25 percent of the vote in two-thirds of the states.
   (C) All the seats in the House of Representatives are allocated using a single-member district system.
   (D) Presidential candidates must win at least 50 percent of the popular vote or face a runoff.

3. Militant violence occurs in the Niger Delta because:
   (A) multinational corporations like Shell and Exxon Mobile do not clean up oil spills
   (B) flaring of natural gas causes environmental pollution
   (C) people living in the Niger Delta earn less than $2 a day
   (D) the Nigerian government has failed to reinvest oil revenues in the region

4. The president of Nigeria has which of the following powers?
   (A) Propose the budget
   (B) Make the budget
   (C) Pass the budget
   (D) Mark up the budget

5. What is one way that the Nigerian government has handled the challenge of coinciding cleavages?
   (A) Granting Boko Haram permission to create a political party
   (B) Joining ECOWAS to improve trade with other West African countries
   (C) Moving the Federal Capital Territory to Abuja
   (D) Refusing help from the international community to fight HIV-AIDS

6. Which of the following indicators could NOT be used to characterize Nigeria as a developing country?
   (A) Its population is 190 million people.
   (B) The median age is 18.
   (C) The literacy rate is 60 percent.
   (D) GDP per capita is $2,177.

7. Which of the following groups is correctly matched with its primary geographic region?
   (A) Igbo—southwestern Nigeria
   (B) Yoruba—southeastern Nigeria
   (C) Hausa-Fulani—northern Nigeria
   (D) MEND—Lagos

8. Why is Nigeria considered a rentier state?
   (A) Because it belongs to the oil cartel, OPEC.
   (B) Because of the NNPC's joint ventures with Shell and Exxon-Mobile.
   (C) Because the government's largest source of revenue is from the sale and export of oil.
   (D) Because Nigeria has a culture of corruption called prebendalism.

9. What was unique about the Nigerian presidential election of 2015?
   (A) More than one party competed in the first round of elections.
   (B) The president took office without winning 25 percent of the vote in any southern state.
   (C) The opposition party took office by winning the election.
   (D) A former general who had governed during military rule won office as a civilian.

10. Which of the following economic policies would indicate that a government was following the import-substitution industrialization (ISI) model?
    (A) Tariffs are lowered.
    (B) Firms are nationalized.
    (C) Industry subsidies are eliminated.
    (D) Imports are increased.

Free Response

1. (A) Define social cleavage.
   (B) Describe the characteristics of a coinciding social cleavage.
   (C) Explain why coinciding social cleavages can cause political conflict.
   (D) Explain how governments facing coinciding social cleavages can structure election systems to increase legitimacy.

2. Use the following line graph to complete your answer.

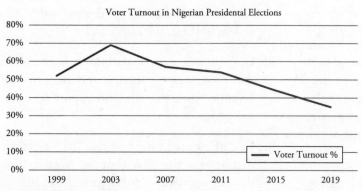

Source: Nigerian INEC

   (A) Using the data in the chart, identify the Nigerian presidential election year with the lowest voter turnout.
   (B) Using the data in the chart, describe a trend in voter turnout for Nigerian presidential elections.
   (C) Define political participation.
   (D) Explain why voter turnout rates are used by political scientists to describe political participation in a country.
   (E) Explain why the trend in voter turnout in (B) is a concern in a state attempting to establish a consolidated democracy.

3. Compare the election systems in states with presidential systems in two different AP Comparative Government and Politics course countries. In your response, you should do the following:
   (A) Define presidential system.
   (B) Explain how the election systems are structured in two different AP Comparative Government and Politics states with presidential systems.
   (C) Explain how each of the election systems in (B) may fail to win the president a clear mandate from the voters.

4. Develop an argument as to whether a unitary or a federal system of government provides more legitimacy for a rentier state.

   Use one or more of the following course concepts in your answer.
   • Corruption
   • Social welfare policies
   • Political participation

   In your response, you should do the following:
   • Respond to the prompt with a defensible claim or thesis that establishes a line of reasoning using one or more of the provided course concepts.
   • Support your claim with at least TWO pieces of specific and relevant evidence from one or more course countries. This evidence should be relevant to one or more of the provided course concepts.
   • Use reasoning to explain why your evidence supports your claim or thesis, using one or more of the provided course concepts.
   • Respond to an opposing or alternate perspective, using refutation, concession, or rebuttal.

› Answers and Explanations

Multiple Choice

1. **B.** A coup is a quick overthrow of a government, typically by military officers.

2. **C.** The purpose of using single-member districts for House elections is to allow the voters to directly elect the person that they want to represent them. To promote national unity, the Nigerian constitution allocated three Senate seats to each state, as well as requiring that presidential candidates not only have to win 50 percent of the vote, but also 25 percent of the vote in two-thirds of the states. Political parties also must draw members from two-thirds of the states.

3. **D.** Although oil spills, bunkering, and flaring cause environmental and health problems in the Niger Delta, and many people do live on less than $2 a day, there would not be militant violence if the people in the area trusted the government to respond to their problems with tangible solutions. Militants use violence to extort oil revenue from the government.

4. **A.** Presidents have the power to propose budgets and laws. Only the legislators can make and pass the budget as well as mark up and amend it.

5. **C.** Because the coinciding cleavages in Nigeria are an intersection of ethnicity, religion, and region, the Nigerian capital was moved from Lagos to Abuja, which is in the center of the country, to be a unifying force.

6. **A.** Population size is not an indicator of economic development. Developing countries tend to have a young median age, lower life expectancy, low literacy rates, and low GDP per capita.

7. **C.** The Hausa-Fulani are found predominately in northern Nigeria. The Igbo are in the southeast, the Yoruba in the southwest, and MASSOB and MEND in the Niger Delta.

8. **C.** A rentier state by definition is one in which the government obtains the majority of its revenue from the sale and export of a natural resource.

9. **C.** The unique aspect of the 2015 election was that it was the first time in Nigerian history that an opposition party gained the presidency through an election. To his credit, Goodluck Jonathan accepted his election loss and stepped down from the presidency. In the past, if the vote was not what the leader wanted, then the election results were nullified.

10. **B.** ISI is employed when a state wants to build up its infant industries and protect them from outside competition. This is accomplished by nationalizing industry and providing subsidies to produce. Structural adjustment policies involve opening up the economy by lowering tariffs and subsidies and reducing government debt burdens by raising taxes.

Free Response

1. (4 points possible)
   (A) A social cleavage is a division in society that separates people in groups, typically based on ethnicity, religion, or class. (1 point)
   (B) A coinciding cleavage is when several social cleavages overlap, thus creating deep divisions in society that result in political conflict. Nigeria's major coinciding cleavage involves ethnicity, religion, and region. For example, the Hausa-Fulani are Muslims living in northern Nigeria, whereas the Igbo are Christians living in southeastern Nigeria. Violent conflict often occurs in the Middle Belt where these two divisions overlap. (1 point)
   (C) Coinciding cleavages cause conflict because any political advantage to one area appears to come at the cost of the other region. Both groups approach the political system as a zero-sum game of winners and losers. For example, in Nigeria, the northern Muslims hold the presidency, and many Igbo, who have never held a presidential position in the Fourth Republic, are agitating for a referendum for an independent Biafra. (1 point)
   (D) Election systems can be structured so that each part of the coinciding cleavage feels that they have access to power, thereby making the system legitimate so that voters accept election results. In Nigeria, seats in the legislature are won in single-member districts so that voters can vote for the person that they want to represent them. Candidates must win a plurality of the vote, and because seats in the House of Representatives are set up by population, each district tends to elect a person who reflects their regional ethnicity/religion, thus securing legitimacy. Presidential elections require the winning candidate to not only win a majority of the vote, but also to win 25 percent of the vote in two-thirds of the states. This system increases legitimacy because the winning president has a clear mandate from the voters and a measure of national support nationwide. (1 point).

2. (5 points possible)
   (A) The presidential election with the lowest voter turnout rate is 2019. (1 point)
   (B) Voter turnout in Nigerian presidential elections has been declining since a high of 69 percent in 2003 to a low of 35 percent in 2019. (1 point)
   (C) Political participation is how individuals and groups engage in behavior that specifically supports or opposes government policymaking. These activities can range from conventional voting in elections to unconventional violent protest. (1 point)
   (D) Political scientists use voter turnout rates as a reliable indicator for conventional political participation because they are easy to calculate and track, especially if compiled by an independent election agency. Particularly in presidential systems, voters are most likely to vote in what is perceived as the most important election. Consequently, in Nigeria, which has a presidential system, voter turnout is an important indicator of conventional political participation. (1 point)
   (E) Nigerian voter turnout in presidential elections has been declining since 2003. States that want to consolidate democracy must consistently have fair, competitive elections over a long period of time. Voters need to feel that their vote matters so that a majority of them will participate and thereby legitimize the election. Because there is a history of coups and corruption in Nigeria, low voter participation is a worrying signal. Were voters concerned about political violence, rigged elections, or simply resigned to Buhari's reelection? Nigeria, like all transitional states, should be concerned when two-thirds of the voters choose not to participate in the country's most important election; such low numbers reflect a true challenge to a democratic state whose legitimacy rests on the republican ideal of people electing their leaders. (1 point)

3. (5 points possible)

(A) A presidential system is one in which the executive (president) is elected in a separate election from the legislature. (1 point)

(B) Both Nigeria and Mexico use presidential systems to organize their executive–legislative relations. This means that both countries allow people to directly vote for president. Each country, however, uses a different direct election system. Mexicans vote for president in a plurality election. Whichever candidate in Mexico receives the most votes wins the presidency. President Calderon and President Peña Nieto, for example, both were elected with less than 40 percent of the popular vote. (1 point) In Nigeria, on the other hand, a presidential candidate must win 50 percent of the popular vote and 25 percent of the vote in two-thirds of the states in order to claim victory or face a runoff. (1 point)

(C) Because Mexico uses a plurality system, the Mexican president often fails to gain a clear mandate from the people. In fact, the first presidential candidate to win a majority since the rigged 1988 election was Lopez Obrador (AMLO) in 2018, when he won 53 percent of the vote. In fact, prior Presidents Calderon and Peña Nieto suffered from their lack of mandate in that AMLO only lost to them each by a few percentage points in 2006 and 2012. This lack of a mandate was most obvious in 2006 when AMLO set up a rival government in Mexico City to protest the elections results. (1 point) Nigeria, on the other hand, has tried to overcome substantial coinciding cleavages with its presidential election system. But Nigerian presidential winners who earn a technical mandate can still fail to unify the country. One example is Goodluck Jonathan, who won a majority of the vote in 2011 and 25 percent of the vote in two-thirds of the states, without a single northern state. Northern states in Nigeria are dominated by Hausa Muslims, who did not support his candidacy and instead preferred Buhari. Violence erupted in the Middle Belt of Nigeria over the election results. (1 point)

4. (5 points possible)

Federal systems enable rentier states to appear more legitimate because by sharing power between national and subnational governments, more government revenue can be dispersed across the country for social welfare programs, thus ensuring acceptance by the people. In a federal system, regional power is guaranteed representation in the legislature, so that all regions, even those without natural resources, are able to create government policy that shares the wealth with all parts of the country, thereby increasing legitimacy. (1 point)

Nigeria is a rentier state that has benefited from using federalism to increase legitimacy. Since its independence from Great Britain, Nigeria has expanded the number of states within Nigeria. More states mean more seats in the Senate, where each state gets three senators. Each of these states is typically created to give power to a specific ethnic group, thus ensuring the group is involved in the process of creating Nigeria's budget to dispense the revenues through social welfare programs earned from the sale of Nigerian oil. Having a regional vote in the budget process ensures that all regions are more likely to support the process, thus increasing legitimacy. (1 point)

In addition, the Nigerian political system uses the federal character principle to ensure that each state has one member on the president's cabinet. In this way, each region has a voice in the creation of the budget, thereby increasing the likelihood that people will accept the government's authority because their leaders are positioned to ensure that its voters get their share of the government revenue gained from the sale of oil. Unfortunately, this power over revenue incentivizes corruption as well. But people are more likely to accept the system as long as they feel that they are receiving their fair share of the cake. (1 point)

Rentier states gain the majority of their government revenue from the sale/export of a natural resource. Legitimate governments must construct a system that fairly distributes this revenue to all regions in the country in order to gain the acceptance of the people. Federal systems, which divide power between levels of government, allow regional governments to have some control over policymaking, especially the ability to spend funds to benefit the region. Consequently, states like Nigeria that use a federal system can ensure that regional groups have representation in the upper house of the legislature and in the cabinet to craft a budget that ensures that the funds are dispersed regionally, although often corruptly, to increase legitimacy. (1 point)

Many critics of federalism would point to the political violence in the Niger Delta as an example of why shared power between the national and subnational governments in a rentier state doesn't increase legitimacy. In fact, terrorist and activist groups in the Niger Delta are critical of a political system that funnels the oil revenue to the government and doesn't use that money to improve the living and environmental conditions for the people where the oil is located. Niger Delta representation in the Senate and the Cabinet does not result in popular acceptance of the government. It more likely results in violent protest and corruption. Consequently, an argument could be made that a unitary system of power would enable the government to make uniform funding grants a priority and thus increase legitimacy. The problem would remain, however, that the diversity of interests in Nigeria makes it difficult to craft a uniform policy that would win acceptance by the people. An advantage of federalism is that local governments are enabled to devise local solutions to their problems. Dispersing the revenue gained from the sale of a natural resource to local governments to use makes federalism the system most likely to be viewed as legitimate. (1 point)

› Rapid Review

- The Federal Republic of Nigeria (Nigeria) has a complex history of colonialism, military rule, and democratic transitions. The current system is known as the Fourth Republic.
- Great Britain colonized Nigeria in 1914 and granted its independence in 1960.
- Initially, Nigeria established a Westminster system of parliamentary government, but switched to a presidential system during the Second Republic. Military coups frequently disrupted attempts to establish a more democratic system.
- The 1999 constitution of the Fourth Republic is based on the U.S. presidential model, with a directly elected president, bicameral legislature, and Supreme Court.
- Nigeria has a diverse population of over 250 ethnic groups. The state confronts powerful coinciding cleavages, especially with its three largest groups. The Hausa-Fulani living in northern states are Muslim, while the Yoruba and Igbo living in the southern states are Christian.
- Nigerian political leaders attempted to mitigate conflict between groups by increasing the number of states over time. Each state has equal representation in the Senate along with a guaranteed cabinet position because of the "federal character principle."
- The Nigerian president must win a majority of the popular vote in a two-ballot system, along with winning at least 25 percent of the votes in two-thirds of the states. The 2015 presidential election was significant because of the peaceful transfer of power by PDP President Goodluck Jonathan to his winning opponent All Progressive Congress (APC) leader Muhammadu Buhari.
- The People's Democratic Party (PDP) successfully controlled the national government from 1999 to 2015 by dominating the SMD election system. The APC was formed as a coalition of smaller opposition parties to compete in 2015. In addition to the presidency, the APC won a majority in the Senate and the House in both 2015 and 2019.
- The bureaucracy in Nigeria is large and corrupt. Nigerians commonly pay bribes for government services. This level of corruption is called prebendalism, an extreme form of patron-clientalism where officeholders use their position to enrich themselves.
- Nigerian civil society is characterized by an independent press and freedom of association. Social movements are formed to pressure the government to make changes. Many of these movements are associated with returning the revenues from the sale of oil from the Niger Delta to people who live in the region.
- Nigeria is a rentier state where the majority of government revenues are received from the export of oil by the state-owned Nigerian National Petroleum Corporation (NNPC). The NNPC relies on joint ventures with foreign multinationals (MNCs) to extract the oil.
- Religious conflict in Nigeria is a serious challenge for the state. The government has allowed northern Nigerian states to adopt sharia as a legal system in contrast to using common law as is traditional in former British colonies. Boko Haram, a radical terrorist group operating in northeastern Nigeria, wants to establish an Islamic caliphate and is willing to use violence to accomplish its goals. Military force has been used to try to stop it, but eight years later, the problem remains.

STEP 5

Build Your Test-Taking Confidence

AP Comparative Government and Politics Practice Exam 1
AP Comparative Government and Politics Practice Exam 2

AP Comparative Government and Politics
Practice Exam 1

Section I: Multiple-Choice Questions

ANSWER SHEET

1 (A) (B) (C) (D)	16 (A) (B) (C) (D)	31 (A) (B) (C) (D)	46 (A) (B) (C) (D)
2 (A) (B) (C) (D)	17 (A) (B) (C) (D)	32 (A) (B) (C) (D)	47 (A) (B) (C) (D)
3 (A) (B) (C) (D)	18 (A) (B) (C) (D)	33 (A) (B) (C) (D)	48 (A) (B) (C) (D)
4 (A) (B) (C) (D)	19 (A) (B) (C) (D)	34 (A) (B) (C) (D)	49 (A) (B) (C) (D)
5 (A) (B) (C) (D)	20 (A) (B) (C) (D)	35 (A) (B) (C) (D)	50 (A) (B) (C) (D)
6 (A) (B) (C) (D)	21 (A) (B) (C) (D)	36 (A) (B) (C) (D)	51 (A) (B) (C) (D)
7 (A) (B) (C) (D)	22 (A) (B) (C) (D)	37 (A) (B) (C) (D)	52 (A) (B) (C) (D)
8 (A) (B) (C) (D)	23 (A) (B) (C) (D)	38 (A) (B) (C) (D)	53 (A) (B) (C) (D)
9 (A) (B) (C) (D)	24 (A) (B) (C) (D)	39 (A) (B) (C) (D)	54 (A) (B) (C) (D)
10 (A) (B) (C) (D)	25 (A) (B) (C) (D)	40 (A) (B) (C) (D)	55 (A) (B) (C) (D)
11 (A) (B) (C) (D)	26 (A) (B) (C) (D)	41 (A) (B) (C) (D)	
12 (A) (B) (C) (D)	27 (A) (B) (C) (D)	42 (A) (B) (C) (D)	
13 (A) (B) (C) (D)	28 (A) (B) (C) (D)	43 (A) (B) (C) (D)	
14 (A) (B) (C) (D)	29 (A) (B) (C) (D)	44 (A) (B) (C) (D)	
15 (A) (B) (C) (D)	30 (A) (B) (C) (D)	45 (A) (B) (C) (D)	

AP Comparative Government and Politics
Practice Exam 1

Section I: Multiple-Choice Questions
Time—60 minutes
55 Questions

Directions: Each of the questions or incomplete statements below is followed by four answer choices. Select the one that best answers each question and then fill in the corresponding oval on the answer sheet.

Questions 1 and 2 refer to the following speech.

Source: Queen's Speech delivered in House of Lords on December 19, 2019, www.uk.gov

My Lords and Members of the House of Commons.

My Government's priority is to deliver the United Kingdom's departure from the European Union on 31 January. My Ministers will bring forward legislation to ensure the United Kingdom's exit on that date and to make the most of the opportunities that this brings for all the people of the United Kingdom.

Thereafter, my Ministers will seek a future relationship with the European Union based on a free trade agreement that benefits the whole of the United Kingdom. They will also begin trade negotiations with other leading global economies.

The integrity and prosperity of the United Kingdom is of the utmost importance to my Government. My Ministers will work urgently to facilitate talks to restore devolved Government in Northern Ireland.

1. Which of the following statements is supported by the main idea of the passage?
   (A) The majority of voters in the UK rejected the results of the Brexit referendum.
   (B) Prime Minister Boris Johnson is committed to leading the UK out of the European Union.
   (C) Devolved governments in the UK are fully supportive of the Brexit agenda.
   (D) The decision to leave the European Union will only benefit those voters living in London.

2. Which of the following statements is an implication of the argument presented in the passage?
   (A) The UK plans to pursue import substitution industrialization (ISI) policies after Brexit.
   (B) The UK plans to dissolve the Northern Ireland parliament and allow reunification with Ireland.
   (C) The UK parliament will have to pass a law authorizing the government to leave the European Union.
   (D) The UK will still be constrained by the free trade rules established by the World Trade Organization.

Questions 3 and 4 refer to the following passage.

Source: Constitution of the People's Republic of China

Article 33. **Citizenship**

All persons holding the nationality of the People's Republic of China are citizens of the People's Republic of China.

All citizens of the People's Republic of China are equal before the law.

Every citizen is entitled to the rights and at the same time must perform the duties prescribed by the Constitution and the law.

The State respects and preserves human rights.

GO ON TO THE NEXT PAGE

Article 34. **Voting requirements**

All citizens of the People's Republic of China who have reached the age of 18 have the right to vote and stand for election, regardless of ethnic status, race, sex, occupation, family backround, religious belief, education, property status or length of residence, except persons deprived of political rights according to law.

Article 35. **Freedom of speech, press, assembly**

Citizens of the People's Republic of China enjoy freedom of speech, of the press, of assembly, of association, of procession and of demonstration.

Article 36. **Religious freedom**

Citizens of the People's Republic of China enjoy freedom of religious belief.

No state organ, public organization or individual may compel citizens to believe in, or not believe in, any religion; nor may they discriminate against citizens who believe in, or do not believe in, any religion.

3. Which of the following statements is supported by the main idea of the passage?
   - (A) The Chinese government is required by law to protect the civil liberties of all Chinese people.
   - (B) The Chinese Communist Party is in charge of making sure that the rights of the Chinese people are protected.
   - (C) The citizens of the People's Republic of China formally have substantial civil liberties and political rights.
   - (D) The Chinese people have the right to vote in national-level elections.

4. Given your knowledge of Chinese politics, which of the following statements is an implication of the argument presented in the passage?
   - (A) The People's Republic of China is a state with a constitution but without a constitutional government.
   - (B) Rule of law exists in China because the constitution clearly protects civil liberties.
   - (C) The Supreme Court of the People's Republic of China effectively uses the constitution to protect civil liberties.
   - (D) China has an independent press to serve as an effective check on the government.

Questions 5 and 6 refer to the following table.

Democracy Index 2019

REGIME TYPE	# OF STATES	% OF COUNTRIES	% OF WORLD'S POPULATION
Full Democracy	22	13.2%	5.7%
Flawed Democracy	54	32.3%	42.7%
Hybrid Democracy	37	22.2%	16.0%
Authoritarian	54	32.3%	35.6%

Source: Economist Intelligence Unit

GO ON TO THE NEXT PAGE

5. Using the data in the table, under which type of regime do the fewest number of individuals in the world live?
   (A) Full Democracy
   (B) Flawed Democracy
   (C) Hybrid Democracy
   (D) Authoritarian

6. This report describes authoritarian regimes as lacking an independent judiciary and a free press, repressing civil liberties and manipulating elections. Using your knowledge of the six AP Comparative Government and Politics countries, which three does this report identify as authoritarian?
   (A) China, Iran, and Mexico
   (B) Iran, Russia, and Nigeria
   (C) UK, Nigeria, and Mexico
   (D) Russia, Iran, and China

Questions 7 and 8 refer to the following table.

Democracy Index 2019

COUNTRY	GINI INDEX
CHINA	38.6
IRAN	40
MEXICO	48.3
NIGERIA	43
RUSSIA	37.7
UNITED KINGDOM	33.2

Source: World Bank

7. The GINI Index is a measure of income inequality. According to the table above, which country has the widest gap between rich and poor?
   (A) China
   (B) Iran
   (C) Mexico
   (D) United Kingdom

8. Which of the following policies would most directly reduce income inequality?
   (A) The executive raises tariffs on imports of foreign goods.
   (B) The legislature passes a law to increase funding for a national health service.
   (C) The judiciary overturns a law that restricted Internet use.
   (D) The bureaucracy implemented anti-corruption measures.

Questions 9 and 10 refer to the following line graph.

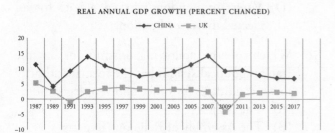

REAL ANNUAL GDP GROWTH (PERCENT CHANGED)

GO ON TO THE NEXT PAGE

9. Using the data in the line graph, which of the following is the best statement about the relationship?
   (A) From 1989 to 2017, the real annual GDP growth rate in China was perfectly correlated with the real annual GDP growth rate in the UK.
   (B) The real annual GDP growth rate in China in 2007 caused the fall in the real annual GDP growth rate in the UK in 2007.
   (C) The real annual GDP growth rate in China will always be greater than the real annual GDP growth rate in the UK.
   (D) From 1989 to 2017, the real annual GDP growth rate in China exceeded that of the real annual GDP growth rate in the UK.

10. What are the implications of the trends shown in the graph?
    (A) After sustaining such high growth rates for decades, pressure will be put on the Chinese government to develop new strategies to deal with a declining real annual GDP growth rate.
    (B) The UK government will be forced to pursue austerity measures to raise the UK's real annual growth rate above 10%.
    (C) Economists would recommend that China pursue import substitution industrialization (ISI) policies to increase real annual GDP growth rates.
    (D) Now that the UK has left the European Union, it can be predicted that their real annual GDP growth rates will quickly surpass those of China.

11. Which of the following conditions best describes a democratic political system?
    (A) A military general serves as the head of state as well as the commander of the armed forces.
    (B) Interest groups are required to register with a state bureaucratic agency that oversees nongovernmental organizations.
    (C) An independent election commission oversees elections to ensure that they are fair and competitive.
    (D) All government officials, both elected and appointed, must be members of the ruling political party.

12. Which of the following groups of countries are governed by a presidential system?
    (A) Iran, Great Britain
    (B) Mexico, Nigeria
    (C) Russia, China
    (D) Great Britain, Mexico

13. A dominant party system is one in which:
    (A) election law prohibits the formation of any party except the ruling party
    (B) multiple parties compete in elections, but the same party is continuously assured of a large majority
    (C) two major parties continuously win because of the use of single-member districts
    (D) all political parties have the power to nominate their own candidates without primaries

14. Which of the following policy changes is an indicator of economic liberalization?
    (A) The government nationalizes foreign-owned oil companies to obtain new sources of revenue.
    (B) The government creates numerous state-owned enterprises to create new jobs for the unemployed.
    (C) The government enforces price controls and highly subsidizes consumer products to end poverty.
    (D) The government adopts structural adjustment programs as recommended by the World Bank and IMF.

15. Which of the following was a result of a referendum held in Great Britain since 1997?
    (A) Voters in Scotland rejected a vote for independence from Great Britain.
    (B) Voters in Wales rejected a vote for an elected Welsh Assembly.
    (C) Voters in Northern Ireland rejected a vote for independence from Great Britain.
    (D) Voters in London rejected a vote for an elected mayor of London.

16. Which of the following institutions in the Iranian political system has the formal authority to vet candidates for office and veto legislation?
    (A) The Majles
    (B) The Assembly of Religious Experts
    (C) The Expediency Council
    (D) The Guardian Council

13/16

GO ON TO THE NEXT PAGE

17. Which of the following policies does the Chinese government follow to address ethnic cleavages in China?
    (A) The Chinese government refuses to allow any ethnic minorities the right to practice their own religion or to speak their own language.
    (B) The Chinese government has created five autonomous regions for groups of ethnic minorities where limited self-government is allowed.
    (C) The Chinese government has encouraged independence movements by ethnic minorities as a way to reduce tension between groups.
    (D) The Chinese government has discouraged Han Chinese from moving to ethnic minority populated areas in order to slow down economic development.

18. Why is Nigeria characterized as a rentier state?
    (A) Nigeria is a member of OPEC and its government follows the agreements of the cartel.
    (B) Nigeria is considered by the World Bank to be a developing nation with low GDP.
    (C) Nigeria has a high percentage of its population living in poverty.
    (D) The Nigerian government earns a large percentage of its revenue from the sale of oil to foreign countries.

19. Mexico's structural adjustment policy was designed to:
    (A) give all parties free and equal media access during election campaigns
    (B) increase the power of the Supreme Court
    (C) devolve more power from the central government to the states
    (D) address serious economic problems by liberalizing trade

20. Which of the following is the best example of a causal statement?
    (A) As access to the Internet increases around the world, it appears that more women are attending college.
    (B) Increased usage of social media has led to an increased level of political participation.

(C) Literacy rates and Internet usage are increasing worldwide.
(D) Authoritarian regimes have been increasing restrictions on social media.

21. Russian oil and natural gas reserves are:
    (A) limited, which has caused the Russian government to invest heavily in solar and wind power
    (B) not regularly exported to Europe, thereby limiting the effects of UN sanctions
    (C) extensive, and the central government effectively controls the production and export of this valuable resource
    (D) rapidly depleting, therefore requiring that the Russian government import these resources from China

22. What is the typical goal of a social movement?
    (A) To nominate candidates and win elections
    (B) To force the government to make significant reforms
    (C) To kick-start a violent revolution
    (D) To increase awareness of an issue and raise funds

23. What is the advantage to Nigeria in using a federal system of government?
    (A) It allows the states to enact public policies that address local concerns.
    (B) It reduces corruption at the national level by centralizing power.
    (C) It protects civil liberties by having a unified, consistent legal system.
    (D) It ensures universal suffrage and fair, competitive elections.

24. Which of the following is a correct statement about Mexican political parties?
    (A) The PRD is a conservative political party with strongest support in the north.
    (B) The PRI has support only in the south and is primarily a far-left party.
    (C) There are only three political parties represented in the Mexican legislature.
    (D) Parties are subject to the 40% gender rule for the proportional seats in the legislature.

GO ON TO THE NEXT PAGE

25. Political socialization is:
    (A) the deeply held, shared attitudes held by citizens about their government
    (B) the process of communicating about global events using social media
    (C) how people acquire their attitudes about government and politics
    (D) the belief that a citizen can actively participate in the political system

26. The supreme leader appoints all the members of which of the following institutions?
    (A) The Expediency Council
    (B) The Guardian Council
    (C) The Assembly of Experts
    (D) The cabinet

27. The most powerful institution in the Chinese political system is the:
    (A) National People's Congress
    (B) National People's Supreme Court
    (C) State Council
    (D) Politburo Standing Committee

28. In Russia, which of the following is head of government?
    (A) The president
    (B) The prime minister
    (C) The head of the Communist Party
    (D) The head of the State Duma

29. How is the prime minister of Great Britain chosen?
    (A) The prime minister is elected directly by the people and formally appointed by the queen.
    (B) The prime minister must first be elected as a member of Parliament and then selected by the majority party or coalition to be the prime minister.
    (C) The prime minister is voted on by the cabinet as "the first among equals."
    (D) The prime minister is appointed by the queen and confirmed by the House of Lords.

30. Which of the following would be an accurate description of an illiberal democracy?
    (A) A government that holds elections that are neither competitive or fair
    (B) A government that protects rule of law with an independent judiciary
    (C) A government that requires business licenses to operate private firms
    (D) A government that mandates only registered voters can participate in elections

31. Which of the following is a power of the president of the Iran?
    (A) Appoint members of the Guardian Council
    (B) Appoint judges for both trial and appellate courts
    (C) Appoint leaders of the state television and radio networks
    (D) Appoint members of the cabinet

32. Which elections in Great Britain consistently have the highest voter participation rates?
    (A) Elections for the European Parliament
    (B) Elections for the House of Commons
    (C) Elections for the Scottish Parliament
    (D) Elections for the Welsh Assembly

33. Which of the following forms of government has Nigeria had since independence?
    (A) Presidential and theocratic
    (B) Parliamentary and presidential
    (C) Theocratic and parliamentary
    (D) Theocratic and military dictatorship

34. Selection bias is a challenge in comparative politics because:
    (A) not all countries are democratic or authoritarian
    (B) not all countries have English speakers
    (C) the country case studies selected can influence the conclusions
    (D) the countries selected as case studies may prohibit polling

35. Which of the following is a correct statement of Putin's policy toward civil society?
    (A) Only Communist Party–affiliated organizations are legal.
    (B) Severe restrictions have been placed on the activities of the Russian Orthodox Church.
    (C) Only national organizations with chapters in all 21 Republics can form.
    (D) All organizations receiving foreign funds must register as foreign agents.

GO ON TO THE NEXT PAGE

36. Globalization is promoted by which of the following groups?
    (A) Great Britain's UKIP party
    (B) Iranian conservatives
    (C) The WTO
    (D) Boko Haram

37. Muhammadu Buhari's election victory in 2015 is significant because:
    (A) it was the first time that an incumbent president was defeated in an election
    (B) it was the first election held under the Fourth Republic
    (C) it was the first win for the PDP, the new dominant political party in Nigeria
    (D) he was the first candidate to win who had never been a general

38. Which of the following policies is most clearly pursing the goal of sustainability?
    (A) China's plan to build more windmills to meet growing energy needs
    (B) Russia's increased state ownership over oil and natural gas production
    (C) Mexico's increased drilling for oil in the Gulf of Mexico
    (D) Nigeria's continued deforestation to increase urban development

39. Special economic zones refer to:
    (A) agricultural areas farmed for exporting goods
    (B) traditional communal properties primarily used by ethnic minorities
    (C) industrial zones where the business and trade laws are different from those in the rest of the country
    (D) areas within which military weapons are built

40. How did Margaret Thatcher create a more pluralist interest group system in Great Britain?
    (A) By signing the Single European Act, a precursor to the European Union
    (B) By eliminating the corporatist relationship trade unions had with the state
    (C) By privatizing council housing and increasing home ownership
    (D) By maintaining support for the state-owned National Health Service (NHS)

41. Which of the following is a correct statement about the Supreme Court of Mexico?
    (A) It is composed of lifetime judges.
    (B) Judges are appointed by each of Mexico's states.

    (C) Nominees require a two-thirds vote by the Chamber of Deputies.
    (D) A supermajority of judges are required to overturn a law.

42. Why do executives call for referendums?
    (A) To address concerns from foreign NGOs
    (B) To respond to criticisms from the United Nations
    (C) To ensure cooperation from multinational corporations
    (D) To gain democratic legitimacy from the voters

43. To escape the resource curse, Nigeria must:
    (A) produce more oil
    (B) become less dependent on oil production
    (C) withdraw from OPEC
    (D) nationalize the oil industry

44. How does an independent media support civil society?
    (A) It is subsidized by government funding to increase group access.
    (B) It serves as a linkage institution to bring government attention to issues.
    (C) It broadcasts government propaganda to ensure compliance.
    (D) It restricts access to pro-government groups to decrease opposition.

45. A state that follows rule of law is characterized by
    (A) arbitrary enforcement of laws
    (B) transparent government policymaking
    (C) elevated levels of official corruption
    (D) high rates of incarceration of political prisoners

46. Which of the following is a correct statement about how Russian presidents are selected?
    (A) They are elected to a four-year term and cannot be reelected.
    (B) They are appointed by the prime minister.
    (C) They are elected to a six-year term and may serve two consecutive terms.
    (D) They must receive a majority of votes in each of Russia's Federation districts or face a runoff election.

47. What government position has usually been held by the general secretary of the Chinese Communist Party since the 1990s?
    (A) Premier of the National People's Congress
    (B) President of the People's Republic of China

(C) Member of the Standing Committee of the Politburo

(D) Paramount Leader

48. Which of the following is a correct statement about the Hausa Fulani ethnic group?

(A) They are a Christian group located in northern Nigeria.

(B) They are a Christian group located in southern Nigeria.

(C) They contain several different religions and are spread throughout Nigeria.

(D) They are a Muslim group located in northern Nigeria.

49. What is an advantage to using a single-member district election system?

(A) The ability to require a gender quota on the party lists to increase the percentage of women serving in the legislature

(B) The tendency to create a two-party system with one party winning a legislative majority to provide stability

(C) The tendency to create a multiparty system requiring a coalition government

(D) The tendency to cause a number of "wasted votes" that discourage voter turnout

50. What is a legitimate reason for a democracy to regulate the media?

(A) To protect individuals from libel

(B) To protect government officials from criticism

(C) To prohibit the media from earning a profit

(D) To conceal public spending

51. Which of the following is only a characteristic of an authoritarian regime?

(A) Fair and competitive elections

(B) Independent judiciary

(C) Patronage appointments to the bureaucracy

(D) One-party system

52. Civil society consists primarily of:

(A) a few peak associations representing labor, business, and government interests

(B) numerous, autonomous organizations: churches, clubs, and interest groups

(C) many government-organized NGOs called GONGOs

(D) quasi autonomous NGOs called quangos

53. Which of the following groups of people voted for Great Britain to leave the EU?

(A) Young, college-educated individuals

(B) Supporters of the Scottish National Party

(C) Older, retired members of the working class

(D) Urban professionals

54. As a country develops economically:

(A) literacy rates decline

(B) infrastructure crumbles

(C) life expectancy falls

(D) women have fewer children

55. Which of the following is a normative statement?

(A) Democratic regimes have a higher GDP per capita than authoritarian regimes.

(B) Authoritarian regimes should pursue political liberalization policies.

(C) Many postindustrial economies have aging populations.

(D) Service-based economies participate in global trade for manufactured goods.

45/55

STOP: END OF SECTION I.

Section II: Free Response

Time—1 Hour and 30 Minutes

Directions: The Free-Response Section includes four questions. You need to answer all parts of all four questions. Write your answers on a separate sheet of paper, making sure to number your answers as the questions are numbered below. Before answering an essay question, take a few minutes to plan and outline your answer. Include specific examples in your answers to the essay questions where appropriate.

1. (A) Define sovereignty. *A nation's ability to govern w/o interference from foreign or domestic groups*
    (B) Describe an internal force challenge to state sovereignty. *Cleavages that lead to regionalism and decrease the stability and legitimacy of the govt.*
    (C) Explain how a state could respond to the challenge to state sovereignty in (B) without using coercion. *could use devolution of powers and return to make sure things are being resolved and that everyone has a say.*
    (D) Explain why an authoritarian state would prefer not to use coercion to protect sovereignty. *Further decrease legitimacy and potentially expose more negative aspects of the regime.*

2. Use the following table to answer the question.

Corruption Perception Index 2019

COUNTRY	SCORE: OUT OF 100	WORLD RANK: OUT OF 180
World Average	43	
China	41	80
Iran	26	146
Mexico	29	130
Nigeria	26	146
Russia	28	130
United Kingdom	77	12

Source Transparency International

   (A) Using the data in the table, identify the country with the worst corruption perception score.
   (B) Using the data in the table, make an empirical statement about the perception of corruption.
   (C) Define corruption.
   (D) Explain how Transparency International would be able to determine the perception of corruption in a country.
   (E) Explain how governments can take steps to reduce corruption.

3. Compare the state response to civil society action regarding the environment in two different AP Comparative Government and Politics countries.
    (A) Define policy agenda.
    (B) Describe civil society action regarding the environment in two different AP Comparative Government and Politics countries.
    (C) Explain how responsive the government was to making the changes requested by civil society groups in (B).

4. Develop an argument as to whether holding elections in an authoritarian regime contributes to or weakens political stability.

    Use one or more of the following course concepts in your response:
    • Transparency
    • Rule of Law
    • Sovereignty

In your response, you should do the following:
- Respond to the prompt with a defensible claim or thesis that establishes a line of reasoning using one or more of the provided course concepts.
- Support your claim with at least TWO pieces of specific and relevant evidence from one or more course countries. This evidence should be relevant to one or more of the provided course countries.
- Use reasoning to explain why your evidence supports your claim or thesis, using one or more of the provided course concepts.
- Respond to an opposing or alternate perspective, using refutation, concession, or rebuttal.

› Answers and Explanations

Section I: Multiple Choice

1. **B.** The queen reads the speech that is written for her by the prime minister. PM Johnson won an election with the promise to take the UK out of the European Union. His plan will benefit everyone. The devolved parliament in Northern Ireland is a separate issue.

2. **C.** Because of parliamentary sovereignty, it is the UK parliament that must pass a law to dissolve the agreement with the EU; a referendum is not enough. Although the Northern Ireland border is a problem, there is no plan to reunify with Ireland. The UK will pursue new trade agreements, but there is no mention of WTO constraints.

3. **C.** Formally, in the Chinese constitution, the Chinese people have civil liberties and political rights. There is no reference here to the responsibility of the Chinese government, the CCP, or actual election rights, as there are no national elections in China.

4. **A.** China clearly has a constitution, but it is not a constitutional government because these rights are not actually protected by rule of law. The Chinese government is authoritarian and arbitrarily applies the law.

5. **A.** Only 5.7% of the world's population have full democracy.

6. **D.** Russia, Iran, and China are authoritarian according to this report.

7. **C.** Mexico has a GINI Index of 48.3, which is the highest level of income inequality of the six countries.

8. **B.** A national health service would provide universal care for all, including the poor.

9. **D.** The line graph shows that during the years listed, China's growth rate exceeded that of the UK's. There is not a perfect correlation, particularly during the Great Recession. In addition, there is no way to predict that the growth rate of China will always be greater.

10. **A.** The Chinese government is under increasing pressure to maintain high economic growth rates or face civil unrest at home. Austerity measures involve raising taxes and cutting spending, not effective policies for increasing economic growth, which requires spending. The UK, a post-industrial economy, will not attain the growth rates of a modernizing economy.

11. **C.** Free and fair (competitive) elections are a defining characteristic of a democracy. A is incorrect because it refers to a situation found in military dictatorships. B is incorrect because in a democracy, interest groups are not overseen by the government. This policy would be found in an authoritarian political system. D is incorrect because it negates the principle of free and fair elections. Only members of the dominant party can be elected.

12. **B.** Mexico and Nigeria both have presidential systems. A is incorrect because Great Britain has a parliamentary system headed by a prime minister and the president in Iran is responsible to the supreme leader. C is incorrect because in China the president is largely a ceremonial head of state and not head of the government. Russia is classified as a semi-presidential system in which the president and prime minister share powers. D is incorrect because Great Britain is a parliamentary system headed by a prime minister.

13. **B.** The definition of a dominant party system is one in which there are multiple political parties but elections are not competitive and one party continuously wins elections. A is incorrect because there are multiple political parties in a dominant party system. C is incorrect because in a dominant party system only one party continuously wins elections. D is incorrect because it does not refer to the outcome of elections, which is the defining feature of a dominant party system.

14. **D.** The IMF's structural adjustment programs require countries to reduce government budgets, promote free trade, and limit government involvement in the economy. All of these are characteristics of economic liberalization. A is incorrect because

governments owning oil companies goes against the principle of free trade and minimum involvement of government in the economic sphere. B is incorrect for similar reasons as A. Large-scale government enterprises are characteristics of command economies and not economic liberalism. D is incorrect because government price controls and subsidies run counter to the principle of minimum government involvement in the economy.

15. **A.** In a 2014 referendum, 55.3 percent of those voting voted no and 44.7 percent voted yes. B is incorrect because in a 1997 referendum a small majority voted in favor of creating a Welsh Assembly. C is incorrect because no referendum on Northern Ireland independence has been held. D is incorrect because a 1998 referendum supported electing London's mayor.

16. **D.** Vetting candidates for office and veto legislation are powers of the Guardian Council. A is incorrect because the Majlis is Iran's legislative body. B is incorrect because the Assembly of Religious Experts has the power to select and dismiss the supreme leader. C is incorrect because the Expediency Council is empowered to reconcile differences between the Majlis and the Guardian Council.

17. **B.** The designated autonomous regions are Guangxi (for the Zhuang minority), Inner Mongolia (Mongols), Tibet (Tibetan), Xinjiang (Uyghur), and Ningxia (Hui). A is incorrect because China has recognized a number of religions and has permitted the use of these languages in autonomous regions. C is incorrect because China always has rejected recognizing ethnic areas as independent countries. D is incorrect because China has not discouraged the Han from doing so and a significant number have migrated to these areas as their economies have grown.

18. **D.** The definition of a rentier state is one that receives a significant portion of its revenue from "rent" or sale of natural resources. Nigeria receives a high percentage of its revenue from oil sales. A is incorrect because membership in an organization such as OPEC is not required to be a rentier state. What is required is that the government is financially dependent on selling the natural resource. B is incorrect because the overall level of economic development is not a defining characteristic of a rentier state. The focus is on the source of government income. C is incorrect for the same reason. The degree of poverty in a country is not central to the definition of a rentier state.

19. **D.** Structural adjustment policies were put forward by the IMF and other international lenders as economic liberalization policies that had to be put in place if countries such as Mexico that were running large international debts would receive additional loans and debt forgiveness. A is incorrect because structural adjustment policies are economic policies. B is incorrect for similar reasons. C is incorrect because structural adjustment polices do not involve a transfer of power from national to regional governments. They require changes in national economic policy that gives more power to the marketplace and reduce government involvement in the economy.

20. **B.** Causal statements link two events or processes together with one resulting in or producing the second. Here, increased social media results in increased political participation. A is incorrect because it is a speculative statement, more of a hypothesis. C is incorrect because it is a statement of fact or observation. D is incorrect because it is a statement of fact or an observation.

21. **C.** This statement accurately describes both the Russian dependence on natural resources (oil and natural gas) as a source of wealth and the high degree of state control over these resources. A is incorrect because it neither correctly identifies the resources that the Russian economy is built around nor the amount of power possessed by the state. B is incorrect because Europe is the largest importer of Russian natural gas and thus makes Russia vulnerable to international sanctions, which would not be the case if Russian energy were consumed domestically rather than sold abroad. D is incorrect because China is not an exporter of energy.

22. **B.** A central theme running through the literature on social movements is that they are groupings of individuals and organizations that seek to

change major government policies by mobilizing citizens and those outside the normal political process. A is incorrect because social movements do not run candidates in elections. Their focus is on protest and lobbying. B is incorrect for similar reasons. Social movements operate from society to produce change, not from within governments. C is incorrect because social movements are not revolutionary movements that seek to overthrow governments. They seek to bring about changes in policy. D is incorrect because their goal is much more than raising awareness and funds. It is to bring about change.

23. **A.** Among the primary advantages of federalism over a unitary system are that it permits citizens to have a greater voice in local matter, allows for greater innovation in laws and policies, and holds the potential for greater efficiency in policymaking and implementation. B is incorrect because dispersing power among states or regions by definition does nothing to reduce corruption. C is incorrect because federalism potentially moves in the opposite direction of protecting civil liberties through the absence of a centralized legal system. D is incorrect for similar reasons. The use of federalism does not ensure democratic rule or the protection of universal suffrage.

24. **D.** Mexico has passed a series of constitutional amendments to increase the level of participation by women. This quota was originally adopted in 2002 and had requirements for both single-member districts and proportional representation districts. It was raised from 30 percent to 40 percent in 2008. A is incorrect. The PRD is a socialist oriented party and is strongest in the south. B is incorrect because the PRI is a centrist party and is a political factor in all regions of Mexico. D is incorrect because while there are three major parties in Mexico, the Mexican legislature has representatives from many minor parties including a Citizens Movement Party, a National Regeneration Movement, and an Ecologist Green Party.

25. **C.** Political socialization is the process by which individuals develop ideas and attitudes toward politics, political activity, and government rule. A is incorrect because political socialization is about a process of acquiring beliefs and values;

it is not about what they are or how widely they are shared. B is incorrect because it is not strictly about global events nor does it specify how those ideas are developed and communicated. D is incorrect because political socialization does not specify the content of the beliefs held by citizens.

26. **A.** All members of the Expediency Council are appointed by the supreme leader for five-year terms. B is incorrect because the members of the Guardian Council are (1) appointed by the chief justice and approved by Majlis or (2) clerics appointed by the supreme leader. C is incorrect because the Assembly of Experts is popularly elected. D is incorrect because the president appoints the cabinet.

27. **D.** China is a communist state. The most powerful institution within a communist party is the Politburo Standing Committee. A is incorrect because while technically the National People's Congress is the highest political body in China, it is less powerful than the communist party. B is incorrect because the Supreme Court in China does not exercise a voice independent of the party or government. C is incorrect because the State Council is part of the executive branch and is primarily concerned with implementing economic policy.

28. **B.** Officially the Chairman of the Government of the Russian Federation, the prime minister is the constitutional head of government. A is incorrect because the president in Russia is the head of state and commander in chief of the armed forces. C is incorrect because the head of government is a political position. Additionally, Russia is no longer a communist state. D is incorrect because the State Duma is the lower branch of the Federal Assembly, Russia's legislative body, and not part of the executive branch.

29. **B.** British prime ministers are elected members of Parliament whom the majority party or a coalition designates to be prime minister. A is incorrect because while directly elected to Parliament, it is not the monarch but the majority party that makes the selection. The monarch then officially appoints the individual as prime minister.

C is incorrect because the prime minister is not selected by the cabinet. The prime minister selects the cabinet. D is incorrect because the House of Lords is not involved in the selection of the prime minister.

30. **A.** The core characteristics of liberal democracy are liberty, rule of law, and popular participation in governing. Illiberal democracies are generally seen as being partial democracies in which elections take place but civil liberties go unprotected and are abused by those in power. The result is elections that are symbolic but not meaningful. B is incorrect because the rule of law and independence of the judiciary are absent in an illiberal democracy, thus placing civil liberties at risk. C is incorrect because virtually all political systems require business licenses. D is incorrect because full or liberal democracies also limit voting to those who are registered.

31. **D.** Appointing members of the cabinet is one of the key powers of the Iranian president. A is incorrect because members of the Guardian Council are (1) appointed by the chief justice and approved by Majlis or (2) clerics appointed by the supreme leader. B is incorrect because trial and appellate judges are appointed by the chief justice. C is incorrect because the supreme leader has the power to appoint and dismiss the head of the state television and radio network.

32. **B.** Typically elections for the House of Commons produce 60–70 percent voter turnout. A is incorrect because elections for the European Parliament produce about 30 percent voter turnout. C is incorrect because elections to the Scottish Parliament produce about 55 percent voter turnout. D is incorrect because elections for the Welsh Assembly produce about 40 percent voter turnout.

33. **B.** Nigeria was originally established as a parliamentary system and adopted a presidential system with the creation of the Second Republic. A is incorrect because Nigeria was never a theocracy. C is incorrect for the same reason. D is incorrect because Nigeria was never a theocracy, although it was ruled as a military dictatorship for periods of time.

34. **C.** Selection bias refers to situations in which cases are selected for study in such a way that they prove or disprove the argument being made but are presented as neutral cases where the outcome is in doubt. A is incorrect because examining a variety of political systems might be crucial to establishing an argument where selection bias would be having only one type of political system. B is incorrect for similar reasons with respect to language or culture. D is incorrect because polling may be irrelevant to the question being studied and thus not contribute to a biased outcome.

35. **D.** Russia's "foreign agent law" passed in 2012 requires that all nonprofit organizations receiving funds from outside Russia that engage in political activity must register as foreign agents.

36. **C.** The World Trade Organization (WTO) is a primary supporter of free trade agreements that are central to globalization. A is incorrect because UKIP is a Eurosceptic party that opposes membership in the EU. B is incorrect because Iranian conservatives are especially concerned with foreign influence in Iran, something that would get more prevalent with globalization. D is incorrect because Boko Haram is a terrorist group.

37. **A.** In 2015, Muhammadu Buhari beat incumbent Goodluck Jonathan by more than 2.5 million votes. B is incorrect because the Fourth Republic held its first presidential election in 1999. C is incorrect because the PDP candidate won the presidency in the 1999 election. D is incorrect because Buhari is a retired major general. E is incorrect because Buhari was not an independent candidate. His party, the All Progressives Congress, was formed as an alliance of opposition parties.

38. **A.** Sustainability is a policy that emphasizes political and economic action that protects and preserves the environment for the future. B is incorrect because government ownership does not necessarily produce sustainability and Russia's policy is geared toward production, not conservation. C is incorrect because increased drilling for oil runs counter to sustainability. D is incorrect because continued deforestation is one of the major concerns of those advocating sustainability.

39. C. Special economic zones were established in China as a way of attracting foreign investment into China by establishing special laws and regulations while at the same time continuing to place the rest of China under tighter communist economic control. A is incorrect because these are not rural, agricultural production areas. B is incorrect because they focus on attracting international business and not protecting traditional economic practices. D is incorrect because they do not focus on the production of military weapons but on goods to be sold on international markets.

40. B. In a corporatist system select interest groups within policy areas are favored over others by the government giving them an advantage in being able to influence government decisions and lobby government officials. A is incorrect because the Single European Act was not about the British government's relations with interest groups but about its relationship with Europe. C is incorrect because increasing home ownership is not fundamental to increasing competition among interest groups. D is incorrect because continuing state-owned health care would reinforce corporatist ties and not lessen them.

41. D. According to legislation introduced in the 1980s a supermajority, 8 of the 11 judges, must vote to overturn a law. A is incorrect because judges are limited to a 15-year term. B is incorrect because judges are appointed by the president. C is incorrect because judges must be approved by a two-thirds vote of the Senate.

42. D. Referendums are votes by citizens on policy questions. They are designed to obtain information on what citizens think, gain support for government action, and approve or reject policies. A is incorrect because organizations, domestic or foreign, do not vote in referendums. B is incorrect because they are not set in motion by UN criticisms of government policy. They are also framed in a yes/no manner around policy questions. C is incorrect because they are not designed to create cooperation with multinational corporations.

43. B. The resource curse refers to situations where countries are so dependent on the production of a natural resource such as oil that they are unable to develop economic policies to diversify their economies, thus becoming trapped by future reductions in demand and price. A is incorrect because producing more oil only makes the danger of the resource curse greater. C is incorrect because withdrawing from OPEC does not reduce the curse unless the Nigerian economy becomes less dependent on oil for revenue. D is incorrect because ownership of the natural resource is irrelevant to the resource curse.

44. B. Civil society consists of nongovernmental interest groups, clubs, social movements, and other organizations that operate without government control and seek to influence policy by mobilizing citizens. A free media is vital to the ability of these groups to work together and distribute information. A is incorrect because government-supported media potentially would reduce the independence of civil society groups from the government. C is incorrect because civil society is seen as a check on government and not an instrument of governance. D is incorrect because an independent media should not restrict access by civil society groups, nor is civil society restricted to anti- or pro-government groups.

45. B. The principle of the rule of law emphasizes the accountability of government officials to the public and the universal application of law to all in society. Transparency is a key requirement for the rule of law to operate successfully. A is incorrect because the arbitrary enforcement of laws runs against its core principles. C is incorrect because the rule of law should work to reduce corruption. D is incorrect because under the rule of law political opponents should be protected from arbitrary arrest and convictions by the government.

46. C. According to the Russian constitution the president is elected for a six-year term and may serve two consecutive terms. After sitting out a term, individuals are allowed to become president again. A is incorrect both in terms of the length of term and the ability to be reelected. B is incorrect because presidents are directly elected by popular vote. D is incorrect because there is no requirement for receiving a majority of votes in each Federation district.

47. **B.** Since the 1990s, the general secretary of the Chinese Communist Party has generally served as president of the People's Republic of China except briefly in cases of leadership transition. A and C are incorrect because they are not positions that the general secretary has held. D is incorrect because Paramount Leader is an informal term and not an official position.

48. **D.** The Hausa Fulani ethnic group makes up 29 percent of Nigeria's population. The Hausa Fulani are a Muslim group concentrated in western Africa. Some 30 million live in northern Nigeria. A is incorrect because it identifies the Hausa Fulani as Christian. B is incorrect for the same reason and because it incorrectly identifies the region of Nigeria in which the Hausa Fulani are located. C is incorrect both in terms of its religious and geographic identification of the Hausa Fulani.

49. **B.** This is the dominant argument given by advocates of a single-member district electoral system. A is incorrect because party lists are associated with proportional representation electoral systems with multiple candidates elected from a district. C is incorrect because a single-member district electoral system does not tend to produce a multiparty system. D is incorrect because the concept of wasted vote is generally applied to multiparty systems where there is no ability to transfer a vote from a poor performing candidate to a stronger candidate who can get elected.

50. **A.** Freedom of speech and freedom of the press are central to the operation of democracy, but democracies place limits on what can be said to protect individuals. Libel is an untruth published in print or broadcast that does harm to individuals. B is incorrect because free speech does not protect government officials from criticism. C is incorrect because neither free speech nor free press relate to the ability of the media to earn a profit. D is incorrect because transparency is central to the operation of a democracy.

51. **D.** One of the fundamental features separating democracies from authoritarian regimes is free and fair elections that produce electoral competition. Authoritarian regimes lack such competition because they have only one meaningful political party. A is incorrect because free and fair elections are defining features of democracies. B is incorrect because an independent judiciary is central to the principle of rule of law. C is incorrect because democracies and authoritarian regimes both rely on patronage to fill bureaucratic positions.

52. **B.** By definition civil society is composed of autonomous organizations and groups. The positions advocated by these groups are not part of the definition, nor is civil society limited to certain types or sizes of groups. A is incorrect because it overly restricts the makeup of civil society. C is incorrect because civil society groups are autonomous and not government controlled or created. D is incorrect for similar reasons.

53. **C.** The referendum vote on Brexit revealed a highly divided British public in terms of education, age, and occupation. Those most in favor of leaving the EU were older, retired, working-class individuals. All other choices for this question are incorrect because the groups identified voted to remain in the EU. For example, 71 percent of those with a higher education degree voted to stay; 66 percent of those with a high school degree voted to leave; 62 percent of voters in Scotland voted to stay; 61 percent of those over 40 voted to leave; and 75 percent of those under 24 voted to stay.

54. **D.** Economic development is known to have a significant effect on the quality of life of those who live in these societies. One of the major effects is that families are smaller because large numbers of children are not necessary to ensure the well-being of parent in their old age. A is incorrect because literacy increases with economic development. B is incorrect because a key aspect of economic development is attention to building and maintaining infrastructure. C is incorrect because life expectancy rises with economic development.

55. **B.** Normative statements are those that make a value statement as to what should be done or should be avoided, or indicate which policy options are preferable. A is incorrect because it is a statement of fact. C is incorrect because it is a statement of fact. D is incorrect because it is a statement of fact.

Section II: Free Response

Note: *The examples here are not the only correct answer to the free-response questions. There almost always exists more than one correct answer for each part of the free-response questions. Gaining full credit for a response requires answering all parts of the question.*

1. (4 points possible)
   A. Sovereignty is the ultimate authority over territory by the state. (1 point)
   B. An internal force challenging state sovereignty can be a domestic terrorist group, such as the Provisional Irish Republican Army (IRA), which sparked "The Troubles" during the 1970s. The IRA wanted the reunification of Ireland and was willing to use violence to try and force the government to allow the separation to occur. (1 point)
   C. Although the British government did use force against the IRA, the conflict was not resolved until the Good Friday Peace Accord was passed, allowing for a devolved parliament with executive power sharing between Catholics and Protestants. The agreement gave both groups representation and a voice in the government, and so they agreed to stop fighting. (1 point)
   D. Any regime, democratic or authoritarian, seeks legitimacy. Acceptance by the people is best earned through recognition or representation or some funding before a government has to force people to comply. (1 point)

2. (5 points possible)
   A. Iran and Nigeria are tied for the worst corruption perception score with 26/100. (1 point)
   B. Of the core six countries, only the UK has the perception of not being a corrupt country with a score of 77/100. (1 point)
   C. Corruption is the misuse of official power. (1 point)
   D. The key is the word "perception." Transparency International had to ask people what they thought, so a survey was used to poll people. (1 point)
   E. Governments can undertake anti-corruption campaigns such as President Xi has done in China where he uses the Discipline Committee of the CCP to prosecute corrupt officials. (1 point)

3. (5 points possible)
   A. The policy agenda is the concept that the government can only focus its attention on a limited number of policies at one time. (1 point)
   B. In the UK, environmental groups have been staging protests in London to pressure the government to take action on climate change. (1 point)

   In Nigeria, groups like the Delta Avengers terrorize the area to force the government to redistribute oil revenues to help the poor and to clean up the oil spills. (1 point)
   C. The UK has allowed the weekly protests to occur, even as they disrupt traffic. Local governments have banned plastic bags, and Parliament has increased funding for alternative energy sources. The UK has also signed the Paris Climate Accords. (1 point)

   Nigerian government responses to militant groups in the Niger Delta has been to disperse them by force. Only limited government resources have been sent to the Delta for cleanup of the oil. (1 point)

4. (5 points possible)

   Holding elections in an authoritarian regime contributes to political stability because if properly managed, elections give the illusion that the people of the state have some say in the government. This illusion provides legitimacy for the government to exercise sovereignty, or ultimate authority, over the territory. (1 point)

Russia is an example of "managed democracy." Putin has centralized his control over the state by manipulating election system rules to create and maintain his dominant party, United Russia. When the people protested in 2011–12 over the Medvedev–Putin switch, Putin changed the system back to a mixed system of PR and SMD to placate voters, thus maintaining political stability for the authoritarian regime. (1 point)

The Islamic Republic of Iran also holds regular elections despite being a theocracy. After the revolution, the regime sought the legitimacy to exercise sovereignty by allowing the people to vote for president, the Majlis, and the Assembly of Experts. This right to vote is controlled by the Guardian Council vetting candidates, but it still is an important element of the system. When people felt like the election was stolen in 2009, they protested and had to be violently repressed. Allowing managed election results maintains political stability, which has returned to Iran in subsequent elections. (1 point)

In a globalized world where most people have some political rights, it is very difficult to justify not giving the people some say in their government. Authoritarian regimes, like Russia and Iran, that allow some elections are able to use them as a safety valve of legitimacy to maintain sovereignty and stability. (1 point)

Critics may charge that the best way for an authoritarian government to maintain political stability would be to not hold national elections as China does. Then there is no chance of people being upset about a stolen election, thereby keeping political stability. But the long-term threat of civil unrest when the people do not have a tangible way to hold the government accountable through something like elections will ultimately lead to the end of political stability. (1 point)

Scoring Conversion

You can get a rough approximation of your score on the AP Comparative Government and Politics exam. Use the answer explanations to award yourself points on the free-response questions. Then compute your raw score using the worksheet below. Finally, refer to the table to translate your raw score to an AP score of 1 to 5.

Section I: Multiple Choice

Number of questions correctly answered $100\% \times 1.0909$ = (a) _____

Section II: Free Response

Points Earned Question 1 (4 possible)   _____ $\times 3.3 =$ _____

Points Earned Question 2 (5 possible)   _____ $\times 3 =$ _____

Points Earned Question 3 (5 possible)   _____ $\times 3 =$ _____

Points Earned Question 4 (5 possible)   _____ $\times 3.36 =$ _____

TOTAL points earned on Section II   (b) _____

RAW SCORE: Add lines (a) and (b) = _____

Conversion Table

RAW SCORE	APPROXIMATE AP SCORE
Mid 70s–120	5
Mid 60s–mid 70s	4
Mid 50s–mid 60s	3
Mid 30s–mid 50s	2
0–mid 30s	1

AP Comparative Government and Politics
Practice Exam 2

Section I: Multiple-Choice Questions

ANSWER SHEET

1 Ⓐ Ⓑ Ⓒ Ⓓ	16 Ⓐ Ⓑ Ⓒ Ⓓ	31 Ⓐ Ⓑ Ⓒ Ⓓ	46 Ⓐ Ⓑ Ⓒ Ⓓ
2 Ⓐ Ⓑ Ⓒ Ⓓ	17 Ⓐ Ⓑ Ⓒ Ⓓ	32 Ⓐ Ⓑ Ⓒ Ⓓ	47 Ⓐ Ⓑ Ⓒ Ⓓ
3 Ⓐ Ⓑ Ⓒ Ⓓ	18 Ⓐ Ⓑ Ⓒ Ⓓ	33 Ⓐ Ⓑ Ⓒ Ⓓ	48 Ⓐ Ⓑ Ⓒ Ⓓ
4 Ⓐ Ⓑ Ⓒ Ⓓ	19 Ⓐ Ⓑ Ⓒ Ⓓ	34 Ⓐ Ⓑ Ⓒ Ⓓ	49 Ⓐ Ⓑ Ⓒ Ⓓ
5 Ⓐ Ⓑ Ⓒ Ⓓ	20 Ⓐ Ⓑ Ⓒ Ⓓ	35 Ⓐ Ⓑ Ⓒ Ⓓ	50 Ⓐ Ⓑ Ⓒ Ⓓ
6 Ⓐ Ⓑ Ⓒ Ⓓ	21 Ⓐ Ⓑ Ⓒ Ⓓ	36 Ⓐ Ⓑ Ⓒ Ⓓ	51 Ⓐ Ⓑ Ⓒ Ⓓ
7 Ⓐ Ⓑ Ⓒ Ⓓ	22 Ⓐ Ⓑ Ⓒ Ⓓ	37 Ⓐ Ⓑ Ⓒ Ⓓ	52 Ⓐ Ⓑ Ⓒ Ⓓ
8 Ⓐ Ⓑ Ⓒ Ⓓ	23 Ⓐ Ⓑ Ⓒ Ⓓ	38 Ⓐ Ⓑ Ⓒ Ⓓ	53 Ⓐ Ⓑ Ⓒ Ⓓ
9 Ⓐ Ⓑ Ⓒ Ⓓ	24 Ⓐ Ⓑ Ⓒ Ⓓ	39 Ⓐ Ⓑ Ⓒ Ⓓ	54 Ⓐ Ⓑ Ⓒ Ⓓ
10 Ⓐ Ⓑ Ⓒ Ⓓ	25 Ⓐ Ⓑ Ⓒ Ⓓ	40 Ⓐ Ⓑ Ⓒ Ⓓ	55 Ⓐ Ⓑ Ⓒ Ⓓ
11 Ⓐ Ⓑ Ⓒ Ⓓ	26 Ⓐ Ⓑ Ⓒ Ⓓ	41 Ⓐ Ⓑ Ⓒ Ⓓ	
12 Ⓐ Ⓑ Ⓒ Ⓓ	27 Ⓐ Ⓑ Ⓒ Ⓓ	42 Ⓐ Ⓑ Ⓒ Ⓓ	
13 Ⓐ Ⓑ Ⓒ Ⓓ	28 Ⓐ Ⓑ Ⓒ Ⓓ	43 Ⓐ Ⓑ Ⓒ Ⓓ	
14 Ⓐ Ⓑ Ⓒ Ⓓ	29 Ⓐ Ⓑ Ⓒ Ⓓ	44 Ⓐ Ⓑ Ⓒ Ⓓ	
15 Ⓐ Ⓑ Ⓒ Ⓓ	30 Ⓐ Ⓑ Ⓒ Ⓓ	45 Ⓐ Ⓑ Ⓒ Ⓓ	

AP Comparative Government and Politics
Practice Exam 2

Section I: Multiple-Choice Questions
Time—60 minutes
55 Questions

Directions: Each of the questions or incomplete statements below is followed by four answer choices. Select the one that best answers each question and then fill in the corresponding oval on the answer sheet.

Questions 1 and 2 refer to the following passage.

Source: President Vladimir's Address to the Federal Assembly on January 15, 2020

Colleagues: Russia's future and historical perspective depend on how many of us there are (I would like to start the main part of my Address with demography), how many children are born in Russian families in one, five or ten years, on these children's upbringing, on what kind of people they become and what they will do for the country, as well as on the values they choose as their mainstay in life.

There are nearly 147 million of us now. But we have entered a difficult, a very difficult demographic period. The measures we took starting in the mid-2000s have had a positive effect on demography. We have even reached a stage of natural increase. This is why we have more children at schools now. However, new families are being created now by the small generation of the 1990s. And the birth rate is falling again. This is the main problem of the current demographic period in Russia. . . .

I want to say once again that we are alarmed by the negative demographic forecasts. It is our historic duty to respond to this challenge. We must not only get out of this demographic trap but ensure a sustainable natural population growth by 2025. The aggregate birth rate must be 1.7 in 2024. Demography is a sector where universal or parochial solutions cannot be effective. Each step we take and each new law or government program we adopt must be scrutinized from the viewpoint of our top national priority—the preservation and increase of Russia's population.

What decisions have already been made? . . . Additionally, with the support of the federal budget we have started paying benefits for the third child and subsequent children in 75 constituent entities, now including all regions in the Urals, Siberia and the Far East.

All of this amounts to substantial support. But the following thought has crossed my mind, and I believe that you also realize this. Parents stop receiving payments when their child turns three, and this means that their family can immediately face financial problems. To be honest, this is happening already. We must prevent this, especially since I realize that mothers often find it hard to combine working and caring for their children before they start school. We know from the experience of our own children and grandchildren that they often fall ill. Their mothers are therefore unable to work. In this connection, I suggest we introduce monthly payments for children aged between three and seven starting already from January 1, 2020.

1. Which of the following statements is supported by the main idea of the passage?
   (A) President Putin believes that Russian society is facing an overpopulation problem as life expectancy increases and families have more children.
   (B) President Putin believes that one of the most important challenges facing the Russian society is a shrinking population.
   (C) President Putin believes that the task of incentivizing families to have more children is the job of local and regional governments, not the federal government.
   (D) President Putin believes that every family should be required to have a minimum of three children to increase Russia's population.

GO ON TO THE NEXT PAGE

2. Which of the following statements is an implication of the argument presented in the passage?
   (A) President Putin is using coercive policies to force Russian families to comply with his demand to have more children.
   (B) President Putin is more concerned about the effects of a declining population than he is about proposing solutions to fix the problem.
   (C) President Putin has hypothesized that small Russian families occur because of financial challenges and so he proposes increasing government transfer payments to families.
   (D) President Putin is only concerned about the growth in ethnic Russian families and is not offering any financial incentives to other ethnic groups in regions in the rest of the Russian Federation.

Questions 3 and 4 refer to the following passage.

Source: President Muhammadu Buhari, President of the Federal Republic of Nigeria at the World Economic Forum on the Middle East and North Africa, April 6, 2019.

As Nigeria celebrated being the largest economy in Africa and one of the fastest growing economies in the world, Nigerians were migrating in droves through harsh desert conditions and across treacherous seas to seek what they believe would be a better life in Europe.

Ladies and gentlemen, I strongly believe that the lack of social and economic inclusion was the root cause of many challenges we are experiencing.

Today, our population is one hundred and ninety million people. By 2050, it is estimated that we hit three hundred and ninety million making us the third most populous country in the world. This means we must start working now to ensure this population is productively engaged.

In the last four years, we focused on security while implementing inclusive policies. On the security front, we made significant gains in fighting Boko Haram. We have recaptured all territories held by Boko Haram in 2014. We have liberated thousands of Nigerians held against their will. Today, I am pleased to say no territory in the Federal Republic of Nigeria is held or controlled by Boko Haram. . . .

Furthermore, our economic diversification and social inclusion policies are also yielding positive results. Our country has now returned to the path of growth. We are making gains in the ease of doing business indices. A key driver for growth is the agricultural sector where we aggressively pushed agricultural policies that empowered millions of our rural citizens. . . .

Nigeria is now at a new dawn and embarking on a new development trajectory. We are determined to industrialize. Nigeria leveraging our comparative advantage. . . . Our new, inclusive and diversified Nigeria is definitely open for business. Our population, resources, policies and programs make it the most attractive investment destination in Africa.

3. Which of the following statements is supported by the main idea of the passage?
   (A) The Nigerian government is only focused on national security issues like removing Boko Haram from its borders.
   (B) The Nigerian population will decline in the future as more Nigerians seek a better life in Europe.
   (C) The Nigerian economy is dominated by the agricultural sector, and the government has no plans to diversify it.
   (D) President Buhari feels that the economic future of Nigeria is positive with a large supply of labor and effective public policies.

4. Which of the following statements is an implication of the argument presented in the passage?
   (A) Nigeria is a highly developed post-industrial economy with only modest plans for economic growth.
   (B) Nigeria is a failed state that has failed to stop internal threats from terrorist organizations like Boko Haram.
   (C) Nigeria has the typical challenges facing a developing nation, such as finding jobs for a young, growing population and diversifying its economy.
   (D) Because so many people are leaving Nigeria, the government faces a demographic problem of declining life expectancy.

GO ON TO THE NEXT PAGE

Questions 5 and 6 refer to the bar graph below.

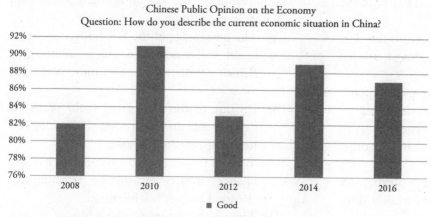

Source: Pew Global Indicator Survey (pewresearch.org/global)

5. According to the data in the bar graph, which of the following statements is correct?
    (A) The majority of Chinese people surveyed consistently believe that the Chinese economy is doing well.
    (B) From 2008 to 2016, there was a wide variation in how Chinese people surveyed felt that the economy was doing.
    (C) Based on the survey data, it is clear that the Chinese government is in danger of losing popular support due to its mishandling of the economy.
    (D) The Chinese economy has been growing at an average rate of 84% since 2008.

6. What are the limitations of the data in the bar graph?
    (A) There is no way to know how many Chinese people surveyed felt that the Chinese economy was doing poorly.
    (B) The listed percentages on the y-axis are too narrowly spaced. The bar graph as drawn implies that there was a large decrease in 2012 in the percentage of Chinese people surveyed who felt the economy was good.
    (C) The years listed on the x-axis are too widely spaced. A two-year interval is too long a time between surveying people about the economy.
    (D) It is difficult to believe the results of the survey because people in China would be afraid to criticize the government's handling of the economy.

Questions 7 and 8 refer to the pie charts below.

Change in proportion of public services budget spent on health

■ NHS ■ Rest of budget

1955–56   11.2%

2016–17   30.1%

Source: IFS

B B C

Source: BBC, "10 Charts that show why the NHS is in trouble." May 24, 2018

GO ON TO THE NEXT PAGE

7. Using the data in the pie chart, why is the National Health Service (NHS) in trouble in the UK?
   (A) In 60 years, the percentage of the UK budget spent on health almost tripled from 11% to 30%.
   (B) In 60 years, the percentage of public spending on defense and education declined.
   (C) Since 1955, the UK government spent more money on the NHS than any other program.
   (D) In 2016, the UK government spent more money on the NHS than it had ever done before.

8. Using the data in the pie chart, what are the implications for the UK government because of change in spending?
   (A) The percentage of the UK budget spent on health will continue to increase as an aging British population requires more NHS services.
   (B) Because of the end of the Cold War, UK defense spending decreased so spending on health appears to increase.
   (C) The total spending on the NHS has not changed over time; only the percentage of the total budget has increased.
   (D) The UK government can no longer support the NHS as part of the welfare state.

Questions 9 and 10 refer to table below.

Presidential Election Results

Candidate A	38%
Candidate B	32%
Candidate C	25%
Candidate D	5%

9. According to the rules of presidential elections in Iran, what happens next?
   (A) Candidate A has a plurality of the votes, so Candidate A becomes the president.
   (B) Because no candidate has a majority, a run-off between Candidate A and Candidate B will be scheduled.
   (C) Because no candidate has a majority, the supreme leader will appoint a president.
   (D) Because no candidate has a majority, the votes for Candidate C and Candidate D will be redistributed to the top two candidates.

10. According to the rules of presidential elections in Russia, what happens next?
   (A) Candidate A has a plurality of the votes, so Candidate A becomes the president.
   (B) Because no candidate has a majority, a run-off between Candidate A and Candidate B will be scheduled.

   (C) Candidate A will become the president, and Candidate B will become the prime minister.
   (D) Because no candidate has a majority, the votes for Candidate C and Candidate D will be redistributed to the top two candidates.

11. What kind of interest group system is characterized by numerous groups competing for access to government institutions?
   (A) Authoritarianism
   (B) Corporatism
   (C) Imperialism
   (D) Pluralism

12. China's Great Leap Forward was:
   (A) an economic reform policy designed to make the country more industrial
   (B) a social policy to encourage equality among ethnic groups

GO ON TO THE NEXT PAGE

(C) a nuclear weapons development policy

(D) a policy to outlaw competitive political parties

13. Sovereignty is:
(A) defined as a state having ultimate authority over a territory
(B) shared between the national and state governments in a unitary system
(C) not relinquished in any way when a state joins a supranational organization
(D) only legitimate if granted through competitive elections

14. Which of the following is an empirical statement?
(A) Less-developed countries need to adopt more structural adjustment policies.
(B) Increased global trade should dramatically improve their GDP.
(C) Less-developed countries employ a sizable percentage of their workers in agriculture.
(D) Allowing more foreign direct investment should increase access to capital.

15. Democratic regimes are best characterized by:
(A) protection of individual liberties
(B) state-run media
(C) state-organized interest groups
(D) protection of patron–client relationships

16. A runoff presidential election is required in Nigeria if no candidate receives:
(A) 60 percent of the popular vote
(B) a majority of the votes of the electoral college
(C) the endorsement of a majority of Nigeria's state legislatures
(D) 25 percent of the popular vote in two-thirds of the states

17. Which of the following countries in the AP Comparative Government and Politics course is often discussed as being dominated by an oligarchy?
(A) Russia
(B) Iran
(C) Mexico
(D) Nigeria

18. According to dependency theorists, what are the necessary elements of import substitution?
(A) Lower tariffs to increase foreign trade
(B) Raise tariffs to protect infant industries

(C) Raise taxes to provide revenue for improvements in infrastructure

(D) Lower subsidies to encourage market efficiencies

19. If a state were to adopt a single-member district election system, what kind of party system should it expect to foster?
(A) One-party system
(B) Two-party system
(C) Multiparty system
(D) Dominant party system

20. Which of the following Iranian institutions are directly elected by the voters?
(A) Supreme leader
(B) Expediency Council
(C) Guardian Council
(D) Assembly of Experts

21. The zoning system of alternating presidents from Nigeria's north and south is:
(A) part of the 1999 constitution
(B) an informal agreement among political parties
(C) a policy imposed by the military as a condition of giving up power
(D) a policy that originated with a coalition of civil society groups

22. Why is an independent judiciary essential to a liberal democracy?
(A) To ensure that no conservative political parties compete for the presidency
(B) To protect the executive from electoral challenges
(C) To check the power of the executive and legislative branches
(D) To guarantee that the government's policies are implemented

23. Which of the following political systems is best characterized as semi-presidential?
(A) Iran
(B) Mexico
(C) China
(D) Russia

GO ON TO THE NEXT PAGE

24. An example of a regime change is:
    (A) a military coup that removes a military government from power
    (B) a change from a democratic to an authoritarian government
    (C) a change from a unitary to a federal system
    (D) a change from a two-party to a multiparty system

25. Which of the following individuals is LEAST likely to be a voter?
    (A) A party activist
    (B) A government official
    (C) A highly educated professional
    (D) A young, unemployed immigrant

26. What is the major difference between a presidential and a parliamentary system?
    (A) Presidents govern in federal systems, while prime ministers govern in unitary systems.
    (B) Presidents propose budgets, while prime ministers implement budgets.
    (C) Presidents can only be a head of state, whereas prime ministers can only be the head of government.
    (D) Presidents are elected separately from the legislature, while prime ministers are selected from the legislature.

27. What is a major disadvantage of a market economy for a communist government?
    (A) Competition allows for individual consumer choice.
    (B) Competition promotes efficiency in production.
    (C) Competition reduces the government's control over the economy.
    (D) Competition generates tax revenue for spending on infrastructure.

28. Which political party in Mexico was the dominant party from 1929 to 2000?
    (A) PAN
    (B) PRI
    (C) PRD
    (D) United Mexico

29. Question time is when the prime minister responds to questions from the:
    (A) parliament
    (B) news media
    (C) party caucus
    (D) cabinet

30. In making appointments to the cabinet, Nigerian presidents must take which of the following into account?
    (A) There must be gender balance.
    (B) All federal states must be represented.
    (C) All appointees must also serve in the national legislature.
    (D) All political parties must be represented.

31. Which of the following is true of the Mexican legislature?
    (A) It is asymmetrically bicameral with the Chamber of Deputies having more power than the Senate.
    (B) The election system for both houses is proportional representation.
    (C) The election system for the Senate is proportional representation, and the Chamber of Deputies is single-member district.
    (D) The election system for both houses is a mixture of proportional representation and single-member districts.

32. How is the prime minister of Russia formally selected?
    (A) By the majority party in the State Duma
    (B) By direct election from the voters
    (C) By appointment by the president and confirmation by the State Duma
    (D) By appointment by the State Duma and confirmation by the Federation Council

33. In general, who has the power to appoint the cabinet?
    (A) Head of state
    (B) Head of government
    (C) Chief justice of the supreme court
    (D) Head of the bureaucracy

34. Regional and local governments in Russia:
    (A) are controlled by the siloviki
    (B) are controlled by the oligarchs
    (C) all have very little power relative to the national government
    (D) vary in the amount of power they have relative to the national government

GO ON TO THE NEXT PAGE

35. In Mexico and Nigeria, federal states are formally represented in the national government through:
    (A) seats in the Senate
    (B) special cabinet positions
    (C) seats in the supreme court
    (D) quotas in the senior military officer corps

36. Who is the head of government in Iran?
    (A) The president
    (B) The supreme leader
    (C) The prime minister
    (D) The head of the Majlis

37. Which of the following is a correct statement about the Mexican constitution of 1917?
    (A) It initially created a parliamentary system, but was amended to create a presidential system.
    (B) It initially created a unitary system but, was amended to create a federal system.
    (C) It initially had judges serve for life, but was amended to allow judges 15-year terms.
    (D) It initially mandated a one-party system, but was amended to mandate a multiparty system.

38. Which of the following is a true statement about the Nigerian military?
    (A) It formed the first government after Nigeria became independent.
    (B) It directly rules all territories where Nigerian oil is produced.
    (C) It is controlled by the federal states and not the national government.
    (D) It has not carried out a successful coup attempt since the creation of the Fourth Republic.

39. Which of the following is a correct statement about the siloviki in Russia?
    (A) They are part of the Russian Orthodox Church.
    (B) They are a pro-democracy social movement.
    (C) They are an informal elite group around Putin.
    (D) They are the Russian national oil company.

40. What is a rentier state?
    (A) A state where private homeownership is banned
    (B) A state that receives the majority of its revenue from the export of a natural resource
    (C) A state that taxes rental property more than commercial property
    (D) A state that protects its natural resources from being exploited by foreign companies

41. Since the adoption of the Russian constitution in 1993, the election system for the State Duma has changed three times. Which is the correct order of election systems used from 1993 through 2016?
    (A) Single-member district, proportional representation with 2 percent threshold, single-member district
    (B) Single-member district, proportional representation with 7 percent threshold, mixed SMD and PR system
    (C) Mixed SMD and PR system, proportional representation with 7 percent threshold, mixed SMD and PR system
    (D) Mixed SMD and PR system, single-member district, proportional representation with 5 percent threshold

42. The Tiananmen Square protests in China in 1989 centered on demands for:
    (A) ethnic minority rights
    (B) political reforms
    (C) environmental cleanup
    (D) ending the One Child policy

43. What is the main difference between a state and a nation?
    (A) A state is permanent, whereas a nation changes over time.
    (B) A state is authoritarian, whereas a nation is democratic.
    (C) A state has a command economy, whereas a nation has a market economy.
    (D) A state has officials, whereas a nation has people with a shared identity.

44. Maquiladoras are most closely associated with which of the following?
    (A) Import substitution
    (B) One-party authoritarian rule
    (C) NAFTA
    (D) Military rule

GO ON TO THE NEXT PAGE

45. Why is Great Britain referred to as a devolved unitary state rather than a federal state?
    (A) The British system is still governed by parliamentary sovereignty.
    (B) Devolution means that newly created parliaments are sovereign as opposed to sharing sovereignty with Westminster.
    (C) Because devolution came as the result of referendums, there is only popular sovereignty.
    (D) Only the queen is sovereign, so there is no shared sovereignty.

46. Why has a more stringent environmental law not brought about rapid improvements in China?
    (A) Foreign firms are not subject to Chinese law.
    (B) Rural farmers still use primitive farming equipment.
    (C) The law does not apply to state-owned enterprises (SOEs).
    (D) Local officials are more focused on economic growth than enforcement.

47. What was the Iranian government's response to the Green Movement in 2009?
    (A) The supreme leader nullified the presidential election results and held new elections as the protesters demanded.
    (B) President Ahmadinejad praised the protesters for expressing their views and being willing to demonstrate against the fraudulent election.
    (C) The government put opposition leader Mousavi under house arrest and also arrested many of the protesters.
    (D) The Ministry of Information relaxed censorship of the Internet so that the protesters could communicate effectively.

48. To allow for some privatization of PEMEX, Mexico's state-owned oil company, President Pena Nieto had to:
    (A) get two-thirds of both houses of the legislature and a majority of the states to amend Article 27 of the constitution
    (B) issue an executive order to PEMEX to require it to cut back on production
    (C) issue a decree that PEMEX was now a private company
    (D) propose legislation to Congress for a law that would allow some privatization of PEMEX

49. Country S has 100 million people, a GDP per capita of $30,000, and 70 percent of its working-age population is employed in the service sector. Country S is most likely:
    (A) a democratic state
    (B) an authoritarian state
    (C) an economically developing country
    (D) an economically developed country

50. A country is considered to be a welfare state if:
    (A) it ensures that all workers have a job
    (B) it provides primary school education
    (C) it charges income taxes to pay for military defense
    (D) it provides universal access to health care, education, and pensions

51. How are bureaucratic officials selected in a merit-based system?
    (A) Officials are selected for their expertise in the field.
    (B) Officials are selected for their party loyalty.
    (C) Officials are selected because of their family position.
    (D) Officials are appointed because of their work on the campaign.

52. If a government is pursuing an austerity program, it will:
    (A) cut taxes and increase spending
    (B) cut taxes and decrease spending
    (C) raise taxes and decrease spending
    (D) raise taxes and increase spending

53. The Falun Gong in China is best described as:
    (A) an opposition social movement
    (B) the ruling elite within the politburo
    (C) the secret police
    (D) the only legal opposition party

GO ON TO THE NEXT PAGE

54. A vote of no confidence means:
    (A) the president is removed from office by the Senate
    (B) the prime minister and the rest of the government must resign
    (C) the supreme court has overturned a law for being unconstitutional
    (D) the military is staging a coup

55. MOSAP and MEND were:
    (A) social movements to bring political and economic justice to the people of the Niger Delta
    (B) Nigerian political parties determined to nominate officials from the Niger Delta
    (C) Nigerian radio networks broadcasting the situation from the Niger Delta
    (D) international interest groups determined to raise awareness about the problems in the Niger Delta

STOP: END OF SECTION I.

Section II: Free Response

Time—1 Hour and 30 Minutes

Directions: The Free-Response Section includes four questions. You need to answer all parts of all eight questions. Write your answers on a separate sheet of paper, making sure to number your answers as the questions are numbered below. Before answering an essay question, take a few minutes to plan and outline your answer. Include specific examples in your answers to the essay questions where appropriate.

1. (A) Define party system.
   (B) Describe the relationship between party systems and election systems.
   (C) Explain why a government would establish a mixed election for voters.
   (D) Explain why an authoritarian government would choose a specific type of party system.

2. Use the following table to answer the question that follows.

Percent of Women in the National Legislature

COUNTRY	LOWER HOUSE	UPPER HOUSE
China	24%	
United Kingdom	32%	26%
Iran	6%	
Mexico	48%	49%
Nigeria	6%	6%
Russia	16%	18%

Source: Inter-Parliamentary Union (10/2018)

   (A) Using the data in the table, identify the country with the highest representation of women in the national legislature.
   (B) Using the data in the table, make an empirical statement about female representation in national legislatures.
   (C) Define gender parity law.
   (D) Explain how Mexico used a gender parity law to increase female representation in the Mexican legislature.
   (E) Explain why female representation in the legislature is a goal for both democratic and authoritarian governments.

3. Compare types of political change in two different AP Comparative Government and Politics course countries. In your response, do the following:
   (A) Describe the difference between a coup and a revolution.
   (B) Describe the reasons for a coup or revolution in two different AP Comparative Government and Politics course countries.
   (C) Explain the effect of the coup or revolution in (B) on the type of regime in each of the two different AP Comparative Government and Politics course countries.

GO ON TO THE NEXT PAGE

4. Develop an argument as to whether a democratic or authoritarian government is more effective at helping a developing economy modernize.

   Use one or more of the following course concepts in your response:
   • Economic liberalization
   • GDP per capita
   • Legitimacy

   In your response, you should do the following:
   • Respond to the prompt with a defensible claim or thesis that establishes a line of reasoning using one or more of the provided course concepts.
   • Support your claim with at least TWO pieces of specific and relevant evidence from one or more course countries. This evidence should be relevant to one or more of the provided course countries.
   • Use reasoning to explain why your evidence supports your claim or thesis, using one or more of the provided course concepts.
   • Respond to an opposing or alternate perspective, using refutation, concession, or rebuttal.

GO ON TO THE NEXT PAGE

❯ Answers and Explanations

Section I: Multiple Choice

1. **B.** President Putin begins the speech by saying that a shrinking population is so important that he is starting his speech by discussing the problem. He also includes federal, not just local or regional, solutions to the problem.

2. **C.** Putin specifically discusses financial incentives, not coercive policies, to convince Russians to have more children.

3. **D.** President Buhari is clearly communicating to the World Economic Forum that despite challenges, the future of Nigeria is positive with a growing population and a diversifying economy.

4. **C.** Because of a fast-growing population and a large agriculture sector, Nigeria is a developing nation with an economy that is in the process of industrializing.

5. **A.** From 2008 to 2016, more than 80 percent of Chinese people surveyed felt that the Chinese economy was doing well. There is not a wide variation in opinion if the range is between 90 and 82 percent.

6. **B.** The bar graph divisions look like there were huge divisions in popular opinion but 90–82 percent is not a big range. One can surmise that percentage of people who felt the economy was doing badly is less than 20 percent.

7. **A.** The pie chart shows a growth in the percent of the budget from 11–30 percent. There is no indication on what happened to other spending programs or the total pounds spent.

8. **A.** The trend would suggest that the percentage on health spending will get larger as time goes on. There is no indication on what happened to other spending programs or the total pounds spent.

9. **B.** Iranian presidential elections require the candidate to win a majority of the vote.

10. **B.** Russian presidential elections require the candidate to win a majority of the vote.

11. **D.** When used with reference to the structure of a political system, pluralism refers to the presence of multiple groups within society competing for influence, with no one group being able to dominate others. A is incorrect because in authoritarian political systems there is only one dominant group controlling political power. B is incorrect because under corporatism the government favors some interest groups over others, giving them greater access to power. C is incorrect because imperialism refers to a foreign policy of domination and control by one country over others.

12. **A.** The Great Leap Forward was instituted in 1958 and was an economic policy under Mao to rapidly turn China from an agricultural economy into a modern socialist-collective society. B is incorrect because equality among ethnic groups was not its focus and some ethnic groups rebelled against the policies being put into place. C is incorrect because it was not a military policy. D is incorrect because political parties were already outlawed by the establishment of communist rule in China.

13. **A.** Sovereignty is a key concept in international politics. It is seen as challenged or weakened today by globalization as states are no longer able to fully control economic activity within their borders. B is incorrect because it does not apply to the distribution of power within a country. C is incorrect because when states join a supranational organization (as opposed to an international organization) they relinquish all or part of their sovereignty. D is incorrect because the existence of sovereignty does not rest on how a government is formed or leaders are chosen.

14. **C.** An empirical statement is a statement of fact. It is not a statement of opinion or a policy recommendation. A, B, and D are all incorrect because they are statements of opinion and policy recommendations.

15. **A.** Along with holding free and fair elections, one of the founding principles of democracy is the protection of civil rights and civil liberties. B is

GO ON TO THE NEXT PAGE

incorrect because a state-run media runs counter to the principle of free and fair elections because it holds the potential for limiting access to the media by opposition groups. C is incorrect because state-organized interest groups run counter to the principle of free and fair elections because some groups are favored over others. D is incorrect because patron–client relations are associated with authoritarian regimes or fragile democratic systems and are a means of concentrating political power in the hands of an elite.

16. **D.** In an effort to promote national unity, Nigerian law requires that to be elected president, a candidate must receive a majority of the vote and at least 25 percent of the vote in two-thirds of the states. If this does not happen, a runoff election is held. A is incorrect because the vote total is too high. B is incorrect because there is no electoral college. C is incorrect because the president is elected by popular vote.

17. **A.** An oligarchy is defined as a political system in which power is concentrated in the hands of a small number of wealthy people, or government by the few with few if any legal constraints. It is common to identify Russians close to Putin who profited greatly by the transition from communist rule as the Russian oligarchs. B is incorrect because Iran is considered to be a theocracy in which religious leaders play a dominant role. C is incorrect because while long ruled by the PRI, Mexico is now a more competitive democratic system. D is incorrect because Nigeria has a strong patron–client system, but this falls short of being an oligarchy because an element of political competition exists.

18. **B.** Import substitution is a development strategy that seeks to restrict foreign economic competition in domestic markets by providing domestic producers with protection in the form of tariffs, import quotas, and other measures to make foreign-made goods more expensive. A is incorrect because lower tariffs would increase foreign competition in domestic markets. C is incorrect because raising taxes would harm the ability of domestic firms to compete with foreign competition. D is incorrect because subsidies lower the cost of domestic production, thus making their products more competitive.

19. **B.** The major advantages of single-member district elections are that they favor a two-party system, which in turn promotes the establishment of majority governments and reduces the likelihood of coalition governments. A is incorrect because a one-party rule is not seen as a function of the type of electoral system as much as it is of other traits such as authoritarian, communist, or oligarchic rule. C is incorrect because multiparty systems are associated with proportional representation electoral systems. D is incorrect because a dominant party system as with a one-party system is seen as the result of factors other than the nature of the electoral system.

20. **D.** Members of the Assembly of Experts are chosen by popular vote for an eight-year term. A is incorrect because the supreme leader is selected by the Assembly of Experts. B is incorrect because the Expediency Council is selected by the supreme leader. C is incorrect because the half the Guardian Council is selected by the chief justice and the other half by the supreme leader.

21. **B.** Zoning is an informal policy not found in laws or the constitution but has widespread support among political parties and societal groups. A is incorrect because the 1999 constitution is modeled on the U.S. Constitution and the idea of zoning has been linked to a proposal by the national student association during military rule. C is incorrect because it was not a condition put forward by the military for reestablishing a democracy. D is incorrect because the African Union made no such proposal.

22. **C.** Democracies are built around the principle of rule of law. A prerequisite for the rule of law to be operational is the existence of an independent judiciary. A is incorrect because democracies are also built around the idea of free speech. B is incorrect because one means by which government officials are held accountable in a democracy is through election challenges. D is incorrect because policy implementation is the task of the bureaucracy.

23. **D.** A semi-presidential system is one that has both a president who is popularly elected and a prime minister who along with the cabinet is

responsible to the legislature. To varying degrees both share political power. A is incorrect because Iran is a theocracy and has a president. B is incorrect because Mexico has a presidential system. C is incorrect because China is a communist state.

24. **B.** A regime change involves a change in the structure of the political system. A governance change only involves a change in the nature of governance within a regime such as a new party taking power or changes in the rules and pattern of governance. A is incorrect because it only involves replacing one military government with another military government. C is incorrect because it involves a change in the structure of governance. D is incorrect because it involves a change in the structure of governance.

25. **D.** Voting studies make it clear that not all citizens are equally likely to vote. Among the characteristics that are most associated with voting are knowledge about politics, education level, wealth, and age, with the very young being unlikely to vote. Young, unemployed immigrants fit the profile of someone unlikely to vote. All the other answers are consistent with the profile of citizens likely to vote due to their education level, exposure to politics, and age.

26. **D.** Presidents and prime ministers differ in how they are selected and who they are responsible to. Presidents are elected by popular vote and thus responsible to the electorate. Prime ministers are chosen by the major party or coalition in the legislature and therefore responsible to the legislature. A is incorrect because presidents and prime ministers may lead either federal or unitary systems. B is incorrect because there is no definitional difference in budgetary power that separates presidents and prime ministers. C is incorrect because both presidents and prime ministers serve as heads of government.

27. **C.** Free market competition reduces the ability of the government to control the economy through economic planning and over time produces demands for the government to reduce other forms of intervention and give citizens a greater say in government. A is incorrect because great consumer choice is not necessarily a threat. It

can increase public support for the government. B is incorrect for the same reason. Increased efficiency might increase public support of the government. D is incorrect because a communist government can still tax firms.

28. **B.** Founded as the National Revolutionary Party in 1929, renamed the Party of the Mexican Revolution in 1938, and today known as the Institutional Revolutionary Party, the PRI ruled Mexico from 1929 to 2000. A and C are incorrect because while both are current political parties, neither was the historically dominant political party. D is incorrect because United Mexico is not a political party.

29. **A.** Question time in Great Britain takes place Monday to Thursday. Each day questions are directed at a specific government speaker. Wednesdays are reserved for questions to the prime minister. Oral questions are known ahead of time but must be answered. The remaining answers identify government and nongovernment organizations that might pose questions to a prime minister but do not constitute question time.

30. **B.** The Nigerian constitution specifies that all federal states must be represented in the cabinet. This is referred to as the Federal Charter Principle. A is incorrect because the constitution does not specify gender balance. C is incorrect because there is no requirement that cabinet members also serve in the national legislature in Nigeria's presidential system. D is incorrect because there is no requirement that all parties be represented in the cabinet.

31. **D.** The Mexican Chamber of Deputies has 500 members, 300 of whom are elected from single-member districts. The other 200 are elected by proportional representation. The Senate has 128 members; 32 are elected in a countrywide proportional representation election. The other 96 are elected in multiseat constituencies. A is incorrect because while the two chambers do not have identical powers, they are relatively equal and thus symmetrical. B is incorrect because members are elected in single-member districts. C is incorrect because there are multiple election formats in each chamber.

32. **C.** According to the Russian constitution, the prime minister of Russia is appointed by the president but must be confirmed by the Duma. A is incorrect because the Duma approves the prime minister but does not have the power to appoint him. B is incorrect because it is the president and not the prime minister who is directly elected. D is incorrect because the Federal Council plays no role in this decision and the State Duma does not appoint the prime minister.

33. **B.** The head of government oversees the executive branch in which the cabinet consists primarily of the heads of major bureaus and departments. A is incorrect because the head of state generally is largely a symbolic figure without day-to-day responsibilities in managing the government. C is incorrect because the chief justice is not part of the executive branch and has no operational responsibilities. D is incorrect because there is no formal position of the head of the bureaucracy.

34. **D.** The relationship between the national government and regional governments in Russia is complex. The national government has changed the way in which governors and key officials are selected, and some regional authorities have successfully challenged the national government, while others have failed, leading many to refer to the situation as one of asymmetrical federalism because of the power differences among regional units. A is incorrect because the siloviki are KGB and military veterans who dominate these services and are found in Putin's inner circle of advisors. B is incorrect because the oligarchs are wealthy Russians closely identified with Putin who profited greatly from the privatization of state firms with the end of the Soviet Union. C is incorrect because it does not identify the variation in power in the national-local relationship that exists.

35. **A.** Both Mexico and Nigeria are federal systems in which states are represented in the upper house. B is incorrect because neither state has special cabinet positions for representatives of states. Nigeria does require states to be represented in the cabinet. C is incorrect because Supreme Court seats are not filled by state representatives in either country. D is incorrect became neither Mexico nor Nigeria has a quota system for the military or civil service, although ethnic representation in these areas is politically important in Nigeria and operates through a patron–client system.

36. **A.** The president of Iran is the head of the government. B is incorrect because the supreme leader is head of state. C is incorrect because there is no prime minister in Iran. D is incorrect because the Majlis is headed by the Speaker of the House.

37. **C.** The constitution was amended to change the term of office from a lifetime appointment to a 15-year term. A is incorrect because the Mexican constitution was modeled on the U.S. Constitution and never was a parliamentary system. B is incorrect because Mexico was created as a federal system. D is incorrect because while long dominated by the PRI, Mexico was not a one-party system.

38. **D.** A coup plot involving the Nigerian military was discovered in 2004, but the military has not carried out a successful coup since the creation of the Fourth Republic. A is incorrect because Nigeria was not ruled by a military government immediately after independence. B is incorrect because it does not directly rule over oil territory in Nigeria. C is incorrect because the military is not controlled by the federal states.

39. **C.** The siloviki are a group of former KGB and military officials who are closely aligned with Putin. They promote a hard-line law-and-order approach to domestic dissent and calls for political reform. A is incorrect because they are not made up of Russian Orthodox clergy. B is incorrect because they are not a reformist social movement. D is incorrect because the siloviki are not the Russian national oil company.

40. **B.** The definition of a rentier state is one that receives a significant portion of its revenue from "rent" or sale of natural resources. Nigeria and Iran are seen as rentier states because of their dependence on the sale of oil. Russia also qualifies as a rentier state in the view of some. A is incorrect because the concept of a rentier state does not apply to homeownership or private property. C is incorrect because it does not

involve tax policy on rented land but natural resources as a source of income. D is incorrect because rentier states exploit natural resources for profit. They do not protect them.

41. **C.** The correct order is (1) a mixed single-member district and proportional representation system (1993), (2) a proportional representation system with a 7 percent threshold (2003), and (3) a return to a mixed single-member district and proportional representation system (2103). The other potential answers have some combination of the incorrect order of electoral systems and the incorrect vote threshold.

42. **B.** The 1989 Tiananmen Square protestors put forward a number of demands. Prominent among them were calls for greater political accountability of government officials and an end to corruption, increased political rights in the areas of free speech and free press, and greater opportunities for political participation. All other possible answers identify policy issues that were not central to the Tiananmen Square protests.

43. **D.** A state refers to a political territory. A nation refers to a group of people who share an identity. A is incorrect because states may change boundaries and become parts of larger political units. The boundaries of nations may change as people's self-identity changes. B is incorrect because authoritarianism and democracy are two forms of state government. C is incorrect because command and market economies are different forms of economic systems in a state.

44. **C.** Maquiladoras are industries located in northern Mexico that primarily produce for export to the United States. They grew in number with the signing of NAFTA, which permitted greater trade between the United States and Mexico. A is incorrect because import substitution is an economic policy that seeks to reduce foreign trade. B is incorrect because maquiladoras are businesses and not political parties. D is incorrect because Mexico is not ruled by the military.

45. **A.** Devolution does not involve the permanent transfer of power from the national government to regions within Great Britain. In a federal state, the regions possess constitutionally protected powers that are beyond the reach of the national government. In Great Britain, all constitutional power still resides with Parliament. B is incorrect because devolution did not transfer sovereign power on a permanent basis. C is incorrect because referendums are not binding on Parliament, which is sovereign. D is incorrect because the queen is head of state and not head of the government.

46. **D.** One of the policy challenges facing China is the tension between economic growth policies and environmental protection policies. Economic growth has been stressed over environment protection policies by local officials. A and C are incorrect because all of these firms are subject to Chinese law. B is incorrect because primitive farming equipment is not a primary cause of environmental destruction.

47. **C.** The Green Movement was a political protest movement that arose in response to the 2009 presidential election in which the incumbent Mahmoud Ahmadinejad, whose first term in office was linked to major human rights violations, defeated Hossein Mousavi. Both claimed victory. A is incorrect because Ahmadinejad did not call for new elections. B is correct because the protestors were arrested, interrogated, and officially linked to foreign media. D is incorrect because censorship was not relaxed.

48. **A.** Private investment in the Mexican oil industry is forbidden by the constitution. The oil industry was nationalized in 1938. Amending the constitution requires two-thirds approval of both houses and the support of a majority of the states. B is incorrect because it is not a method of amending the constitution. C is incorrect because it is not a method of amending the constitution. D is incorrect because it would violate the constitution.

49. **D.** In economically developed counties as opposed to less-developed countries a far greater percentage of the workforce is employed in the service sector. These states also have a much higher per capita GDP. A and B are incorrect because the question refers to the structure of the economy and not the nature of the political system. C is incorrect because the characteristics listed in the question will not be found in states with developing economies.

50. **D.** The concept of a welfare state refers to a political system that provides basic services to protect the socioeconomic well-being of all of its citizens. It is not a system of poverty relief but one designed to provide an equal measure of services to all in society. A is incorrect because welfare states do not guarantee employment. B is incorrect because primary education is not a sufficient level of education to provide for the well-being of citizens. C is incorrect because military defense is not an element of the welfare state.

51. **A.** In a merit-based system expertise and skills are valued over political affiliation; family ties; ethnic, religious, or class identity, or military experience. All other answers identify; non-skill-based criteria as being the basis for being hired into the bureaucracy.

52. **C.** Austerity programs are a set of policies adopted by governments to cut government spending and at the same time increase revenues by raising taxes in order to reduce budget deficits. A is incorrect because the policies listed there work in the opposite direction of austerity programs. B is incorrect because cutting taxes is not part of an austerity program. At best, taxes would be left in place. D is incorrect because there would not be an increase in spending in an austerity program.

53. **A.** Falun Gong is a Chinese social protest movement that was founded in 1992 after Tiananmen Square and has staged large protests that prompted a strong and harsh crackdown by the government leading to charges of human rights violations. B is incorrect because it is not a protest movement within the communist party. C is incorrect because it is not the secret police. D is incorrect because it is not an opposition political party.

54. **B.** By tradition, a parliamentary vote of no confidence forces the government to resign and be replaced by a new government either through elections or the selection of a new prime minister by the majority party or coalition in Parliament. A is incorrect because there is no president in a parliamentary system. C is incorrect because actions of the Supreme Court do not qualify as a vote of no confidence. D is incorrect because a military coup is not a parliamentary vote of no confidence.

55. **A.** MOSOP (Movement for the Survival of the Ogoni People) and MEND (Movement for the Emancipation of the Niger Delta) are two of the most active social movements in Nigeria. Both have been linked to violent action directed at the government and foreign oil companies. B is incorrect because social movements are not political parties. C is incorrect because they are not media organizations. D is incorrect because they are not international interest groups by social movements organized and operating in the Niger Delta.

Section II: Free Response

Note: The examples here are not the only correct answer to the free-response questions. There almost always exists more than one correct answer for each part of the free-response questions. Gaining full credit for a response requires answering all parts of the question.

1. (4 points possible)
   - (A) A party system categorizes the number of parties in a political system that have the chance to win seats in the legislature. Party systems are either one-party, dominant party, two-party, or multiparty systems. (1 point)
   - (B) There is a clear relationship between election systems and party systems. Single member district plurality (SMDP) election systems result in two-party systems, whereas proportional election (PR) systems result in multiparty systems. (1 point)
   - (C) A government will use a mixed election system for voters to minimize wasted votes. Voters get to try to pick the representative that they want in the SMDP system and then pick a party in the PR system with the hopes that if their chosen rep doesn't win, at least a member of their party will get a seat. This boosts the legitimacy of the election because more people feel represented. (1 point)
   - (D) Authoritarian governments want to keep power and not be elected out of office. Therefore, these governments use a one-party or dominant party system to ensure that their party won't lose. (1 point)

2. (5 points possible)
   - (A) Mexico has the highest percentage of women in the legislature. (1 point)
   - (B) In most countries, women make up less than a third of the percentage of legislators. (1 point)
   - (C) Gender parity laws are legal requirements for political parties to increase the number of female candidates for office. (1 point)
   - (D) Mexico required gender parity for the PR seats in both the upper and lower house elections. The result is one of the highest number of female legislators in a national body. (1 point)
   - (E) One function of a legislature is to represent the people. Descriptive representation or having a legislature that reflects the gender, ethnic background, or religion of the population as a whole makes the body more legitimate even if it already does a good job of substantively passing legislation to benefit all people. (1 point)

3. (5 points possible)
   - (A) A coup occurs when a group of elites, often military, seizes executive power. Revolutions, on the other hand, are transformational in that many groups across the society rise up to overthrow the current regime. (1 point)
   - (B) Nigeria was plagued with military coups during much of the time from 1960 to 1999. Each time that the military seized power, it was to "restore law and order." (1 point)

     Iran had a revolution in 1979 where many groups of people rose up to overthrow the Shah. The Shah had been a repressive, corrupt leader who made enemies of political dissidents, merchants, and the religious followers of the exiled Ayatollah Khomeini. (1 point)
   - (C) The Nigerian coups did not lead to substantial regime change, because even though some leaders would give up power to a democratic government, another coup would occur. That is, until the last one under Sani Abacha. After his death, a new power-sharing constitution was written, and the transition to a democratic regime in 1999 was successful. (1 point)

     The Iranian revolution led to regime change, although it remained authoritarian after the Ayatollah Khomeini consolidated his power. But instead of being a monarchy, the Iranian Revolution resulted in a theocracy, the Islamic Republic of Iran. (1 point)

4. (5 points possible)

An authoritarian government is more effective at modernizing an economy than a democracy because the authoritarian government won't hesitate to ruthlessly move labor and capital around to create new industries. People accept the government's authority or legitimacy because the rapid industrialization typically leads to an increase in GDP per capita or the country's standard of living. (1 point)

The Soviet Union under Stalin is one effective modernizing example. By moving people and collectivizing factories and farms, he put the USSR on a quick industrializing path. His ruthless, totalitarian methods are not anything to emulate but they were effective at building the Soviet war machine. (1 point)

China, under the leadership of Deng Xiaoping, was able to steadily modernize the Chinese economy by building SEZs, allowing FDI, and unleashing the power of TVEs. Under his leadership and policies, China grew at a rate over 10 percent a year, increasing GDP per capita and lifting millions of people out of poverty. (1 point)

Modernizing an economy means moving an agricultural-based economy to industrialize so that it produces more products and raises GDP. An authoritarian government, like that of the former Soviet Union or China, is willing to use force to make the changes happen. (1 point)

Critics would charge that the first industrializing countries, the UK and the United States, were democracies and that markets work better when individuals make the decisions. Yet while it is true that markets are more efficient, the actual modernization process can happen more quickly and effectively if steered by an authoritarian government. (1 point)

Scoring Conversion

You can get a rough approximation of your score on the AP Comparative Government and Politics Exam. Use the answer explanations to award yourself points on the free-response questions. Then compute your raw score using the worksheet below. Finally, refer to the table to translate your raw score to an AP score of 1 to 5.

Section I: Multiple Choice

Number of questions correctly answered _____ × 1.0909 = (a) _____

Section II: Free Response

Points Earned Question 1 (4 possible) _____ × 3 3 = _____

Points Earned Question 2 (5 possible) _____ × 3 = _____

Points Earned Question 3 (5 possible) _____ × 3 = _____

Points Earned Question 4 (5 possible) _____ × 3.36 = _____

TOTAL points earned on Section II   (b) _____

RAW SCORE: Add lines (a) and (b) = _____

Conversion Table

RAW SCORE	APPROXIMATE AP SCORE
Mid 70s–120	5
Mid 60s–mid 70s	4
Mid 50s–mid 60s	3
Mid 30s–mid 50s	2
0–mid 30s	1

NOTES